International Migration

How does immigration affect the economy? What are the right immigration policies? Does greater cooperation in trade stimulate or slow the pace of migration between countries? How can we predict future migration flows and how effective are the existing measures to control their magnitude and composition?

International migration, legal as well as illegal, presents a wide range of opportunities, challenges and risks for both the countries of immigration and emigration. This book provides an in-depth analysis of the issues which lie at the centre of academic and policy debates on the subject. It covers topics such as:

- Political economy of immigration policy, migration and the welfare state
- Economic impact of immigration and the role of selection criteria
- Trade and migration
- Illegal immigration, amnesties
- Return migration, remittances

This work draws together the research and findings of leading specialists in the field of international migration to provide a wide-ranging and definitive treatment of the subject. Graduate and advanced undergraduate students, professional economists and policy makers will all find this book a valuable resource.

Slobodan Djajić received his PhD in international economics at Columbia University in 1979. He has held teaching appointments at Queen's University, Columbia University, and the Graduate Institute of International Studies. His main research interests concentrate on trade and international migration. He has published numerous articles in scholarly journals on temporary migration, illegal immigration, and immigration policy.

Routledge contemporary economic policy issues

Series Editor Kanhaya Gupta

This series is dedicated to new works that focus directly on contemporary economic policy issues. It aims to include case studies from around the world on the most pressing questions facing economists and policy makers at both a national and international level.

1 Regionalism and Globalization: Theory and Practice
Edited by Sajal Lahiri

2 The Political Economy of Corruption
Edited by Arvind K. Jain

3 International Migration: Trends, Policies and Economic Impact
Edited by Slobodan Djajić

International Migration

Trends, policies and economic impact

Edited by
Slobodan Djajić

London and New York

First published 2001 by Routledge
11 New Fetter Lane, London EC4P 4EE

Simultaneously published in the USA and Canada
by Routledge
29 West 35th Street, New York, NY 10001

Routledge is an imprint of the Taylor & Francis Group

Typeset in Baskerville by Exe Valley Dataset Ltd, Exeter
Printed and bound in Great Britain by
T J International Ltd, Padstow, Cornwall

British Library Cataloguing in Publication Data
A catalogue record for this book is available
from the British Library

Library of Congress Cataloging in Publication Data
International migration: trends, policies, and economic impact / Slobodan
Djajić, editor.
p. cm.
Includes bibliographical references and index.
1. Emigration and immigration – Economic aspects. 2. Emigration and immigration – Government policy. I. Djajić, Slobodan.

JV6217.I59 2001
331.6'2—dc21 00–051773

ISBN 0–415–23782–3

Contents

Tables

Figures

Contributors

Barry R. Chiswick is Research Professor and Head of the Department of Economics at the University of Illinois at Chicago. For nearly 25 years he has done extensive research on immigration policy and on the economic adjustment and impact of (legal and illegal) immigrants and racial, ethnic and religious minorities in a range of developed and less developed countries. His most recent research interest has been in the economics of language.

Don DeVoretz is Professor of Economics and co-director of Research and Integration in the Metropolis (RIIM) at Simon Fraser University, Burnaby, Canada. A collection of his work on the economics of immigration is available in *Diminishing Returns: The Economics of Canada's Immigration Policy* (C.D. Howe, Toronto, 1995).

Slobodan Djajić is Professor of Economics at the Graduate Institute of International Studies in Geneva, Switzerland. His main research interests concentrate on trade and international migration. He has published numerous articles on temporary migration, illegal immigration, and immigration policy.

Christian Dustmann is Senior Lecturer in the Department of Economics at University College London, a Research Fellow of both the Center for Economic Policy Research (CEPR), London, and the Institute for the Study of Labor (IZA), Bonn, and a Research Associate of the Institute of Fiscal Studies (IFS), London. His research interests cover microeconometrics, labour economics, and population economics. He has published papers on migration, education, and other aspects of labour economics in many leading journals.

Michael Fertig is a PhD student at the University of Heidelberg under the supervision of Christoph M. Schmidt. Since 2000 he has been a Research Affiliate at the Institute for the Study of Labor (IZA) in Bonn. His research interests include applied econometrics in the field of international migration and programme evaluation, with a particular emphasis on active labour market policy.

Nicholas P. Glytsos is Head of the Labour Economics Division at the Centre of Planning and Economic Research (KEPE) in Athens, Greece. His research interests include labour market issues, international migration and the economics of education, and human capital. He has published numerous articles on these topics in scholarly journals and collected volumes of essays.

Jean-Marie Grether is Professor of Economics at the University of Neuchâtel. He has taught as a Lecturer at the University of Lausanne and at the University of Geneva. His research interests include international trade, migration and economic development.

Evgenia Markova is a PhD candidate under an ACE scholarship in the Department of Economics at the University of Athens, Greece. She holds a Master's degree from the Mediterranean Agronomic Institute of Chania and her research interests are in immigration studies and policy.

Philip L. Martin is Professor of Agricultural and Resource Economics at the University of California-Davis, and chair of the University of California's Comparative Immigration and Integration Program. He is editor of *Migration News* and *Rural Migration News*, and his book on collective bargaining in Californian agriculture, *Promises to Keep*, won the Richard Lester Award as the Outstanding Book in Labor Economics and Industrial Relations published in 1996.

Jaime de Melo is Professor of Economics at the University of Geneva and Professeur Invité at the Université d'Auvergne. He has worked at the research department of the World Bank (1980–93) and has taught at Georgetown University. He is a Research Fellow in the International Trade Programme of the Center for Economic Policy Analysis.

Tobias Müller is Maître d'Enseignement et de Recherche at the University of Geneva. He has worked as consultant at the World Bank and taught as Professeur Invité at the University Laval in Quebec, Canada. His research interests include migration, regional integration and environmental policies.

Assaf Razin is the Mario Henrique Simonsen Professor of Public Economics at Tel Aviv University, Research Associate of the National Bureau of Economic Research (NBER), Research Fellow of the Centre for Economic Policy Research (CEPR) and Research Fellow of CES-ifo.

Gaston Repetto is a doctoral student in economics at the University of Illinois at Chicago. His dissertation is on the role of human capital in the economic development of Argentina. His current research includes a study of the effect of country of origin and mother tongue on Hebrew language skills among immigrants in Israel.

Francisco L. Rivera-Batiz is Associate Professor in the Department of Economics at Columbia University and Associate Professor in the Department of International and Transcultural Studies at Teacher's College, Columbia University. His research interests include international migration, economic development and the economics of education. He has published numerous articles on immigration policy, undocumented workers, migrant education, and the economic consequences of migration flows.

Efraim Sadka is the Henry Kaufman Professor of International Capital Markets at Tel Aviv University and a Research Associate of CES-ifo.

Alexander Sarris is Professor of Economics at the University of Athens, Greece. He has published widely in the fields of agricultural development and food policy, applied international trade, income distribution and poverty analysis, international migration, and commodity risk management. He has also acted as a consultant for various UN and other multilateral organisations.

Christoph M. Schmidt is a Professor at the University of Heidelberg, where he teaches econometrics and labour economics. Since 1996 he has been a Research Fellow of the Centre for Economic Policy Research (CEPR) in London, and since 1998 a Research Fellow at the Institute for the Study of Labor (IZA) in Bonn. He has published articles on migration, the wage structure and employment flows, and on the evaluation of labour market programmes in many international journals.

Rainer Winkelmann is currently Senior Research Associate at the Institute for the Study of Labor (IZA) in Bonn. He previously held positions at Dartmouth College, Hanover, USA, and at the University of Canterbury, Christchurch, New Zealand, where he co-authored a report on the labor market outcomes of New Zealand's immigrants for the Department of Labor.

Acknowledgements

The author acknowledges with thanks the permission of Cambridge University Press to reprint Chapter 4, "Interactions Between International Migration and the Welfare State," by A. Razin and E. Sadka, which is based on material published in Assaf Razin and Efraim Sadka, *Labor, Capital and Finance: International Flows* (Cambridge: Cambridge University Press, forthcoming). The paper on "Immigrant Adjustment in Israel: Literacy, Fluency in Hebrew and Earnings," by B.R. Chiswick and G. Rapetto, is a revised version of a paper by the same title published in S. DellaPergola and J. Evans (eds), *Papers in Jewish Demography 1997* (Jerusalem: The Hebrew University, Jewish Populations Studies 29, forthcoming). Permission to publish the paper as Chapter 10 of this volume is acknowledged with thanks.

Introduction

Slobodan Djajić

Throughout much of our history, immigration has been relatively unrestricted in most parts of the world. The state typically represented the interests of landowners who were rather receptive to inflows of foreign labor. Both voluntary and forced immigration, as in the case of slave labor, served to increase land values and rents. Following the industrial revolution and the ensuing socioeconomic and political changes, capital owners became more influential in setting economic policy. Their attitude towards immigration, however, was not very different from that of the landlords. In consequence, immigration remained relatively unrestricted in most countries well into the first decades of the twentieth century. When restrictions were applied, exclusion of foreigners was based primarily on racial discrimination, public health considerations, and national security concerns rather than economic objectives.

The twentieth century was one of great change. Workers in the advanced market economies witnessed significant improvements in their economic, social, and political status. They became partners with other factor owners in sharing the fruits of economic progress. High labor standards, collective bargaining, and the welfare state have brought an end to the regime of sweatshops and subsistence wages. Unfortunately, the same level of progress has not been achieved in many of the developing countries. This has contributed to an expansion of the income differentials between workers of rich and poor nations. At the same time, technological advances in transportation and communications have sharply reduced the cost of international migration. Travel to a foreign country, or even intercontinental travel, has become increasingly more accessible to potential migrants. So has information concerning the standard of living and economic opportunities available abroad, not only through films, television and other forms of entertainment and news media, but also through personal communications networks. Low cost travel and telecommunications contribute, in addition, to a reduction in the psychic costs of migration by enabling individuals to maintain close ties with family and friends remaining overseas.

A combination of these and other factors has contributed to an increase in migratory pressures along international borders. The receiving countries have responded by trying to restrain immigration. Rules for issuing residence and work permits, tourist visas, and granting refugee status are becoming increasingly restrictive, targeting in particular the nationals of developing countries. In the meantime, boatloads of asylum seekers, truckloads of undocumented foreign workers, and airplanes with visa overstayers continue to arrive with increasing frequency. This is feeding fears in the relatively prosperous countries of being flooded with unwanted immigrants. It is obvious, however, that international migration, legal as well as undocumented, presents a wide range of opportunities in addition to challenges and risks for both the countries of immigration and emigration.

As the destination countries struggle to regain control over the magnitude and composition of their immigration flows, various aspects of the problem have sparked a lively public debate on the subject of international migration. The aim of this volume is to address some of the key issues. How does immigration affect the economy? What is the role of immigration policies? What are the effects of immigration on income distribution and on the attitudes of host country voters to immigration and redistribution policies of the state? Does greater cooperation in trade stimulate or slow down the pace of migration between more and less advanced countries? How can we predict future immigration flows and how effective are the existing measures to control their magnitude and composition? What is being done about illegal immigration? How does it affect the wages and employment of legal residents and the burden of providing public goods and services? What do we know about the characteristics of undocumented immigrants and their economic activities in the host country? How do they respond to amnesty programs? What factors influence the earnings of immigrants, remittance flows to the source country, and the pattern of return migration?

This volume provides an analysis of these and other important current issues with a focus on recent immigration trends and policies and their economic impact. The first two chapters review the recent immigration experience of three economies which continue to encourage immigrants to come, while using explicit points systems to evaluate admissibility of immigrants. Cases of Australia and New Zealand are analyzed and compared in Chapter 1 by Rainer Winkelmann, and the case of Canada is treated by Don DeVoretz in Chapter 2. The focus of these chapters is on the demographic and economic impacts of recent immigration flows, the problems of assimilation, the impact of immigration on the public sector, and the recent changes in immigration policies. The role of selection criteria used by the immigration authorities in the three countries is also evaluated.

In Chapter 3, Jean-Marie Grether, Jaime de Melo, and Tobias Müller utilize a direct-democracy framework to analyze the determinants of national attitudes towards immigration. In the context of several variants of a two-sector, specific-factors model of an open economy, the study examines how the distribution of factor ownership over a population determines whether voters will choose restrictive or liberal immigration policies. The purpose of the analysis is to help interpret a number of stylized facts about recent immigration policies of the industrial countries. These include restrictive attitudes towards inflows of unskilled workers, lax enforcement of legislation related to employment of illegal aliens, preference for guest-workers over permanent migrants, and application of strict eligibility criteria for new immigrants.

The redistribution of income through the tax-transfer mechanism is becoming a key issue in the debate on the welfare consequences of international migration. Many consider the income-redistribution feature of the welfare state to serve as a magnet for immigrants. In Chapter 4, Assaf Razin and Efraim Sadka examine the political-economy determinants of the scope of the welfare state in the presence of migration. They also consider the implications of various redistribution policies for attitudes of native-born residents towards immigrants. Finally, they investigate whether unrestricted immigration would tend to generate a larger inflow of immigrants in a laissez-faire economy (no redistribution) or in a welfare state (with redistribution).

In Chapter 5, Philip Martin studies the various links between trade liberalization policies and migration flows in the context of NAFTA. Expanded trade between Mexico and the United States can be expected to reduce unwanted migration in the long run, while the development process itself tends to stimulate migration in the short to medium term. This gives rise to what is referred to as a migration hump. The chapter reviews five plausible scenarios under which migration humps are likely to occur and considers policy measures that may be useful in reducing their magnitude and duration. The problem of assessing migration potential and predicting future migration streams is also addressed by Michael Fertig and Christoph M. Schmidt in Chapter 6. They provide a critical survey of existing aggregate-level migration studies and go on to develop their own approach to the problem of predicting future migration streams from Eastern Europe to the European Union. Data for the post-World War II period is then used to generate concrete predictions of immigration flows under various identification strategies.

Illegal immigration in its various forms is becoming an increasingly important policy issue in most of the advanced economies. In my Chapter 7, I review the recent illegal immigration trends and discuss the effectiveness of policies used by the authorities of destination countries in an effort to control illegal entry, residence, and employment of undocumented foreign workers. The chapter also includes a discussion on the economic impact of illegal immigration. Alexander Sarris and Evgenia Markova consider in Chapter 8 the problem of legalizing illegal aliens. It is typically the case that not all illegal immigrants opt for legalization. This chapter examines the decision problem of the illegal immigrant *vis-à-vis* legalization, highlighting the role of the intended duration of stay in the host country and the costs of complying with the legalization requirements.

The study is based on the evidence from a survey of illegal Bulgarian immigrants reacting to a recent legalization drive in Greece. Also on the subject of illegal immigration, in Chapter 9, Francisco L. Rivera-Batiz uses a recently released national sample of illegal immigrants in the United States to examine their labor market performance and compare it to that of legal immigrants. He estimates human capital earnings functions, analyzing the role of education, age, location, and other factors in determining the earnings of Mexican and non-Mexican illegal immigrants. While the popular perception of illegal immigrants in the United States characterizes them as predominantly unskilled workers with low levels of schooling, the findings presented in this study provide a sharply different picture.

In Chapter 10, Barry R. Chiswick and Gaston Repetto provide an empirical analysis of the determinants of earnings and Hebrew language skills among adult male Jewish immigrants in Israel. They consider the role of schooling, pre-migration employment experience, duration in Israel, age, family structure, country of origin, and other variables. The study reports large effects on earnings of Hebrew language skills and correspondingly high estimates of the rate of return to investment in language training. In Chapter 11, Christian Dustmann provides an analysis of the conditions under which it is optimal for migrants to return to their countries of origin. The focus here is on the consumption-saving decision of temporary migrants and the determinants of their length of stay in the host country. Of the factors influencing behavior of migrants, emphasis is placed on international differences in purchasing power of savings, the effect of location on the utility of consumption, and the role of human capital accumulation by migrants in the host country. Finally, the chapter looks at the implications of the theoretical analysis for the specification of empirical models.

International migration is also a very important issue from the perspective of the source countries. One reason is that roughly $65 billion is transferred by migrants every year back to their countries of origin. For some of the countries, this constitutes a major portion of their foreign-exchange earnings. In such cases the flow of remittances has a significant impact on the distribution of income and the pattern of household spending on consumption as well as investment goods. In the closing chapter of the volume, Nicholas Glytsos reviews the literature on remittances, focusing on the analysis of the motives for remitting and the various factors that influence the flow of such transfers. The impact of remittance payments on the expenditure pattern of recipients as well as on the macroeconomic variables of source-country economies is examined on the basis of existing theoretical and empirical studies.

1 Immigration policies and their impact

The case of New Zealand and Australia

Rainer Winkelmann[1]

Introduction

Australia and New Zealand have much in common. Given their geographic proximity, their shared colonial past, and their close economic integration, it should not be surprising that their current approaches to immigration policy are in many ways similar. In particular, both countries emphasize the economic contribution immigrants are expected to make. Yet, there are small but important differences in policy as well. A study of the differences in post-migration outcomes, if any, can thus shed some light on the role of the selection system for the economic success of immigrants. To this end, the chapter provides an analysis of the recent immigration history of the two countries, including aspects of quantity, quality, and policy.

The next section starts with a description of the quantitative dimension of immigration: how many immigrants entered the two countries, and what were the contributions of external migration to population growth. The following section considers qualitative aspects of migration. Finally, an attempt is made to evaluate policy outcomes using empirical evidence on immigrants arriving in the 1990s. It is found that with a limited worldwide supply of internationally mobile skilled migrants, geography and macro-economic performance appear more important than policy in determining the size and the skill-composition of a country's potential immigration flows.

Immigration in New Zealand and Australia: a quantitative view

In this section, I will assess the status of Australia and New Zealand as immigration countries in the last decade(s) of the twentieth century.[2] Both New Zealand and Australia remain relatively unpopulated countries, and hence offer ample opportunity for population growth.[3] How were these opportunities perceived and dealt with, and what were the results that followed? An early report of the then just founded Australian Department of Immigration defined in 1945 that Australia's need for a greater population for the purposes of defence and development would be served well by a population growth rate of 2 percent per annum, 1 percent from natural increase and 1 percent from immigration (Price, 1998). Towards the end of the 1990s, New Zealand's government set the target for the annual number of residence approvals at 35,000, again about 1 percent of the population, although based more on a judgement of the society's absorptive capacities rather than on an overall population goal. Thus, it appears that this "1 percent" immigration rule is a useful point of reference against which the empirical evidence can be gauged.

A possible metric for assessing the openness of a country and the effects of international movements of people on its population size is net permanent and long-term (PLT) migration. As island states, both Australia and New Zealand can keep relatively reliable records of border movements through arrival and departure cards. While some details of the system differ in the two countries, the general idea is to ask people arriving (leaving) about their intended duration of stay in the country of arrival (or the country they departed for). Responses of 12 months or longer (but not permanent) are classified as "long-term" migration. Apart from some other socio-demographic characteristics, these cards also contain information on country of birth, country of citizenship, and residence status in the local country.

Table 1.1 provides information on population sizes and net-PLT migration for New Zealand and Australia between 1979 and 1996. New Zealand's population grew by 16 percent (or 0.8 percent per year) from 3.1 million to 3.6 million. Australia's population grew by 26 percent (or 1.3 percent per year) from 14.5 million to 18.3 million. Hence, both countries fell short of the overall 2 percent yardstick (for natural increase plus net-migration), but the discrepancy was particularly large for New Zealand. The main culprit was its negative cumulative net-PLT migration, i.e. more people left New Zealand long-term or permanently than arrived. Australia by contrast gained 1.6 million people through external migration, 43 percent of the overall increase in population. However, even Australia's net-PLT migration never reached the aforementioned 1 percent of the population, with an average net-migration rate of 0.59 percent.

Despite the finding of negative net-migration for New Zealand over most of the period,[4] New Zealand was an immigration country as well as an emigration country. This apparent contradiction is resolved when New Zealand nationals are considered separately from non-nationals. The third column of Table 1.1 gives the net-PLT migration statistics for non-New Zealand nationals only. It is found that non-New Zealand PLT migration generated a substantial surplus of 240,000 people between 1979 and 1996, 48 percent of the total population growth over the period. Moreover, the trend in non-New Zealand PLT migration is upward, reaching more than 1 percent of the population in 1996. In the early and mid-1990s, New Zealand's immigration program was substantially larger than Australia's in relative terms. However, the substantial inflow of immigrants was more

Table 1.1 Permanent and long-term (PLT) migration, New Zealand and Australia, 1979–1996

	New Zealand					Australia		
	Population (in thousands) (1)	*Net-PLT migration (2)*	*Net-non-NZ PLT migration (3)*	*(2)/(1)×100*	*(3)/(1)×100*	*Population (in thousands) (4)*	*Net-PLT migration (5)*	*(5)/(4)×100*
1979	3,137.8	−40,200	−2,776	−1.28	−0.09	14,515.7	55,100	0.38
1980	3,144.0	−34,417	2,603	−1.09	0.08	14,695.4	75,900	0.52
1981	3,156.7	−28,479	1,331	−0.90	0.04	14,923.3	119,200	0.80
1982	3,180.8	−11,482	8,689	−0.36	0.27	15,184.2	128,100	0.84
1983	3,221.7	3,180	10,685	0.10	0.33	15,393.5	73,300	0.48
1984	3,252.8	6,558	8,276	0.20	0.25	15,579.4	49,100	0.32
1985	3,271.5	−8,084	6,648	−0.25	0.20	15,788.3	73,700	0.47
1986	3,277.0	−21,613	6,420	−0.66	0.20	16,018.4	100,400	0.63
1987	3,303.6	−14,269	11,453	−0.43	0.35	16,263.9	125,700	0.77
1988	3,317.0	−15,625	12,353	−0.47	0.37	16,532.2	149,300	0.90
1989	3,330.2	−24,708	12,477	−0.74	0.37	16,814.4	157,400	0.94
1990	3,362.5	−4,018	14,624	−0.12	0.43	17,065.1	124,600	0.73
1991	3,406.2	11,616	15,555	0.34	0.46	17,284.0	86,400	0.50
1992	3,442.5	4,287	12,289	0.12	0.36	17,494.7	68,600	0.39
1993	3,480.2	6,848	15,570	0.20	0.45	17,667.1	30,000	0.17
1994	3,526.4	15,587	23,706	0.44	0.67	17,854.7	46,500	0.26
1995	3,580.0	21,697	33,756	0.61	0.94	18,071.8	80,100	0.44
1996	3,640.0	29,832	44,952	0.82	1.23	18,310.7	104,100	0.57
Change 1979–96 (in thousands)	+502.0	−103.3	+238.6			+3,795.0	+1,647.5	

than offset by international movements of New Zealand nationals who generated a combined deficit of 342,000 between 1979 and 1996. While there was a net loss of New Zealand nationals in every year, the magnitude was quite volatile, ranging from almost 40,000 in 1979 to less than 2,000 in 1984.

Most outmigrating New Zealand nationals leave for Australia. The Trans-Tasman Travel Agreement gives full freedom of movement, i.e. nationals can live and work anywhere in the two countries without a requirement of residence or work permits. As a rule of thumb, one in ten New Zealanders can be found in Australia.[5] Of course, many migrants return, and "permanent migration" is difficult to define in this context. However, of the estimated 404,750 New Zealand nationals who were present in Australia at June 30, 1999, slightly more than half had been there for more than 12 months (DIMA, 2000).[6] In principle, the Trans-Tasman Travel Agreement would also allow Australians to settle in New Zealand. But this option is taken up much less frequently, and only 54,708 Australia-born people were enumerated in the 1996 New Zealand Census. Hence, Trans-Tasman migration is to a large extent a "one-way street."

Of course, the emigration decisions of a country's nationals are not (at least not directly) subject to government policy. By contrast immigration policy directly affects the inflow of non-nationals, whereas settlement policy is one of the determinants of outflow of non-nationals. Hence, one could focus on the gross or net inflow of non-nationals as an indicator of the stance of immigration and settlement policy, rather than on overall net-migration. By this measure, the gap between New Zealand and Australia is reduced indeed. The net-inflow of immigrants, as defined by net-PLT migration, was on average 0.38 percent of the population in New Zealand. In the period 1991–96, the average net-migration rate of non-nationals was 0.68 percent for New Zealand, much higher than the overall net-migration rate of 0.39 percent for Australia.

The long-term importance of immigration for Australia and New Zealand can be assessed also by analyzing the composition of the population at one point in time. Common measures used in this context are the composition of the population by place of birth (i.e. foreign- or overseas-born versus native), the composition including second-generation immigrants, or, more generally, the ethnic composition. These are long-term measures, since depending on mortality, age-at-arrival and the population increase of the native population, the proportion of migrants is affected by the cumulative immigrant flows over the last half century and longer, and there is no simple link between the more recent flows and the overall stock of migrants.

The proportion of foreign-born residents is substantial in both countries: 17.6 percent of New Zealand residents were foreign-born in the last available census of 1996 (Cook, 1997); 23.3 percent of the Australian population were foreign-born as of June 30, 1997.[7] This gives Australia the lead among the traditional immigration countries. For instance, 17.4 of the Canadian population was born overseas in 1996, and 9.3 percent of the US population. The gap between the proportion of foreign-born New Zealand residents and foreign-born Australian residents mainly reflects historically higher net-migration gains in Australia, built up since World War II. At current immigration rates, the share will stabilize or decline in Australia, but further increase in New Zealand as both the departure of New Zealand-born people and the arrival of overseas settlers push up the proportion of foreign-born. For instance, between 1986 and 1996, i.e. in just ten years, the proportion of foreign-born among New Zealand residents increased by more than two percentage points from 15.4 to 17.5 (Winkelmann and Winkelmann, 1998a).

Immigration in New Zealand and Australia: a qualitative view

In any classical immigration country, a distinction can be made between economic and social migrants. The social stream has again two components, one being family reunification, the other humanitarian. While the humanitarian program tends to be the smallest among the three in Australia and New Zealand (this program includes an annual refugee allocation of 4,000 to Australia and 800 to New Zealand by the United Nations High Commissioner of Refugees, but the total size usually is two or three times as large), family reunification is a major factor, even though various steps have been undertaken over the years to limit the size of this stream.

The emphasis of the further analysis will be on Australia's and New Zealand's policy rules for the selection of economic migrants. Only this category provides the immediate possibility of selecting migrants based on personal characteristics and thus exerting a direct influence on "quality" aspects of migration. For New Zealand and Australia, two themes stand out behind the policy changes of the last half-century. The first is the abolition of ethnic background considerations; and the second is the shift from an "occupational needs principle" towards a "general skills principle," reflecting a change in the perception of the economic benefits of the types of skills that are involved.

Occupational migration

Traditionally, successive New Zealand and Australia governments from the 1950s and 1960s onwards regarded economic immigration as an instrument of labor market policy, to be applied to alleviate skill shortages in particular sectors, rather than as a force for broader economic growth. The mechanism used to control entry on this basis was an "Occupational Priority List." Employers wanting to recruit persons for occupations not on the list had to demonstrate that no suitable local resident was available or readily trained. In the 1990s the two countries' policies on this issue started to diverge. While New Zealand completely abandoned occupational targeting in 1991, Australia weakened its importance but nevertheless kept various direct and indirect instruments of occupational selection in place. For instance, preference is given in general to migrants in occupations that are part of a so-called "Migration Occupations in Demand List" (MODL). Moreover, the economic migration program continues to include a so-called Employer Nomination Scheme for skilled persons nominated for a specific skilled position by an Australian employer who has not been able to fill a vacancy from the local labor market or by training.

Cultural diversity

The second important characteristic of immigration policy is its ethnic dimension. The colonial past shaped immigration policy in both countries well into the second part of the twentieth century. For instance, in New Zealand, Commonwealth citizens of European ancestry and Irish citizens had unrestricted right of entry for residence until 1974. A complete break with an ethnic preference system did not occur until 1987 in New Zealand, when a "non-discriminatory" immigration policy was officially adopted. Prior to 1987, workers from so-called "Traditional Source Countries" were given priority in filling positions on the occupational priority list. To recruit from a non-traditional migrant source country, an employer had to show they could not recruit either in New Zealand or from a traditional source country and that the skills were not in demand in the country of origin (NZIS, 1997). This was a substantial constraint on occupational entry from non-traditional countries.

Traditional source countries were those from which New Zealand had previously taken substantial numbers of immigrants and/or which had vocational training schemes similar to its own. Initially, this list included most countries from Western and Northern Europe, plus Italy and the United States. This was effectively a "white New Zealand" policy, although it was not phrased that way at the time. In the mid-1970s, however, the list of countries was extended, opening up the possibility for large-scale immigration for Pacific Islanders. Pacific Island immigration was also given a boost by a general amnesty in 1976 for a large number of *de facto* immigrants who had come to New Zealand with temporary work permits and were given permanent residence status. Pacific Island immigration remained important throughout the 1980s.

A review of New Zealand's immigration policy was conducted in 1986. Factors motivating this review included a desire to acknowledge explicitly New Zealand's location in the Asia-Pacific region (considering that immigration from within this region might foster trade, attract investment, and increase cultural diversity), and a desire to tidy up some of the administrative and legal shortcomings of the old legislation (Burke, 1986).

The resulting Immigration Act 1987 abolished the "traditional source" preference list. It maintained the system of an occupational priority list until it was finally abandoned in 1991.

Australia was notably faster in formally giving up its "White Australia" policy of immigration. The gradual process took place over a period of 25 years and came to a conclusion as early as 1966 when Immigration Minister Opperman, after a review of the non-European immigration policy, announced applications for migration would be accepted from well-qualified people on the basis of their suitability as settlers, their ability to integrate readily and their possession of qualifications deemed useful to Australia.

At the same time, the government decided that a number of non-Europeans who had been initially admitted as "temporary" residents, but who were not to be required to leave Australia, could become residents and citizens after five years (i.e. the same as for Europeans), instead of 15 years previously required. These policy changes triggered a period of steady expansion of non-European migration, and the non-discriminatory immigration policy was reconfirmed and strengthened by various policy reviews in 1973 and 1978, among others.

The cumulative quantitative effects of these policies are visible in Table 1.2, which shows the distribution of the foreign-born population by region of birth for the two countries in 1995/1996. In both Australia and New Zealand, UK and Ireland constituted the most important countries of origin. However, the dominance was much less pronounced in Australia, where other European countries were more represented and, when combined, almost reached the share of UK and Ireland. This reflects the fact that at various times in the 1950s and 1960s, the Netherlands, Germany, Italy, Greece, Turkey and Yugoslavia were important migrant source countries for Australia. For New Zealand, however, the only substantial non-UK inflow from Europe was a Dutch migration wave in the 1950s.

Table 1.2 Foreign-born population by region of birth, 1995/1996

	New Zealand	*Australia*
Oceania	26.30	9.24
UK and Ireland	38.62	28.70
Other Europe	6.93	27.74
Middle East and North Africa	0.73	5.25
Asia	21.81	21.92
North America	3.37	2.20
South and Central America	0.00	2.05
Africa	2.24	2.90
Total	100.00	100.00

Sources: New Zealand: Winkelmann and Winkelmann (1998a), Table A3. Data come from the 1996 Census and include working age population only (15–64). Based on a list of countries that had at least 1,000 migrants enumerated in the census (34 countries met this criterion). Australia: DIMA Online publication. Reference date is June 30, 1995.

Moreover, Australia in 1995 had a much larger share of immigrants from the Middle East and North Africa, as well as South and Central America, than New Zealand. On the other hand, a disproportionate number of New Zealand's immigrants came from Oceania, i.e. mainly the Pacific Islands. The share of Asian immigrants was about the same in the two countries, one in five. Overall, though, one can clearly uncover the earlier commitment of Australia to a policy of diversified immigration. Apart from Asian and Pacific Island immigration, New Zealand drew immigrants mainly from two countries, the UK and the Netherlands, whereas Australia attracted migrants from a much wider pool of countries.

Current policy

At first glance, current immigration policies in Australia and New Zealand are very similar. The similarity starts with the official policy objectives. For New Zealand, official statements define goals such as "to allow entry to migrants who would make the highest contribution to employment and income growth" and "to maximise the gain in productive human capital while maintaining provisions for migrants to enter New Zealand for social and humanitarian reasons" (NZIS, 1997). Similarly, for Australia, one finds quotes that immigration should deliver an intake that "has broad-based skills with the capacity to contribute to Australia's economy" (DIMA, 2000).

In both cases, economic migration is deemed to bring into the country "productive human capital" or "broad based skills." The motive of short-term fixes for occupational labor market imbalances has been replaced by a longer-term perspective that fits into the current emphasis on a "knowledge society." In fact, Australia advertises its multicultural society as a competitive advantage: "'Productive Diversity' is an expression which recognises the economic value of Australia's culturally diverse society. Through 'Productive Diversity', companies can develop a competitive advantage by leveraging their most valuable resource: their people" (DIMA, 2000, Fact Sheet 12).

Further similarities concern the general structure of the immigration program, with its division into economic, family and humanitarian migration. And finally, the economic program in both countries is implemented as a point system. Points are allocated for employability, age and settlement factors, and an adjustable pass mark is set in order to meet a given target number of successful applications. In Australia's case, the target is an upper limit, whereas New Zealand operates a soft target that can be exceeded in single years.

The point system

Points are awarded in a way that is thought to promote a selection of "the most productive" applicants. From the perspective of human capital theory, the task is to determine the value of the transferable human capital a person is endowed with (or, more precisely, the present value of the stream of income associated with that human capital). Not surprisingly, then, the factors entering the point system are similar to those one would find in a typical Mincerian earnings function, augmented by life-cycle considerations: e.g. the level of schooling, actual labor market experience, language proficiency, and age. The points awarded to each characteristic could be seen as an assessment of the returns to these productive characteristics (in terms of higher life-time productivity/income) in the host country labor market.

Table 1.3 gives the current structure of the point system for skilled migrants in the two countries.[8] The guiding principles of the human capital model can be identified in both systems, although it is more purely presented in New Zealand. The current New Zealand pass mark is set at 25 points. A maximum of 12 points can be obtained for formal qualifications (Master degree or higher), a maximum of 10 points for experience (1 point for each two years), and a maximum of 10 points for age (25–29 years). An offer of employment brings 5 points, and a variety of other settlement factors can bring a maximum of 7 additional points.

There is a trade-off between age at the time of application and labor market experience that can be illustrated with some simple calculations. Assume that an applicant had an uninterrupted working career. In this case someone who started to work at the age of 18 obtains a maximum of 16 points for age and experience if aged 29–39 at the time of the application. For a starting age of 20 years, 16 points are reached for those aged 39 on application. If the applicant started to work at the age of 25, the maximum achievable number of points is 14 when aged 44. Despite the step-wise nature of the system, a general pattern emerges: in general, it is better to have started the working career at an early age. The optimal migration age is an increasing function of age at entry into the labor market. Interestingly, the inclusion of points for experience leads to a system where immigrants tend to be older (the prime-age range is between 29 and 44), and one can question whether the system sufficiently appreciates the common research finding that younger immigrants tend to be more easily integrated into the host country labor market than older immigrants.

The pattern is complicated, though not overturned, by including also qualifications, as qualifications and experience, for a given age, are negatively related. It is interesting to note that a minimum base qualification is not necessary to get over the pass mark if an offer of employment and other settlement factors exist. However, if settlement factors do not apply, then both a qualification and, in most cases, an offer of employment will be necessary to gain entry into New Zealand. The "returns" to a qualification beyond the base qualification are not very high (or even negative, if other factors are taken into account). In general, a PhD is worse than a Bachelor's degree because the years spent as a student do not qualify for work experience.

Table 1.3 Summary of points scored in general skills/skill independent category

	New Zealand	*Australia*
Qualifications	10 points for base qualification; 11 points for advanced qualification; 12 points for Master degree or higher (compulsory registration for certain occupations).	40 points for occupations which require diploma or advanced diploma level qualifications; 50 points for 'generalist' occupations which require degree level qualifications; 60 points for occupations that require degree (or higher) or trade level qualifications where entry to the occupation requires training which is specific to the occupation.
Host country qualification	2 points for a New Zealand qualification that is recognized for points.	Five points will be awarded where the applicant obtained a diploma, trade qualification or degree (this was introduced on July 1, 1998); or 10 points if the applicant holds an Australian PhD (doctorate degree) (introduced on November 1, 1999) from an Australian educational institution.
Work experience	1 point for each completed two years of experience, up to a maximum of 10 points.	5 points for applicants who have been employed in an occupation on the skilled occupation list for three out of the four years before applying; 10 points for applicants nominating an occupation which attracts 60 points under the skill factor, and who have worked in their nominated, or a closely related, occupation for three of the four years before applying.
Offer of employment/ occupational targeting	5 points for offer of ongoing full-time employment; no occupational targeting.	5 points for applicants whose skills are in short supply in Australia. These occupations will be included on a Migration Occupations in Demand List (MODL). A further 5 points will be awarded to applicants who have a genuine job offer in an occupation included on the MODL. (Note that Australia also operates a separate Employer Nomination Scheme.)

Age	8 points if 18–24 years; 10 points if 25–29 years; 8 points if 30–34 years; 6 points if 35–39 years; 4 points if 40–44 years; 2 points if 45–49 years;	30 points if 18–24 years; 30 points if 25–29 years; 25 points if 30–34 years; 20 points if 35–39 years; 15 points if 40–44 years.
	Migrants must be younger than 55	Migrants must be younger than 45
English language	All principal applicants and any accompanying family members aged 16 years and over must meet band score of 5 in each component of the IELTS test or having an English-speaking background. Principal applicants must meet the English language standard. Accompanying family members can instead pre-purchase language training. The cost depends on the applicant's current level of English (NZ$1,700–NZ$6,500).	15 points for applicants who achieve a score of at least 5 on each component of the IELTS; 20 points for applicants who obtain an IELTS score of 6 or more for each of the four components.
Settlement funds	1 point for $100,000. 2 points for $200,000.	5 bonus points possible for $100,000.
Spouse skills	1 point for base qualification. 2 points for advanced qualification.	5 points will be awarded where the applicant's spouse also meets the minimum requirements for skills (including work experience), age and English language ability.
Host country work experience	1 point per year up to 2 points.	5 bonus points possible.
Family sponsorship	3 points	Not available.
Passmark	25 points.	110 points.
Fees	NZ$700 and a settlement fee of NZ$180 per person (NZ$720 maximum per family) payable upon arrival in New Zealand.	AUS$ 1075, 2nd Instalment of AUS$2275 for insufficient language.

Finally, it is of importance how the language requirement is implemented. This was, and remains, one of the more contentious areas of the system, as reflected in the fact that rules were changed substantially on two occasions since the introduction of the point system in 1991. Initially, the English language requirement affected the principal applicant only. In contrast to Australia, no points were awarded but a certain level of proficiency was a non-negotiable requirement. In October 1995, the English language requirement was extended from just the principal applicant to all adult family members. A bond had to be paid per non-speaker to the government. The bond was refunded if sufficient English skills were acquired within a certain period of residence. A further change in 1999 replaced the bond-system by the requirement to pre-purchase English language training in New Zealand. Australia operates *de facto* a similar system: although migrants are entitled to 510 hours of government-funded tuition (or the number of hours it takes to reach functional English), adults with insufficient English proficiency are liable for a so-called second instalment payment upon arrival (that tends to be somewhat below the pre-purchase amount required in New Zealand).

The Australian system features a current pass mark of 110 points. Qualifications are not rewarded *per se*, but rather in relation to occupations they lead into. Up to 60 points can be obtained here. No special mention is made of high-level academic training. A PhD is not rewarded, unless it comes from an Australian university (which, of course, is a good way to "sell" Australian education programs in the Asian market).[9] Points for experience are awarded if the person worked in a skilled occupation for at least three out of the last four years. This ruling tends to favor younger immigrants (relative to the New Zealand system). This effect is reinforced by the maximum age, which is set at 45 years for Australia but at 55 years for New Zealand. It was already mentioned before that occupation still plays an active role in the Australian selection process, whereas it does not in New Zealand. Australia operates a "Migration Occupation in Demand List," and 5 extra points are awarded for occupations on that list, 10 extra points if employment for such an occupation has been offered. Finally, English proficiency is part of the point system in Australia. This has two consequences. First, non-proficient principal applicants are not *a priori* excluded from consideration. And second, it becomes possible to distinguish between levels of proficiency, as "very proficient" speakers (competent English) are awarded 5 more points over "proficient" speakers (vocational English).

In summary, although both countries operate a point system to select skilled economic migrants, the relative valuation of a potential migrant's characteristics is not the same. The Australian system prefers younger migrants with specific occupational skills. The New Zealand system generally provides less room for differentiation. Most importantly, it does not target specific skills but rather adheres to the "general skills principle." This "hands-off" policy is consistent with the devolution and reduction of government influence that came to be associated with the New Zealand reform agenda starting in 1984. While the resulting system has the advantage of simplicity, transparency, and conformity to the prevailing economic paradigm, it is not clear whether it leads to results that are superior to those of the more pragmatic Australian approach with its larger scope for micro-management. Some tentative empirical evidence on selection outcomes is considered next.

Outcomes

A comprehensive assessment on the relative merits of the two selection processes, in comparison with each other, and in comparison with alternative systems as they are operated in other countries, in the sense of a formal evaluation study, is beyond the scope of this survey. To the best of my knowledge, such an analysis has not been attempted yet. There are certainly immense conceptual and practical problems to overcome. Availability of appropriate data is one, but it is also unclear what exactly should one measure and compare. A paper that touches on the issue (Cobb-Clark and Connolly, 1997) considers the number of applicants to Australia, by country, and acceptance rates as an indicator of quality. However, Cobb-Clark and Connolly concentrate on the effects of inflows to two other major immigration countries (US and Canada, they ignore New Zealand), rather than on features of the Australian system itself. They come to the rather sobering conclusion that the possibilities for being selective are limited: since the pool of qualified internationally mobile migrants is small relative to the overall demand, and since Australia is only a "small player," it must accept most of the applicants, unless the annual intake is to be reduced quite a bit. If this is a valid argument for Australia, then it must be even more so for the even smaller "player" New Zealand.

Of course, for the direct competition between Australia and New Zealand, differences in the details of the migration system may still be decisive. To shed some light on this question, the modest goal of this section is threefold. First, the proportion of skilled migrants among all migrants is analyzed, indicating potential differences in the "bite" of the selection process with regard to the quality of the average migrant. Second, differences in the country-of-origin composition of successful applicants are studied. Third, unemployment rates of recent immigrants are compared.

Prior to presenting the evidence, one should ask, however, whether from a prospective migrant's point of view, the two countries can be considered as good substitutes. In other words, are the two countries likely to draw from the same pool of applicants? The standard model of migrant's choice emphasizes the relative returns to skills in the two countries, and thus inequality, as one factor. But absolute income levels matter as well. And while inequality measures are not so different in Australia and New Zealand

(Deininger and Squire, 1996), absolute income measures increasingly are. For example, between 1949 and 1998, per capita Gross Domestic Product (GDP) increased on average by 2.1 percent per annum in Australia, compared to 1.4 percent in New Zealand (Dalziel, 1999).

Concurrently with the increasing per capita GDP gap, considerable salary differentials have developed between New Zealand and Australia. The difference in growth of economic activity and opportunity not only provides a partial explanation to the observed one-way Trans-Tasman traffic of young New Zealanders to Australia, but is also likely to mean that New Zealand is only second choice for many prospective migrants. It also means that job opportunities for skilled workers tend to be more limited in New Zealand. This should be kept in mind in the following analysis.

One measure of the potential effects of the point systems for skilled migration on the overall immigrant quality is the proportion of points-tested migrants among all migrants in a given year, with family and humanitarian migration being the alternatives. Table 1.4 aggregates these two categories into a single "social"-migration category. It is found for New Zealand that between 1992 and 1998 about one-half to two-thirds of all migrants were subject to the points test.[10] In Australia, where family and humanitarian migration is relatively more important, this proportion was significantly lower, ranging from 25 to 50 percent. Efforts have been made in recent years to increase the share of economic migrants, with some success, as can be seen from Table 1.4.

There is ample research evidence that the country-of-origin composition is one of the main contributing factors to immigrants' labor market success. In particular, in the case of Australia and New Zealand, it is common practice for outcome studies to distinguish between immigrants with English speaking background (ESB) and those with non-English speaking

Table 1.4 People approved for residence by category: economic/social

	New Zealand (by calendar year)						
	1992	*1993*	*1994*	*1995*	*1996*	*1997*	*1998*
Economic	14,188 (0.55)	20,337 (0.69)	31,268 (0.74)	41,994 (0.75)	28,094 (0.66)	14,425 (0.48)	13,699 (0.47)
Social	11,475 (0.45)	9,166 (0.31)	11,200 (0.26)	13,898 (0.25)	14,615 (0.34)	15,380 (0.52)	15,635 (0.53)
	Australia (by business year)						
	1992/93	*1993/94*	*1994/95*	*1995/96*	*1996/97*	*1997/98*	*1998/99*
Economic	21,300 (0.32)	18,297 (0.30)	30,400 (0.35)	24,100 (0.25)	27,550 (0.33)	34,670 (0.44)	35,000 (0.45)
Social	45,300 (0.68)	43,181 (0.70)	57,700 (0.65)	71,752 (0.75)	56,483 (0.67)	43,330 (0.56)	43,400 (0.55)

background (NESB) (see, for instance, Miller, 1986; Beggs and Chapman, 1988; McDonald and Worswick, 1999; Winkelmann and Winkelmann, 1998a, b). It is generally found that NESB migrants have labor market outcomes (e.g. earnings, unemployment rates) that are considerably worse than those of ESB migrants.

Table 1.5 shows the Top-10 countries of origin for the economic migrants who obtained their residence permit in the year ending June 1997. In both countries, UK and Ireland are still the most important single source countries.[11] However, Asian immigration clearly outweighs migration from Europe. The combined share of Asian countries in the Top-10 list was 30 percent in New Zealand and 44 percent in Australia. Furthermore, there was substantial migration from South Africa in both countries, reflecting the political changes taking place in that country. Taken together, about one-half of the approvals in either country were for migrants with an English speaking background, and one-half for those without.

A further point worth noting is the continuing difference in the degree of diversity between the two countries. It was already shown above that Australia's immigration history is characterized by greater ethnic and country-of-origin diversity. Table 1.5 shows that this trend continues into the present. For instance, the Top-3 countries had a combined share of 55 percent of all approvals in the case of New Zealand, but only 39 percent in the case of Australia. One possible explanation can be found in models of "network migration" (for an overview, see Bauer and Zimmermann, 1998), according to which migration may become self-perpetuating because the cost and risks of migration are lowered by social and informational networks that have been built up through previous migrants. Network migration could also explain why New Zealand continues to be an important receiving country for Pacific Islanders, whereas Pacific Island migration is much less important for Australia.

Table 1.5 Top-10 countries of origin among residence approvals in skilled stream, year ending June 1997 (%)

New Zealand	%	*Australia*	%
UK and Ireland	21	UK and Ireland	18
South Africa	19	Hong Kong	11
China	15	South Africa	10
India	7	China	8
Fiji	3	Taiwan	8
Hong Kong	3	India	6
Philippines	3	Indonesia	6
USA	3	Singapore	3
Iraq	2	USA	2
Taiwan	2	Malaysia	2
Other	22	Other	26
Total	100	Total	100

Table 1.6 shows the unemployment rates for recent immigrants in Australia and New Zealand. Unemployment is only one among several possible measures of labor market success. It is chosen here for pragmatic reasons, because of the availability of comparable information for the two countries. While the focus on *recent* immigrants provides an incomplete picture of the overall contribution of immigrants to the economy, as it ignores issues of assimilation and integration, it gives a useful yardstick as it reflects the immediate impact of recent selection policies and as it remains relatively unaffected by selective outmigration.

The Australian statistics are provided by Williams, Brooks and Murphy (1997), based on a sample survey of immigrants in 1994 or 1995. The New Zealand statistics are based on the study by Winkelmann and Winkelmann (1998a) and refer to the 1996 census. Both sources refer to *all* arrivals and do not distinguish between economic and social immigrants. This puts some limits on the interpretation. Also, when comparing the statistics, one should be aware that the base years are not the same, and that the definition of "recent immigrants" differs somewhat, from 3–6 months after

Table 1.6 Unemployment rates of recent immigrants by selected characteristics

	New Zealand	*Australia*
Sex		
Female	0.37	0.41
Male	0.33	0.38
Age		
15–24	0.29	0.43
25–34	0.33	0.34
35–44	0.40	0.40
45–54	0.40	0.60
55–64	0.29	0.68
Region of origin		
Oceania*	0.21	0.39
Europe	0.27	0.27
Southeast Asia	0.33	0.54
Northeast Asia	0.42	0.26
South Asia	0.59	0.50
Total	0.35	0.39

Sources: New Zealand: Winkelmann and Winkelmann (1998a), who analyze the 1996 Census, own calculations. Recent immigrants have spent less than 1 year in New Zealand, i.e. between 0 and 11 months.

Australia: Williams, Brooks, and Murphy (1997), Table 1.4. Results are based on the Longitudinal Survey of Immigrants to Australia (LSIA). The first round of interviews began in 1994 and was completed in 1995. A total of 5,192 immigrants (out of a population of some 75,000) who were principal applicants for permanent resident visas and who arrived in Australia during the period September 1993–August 1995, were interviewed within 3 to 6 months after arrival.

Note: *'Oceania' excludes New Zealand citizens in the case of Australia, but includes Australia-born people in the case of New Zealand.

arrival in Australia to 0–11 months after arrival in New Zealand. The latter difference tends to be in favor of New Zealand's immigrants, although the magnitude of this effect is unclear.

The overall unemployment rates of recent immigrants were 35 percent for New Zealand and 39 percent for Australia. At first, these rates look exorbitantly high, as overall unemployment rates were well under 10 percent over the period. However, one has to recognize that unemployment rates for other new labor market entrants are high as well. Williams, Brooks and Murphy (1997) provide some estimates for Australia. According to these, 27 percent of those who left the education system at the end of 1993 were unemployed five months later. A 1995 survey of Australian first-time labor market entrants (those who just finished the education system plus others) estimated their unemployment rate to be 45 percent.

Table 1.6 also decomposes the unemployment rates by gender, age and region of origin. Women have higher unemployment rates in both countries. The differences are not as large as one might expect though, considering that women are often tied movers who are not screened independently as economic migrants. The age-unemployment patterns are opposite in the two countries: u-shaped (with a low between 25–34) in Australia and inverse u-shaped (with a high between 35–54) in New Zealand. The inverse u-shape in New Zealand is unusual, and it contrasts with the pattern in the New Zealand-born population. Finally, as expected, the table reveals substantial region-of-origin effects: unemployment rates are lowest for Europe-born immigrants and highest for Asian-born immigrants. This discrepancy could be an expression of the "English-language" effect, or capture cultural or some other differences.

Overall, one can conclude from the evidence presented in Table 1.6 that despite some differences between the outcomes of immigrants, none of the two countries stands out as particularly superior. The main impression in fact is one of similarity: immigration is by no means a "painless" process. It is associated with high initial unemployment rates, and European immigrants continue to be better off in the two countries relative to immigrants from other regions.

Summary and conclusions

Throughout the 1990s, New Zealand and Australia experienced substantial immigration, although its effect on overall population growth was small by historical standards. In New Zealand's case, despite a substantial intake, immigration was only partially able to offset the population loss due to New Zealanders leaving. In Australia's case, the immigrant intake was relatively smaller. But with modest outmigration, it nevertheless generated a steady net migration gain.

The most significant policy event over the last half-century was the abolition of the "traditional source country" preference with its resulting ethnic diversification. More recently, both countries refined their selection process with regard to economic migrants. The New Zealand approach is human capital based and emphasizes general skills in its selection. The Australian approach has similar elements, although it appears somewhat more pragmatic by maintaining elements of occupational selection.

In both countries, the region-of-origin composition continues its shift from Europe towards Asia. Immigration is associated with high initial unemployment rates, while European immigrants continue to be better off relative to immigrants from other regions in both countries. It is difficult to draw firm conclusions with respect to the effect of policies on outcomes. One potential lesson is that the limited supply of highly skilled, internationally mobile workers puts a binding constraint on a country's ability to implement a skill-based immigration policy.

Notes

1 I thank Jacques Poot for valuable comments on an earlier draft, and Sibel Duman for her research assistance.

2 Concise summaries of the two countries' earlier migration experiences can be found in Price (1998), Burke (1986), and Shroff (1988).

3 Australia has about 6 inhabitants per square mile and New Zealand about 33. This is well below the United States (74), or Western European countries such as Germany (600) (Statistical Abstracts of the United States, 1994).

4 As a matter of fact, the net migration rate had turned negative again by the end of the decade. For the year ending January 2000 there was a net loss of 9,460 permanent and long-term migrants, up 14 percent on the net outflow of 8,330 in the January 1999 year (Statistics New Zealand, External Migration (January 2000) Media Release).

5 The economic determinants of Trans-Tasman migration have been studied in Brosnan and Poot (1987), Gorbey, James and Poot (1999), Poot (1995), Poot, Nana and Philpott (1988), and Nana and Poot (1996), among others.

6 Of the 24,686 New Zealand permanent migrants to Australia in 1998/99, only 76 percent were born in New Zealand. The rest were "step-migrants" (DIMA, 2000). New Zealand permanent residents can apply for citizenship after three years of residence (citizenship can be obtained after two years of residence in Australia).

7 On June 30, 1997, a further 19.2 percent were Australia-born but had at least one parent born overseas.

8 These tabulations are made available by the respective immigration services over the internet. In fact, it is possible for prospective immigrants anywhere in the world to conduct a self-assessment and to find out whether or not the combined number of points is sufficient for immigration. The transparency of the system is somewhat diminished in Australia, since the various occupational classifications require judgements that may not be immediately available to the individual.

9 People with outstanding academic or other abilities can apply under different programs, such as the "Distinguished Talent Scheme," or the "Employer Nomination Scheme."

10 Literally speaking, not everyone coming through the economic category is points tested, since the points test only involves the principal applicant, although accompanying direct family members are also counted among immigrants in that class.

11 It was mentioned before that New Zealand was the most important country of origin for Australian immigrants in the late 1990s. However, since New Zealanders do not need residence approval, they are not included in this table.

References

Bauer, T. and K.F. Zimmermann (1998) "Causes of International Migration: A Survey," in C. Gorter, P. Nijkamp and J. Poot (eds), *Crossing Borders: Regional and Urban Perspectives on International Migration*, Ashgate: Aldershot.

Beggs, J.J. and B.J. Chapman (1988) "Immigrant Wage Adjustment in Australia: Cross Section and Time-series Estimates," *Economic Record*, 64: 161–167.

Brosnan, P. and J. Poot (1987) "Modelling the Determinants of Trans-Tasman Migration after World War II," *Economic Record*, 63: 313–329.

Burke, K. (1986) "Review of Immigration Policy," *Appendix to the Journals of the House of Representatives*, 1986–87.

Cobb-Clark, D.A. and M.D. Connolly (1997) "The Worldwide Market for Skilled Migrants: Can Australia Compete?" *International Migration Review*, 31: 670–693.

Cook, L. (1997) "New Zealand's Current and Future Population Dynamics," paper presented at the Population Conference held in Wellington on November 12–14, 1997.

Dalziel, P. (1999) "New Zealand's Economic Reforms Failed to Achieve their Ultimate Objectives," mimeo, University of Canterbury.

Deininger, K. and L. Squire (1996) "A New Data Set Measuring Income Inequality," *World Bank Economic Review*, 10 (3): 565–591.

Department of Immigration and Multicultural Affairs (DIMA) (2000), various fact sheets under http://www.immi.gov.au/statistics/migrant.htm

Gorbey, S., D. James and J. Poot (1999) "Population Forecasting with Endogenous Migration: An Application to Trans-Tasman Migration," *International Regional Science Review*, 22: 69–101.

McDonald, J.T. and C. Worswick (1999) "The Earnings of Immigrant Men in Australia: Assimilation, Cohort Effects, and Macroeconomic Conditions," *Economic Record*, 75: 49–62.

Miller, P.W. (1986) Immigrant unemployment in the first year of Australian labor market activity, *Economic Record* 62, 82–87.

Nana, G. and J. Poot (1996) "Trans-Tasman Migration and Closer Economic Relations," in P.J. Lloyd and P.S. Williams (eds), *International Trade and Migration in the APEC Region*, Oxford: Oxford University Press.

New Zealand Immigration Service (NZIS) (1997) "New Zealand Immigration Policy and Trends," paper prepared for the Population Conference held in Wellington on November 12–14, 1997.

Poot, J. (1995) "Do Borders Matter? A Model of Interregional Migration in Australasia," *Australasian Journal of Regional Studies*, 1: 159–182.

Poot, J., G. Nana and B. Philpott (1988) *International Migration and the New Zealand Economy: A Long-Run Perspective*, Wellington: Victoria University Press for the Institute of Policy Studies.

Price, C.A. (1998) "Post-war Immigration: 1947–98," *Journal of the Australian Population Association*, 15: 115–129.

Shroff, G. (1988) "New Zealand's Immigration Policy," *New Zealand Official Yearbook*, 1988–89: 193–207.

Williams, L.S., C. Brooks and J. Murphy (1997) "The Initial Labor Market Outcomes of Immigrants," *Australian Bulletin of Labour*, 23: 193–213.

Winkelmann, L. and R. Winkelmann (1998a) *Immigrants in the New Zealand Labour Market: A Study of their Labour Market Outcomes*, Wellington: New Zealand Department of Labour.

Winkelmann, L. and R. Winkelmann (1998b) "Immigrants in the New Zealand Labour Market: A Cohort Analysis using 1981, 1986 and 1996 Census Data," *Labour Market Bulletin*, 1&2: 34–70.

Winkelmann, R. (2000) "The Labour Market Performance of European Immigrants in New Zealand in the 1980s and 1990s," *International Migration Review*, 34 (1): 33–58.

2 Canadian immigration

Economic winners and losers

Don DeVoretz

Major economic and social impacts have occurred in Canada as a consequence of the almost five million immigrant arrivals circa 1967–96 who now represent 17 percent of Canada's population. Public finance transfers have resulted from this immigrant inflow as well as wage compression and labor displacement and altered savings and wealth accumulation levels. In short, each of these economic arenas has experienced major changes in the demand and supply conditions, which in turn has redistributed resources among old and new immigrants and resident Canadians. It is the primary focus of this chapter to document the winners and losers.

From 1967 until 1975, immigration inflows largely emanated from Europe through three entry gates: an independent class, nominated relatives, and a sponsored group (refugees). The 1951 Immigration Act, which provided the legislative framework for this immigration flow, was reformulated in the 1960s to reduce the inherent racism in Canada's immigration legislation and to focus on the economic attributes of immigrants. In particular, in the late 1960s, Canada instituted a "points system" to assess economic immigrants. This system evaluated the primary independent-class immigrant on the basis of his/her human capital characteristics. A formal test was applied with a passing grade set at 50 points out of a maximum of 70.

Admission in the independent class could be gained through knowledge of English/French, youth, education and job experience (Green and Green, 1995). In addition, the "points system" precluded country or area preferences, and under this new regime a precipitous decline in European immigrants occurred in 1967–76. In 1967, European immigrants accounted for approximately 160,000 immigrants or 70 percent of the total arrivals (222,876), but by 1976 Europeans accounted for less than 33 percent of the 149,429 arrivals.

The year 1976 was a watershed in Canada's immigration policy history since new immigration legislation was brought forward culminating in the 1978 Immigration Act. This act retained the points system for economic applicants in order to meet its defined demographic and economic goals, but also opened two new entry gates for immigrants to Canada. These latter gates were for family reunification entrants and refugees and were intended to meet Canada's humanitarian goals. In addition, the Minister of Immigration was required to announce an annual target for the following year's immigration level.

These innovations had two important economic implications. First, unlike in the 1967–75 period, the percentage of economically assessed immigrants fell as the Ministry attempted to meet yearly quotas by increasing the oversubscribed family class or expanding refugee numbers. In the 1968–76 period (under the 1967 regulations of the 1953 Immigration Act), over 70 percent of immigrants were screened in the independent or economic class. This high percentage of economic immigrants dropped under the 1978 Immigration Act at first below 30 percent (1975–82) and then to about 14 percent of the total flow by the mid-1980s. To partially counteract this decline in the independent entry class, new entry classes were devised under the 1978 act. Self-employed or entrepreneurs and investor (after 1985) immigrants were now separately assessed and admitted based on their ability to be self-financed or to create jobs. Even with these new economic entry gates, however, Canada abandoned a policy of using immigration as an engine of economic growth. During 1982–85, as Canada's unemployment rate soared, policymakers responded by reducing the level of economic immigrants to near zero and the total level to about 84,000. This was an even more precipitous decline than at first appears once we recognize that Canada experiences a 50,000–75,000 yearly emigration outflow, leaving a total net immigrant inflow of less than 30,000 in 1984.

After 1986, a new policy direction was sought and a concerted effort was made to raise the immigrant numbers in the economic class, and as a consequence total immigrant numbers rose to a peak in the early 1990s. The stated policy rationale for this increase was that economic immigrants could stimulate Canada's then weak economy. This policy goal was reflected in the revised points system criteria for entry.

The points system as applied in the 1990s to the independent class is outlined in Table 2.1. In this period, the points system was no longer dominated by the migrant's human capital characteristics of age, education and language. Rather, occupational criteria accounted for 60 or more of the necessary 70 points needed to gain admission. Others have argued that this shifting from human capital or long-run characteristics to immediate job qualifications was an attempt to reduce any welfare or other negative public finance impacts of immigrants. We document this outcome in a later section.

However, political considerations hindered an expansion of the economic class under these revised points criteria. Given that maintenance of the family class was a goal of a large political constituency (five million post-1967 immigrants had rights to sponsorship), the only mechanism open to increasing the economic class was to add these numbers over and above the then dominant family class and not to shrink the family class.

Table 2.1 Canada's points system circa 1990s

Category	*Potential*
Long-term	
Education	12
Age	10
Occupational demand	10
Occupation skill	15
Experience	8
Suitability	10
Short-term	
English/French	15
Arranged employment	10
Levels control	10
Total	100

Source: DeVoretz and Laryea (1998b).

Table 2.2 illustrates that, regardless of the underlying philosophy, the post-1986 increase in net immigrant numbers was still substantial, and this increase in immigrant numbers allowed for a major growth in Asian and African immigration. In particular, almost the entire increase in immigrant numbers between 1986 and 1996 of 126,000 was accounted for by the 103,000 increase in Asian immigrants alone. African immigration also increased by over 10,000 during this period to account for the remainder of this period's increase. Immigration from the USA, other North American and Central and South American regions actually declined during the 1990s as the economy of the United States grew faster than that of Canada, and terrorism in Latin America abated.

In sum, Table 2.2 reveals that Canada's post-1986 immigrant flow by source country approximately reflected the world's population distribution, with over 62 percent of Canada's post-1990 immigrant inflow emanating from Asia. Within the Asian source region, however, there occurred substantial shifts between immigrant source countries over the 1986–96 period. Originally Hong Kong émigrés and later those from China–Taipei dominated Canada's post-1990 immigrant inflow. More recently, immigration from the People's Republic of China has led Canada's Asian immigrant inflow. This post-1986 source country pattern for Canada's immigrants is in sharp contrast to conditions 35 years ago when Asian immigration to Canada was almost non-existent.

Two major forces caused this shift in country of immigrant origin. First, as noted, a deliberate change in Canadian immigration policy occurred after 1967 as Canada went to a "points-assessment system." The second and more important force that caused a shift in source regions was the decline in the demand by Europeans for Canadian immigrant slots as European economic growth outstripped that of Canada. By the 1990s,

Table 2.2 Immigrants to Canada by region of last permanent residence, 1967–1996

Year	*Europe*	*Africa*	*Asia*	*Australia*	*USA*	*Other North/ Central America*	*Caribbean*	*South America*	*Oceania and other Ocean Islands*	*NS**	*Grand total*
1967	159,979	4,608	20,740	6,168	19,038	422	8,582	3,090	–	249	222,876
1968	120,702	5,204	21,610	4,815	20,422	374	7,755	2,693	–	323	183,974
1969	88,383	3,297	23,319	4,411	22,785	593	13,315	4,767	–	681	161,531
1970	75,609	2,863	21,170	4,385	24,424	711	12,660	4,385	–	948	147,713
1971	52,031	2,841	22,171	2,902	24,366	636	11,017	2,902	–	878	121,900
1972	51,293	8,308	23,325	2,143	22,618	865	8,353	2,143	–	792	122,006
1973	71,883	8,307	43,193	2,671	25,242	1,141	19,563	11,057	1,143	–	184,200
1974	88,694	10,450	50,566	2,594	26,541	1,391	23,885	12,528	1,816	–	218,465
1975	72,898	9,867	47,382	2,174	20,155	1,510	17,973	13,270	2,652	–	187,881
1976	49,908	7,752	44,328	1,886	17,315	1,356	14,842	10,628	1,414	–	149,429
1977	40,748	6,372	31,368	1,545	12,888	1,330	11,911	7,840	912	–	114,914
1978	30,075	4,261	24,007	1,233	9,945	950	8,328	6,782	719	13	86,313
1979	32,858	3,958	50,540	1,395	9,617	732	6,366	5,898	726	6	112,096
1980	41,168	4,330	71,602	1,555	9,926	800	7,361	5,433	942	–	143,117
1981	46,295	4,887	48,830	1,317	10,559	1,110	8,633	6,136	934	17	128,618
1982	46,150	4,510	41,617	938	9,360	1,651	8,674	6,870	1,181	196	121,147
1983	24,312	3,659	36,906	478	7,381	3,654	7,216	4,816	735	–	89,157
1984	20,901	3,552	41,896	535	6,992	4,078	5,630	4,084	616	25	88,239
1985	18,859	3,545	38,597	506	6,669	5,016	6,132	4,456	622	–	84,302
1986	22,709	4,770	41,600	503	7,275	6,078	8,874	6,686	724	–	99,219
1987	37,563	8,501	67,337	753	7,967	6,873	11,227	10,801	1,074	2	152,098
1988	40,689	9,380	81,136	745	6,537	5,671	9,439	7,225	1,077	–	161,929
1989	52,105	12,198	93,213	894	6,931	5,870	10,909	8,685	1,147	49	192,001
1990	51,945	13,440	111,739	988	6,084	7,781	11,689	8,989	1,659	7	214,230
1991	48,055	16,087	119,995	952	6,597	13,404	12,922	10,582	2,183	44	230,781
1992	44,871	19,633	139,216	1,191	7,537	12,526	14,952	10,389	2,468	59	252,842
1993	46,602	16,918	147,323	1,319	8,014	7,737	16,563	9,580	1,763	–	255,819
1994	36,641	13,706	141,587	1,108	6,234	3,503	9,980	7,919	1,197	–	223,875
1995	41,266	14,631	129,106	1,049	5,185	2,842	10,056	7,538	831	–	212,504
1996	39,970	14,859	144,210	1,228	5,837	3,409	9,322	6,104	834	–	225,773
67–85	1,132,746	102,571	703,167	43,651	306,243	28,320	208,196	119,778	14,412	4,128	2,667,878
86–96	462,416	144,123	1,216,462	10,730	74,198	75,694	125,933	94,498	14,957	161	2,221,071
67–96	1,595,162	246,694	1,919,629	54,381	380,441	104,014	334,129	214,276	29,369	4,289	4,888,949

Sources: Citizenship and Immigration, Canada: Calendar Years 1967–1996 and Facts and Figures 1998: Immigration Overview.

Canada's immigration policy had been refocused, with the primary goal being to achieve at least 50 percent economic entrants in each arrival cohort.

Table 2.3 provides an outline of the changing composition of Canada's immigration flow by entry category. Several trends emerge from Table 2.3. First, refugee flows (column 3) average generally less than 20 percent of the yearly intake. These refugee admissions are largely beyond the control of Canada's immigrant policymakers since these numbers reflect external pressures.[1] The nature of Canada's immigration selection program, as already noted, divides the remainder of the entry flows into two broad categories – economic or family reunification. Family reunification is narrowly defined in Canada and includes only immediate paternal or maternal relatives. During 1986–96, this family reunification number fluctuated widely from 42,000 to over 112,000. The important point to note, however, is that as a proportion of the entire flow, the family class has never exceeded 50 percent of any annual inflow and generally fell below 30 percent *after 1986*. Thus, since 1986, Canada has implicitly followed the important entry rule of thumb of "cinquante-cinquante" or fifty-fifty. We expand on the importance of this rule of thumb below. In fact, by 1995, approximately 62 percent of the immigrant intake occurred in a broadly defined economic class, with the remaining 38 percent arriving in the family and/or refugee classes.

How were the economic impacts emanating from this large post-1986 immigrant inflow distributed across Canada? And where did these almost three million post-1986 immigrants settle once they arrived in Canada? On

Table 2.3 Immigrants to Canada by category, 1986–1998

Year	*Family class*	*Total refugees*	*Total entre-preneurs*	*Total self-employed*	*Total investors*	*Other immigrants**	*Grand total*
1986	42,197	19,147	5,866	1,629	23	20,774	99,219
1987	53,598	21,565	8,440	2,313	316	65,866	152,098
1988	51,331	26,836	11,372	2,712	1,028	68,650	161,929
1989	60,774	37,004	12,984	2,309	2,271	76,659	192,001
1990	73,457	39,689	12,263	1,974	4,208	84,639	214,230
1991	86,378	53,401	9,901	1,953	5,189	73,959	230,781
1992	99,960	51,875	15,697	2,818	9,628	72,864	252,842
1993	112,266	30,382	16,666	3,384	12,576	80,545	255,819
1994	93,882	20,384	14,166	2,736	10,463	82,244	223,875
1995	77,174	27,990	11,414	2,850	5,164	87,912	212,504
1996	68,229	28,291	11,909	4,371	6,172	106,801	225,773
1997	59,956	24,101	10,404	3,926	5,594	112,058	216,044
1998	50,861	22,644	6,618	2,625	4,535	86,817	174,100
1986–98	930,063	403,309	147,700	35,600	67,167	1,019,788	2,611,215

Sources: Canada (1997, 1999).

Note: *Skilled workers are included under this category.

the surface, since Canada is a large country geographically, it would seem easy for Canada to absorb into the economy 250,000 immigrants per annum since this is only fraction (0.8 of 1 percent) of its base population. Table 2.4 indicates, however, that immigrants do not move to the whole of Canada but rather they move to a select group of Canadian urban centres, thus creating regional economic winners and losers in the process.

The exact urban destination of Canada's immigrants varies over the 1986–96 period but largely depends on individual cities' economic conditions and the source country of immigrants, with the majority of immigrants destined for Canada's three major cities of Toronto, Vancouver and Montreal. Toronto, in turn, is always the primary destination for Canada's immigrants. Over the 1986–96 period, Toronto attracted a near-constant share (30 percent or more) *regardless* of the level of Canada's yearly absolute total immigrant inflow. Vancouver, on the other hand, has become a more favored destination over the more recent period as its share of the yearly immigrant inflow grew from 9 percent to 20 percent, while Montreal suffered a steep decline in absolute numbers as well as percentage share (17 percent to 9.7 percent). The economic decline of Montreal largely explains the diminution of its status as a major immigrant-reception area. The robustness of Vancouver's economy and its Asian heritage accelerated the arrival of Asians to the city in the early 1990s. Toronto, as noted, is the exception. It still remains the favored city of Asians, even though Asian immigrants do not dominate in the city, and Toronto's recession of the early 1990s did not stall the movement of immigrants into the city as it did in Montreal.

One final immigrant destination pattern is important to note, namely the large absolute and percentage size (40 percent) of immigrant movement to the "other" city categories. Mid-size cities such as Ottawa, Calgary, Winnipeg and Hamilton now experience significant in-movements of immigrants to complement their respective cities' periodic spurts in economic growth.

The regional demographic impact derived from this urban post-1986 immigration inflow has fuelled a listless urban population growth when domestic fertility would have implied near-zero urban population growth. For example, during the 1986–96 period, two-thirds of Vancouver's population growth was due to this immigrant in-movement. In fact, in the absence of immigration, Vancouver's population would have grown by less than 0.6 of 1 percent per annum after 1986. A similar pattern holds for Toronto, while Montreal's absolute population decline was partially offset by immigrant arrivals.

In sum, a few cities in Canada were the favored destinations for post-1986 immigrants, with Toronto and Vancouver clearly the winners in the numbers game. How do we assess the impact of this robust and highly urbanized post-1986 immigrant inflow into Canada? As was noted above, Canada's 1978 Immigration Act set a variety of economic, social and

Table 2.4 Immigrants to Canada by city of intended destination, 1986–1996

	Vancouver		*Toronto*		*Montreal*		*Others*		*Grand Total*	
	#	%	#	%	#	%	#	%	#	%
1986	8,914	8.98	29,564	29.30	17,228	17.36	43,513	43.86	99,219	100
1987	14,536	9.56	55,184	36.28	24,141	15.87	58,237	38.29	152,098	100
1988	18,502	11.43	55,832	34.48	22,737	14.04	64,858	40.05	161,929	100
1989	20,611	10.73	63,453	33.05	30,245	15.75	77,692	40.46	192,001	100
1990	23,747	11.08	64,884	30.29	36,917	17.23	88,682	41.40	214,230	100
1991	26,361	11.42	63,891	27.68	46,300	20.06	94,229	40.83	230,781	100
1992	30,796	12.18	74,047	29.29	42,500	16.81	105,499	41.73	252,842	100
1993	37,132	14.60	71,956	28.29	38,482	15.13	106,751	41.97	254,321	100
1994	41,920	18.72	65,667	29.33	22,908	10.23	93,380	41.72	223,875	100
1995	38,166	17.96	66,808	31.44	20,270	9.54	87,247	41.06	212,491	100
1996	44,615	19.91	72,471	32.35	21,871	9.76	85,093	37.98	224,050	100
1986–96	305,300		683,757		323,599		905,181		2,217,837	

Source: Canada (1997).

Note: Total is for CMSAs or cities and not Canada.

demographic goals to assess Canada's immigration program. However, the ultimate goal of this chapter is to assess the economic winners or losers generated by immigrant arrivals. My thesis will argue that, in order to achieve these three goals and minimize negative distributional impacts, Canada required a balanced immigrant entry program. This balanced program I have termed elsewhere as a "cinquante-cinquante" policy with 50 percent economic entrants and 50 percent non-economic (family class and refugees) entrants per year.[2] This operational rule, I argue, has the important distributional consequence of enhancing the welfare of Canada's resident population in general while in particular not harming Canada's poorest.[3] Figure 2.1 provides the theoretical structure to evaluate if immigrants improve or worsen the welfare of resident Canadians in terms of the immigrant's impact on public finances.

In particular, Figure 2.1 presents a life-cycle analysis of public consumption and tax payments over an immigrant household's lifetime. For example, if Canada admits a 25-year-old immigrant, it is argued then that throughout this immigrant's working life (25–65) tax payments (T_i-T_i) will exceed the consumption (C_i-C_i) of public goods as the immigrant's lifetime income increases in the first 10–12 years in Canada.[4] Thus, the discounted lifetime monetized difference between this immigrant's consumption of public goods (C_i-C_i) and his or her tax payments (T_i-T_i) yields the immigrant's surplus to the treasury. The existence of this immigrant surplus implies that immigrants subsidize Canada's resident population and one portion of the DeVoretz criterion for a successful distributional outcome is satisfied. Figure 2.2 depicts the case when immigrants are a net draw on the treasury.

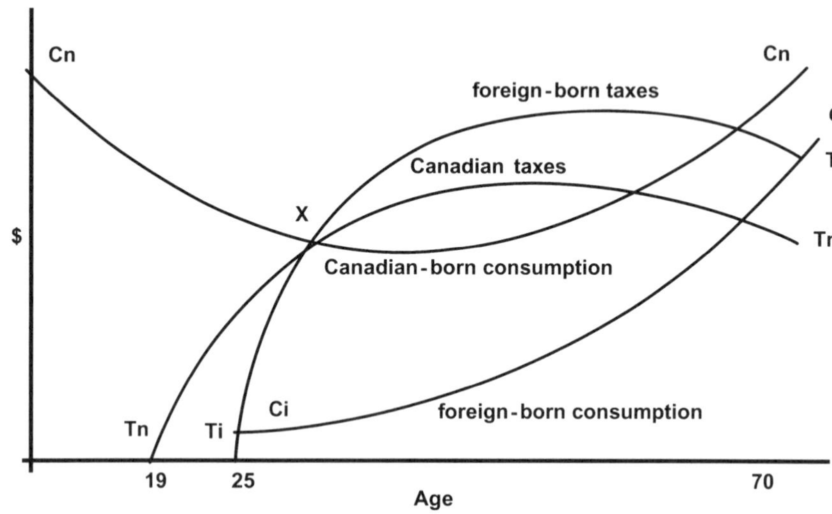

Figure 2.1 Public finance transfer: optimistic case.

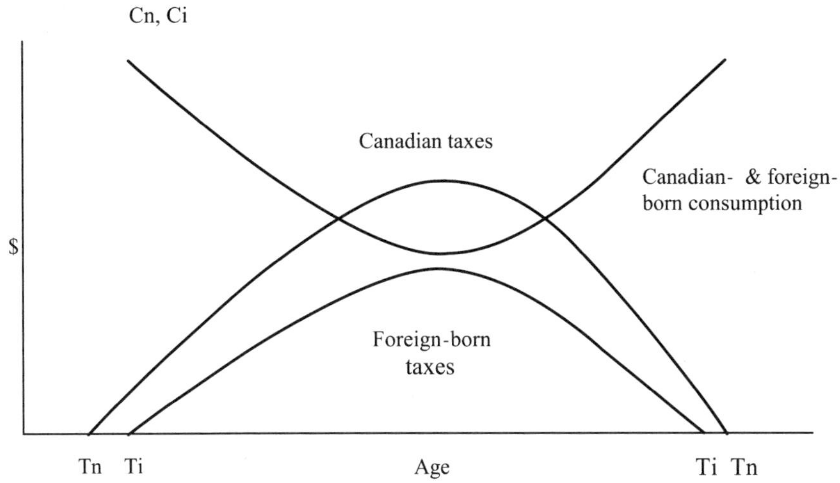

Figure 2.2 Public finance transfer: pessimistic case.

DeVoretz and Ozsomer (1998) provide the most recent Canada-wide evidence to support the proposition that Canada's immigrant population has in fact provided a public finance surplus to Canada's resident population. Between the ages of 20 and 80 Canada's foreign-born population on average contributed $66,156 (1995) more to the treasury in taxes than they used in services. DeVoretz and Ozsomer find that these Canada-wide results conceal more than they reveal, and note that the size of the lifetime public finance transfer is a function of the year of immigrant entry, gender and city of residence.

Table 2.5 depicts the distributional impact of immigrant and foreign-born arrivals on public finance transfers by cities across Canada circa 1995. Citywide variations in immigrant public finance contributions were substantial, with residence in Toronto and Vancouver increasing the foreign-born net discounted lifetime contributions to the treasury to $77,589 and $81,098 respectively. Column 3 indicates the relative contribution of the foreign-born versus the Canadian-born household in each city. In every case, the foreign-born household contributes less than the Canadian-born household does, and in particular Montreal's foreign-born transfer is negative. What caused this reversal in Montreal? DeVoretz and Ozsomer (1998) suggest that the poor economy in Montreal, coupled with its large number of refugee arrivals as opposed to economic immigrants, led to this unique negative finding.

The geographic winners and losers in this public finance transfer process are easy to discern. Toronto and Vancouver were large public finance winners, Canada a more modest winner and Montreal a loser in the transfer process.

Table 2.5 Net present value of public finance transfers by Canadian CMSAs, 1995

Location	*Canadian-born*	*Foreign-born*	*Col 3= (2)/(1)*	*Col 4= (2)-(1)*
Canada	$60,623	$66,156	1.09	+$5,523
Vancouver	$151,324	$81,098	0.54	−$70,226
Toronto	$188,403	$77,589	0.41	−$101,814
Montreal	$92,326	−$1,686	N.A.	−$99,012

Source: DeVoretz and Ozsomer (1998).
Note: CMSA=Census metropolitan statistical area.

If we next decompose the immigrant populations by gender, what new patterns of winners and losers in the public finance sector emerge?

Figure 2.3 depicts the lifetime pattern of tax payments versus government transfers for households headed by foreign-born females. Over their lifetime, except for the years 45–55, foreign-born female households used more in services than they paid in taxes, leading to a lifetime discounted deficit of $47,775 circa 1995 (DeVoretz and Ozsomer, 1998: 27).

However, similar calculations indicate that Canadian-born females' level of public finance deficit (circa 1995) was even more pronounced at –$62,219 than foreign-born females. This relatively poor performance by

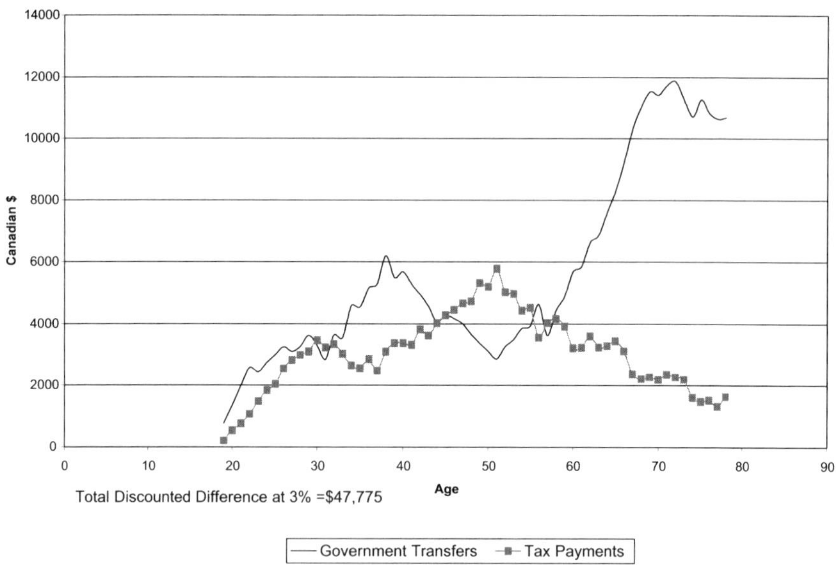

Figure 2.3 Tax payments versus government transfers to female foreign-born households, all of Canada (5-year moving average), 1995.

Source: Head of Household Survey of Consumer Finances (SCF) for census families, 1995 income (direct observation).

Canadian-born females is due to their lower earnings and tax payments and greater use of pensions.

Figure 2.4 illustrates the large net lifetime transfers from male foreign-born households to all other households including female-headed households. In fact, the net discounted transfer was slightly larger from foreign-born male heads of households ($93,086) than that transferred from Canadian-born male heads of households ($92,724). In sum, males, regardless of foreign-birth status, subsidize female-headed households with foreign-born male-headed households providing the largest public finance transfer.

What about transfers across entry cohorts? Do older immigrants finance newer arrivals or vice versa? DeVoretz and Ozsomer (1998) provide extensive evidence that both the use of public services and the net transfer to the treasury is a function of year of entry. For example, pre-1980 entrants are intensive users of Canada's public health and pension schemes, driving down their net treasury transfers. In particular, for the post-1986 entry cohort, the discounted present value of the transfer was $142,562 (circa 1995) for the representative foreign-born household. This extraordinary performance is owing to this entry group's low use of monetized public services ($5,000 per annum per household) combined with high tax payments for those aged 35 to 50.

Now that we have established the public finance transfer resulting from immigration, we turn to the second dimension or labor-market impact of

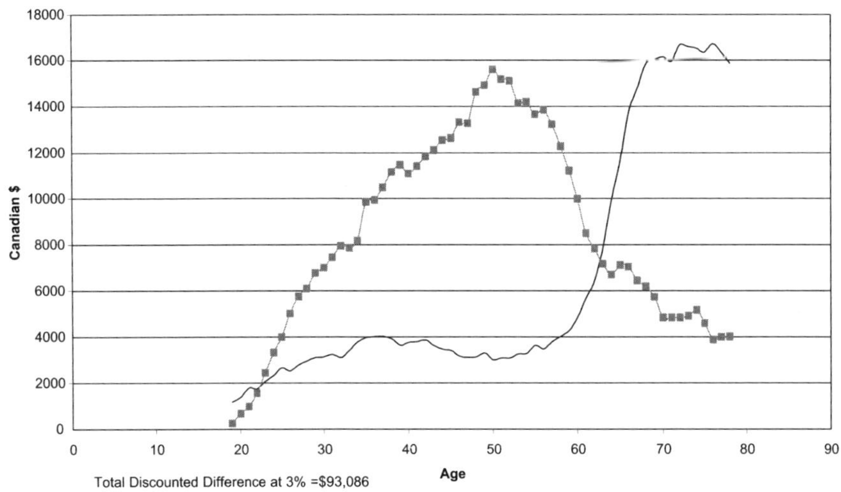

Figure 2.4 Tax payments versus government transfers to male foreign-born heads of households, all of Canada (5-year moving average), 1995.

Source: Head of Household Survey of Consumer Finances (SCF) for census families, 1995 income (direct observation).

the foreign-born population on Canadians. Specifically we ask: how has this foreign-born resident population affected the labor market outcomes of Canadians in terms of their wages and job opportunities? Substantial evidence exists in the Canadian literature and we selectively report the work of Akbari and DeVoretz (1992), Roy (1997) and Laryea (1997) on these issues.

Table 2.6 reports that, economy-wide in Canada circa 1991, there existed no significant labor substitution between either Canadians or the foreign-born or between older immigrants (pre-1980 arrivals) and newer immigrants (post-1980). In fact, the only significant economy-wide finding is that Canadian-born additions to the labor force require a significant increase in capital. For either recent (post-1980) or earlier immigrants (pre-1980 arrivals), no significant increase in the capital stock is required in order to expand their employment opportunities. This latter outcome could be either a function of where immigrants are employed – less capital intensive industries – or the fact that they bring their own financial and human capital.

This finding is in sharp contrast to the findings reported in the United States, and Akbari and DeVoretz argue that this unique outcome is owing to two specific reasons. First, Canadian immigration policy after 1967 was largely predicated on screening immigrants with a "points" system to insure successful labor-market integration. Thus this points policy, unlike the United States policy, kept out unskilled workers. In addition, they argue that for Canada the general economy-wide findings are misleading. In other words, in some sectors labor substitution occurred while in other sectors it did not.

What are these displacement impacts when we again employ a distributional analysis? Do particular industrial sectors or isolated groups at risk suffer more than large and better-protected industrial or skill groups?

First, it should be pointed out that Akbari and DeVoretz found significant substitution between immigrants and the Canadian-born labor force members in those industries which simply had a high percentage of foreign-born. In this foreign-born intensive group, both recent (post-1980) and earlier immigrants substitute for Canadians in these diverse set of foreign-

Table 2.6 Elasticities of factor complementarities, 1991–107 Canadian industries

Elasticity between	*Value*	*Std. error*	*T-value*
Canadian – early immigrants	−0.97	0.48	−0.47
Canadian – recent immigrants	0.96	1.05	1.01
Canadian – capital	0.91	1.02	1.93
Recent immigrants – capital	1.03	0.97	1.00
Old immigrants – recent immigrants	1.18	0.39	0.47

Source: DeVoretz and Laryea (2000).

intensive industries circa 1990. These affected industries ranged from highly skilled professions to semi-skilled workers in clothing manufacturing. In fact, if we rank these affected industries by skill groupings – unskilled (clothing, furniture, meat and poultry), skilled (fabricating, metal stamping) and professional (universities) – we would find that they simply reflect the immigration policy priorities between 1967 and 1996. Moreover, the displacement impact on Canadians was substantial in this foreign-born group. For example, when a 1 percent rise (approximately 17,000) in foreign-born stock occurred in these industries, 4,233 Canadian-born workers were displaced.

How did the substitution patterns appear in other industrial configurations? Two interesting subsets of industries are those characterized by large firm size or unionization.[5] The underlying premise is that size and unionization would reduce the impact of immigrants on the employment opportunities of Canadians. This was the case in Canada (circa 1990) as no significant pair-wise substitution occurred in the Canadian unionized sector. More interesting was the fact that in industries characterized by large-scale firms, a complementary relationship existed between foreign-born and Canadian-born workers. In other words, as more Canadians were hired in these large firms, more foreign-born workers were also hired.

In more-vulnerable industrial groupings – high tariff and female intensive – the substitution between Canadians and foreign-born, regardless of vintage, was significant. In fact, in the low-skilled female-intensive service sector, foreign-born females replaced Canadian-born males in sales, clerical and services. In Canadian tariff-protected industries, both old and new immigrants displaced Canadian-born workers.

In sum, there exist distributional employment effects on vulnerable Canadians from the presence of foreign-born labor in niches of the Canadian labor force. If you are at risk, in a tariff-protected, small or female-intensive industry with less than average unionization rates, then significant job competition occurred from immigrants in the Canadian labor market circa 1990. However, if your industry was large, highly unionized, male dominated and not a foreign-born enclave, then there existed no job competition. In fact, growth of foreign-born jobs could occur as Canadian-born employment increased.

Laryea (1997) and Roy (1997) review the impact of immigrants on Canadian-born wages. The basic argument here is that if minimal Canadian job loss occurred as a result of immigrant arrivals, then immigrants must have affected Canadian wages since immigrants increased the supply of all Canadian workers. Even given this logic, both Laryea and Roy present limited evidence for wage competition. Laryea only cites eight industries in which Canadian wages were suppressed after the arrival of immigrants. Roy analyzed the wage impact from the perspective of source country of the immigrants and notes that only Third World immigrants had a negative affect on the wages of their Canadian counterparts.

Why do these benign labor-market outcomes appear? Essentially for two reasons. First, in the skilled section of the labor market the entrance of highly skilled immigrants increased the employment opportunities of less-skilled Canadians and raised their wages.

There exists, however, a second set of reasons applicable to the less-skilled sector, which rationalizes this limited impact of immigrants in the Canadian labor market. Heibert (1997) argues that the foreign-born are "over represented" in the self-employment sector and are competitive with the Canadian-born in the mainstream labor force. In addition, Pendakur and Pendakur (1997) argue that even if the foreign-born do enter a particular occupation they experience ethnic wage discrimination. In other words, even if the foreign-born population is able to utilize its near equal human capital endowment, it suffers from a diminution in wages of 10 to 30 percent relative to the Canadian-born population if it belongs to an ethnic group of colour.

Given these findings, it is easy to rationalize why the large increase in the post-1986 Asian and African immigrant population did not have a negative impact on Canadians in the labor market. Immigrants of colour have been either marginalized in self-employment or discriminated against in general while mainstream immigrants with human capital raised the employment and wage opportunities of Canadians. An alternative, and more positive explanation of small labor market impacts would arise if large-scale capital inflows occurred as immigrants arrived.

Regardless of the reasons, this limited labor force impact on Canadian wages and jobs by immigrant arrivals reinforces the positive conclusions found in the earlier section on immigrants' impact on Canadian public finances. In short, both the public and private (labor force) impacts of immigration to Canada are either positive (treasury) or benign (labor market). Thus, Canada's immigration policy of balancing economic with family and refugee immigrant inflows have satisfied the DeVoretz rule by providing benefits to the resident Canadian-born population without harming the weaker segments of the Canadian economy in the public finance and labor markets. But what of the goods markets? Have immigrants created winners and losers in the housing and other markets? Have immigrants altered retail expenditure patterns and prices which in turn has redistributed income? If so, is this redistribution through changing goods prices a Canada-wide or citywide phenomenon?

The Canadian popular press has fuelled this stage of the distributional debate. The issues have centered on the alleged impact of immigrants on regional or citywide consumption patterns. Many have argued that immigrants have caused housing speculation and a rise in the price of services and altered the recreational and food choices available within the community at large. Are these casual observations correct? Have new consumption patterns emerged with a new set of relative prices after immigrants arrived in large numbers? We offer evidence for one major immigrant-recipient city – Vancouver – to measure these alleged consumption impacts of immigrants. There are several necessary ingredients to measure before the impact of Vancouver's foreign-born population on its consumption patterns can be determined. First, a measure of differential consumption patterns or household budget weights across consumption groups must be calculated from available survey data. A sample of these budget weights appears in Table 2.7 and establishes that Vancouver consumption propensities vary by foreign-birth status.

Several points emerge from Table 2.7. First, foreign-birth status does affect the average propensities to consume across product groups. In particular, the foreign-born spent a greater share of their budget on shelter (40 percent) and food (21 percent) than the average Vancouver Canadian-born household did. In addition, if we control for length of stay in Canada, these patterns become even more complex, with recent immigrants spending 45 percent of their budgets on shelter while the Canadian-born spent only 31 percent. Next, some commodity groups' clothing and transport are *not* significantly influenced by foreign-birth status. Finally, necessities (food, shelter, clothing and transport) form a much larger portion of the budget for recent immigrants (91 percent) than for the Canadian-born household (72 percent), leaving recent immigrants with less possibility for discretionary expenditures.

The final ingredient necessary to measure the expenditure patterns by birthplace is an estimate of household expenditure elasticities by birth status for these consumption groups. These elasticities measure the response by each group of a rise (1 percent) in their income for selected expenditure categories. The argument in this stage is that both foreign-born and Canadian-born households' income changes over time, specifically in the period 1990–99, and this income effect must be captured.

The expenditure elasticity or driving force behind differential consumption patterns over time is revealed in Table 2.8. In every case except transport, the foreign-born group has a greater response to an increase in total household income than their Canadian-born counterparts for these selected items. Thus, as time in Vancouver increases for the foreign-born and their income rises, the consumption patterns between the foreign-born and

Table 2.7 Budget weights by commodities for Vancouver by place of birth, 1995

Category	*Canadian-born*	*Foreign-born*	*Foreign-born pre-1981*	*Foreign-born post-1980*
Shelter	0.31	0.40	0.37	0.45
Food	0.16	0.21	0.19	0.24
Clothing	0.07	0.05	0.06	0.05
Transport	0.18	0.16	0.16	0.17
Total	0.72	0.82	0.78	0.91

Source: Constructed by author from *Family Expenditure in Canada* (1995).

Table 2.8 Expenditure elasticities of consumption for Vancouver by place of birth, 1995

Category	*Canadian-born*	*Foreign-born*
Food	0.50	0.65
Shelter	0.71	0.83
Furnishings	1.20	1.90
Clothing	1.10	1.60
Transport	1.90	1.60

Source: Constructed by author from Statistics Canada, *Family Expenditure in Canada* (1996).

Canadian-born groups for these selected commodities will diverge. Next, for both groups the expenditure elasticities range in values from almost two to one-half. Thus, as income grows for either Canadians or immigrants, those commodities which obtain an elasticity value greater than unity will grow the fastest, while the inelastic expenditure groups (i.e. those that assume an elasticity less than unity) will stagnate in the Vancouver economy. To project these growth patterns we simply combine estimates of income growth over time from (unreported) age earning profiles for both immigrants and Canadians in Vancouver and their total expenditure elasticities as reported in Table 2.9.[6] This combination leads to Figure 2.5.

In short, the values reported in Figure 2.5 measure the percentage increase in each of 14 major commodity groups in Vancouver over the 1991–99 period given the income growth and expenditure elasticities for the various cohorts reported in Table 2.9.

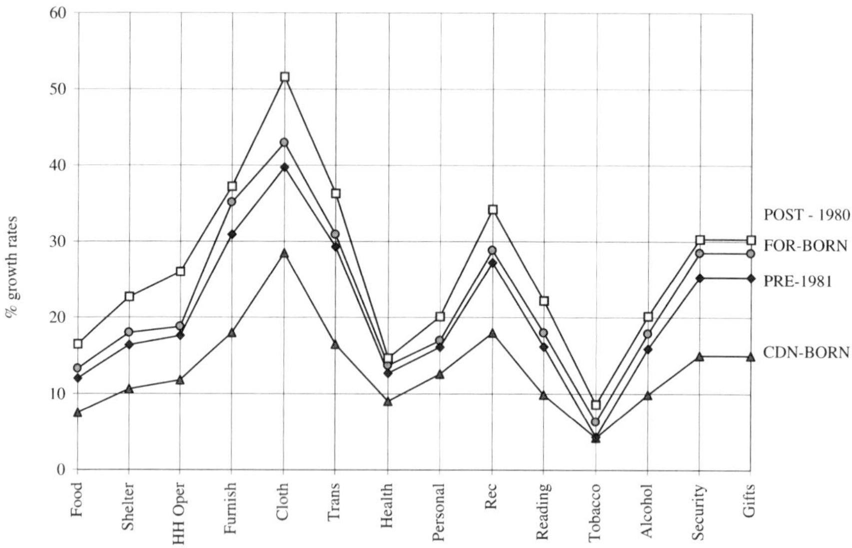

Figure 2.5 Vancouver expenditure growth rates 1990–1999 by birthplace.

Several important phenomena arise from Figure 2.5. First, we pose a counterfactual question. How would Vancouver's expenditure patterns have changed circa 1990–2000 in the absence of immigration to Vancouver after 1981? Furthermore, what would have been the Vancouver expenditure patterns in 1990–99 if no immigrants either pre- or post-1981 had arrived in Vancouver? The underlying premise of both these counterfactuals is that immigrants with different tastes (expenditure elasticities) and income patterns create rents in the retail markets as differential demand grows for particular expenditure groups.

In the counterfactual world of only the Canadian-born in Vancouver, the average expenditure growth for all expenditure groups, with the exception of clothing, is less than 1 percent per annum or in most cases approximately one-half of 1 percent for the decade. Clearly, few rents in the form of rising real prices would appear if no immigrants arrived in Vancouver. Relative real prices would remain unchanged in this counterfactually induced slow-growing retail sector, as supply would easily match the one-half of 1 percent growth rate for commodity expenditures. If we relax the conditions on our counterfactual experiment and create a Vancouver population of only Canadian-born and pre-1981 immigrants, then the counterfactual outcome would realize even smaller, if any, rents than the first case with no immigrants! How do we rationalize this perverse outcome? If we look to the expenditure growth paths of pre-1981 immigrants (lowest line), the average growth rate in total expenditures is slightly negative since expenditures on all items except food declined in the 1990s for this older vintage of immigrants. Why this negative expenditure pattern arose is clear. This pre-1981 group of immigrants is aging (average age 57) and its income has been declining throughout the decade. This decline in household income coupled with positive expenditure elasticities meant that absolute expenditures across all expenditure items declined.

Post-1980 immigrants created the unexpected rents in the Vancouver retail sector in the 1990s. Over that decade, the rise in real expenditures by recent immigrant arrivals was the driving force behind the change in relative prices in the Vancouver retail sector. For example, shelter, furnishings, and household operations consist mainly of non-importables and the rate of increase in real expenditures over the decade was 10 to nearly 30 percent in these categories. Since these commodities could not be imported and supply curves were not perfectly elastic, rents in the form of rapidly rising housing prices and rental rate increases transferred wealth from post-1980 immigrants to Vancouver property-owning residents in the 1990s. In fact, the only category in which recent immigrants' real expenditure growth rates fell below the Canadian average was for tobacco.

In sum, the rents created by immigrant arrivals to Vancouver were greatest in the non-importable housing and associated service sectors. The economic winners in these markets were both the Canadian-born and older immigrants who held real property in their portfolio (Shamsuddin and

DeVoretz, 1997). The losers in this process were the younger generation of residents who did not realize the transitional gains from rising prices in the Vancouver housing market. Thus, the windfall profits created by the post-1980 immigrant arrivals to Vancouver were a result of transfers from both the recent foreign-born and the younger generation of potential household owners to the older resident generation in the Vancouver economy.

But more subtle changes in Vancouver's retail market also created rents. Linguistic and culture differences created barriers and opportunities in both service and specialty items in Vancouver's retail trade. An example should illustrate how these barriers redistributed rents back to immigrants. For jewelry items, language and taste differences between the resident and post-1980 immigrant community implied that ethnic-based business would capture the bulk of the expenditure increase in this item. Thus, Chinese malls with specialty stores transacting only in Cantonese appeared in ethnic enclaves in Vancouver to serve this market. The point to note is that in many cases where language and cultural differences raised transaction costs, the potential gains of rising retail expenditures could not be realized by the resident community.

In sum, the post-1981 immigrant group to Vancouver created a unique set of rents owing to an increase in prices for non-importable expenditure items. In particular, rising prices in Vancouver's housing market provided substantial windfall gains to Vancouver residents at the expense of immigrant arrivals and later generations of Vancouver residents. However, in several service, clothing and recreational markets, rising rents were only partially reaped by resident Canadians given the linguistic and cultural differences in these new markets. In fact, under these circumstances, earlier immigrants reaped the rents.

Conclusions

Canada is a major immigrant-receiving country blessed with a continental economy and extensive geographical space. The introduction of almost five million immigrants or approximately 20 percent of Canada's base population since 1967 has, in fact, had little overall impact on successive generations' economic prospects. However, this is an aggregate picture. If we focus on citywide effects, for a particular set of skill levels and product types immigrants produce extensive impacts with substantial distributional impacts. For the public treasury, Montreal immigrants represent a net drain while immigrants to Vancouver and Toronto produce large, positive treasury transfers. In the latter two cases as well as Canada-wide, male immigrant households provide the largest subsidy to other Canadian residents. More importantly, the latest immigrant cohort (post-1986) produced the most substantial positive treasury transfers to the rest of the Canadian community regardless of city location.

Again in general, immigrants produced no negative impacts in Canada's labor market. However, in particular niches – foreign-born intensive, tariff-protected, female-intensive – negative outcomes arose. In these cases, immigrants displaced both earlier immigrant cohorts and Canadian-born workers. In particular, for the sector which was intensive in foreign labor, displacement of the Canadian-born was substantial in the decade 1980–90. Wage competition or compression, however, was minimal in the Canadian context, with only 17 industries experiencing a wage decline from the added presence of immigrants. The limited distribution of immigrants across occupations led to the limited labor-market effects generated by immigrants. Canadian immigrants were either very high skilled and created employment for Canadians or low skilled and marginalized to the enclave economy.

The retail sector, at least in the Vancouver context, also produced strong distributional effects in the decade of the 1990s. Real wealth was transferred to resident Canadians in the housing market from wealthy immigrants given the immigrants' high expenditure elasticities for shelter. The losers in the real estate sector were both poorer immigrant arrivals and younger-generation Canadians who were marginalized in Vancouver's inflated housing market. In other retail markets (service, recreation, food and clothing), high transaction costs arose due to taste and language barriers and produced gains for foreign-born retailers who could best service these markets.

These distributional consequences in the public treasury, labor and goods markets have substantial implications for the political acceptance of immigrants in Canada. Circa 2000, less than one-third of Canada's population supports an active immigrant program. The support is the lowest in Vancouver. I argue that the distributional consequences of immigration, as outlined above, account for this antipathy or apathy toward Canada's immigrant program. For most Canadians, the 4.8 million post-1967 immigrant arrivals have had a minor economic impact on their households. However, in certain cities and sectors, the impact has been substantial in the form of job competition, higher housing prices and retail activity diverted to immigrant enclaves. This has produced economic losses for some neighborhoods or niches in the economy and resulted in antipathy towards immigrants. The benefits when substantial, such as in the treasury, are either unknown or diffused over a wide population with small, positive impacts and lead to little support for immigration. Thus, in the final analysis, the negative consequences are concentrated and produce vociferous critics to immigration, while the benefits are widely diffused with few supporters amongst this winning constituency.

In sum, Canada's well-run immigration policy, with an overall positive impact, leads to one pessimistic conclusion. If the distributional economic effects are concentrated in cities or enclaves, antipathy towards immigrants is pronounced.

Notes

1 Refugees enter Canada as either asylum seekers or convention refugees. The latter group is an outgrowth of Canada's agreement with the United Nations. The number of asylum seekers has grown in the last ten years and many are under appeal.
2 See DeVoretz (1995).
3 Berry and Soligo (1969) and Rawls (1971) originated these concepts in a general form.
4 Public goods consumption is convex since most expenditures occur in youth (health and educaton) and during old age (pension and health). Tax payments are concave over the immigrant's lifetime because they are directly related to income, which rises upon entry in the labor market and eventually flattens out.
5 Akbari and DeVoretz (1992) define high degrees of unionization as above 50 percent of the labor force in the industry under consideration. In addition, a large firm is one in which the value added per worker exceeds the national average by at least two standard deviations.
6 The age earnings profiles are available by request. E-mail address: devoretz@sfu.ca.

Bibliography

Akbari, A.H. and D.J. DeVoretz (1992) "The Substitutability of Foreign-born Labour in Canadian Production: Circa 1980," *Canadian Journal of Economics*, 25: 604–14.

Berry, R.A. and R. Soligo (1969) "Some Welfare Aspects of International Immigration," *Journal of Political Economy*, 7: 778–794.

Canada (1997) *Annual Report 1986–1996*, Ottawa: Citizenship and Immigration.

Canada (1999) *Facts and Figures: Immigration Overview (1997–1998)*, Ottawa: Citizenship and Immigration.

DeVoretz, D.J. (ed.) (1995) *Diminishing Returns: The Economics of Canada's Immigration Policy*, Toronto: C.D. Howe.

DeVoretz, D.J. and S. Laryea (1998a) *Canadian Human Capital Transfers: The USA and Beyond*, Toronto: C.D. Howe.

DeVoretz, D.J. and S. Laryea (1998b) "Migration and the Labour Market: Sectoral and Regional Effects in Canada," in Migration, Free Trade and Regional Integration in North America, *OECD Proceedings* 30: 135–153.

DeVoretz, D.J. and S. Laryea (2000) "Canadian Immigration Experience: Any Lessons for Europe?," in K. Zimmermann (ed.), *CEPR Conference on European Labour Mobility: Proceedings*, Cambridge: Cambridge University Press.

DeVoretz, D.J. and Y. Ozsomer (1998) "Immigrants and Public Finance Transfers: Vancouver, Toronto and Montréal," Working Paper Series 99–06, Vancouver: Simon Fraser University, Centre for Excellence: Research on Immigration and Integration in the Metropolis (RIIM).

Green, A.G. and D.A. Green (1995) "Canadian Immigration Policy: The Effectiveness of the Points System and Other Instruments," *Canadian Journal of Economics*, 28: 1006–1041.

Heibert, D. (1997) "The Colour of Work: Labour Market Segmentation in Montréal, Toronto and Vancouver," Working Paper Series 97–02, Vancouver: Simon Fraser University, Centre for Excellence: (RIIM).

Laryea, S.A. (1997) "The Impact of Foreign-born Labour on Wages Rates in Canada," unpublished Ph.D. dissertation, Simon Fraser University.

Pendakur, K. and R. Pendakur (1997) "The Colour of Money: Earnings Differentials Among Ethnic Groups in Canada," Working Paper Series 96–03, Vancouver: Simon Fraser University, Centre for Excellence: (RIIM).

Rawls, J. (1971) *A Theory of Justice*, Cambridge, Mass.: Harvard University Press.

Roy, A.S. (1997) "Job Displacement Effects of Canadian Immigrants by Country of Origin and Occupation," *International Migration Review*, 31: 150–161.

Shamsuddin, A. and D.J. DeVoretz (1999) "Wealth Accumulation of Canadian and Foreign-born Households in Canada," *Review of Income and Wealth*, December: 515–553.

Statistics Canada (1996) *Family Expenditure in Canada*, Public Use Microdata File, Catalogue no. 62–554–XPB, Ottawa.

3 The political economy of international migration in a Ricardo–Viner model

Jean-Marie Grether, Jaime de Melo and Tobias Müller

Introduction

Writing about the economic consequences of immigration in receiving countries from the standpoint of a labor economist, Borjas (1995) speaks of a resulting "immigration surplus" to underline that the benefits created by immigration usually outweigh any losses for natives in the receiving country. At the same time he notes that the condition for this gain to materialize is that the wages of natives diminish, which means that gainful immigration will generate distributional conflicts. Under most scenarios the efficiency gains are small relative to the redistribution of income caused by immigration. Yet, given the overall gains and the means at the disposals of the state to redistribute income, on economic grounds, at least, one might be inclined to expect a more positive attitude towards immigration than those expressed in recent surveys (see below). Bhagwati (1991), also writing from the point of view of receiving countries, but from the standpoint of a trade economist, notes that both politicians and economists in the European Union (EU) and the US support free trade while advocating restrictions on migrations, and argues that such attitudes can only be the consequence of being inconsistent in the application of utilitarian logic which would lead to the advocacy of the free immigration solution.

Indeed, any stylized description of the recent evolution of trade and migration policies would conclude that the barriers against the free movements of goods have been less intense than the restrictions countries have imposed on the international movement of labor (while policies with regard to the international movement of capital have also been generally more liberal than labor immigration policies). In other words, countries have been more open to the indirect inflow of factor services embodied in goods and to direct capital flows than to direct inflows of labor.

This chapter is concerned with the determinants of national policies towards immigration in receiving countries and recognizes that immigration policies are the result of the interaction of two factors: (i) standard economic analysis where benevolent policymakers are primarily concerned with efficiency; (ii) the preferences of the electorate which are driven by the impact of immigration on native factor-market returns. This discussion is largely carried out in terms of a small price-taking economy.

Table 3.1 gives characteristics of the labor force in a group of industrialized countries: the share of foreigners in the population (Table 3.1a) and comparative education levels (Table 3.1b). The figures in Table 3.1a show that foreigners' share in population has increased recently in most countries. The increase has been particularly strong in traditional "guest-worker" countries (Austria, Germany and Switzerland). Besides the temporary surge following the collapse of socialist regimes in Eastern Europe, the stylized pattern has been little permanent migration flows, with the flows being mostly for temporary migration and mostly concentrated in skilled labor.[1] The figures in Table 3.1b relate to European countries. They show that the share of low education individuals is generally

Table 3.1 Foreigners and their characteristics

a: Percent of total population

	1987	*1997*
Austria	4.3	9.1
Belgium	8.7	8.9
France	6.8	6.3
Germany	6.9	9.0
Italy	1.0	2.2
Switzerland	14.9	19.0
UK	3.2	3.6
US	6.2	9.3
Canada	15.4	17.4

Source: SOPEMI (1999).

Note: US and Canada: foreign-born population as a percentage of total population.

b: Education levels in EU countries (1995)

	Natives		*Immigrants*	
	Low	*High*	*Low*	*High*
UK	46.5	18.6	57.9	20.4
France	40.3	16.7	53.3	16.0
Germany	19.1	18.9	46.3	10.7
Austria	31.7	6.4	47.4	8.9
Spain	67.8	14.1	47.0	25.6
Italy	64.2	6.3	53.3	16.0
Denmark	25.4	22.1	31.6	29.0
Belgium	45.3	20.6	52.8	19.5
Sweden	27.2	23.3	30.3	24.9
Netherlands	24.0	18.6	40.2	16.0

Source: Razin, Sadka and Swagel (1998: Table 2).

Notes: Low education is less than first stage of secondary level; high education is completed third schooling level; medium (not shown) is the balance.

smaller for natives than for immigrants, though the opposite is the case in Spain and Italy.

Going beyond the data in Table 3.1, recent migration trends raise a number of issues. First, why is it that legal immigrants coexist with illegal immigrants who are often all too visible? Second, why is it that the opposition towards what demographers call "primary migration" is remarkably strong,[2] even though some small economies like the Netherlands and Ireland have acute labor shortages, and in some larger economies like the UK and Germany steps are currently under way to bring in skilled workers?[3] Third, is there a link between the type of immigration and sector of activity? In the US it has been of a permanent kind rather than temporary and of a "melting-pot" type where the intersectoral distribution of immigrants and natives is similar, whereas in some EU countries it has been of a "guest-worker" type, where immigrants are seasonal and concentrated in a few sectors. And fourth, why are countries increasingly resorting to the use of eligibility criteria like capital and/or skill requirements?

The next section introduces the standard economic analysis primarily to identify when there is an immigration surplus. The following sections introduce political-economy elements into the analysis. We use a new specific-factor direct-democracy framework further developed in Grether et al. (2000) to analyze the determinants of attitudes towards immigration. First, we use the model to investigate the conditions under which natives will oppose (be in favor of) certain types of immigration, and how the level of immigration and exogenous changes such as globalization might alter attitudes. Next, we bring a slight modification to the model to show how one may observe simultaneously legal and illegal immigration. We then develop a dual labor market version to compare the "guest-worker" and "melting-pot" immigration systems. Concluding remarks follow in the final section.

Is there an immigration surplus?

In the introduction, our allusion to a "surplus" created by immigration referred to an aggregate model with only one good produced (as in the seminal paper by Berry and Soligo, 1969), thereby excluding trade, and more importantly minimizing the conflicts and controversies surrounding migration policy. In this section we review briefly the robustness to various modifications in an otherwise standard framework where policy choice is carried out by benevolent policymakers. The usefulness of looking into the robustness of the "immigration surplus" result is that if immigration leads to a welfare loss of natives on efficiency grounds, there is no need to extend the analysis along political economy dimensions to explain the resistance to immigration. First, we look for the robustness of the immigration surplus prediction in trade models and for the presence of distributional conflicts. We then consider extensions.

The impact of immigration in an open economy

In the closed-economy model presented by Borjas (1995), immigration alters factor returns so that benefits outweigh losses resulting from income redistribution effects. In fact, this outcome of redistributive conflict with efficiency gain also describes the effects of immigration in the short-run specific-factor model used later in the chapter. Thus, it is legitimate to check the robustness of this result in other international trade models.

Suppose then that the evaluation of the effects of immigration takes place over long periods. Then the long-run condition of zero profits replaces the rents earned by specific factors which are never equalized in the specific-factor model. Let us start with models where immigration takes place in a setting where free entry and exit imply zero long-run profits.

Take first the Heckscher–Ohlin (H–O) model where international trade has a strong disciplining effect on wages. We assume a two country world, where skilled labor, H, and unskilled labor, L, are the two factors entering identical constant returns to scale production functions describing the technology in each of two price-taking sectors. Since, in the absence of transport costs, goods prices will be equalized, unit costs must also be equal, which implies (in the plausible case of no factor intensity reversal) that wages are equalized (Factor Price Equalization or FPE), with wages entirely determined by world prices and technology parameters. The output mix consists of both products so that the economy is "diversified," and so long as it remains so, immigration will have no effect on factor rewards. Arbitrage via trade in goods will eliminate any incentive to migrate, but, in the absence of trade, as first shown by Mundell (1957), international factor mobility will also exhaust arbitrage gains, so that trade in goods and trade in factors are substitutes.[4] In this world where trade eliminates any incentive to migrate, if migration takes place in a small economy for exogenous reasons, it does not alter factor prices, and there is no "immigration surplus."[5]

The FPE proposition being obviously false, Trefler (1993, 1998) has shown that allowing for differences in productivity between sending and receiving countries leads to a modified FPE proposition where productivity-adjusted wages are the same, which rehabilitates empirically both the H–O and FPE theorems. To draw the welfare implications of this amendment, one must determine migrants' attributes. If productivity is an attribute of the worker (a migrant will have low productivity regardless of where he works), we are back in the previous setting and there are no welfare effects of migration. But if productivity is an attribute of the country (low productivity is then the result of poor policies), migration will raise productivity, and there will be a positive welfare effect from migration.

For large countries like the EU and US, sustained migration can, in addition, have income distribution effects. Migration of, say, skilled workers can be equivalent to increasing the relative supply of skilled-intensive goods, thereby lowering their relative price along with the wage of skilled workers. Also there is the possibility of a terms-of-trade effect as the relative price of skill-intensive goods is likely to fall.[6]

The terms-of-trade effect of migration is best captured in a Ricardian model (Findlay, 1982). Consider here a version in which an array of goods are produced with one unit of labor, with sending and receiving countries specialized in the production of different goods. To illustrate the effects of immigration take a three good model in which the destination country produces initially only good 1 so that $w/p_1=1/a_1$, and $w/p_i>1/a_i$, $i=2,3$. With immigration, the equilibrium condition in sector 1 is unaffected but the wage is driven down until $w/p_2=1/a_2$ while in the sending country the wage is bid up until $w^*/p_2=1/a^*_2$, which means, by the likewise equilibrium condition in sector 3, that p_3 has risen in the sending country. It is then clear that real wages per capita, w/p, of natives have fallen in terms of goods 2 and 3. As pointed by Trefler (1998), who develops this case further, what has happened is that by increasing the supply of good 1 and shifting the terms of trade against the host country, immigration serves to reduce the scarcity rents enjoyed by native workers. Thus general equilibrium adjustments result in a negative immigration "surplus."

What about increasing returns to scale? With external returns to scale, it is intuitive that the immigration surplus result will be restored if one thinks, for example, of opening up new land to cultivation like the prairie in nineteenth-century US: without immigrants production would have been insufficient to warrant investment in the railways. Trefler (1998) develops such a model and shows that immigration raises the productivity of domestic labor, though there is also a negative terms-of-trade effect so that it is possible that there is an optimal level of immigration beyond which further immigration reduces domestic welfare.[7]

In Europe, closer integration has increased factor mobility and diminished transport costs, although labour mobility is low, at least compared with the US where up to 20 percent of families move in any given year. Ludema and Wooton (1999) introduce imperfect labor mobility in an economic-geography model à la Krugman (1991). As a result, even though it is again impossible to identify an unequivocal immigration surplus, in this richer model the cumulative causation process triggered by a reduction in transport costs that is welfare-enhancing for the destination country and potentially immiserizing for the sending country may no longer occur. They show that for sufficiently mobile labor, progressive integration may initially lead to agglomeration, then again to diversification as trade costs are lowered further. Temporary dislocations in the face of increased market integration could then be avoided by a temporary restriction on factor movements, as for example in the Europe Agreements, where reduction in barriers to trade take place before migration of people is allowed.

Extensions

Wildasin first (1992, 1994) and subsequently Razin and Sadka (1995) pointed out that immigration will raise the costs of income redistribution if such a 'non-economic' objective is present. This is because factor mobility means that redistributive policies entail interjurisdictional externalities since it is no longer a local public good: redistributive policy from mobile towards fixed factors will be thwarted as mobile factors move (poor flock in and rich leave).

The implications of immigration for the functioning of a welfare system are examined in Razin and Sadka (1999a, 1999b) and Razin, Sadka and Swagel (1998) in an overlapping generations model where life spans two periods (young contribute to a pays-as-you-go pension scheme, while the old draw a pension). In this framework, even if immigrants are net receivers of the welfare system (in the US, according to calculations by Borjas (1994), foreign-born households are 10 percent of households receiving assistance but receive 13 percent of total assistance), so long as immigration (only the young immigrate) has no effect on wages, their arrival provides a positive externality on native population as they make a net contribution to public finances in the period in which they arrive. With immigrants reducing wages upon arrival, the welfare impact becomes ambiguous.

These, and other extensions (such as wage rigidity – see Razin and Sadka, 1995), modify and may reduce the efficiency gains of immigration, potentially pointing towards ambiguous effects of immigration on welfare in a standard optimizing framework. This conclusion is also reached when one introduces cultural preferences in the form of social capital into the analysis as in Schiff (1998, 1999). In this case, not considered here, immigration creates a negative externality that reduces welfare.

Determinants of individual preferences over immigration policy

To explore the political economy of immigration policy, we use the specific-factor or Ricardo–Viner model in a direct-democracy framework. The direct-democracy model is arguably the best-suited framework to represent how preferences over immigration are formed by the population at large. This is due to peoples' perception that absorbing immigrants will be partly via changes in one's wage.[8] Also, its links to the underlying economic model are more transparent than in other political economy approaches like the pressure group model where policy is the result of the maximization of a welfare function whose weights are often arbitrarily chosen.[9] As to the specific-factor model, its time-frame with short-term rents also probably corresponds to the time-frame envisaged by many voters when they form an opinion on immigration policy.[10]

Suppose then that every individual (or household) can vote on migration policy (i.e. whether he or she agrees to accept a given number of immigrants), and that no other issue is on the political agenda. Then preferences are single-peaked and the national stance towards immigration is determined by the median voter. We analyze this institutional setting in the context of a small price-taking open economy. Variations in income determine the attitude towards immigrants. Each native household is endowed with one unit of labor and a certain amount of capital. If immigration lowers a native's income, he or she will oppose it. Here we focus on legal immigration and on the effects of capital distribution among natives, and turn to illegal immigration later.

The economy produces two traded goods: X (import-competing) and Y (exporting), using three factors: unskilled labor (L) which is specific to sector X; skilled labor (H) which is specific to sector Y; and capital (K), which is the mobile factor.[11] Let k_X (k_Y) denote the capital to unskilled (skilled) labor ratio in X (Y). Denote the share of capital used in sector X by $\lambda_K \equiv K_X/\bar{K}$. Let ℓ be the share of unskilled individuals in total population $(\ell \equiv \bar{L}/(\bar{L}+\bar{H}))$. Define the index of between-group inequality in capital distribution, τ, as the ratio between capital per capita of unskilled households and the national capital per capita average. Letting K^L denote total ownership of capital of unskilled households, denote by $\theta_L \equiv K^L/\bar{K}$, the unskilled labor's ownership share of capital. Unskilled (skilled) migrants are denoted by M_L (M_H), and μ (γ) is the share of natives in the population of unskilled (skilled) households. Finally, it will prove useful for the graphical presentation to choose units so that native population equals the capital stock, with both set equal to unity. The following equations conveniently summarize the notation used in this section:

$$
\begin{aligned}
&k_X \equiv K_X/\bar{L}; k_Y \equiv K_Y/\bar{H};\\
&\ell \equiv \bar{L}/(\bar{L}+\bar{H});\\
&\lambda_K \equiv K_X/\bar{K};\\
&\theta_L \equiv K^L/\bar{K}; \qquad (1)\\
&\tau \equiv [K^L/\bar{L}]/[\bar{K}/(\bar{L}+\bar{H})] = \theta_L/\ell\\
&\mu \equiv \bar{L}/(\bar{L}+M_L) \text{ or } \gamma \equiv \bar{H}/(\bar{H}+M_H);\\
&\bar{L}+\bar{H}) \equiv \bar{K} \equiv 1
\end{aligned}
$$

In this model, attitudes towards immigration will be determined by the interaction of three elements: (i) the number of migrants; (ii) the capital distribution among natives; (iii) the capital endowment of immigrants. We start from the simplest case where immigrants bring no capital with them, there are no immigrants initially ($\mu=\gamma=1$), and domestic capital is equally shared among national households ($\theta_L=\ell \Leftrightarrow \tau=1$). We then allow first for sustained immigration, and second for unequal distribution of capital ownership.

Infinitesimal immigration

To illustrate the current immigration policy debate in the majority of industrialized countries, we assume that immigrants are unskilled individuals, and that the export-competing sector is capital intensive (i.e. $k_X<k_Y$).

As the immigration surplus is a second-order efficiency gain, it cannot be reaped with marginal (or infinitesimal) immigration. This implies that global national income is unaffected (zero-sum property) and, as a consequence, if one type of household loses (opposes immigration), the other one necessarily wins (favors immigration). Thus, it is sufficient to analyze the attitude of one household category, say unskilled individuals.

The arrival of unskilled migrants will lead to an expansion of sector X that uses them intensively, through an improvement of the marginal productivity of capital ($V_X \rightarrow V_X'$ in Figure 3.1). The real return to both categories of domestic sector-specific labor factors will decrease, while capital remuneration goes up, so it is *a priori* unclear if unskilled households benefit from immigration. In Figure 3.1, A (D) is the loss of labor income of unskilled (skilled) households and A+B+C+D is the total increase in capital income. As aggregate national income does not change following an infinitesimal inflow of immigrants, the triangular areas B and C are negligible. This means that areas A and A+B are approximately identical, so that unskilled households will be exactly compensated from their labor income loss provided the amount of capital they own (K^L) is equal to the amount of capital which is used in sector X (K_X). In other words, if $K^L{}_C$ is the critical amount of capital owned by unskilled natives which leaves them indifferent to immigration, its value is given by $K^L{}_C=K_X$.

How does the actual capital ownership of unskilled natives compare with this critical amount? With capital evenly distributed among households, the share of capital owned by unskilled households is equal to their share in population (i.e. $\theta_L=\ell$). Indifference towards immigration (i.e. $K^L=K_X$) will arise if the share of capital owned by unskilled labor is equal to the share of capital used in sector X, i.e. if $\theta_L=\lambda_K$. This indifference condition is satisfied along the diagonal of the box represented in Figure 3.2. If $\theta_L=\ell<\lambda_K$, unskilled households own less than the critical amount, and the compensation effect from capital ownership is too weak to compensate for the loss of rents. In other words, unskilled households are, in a sense, "capital-poor": they suffer a net income loss and oppose immigration (this is represented by the dashed area in Figure 3.2). By the same reasoning,

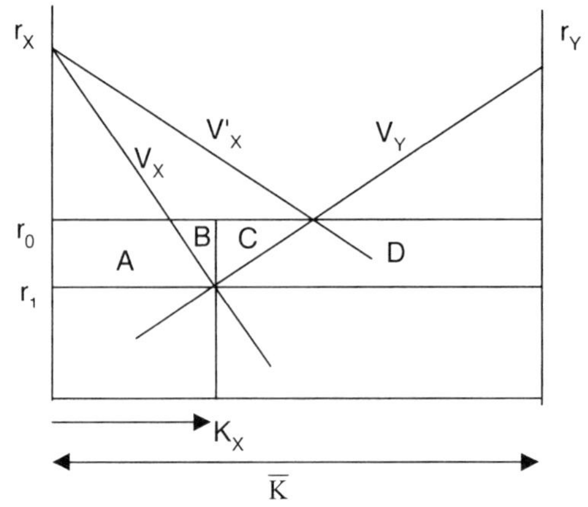

V_X: pre-migration marginal product of capital in sector X
V'_X: post-migration marginal product of capital in sector X
V_Y: marginal product of capital in sector Y

Figure 3.1 Infinitesimal immigration and factor rewards.

unskilled natives' attitudes are favorable towards immigration for points below the diagonal ($\theta_L = \ell > \lambda_K$).

To determine whether unskilled natives will oppose or favor immigration, we need to know whether unskilled labor are "capital-rich" or "capital-poor." Think now of Figure 3.2 as an Edgeworth box which is possible by our choice of units. By the choice of units in equation (1), the share of unskilled labor in total population, ℓ, and the share of capital in sector X, λ_K, are both equal to their respective stocks in the economy, i.e. $\ell = \bar{L}$, $\lambda_K = K_X$, and the choice of units also implies that $\bar{H} = 1 - \ell$ and $K_Y = 1 - \lambda_K$. This means that starting from, say, the SW corner of the box in Figure 3.2, one reads the allocation of unskilled labor to X going to the right along the horizontal axis while, if the NE corner represents the origin for industry Y, one reads the allocation of skilled labor to Y along the horizontal axis going from right to left. Thus any point in the box corresponds to a given allocation of skilled and unskilled labor and of the mobile capital between the two sectors.

Now, since we assumed that sector X is (unskilled) labor-intensive ($k_X < k_Y$), whatever the allocation of capital, the permissible allocation of unskilled labor and of skilled labor will be below the diagonal. This means that, starting from a point like A (which would be on the dashed contract curve line if the economy were in long-run equilibrium), unskilled natives are necessarily capital-rich (since below the diagonal $k_X < k_Y$ or again $\theta_L = \ell > \lambda_K$) and they favor immigration.

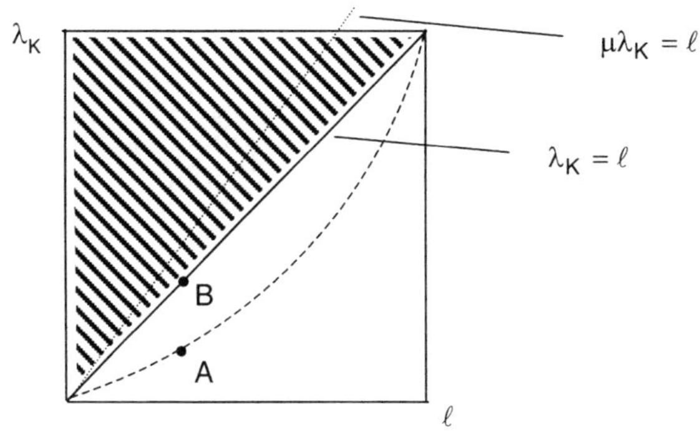

Figure 3.2 Attitude of unskilled natives towards immigration.

What about national attitude? Given the zero-sum property of infinitesimal immigration, skilled natives adopt a position which is systematically opposed to that of unskilled natives (apart from the indifference case). This is represented in Figure 3.3a and b, with reversed dashed areas representing opposition to immigration. Combining both boxes one obtains Figure 3.3c, representing the national stance towards immigration according to which household group has the majority. For example, suppose that $\ell_0<0.5$, then (given that we have also assumed $k_X<k_Y$), the economy is in the shaded area (1) in figure 3.3(c). In that region, unskilled households are favorable to immigrants, but since they are the minority, the national attitude is one of opposition towards immigrants.[12]

Note that all the previous analysis, which was based on an infinitesimal inflow of unskilled immigrants, remains valid if immigrants are skilled individuals. The reason is that both types of labor are analytically symmetric, and a reinterpretation of Figure 3.1 switching X and Y indices would lead exactly to the same results as far as critical capital ownership is concerned. In other words, Figure 3.3 represents the national attitude towards immigration, whatever the immigrants' skills.

In sum, as X is labor intensive and H is the majority group, it turns out that the nation as a whole unequivocally opposes immigration because it leads to a lower income of skilled natives, whose capital ownership is lower than the critical level that would make them indifferent. This result may seem surprising and rather inconsistent with actual immigration policies. In fact, it is highly dependent on the simplifying assumptions that

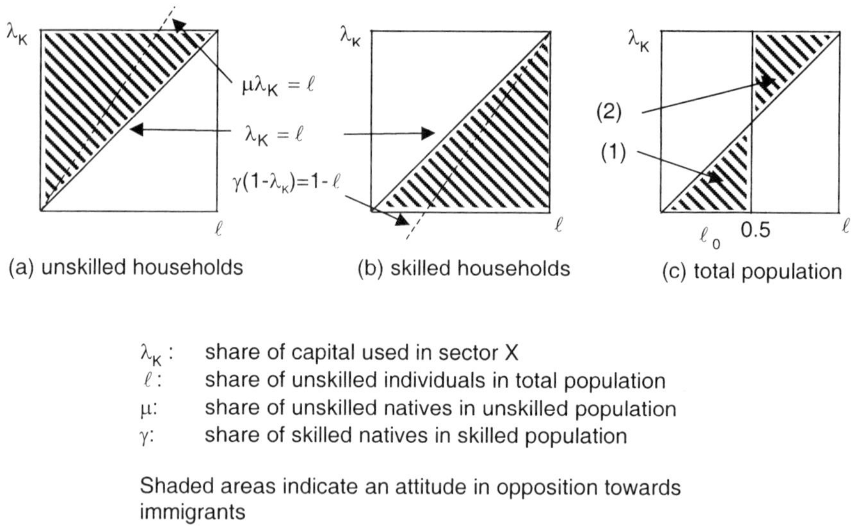

Figure 3.3 National attitude towards immigration.

underline the benchmark case which we adopted for expository purposes rather than for their realism. As will be shown below, relaxing these assumptions leads to a richer pattern of possible attitudes that will provide the basis for an interpretative discussion of results.

Sustained immigration

What happens if immigrants keep on flowing in? A quick, though incorrect, reaction would be to conclude that unskilled natives become progressively less prone to immigration because, as the share of capital used in industry X increases with the expansion of this sector, the critical capital ownership of unskilled natives, K_c^L, becomes closer and closer to their effective capital ownership (an upward move from point A in Figure 3.2).

In fact the reverse is true: the critical capital ownership level of unskilled natives actually decreases, because since immigration is no longer infinitesimal, the zero-sum property no longer holds (one is in the "immigration surplus" situation discussed above). Hence, there is an increasing net gain from immigration that accrues to natives, making them more sympathetic towards immigrants. This "immigration surplus" situation is illustrated in Figure 3.4, where the sequential expansion of capital demand from sector X ($V_X^0 \rightarrow V_X^1 \rightarrow V_X^2$) leads to an ever increasing dashed area representing the net gain from immigration. Now, native unskilled households share their loss in rents with unskilled immigrant households.[13]

For skilled households, the critical capital level remains equal to the level of capital used in sector Y, so the analysis of Figure 3.3b remains unchanged. For unskilled households, because part of their income loss is now absorbed by the migrants already present, the compensatory requirement in terms of capital ownership is smaller. As illustrated in Figure 3.4, the critical amount of capital that leaves unskilled natives indifferent to immigration ($K_c^{L,2}=DE$) is equal to the amount of capital used in sector X ($K_X=DC$) times the share of natives in unskilled population, denoted by μ ($\mu \equiv \bar{L}/\bar{L}+M_L$) where M_L is the number of unskilled migrants, with $\mu=DE/DC$ at point C of Figure 3.4.

In terms of Figure 3.2, and provided ℓ is interpreted as the share of unskilled individuals in the voters' (not total) population, this leads to a rotation of the indifference line towards the left, whose expression is now given by $\mu\lambda_K=\ell$. Again, this is because the critical share of capital ownership for unskilled households is now smaller than the actual share of capital used in sector X, thereby decreasing the relative share of shaded areas in Figures 3.2 and 3.3a. Thus, an initial opposition may be softened and even reversed if a substantial immigration flow leads to sufficiently large net gains. However, recall that the attitude of skilled households (Figure 3.3b) remains unchanged. Thus, in terms of national attitude towards immigration (Figure 3.3c), it is only the shaded area (2) whose share would decrease, leaving area (1) unchanged.

As there is now an asymmetry between skilled and unskilled households, the skill level of immigrants matters. If immigrants are skilled individuals,

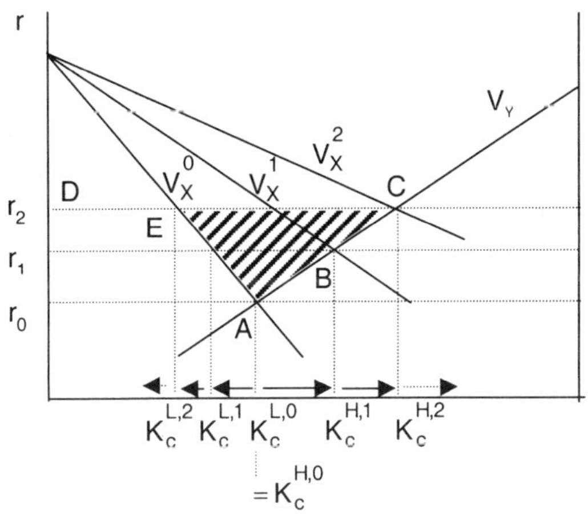

V_X: marginal product of capital in sector X

V_Y: marginal product of capital in sector Y

K_c^V: critical capital ownership of household V (V=L,H)

Figure 3.4 Sustained immigration.

the previous analysis is reversed: the indifference condition for unskilled households ($\lambda_K = \ell$) remains unaltered, but skilled natives become more favorable to immigration. In Figure 3.3b, the indifference line for skilled households is now given by $\gamma(1-\lambda_K)=(1-\ell)$, where γ is the share of skilled natives in skilled population ($\gamma=\bar{H}/\bar{H}+M_H$)), M_H being the number of skilled migrants. In terms of national attitude (Figure 3.3c), area (2) is unchanged but area (1) is reduced.

Concurrently with the changes that have occurred in national attitudes towards immigration since the 1950s and 1960s when unskilled immigrants were welcomed, and the 1980s and 1990s when they were no longer welcome, the share of unskilled households has markedly declined. Suppose then that we apply our framework to a two-period analysis, and assume that $\ell_0 > 0.5 > \ell$, so that native unskilled households started as a majority and became a minority (with a corresponding decrease in λ_K). In the presence of sustained migration, as the non-shaded areas in Figure 3.5a indicate, the median (native) voter changes from being in favor, to being against, unskilled immigration.[14] However, as depicted by Figure 3.5b, if immigrants are skilled and there is a substantial immigration surplus associated with their arrival, it may well be that the majority change leaves unaltered the favorable attitude towards skilled migrants.

Although this direct-democracy framework helps us to understand why attitudes towards skilled immigrants would be more favorable, it is still one in which unskilled natives (who are, according to our definition, "capital-rich") favor immigration, the reverse being true for skilled natives. This is particularly hard to reconcile with the survey-based results reported by Scheve and Slaughter (1999). Their econometric evidence using 1992 household survey data shows that, after controlling for gender, age, ideology, race, less-skilled (more-skilled) people prefer more-restrictionist (less-restrictionist) immigration policy. They also report that these results are robust to choice of the skill measure (occupational wage, years of schooling).

A straightforward extension to accommodate this result would be to assume that skilled (or unskilled) labor, rather than capital, is the mobile factor. In this case, every native would be opposed (favorable) to immigrants who (do not) share his or her skill level, irrespectively of capital ownership. An alternative is to introduce inequality in capital ownership among natives, as we do in the next section.

Unequal capital distribution across households

Relax now the assumption of equal capital ownership share among national households. We shall consider the case where capital is evenly distributed within each household group but capital per capita is different across groups (i.e there is "between" inequality).[15] Now the value of the index of between-group inequality, τ, defined in equation (1), is given by $\tau=\theta_L/\ell$ and

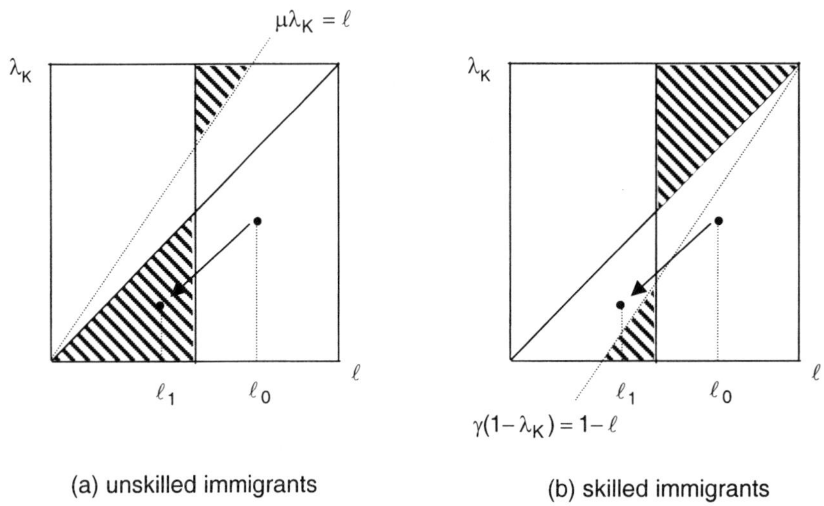

λ_K: share of capital used in sector X
ℓ: share of unskilled individuals in total population
μ: share of unskilled natives in unskilled population
γ: share of skilled natives in skilled population

Shaded areas indicate an attitude in opposition towards immigrants

Figure 3.5 Population shares in the presence of sustained migration.

$\tau<1$, under the plausible assumption that the per capita capital ownership of unskilled households is inferior to their share in total population. Recall that the definition of a "capital rich" ("capital poor") unskilled household is one for which $\theta_L>\lambda_K$,($\theta_L<\lambda_K$), so that the indifference line is now given by $\tau\ell=\lambda_K$.

Figure 3.6 draws the plausible case where $\tau<1$, so that the indifference line ($\lambda_K=\tau\,\ell$) has rotated clockwise with respect to Figure 3.3 ($\tau=1$). This leads to an increase of the area where unskilled (skilled) households are opposed (favorable) to immigrants, an intuitive result as between inequality has lowered the capital ownership of unskilled households. In the limiting case where unskilled natives do not own any capital ($\tau=0$), they become unambiguously opposed to immigration, while skilled natives systematically favor it, a result more consistent with the empirical evidence.

For the whole country, in Figure 3.6c, there is a net increase in the total shaded area (opposition to immigration). This suggests, in a probabilistic approach to reflect ignorance about the economy's parameter values, rising opposition towards immigration. Again, if one interprets these results in the light of the increased income inequality in the US (and to some extent

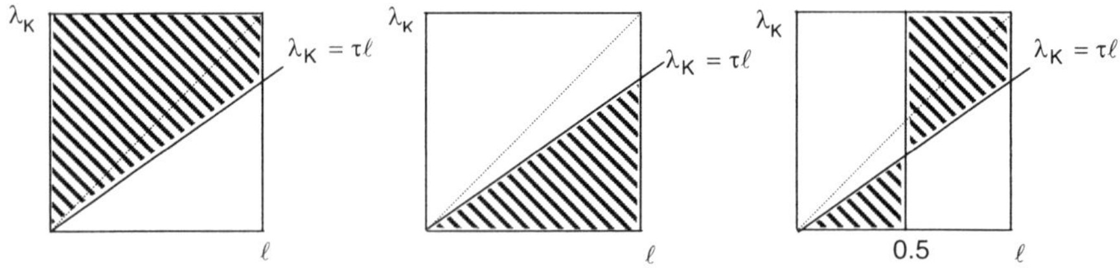

(a) unskilled households (b) skilled households (c) total population

λ_K: share of capital used in sector X
ℓ: share of unskilled individuals in total population
τ: index of between-group inequality in capital distribution

Shaded areas indicate an attitude in opposition to immigrants

Figure 3.6 Inequality in capital distribution between households.

in other receiving countries), the framework can help explain how the recent increase in income inequality is accompanied by a stiffening attitude towards unskilled immigration.

Another source of opposition towards immigration may come from globalization, reflected in an increase in the relative price of the exporting sector. Assume that the price of good Y increases or, alternatively, that a neutral technical progress in the same sector increases the marginal productivity of capital in the exporting sector. How would this affect the attitude towards immigrants? In itself, the shock would alter factor rewards (along the usual lines in the Ricardo–Viner model), but in fact the only thing that matters as far as households' attitudes are concerned is the impact on the critical capital ownership levels. And the answer is straightforward: as the exporting sector expands, so does the share of capital used in sector Y. This means that skilled households face a higher critical capital level, the reverse being true for unskilled households. Thus, starting from an initial national indifference towards immigration (i.e. relaxing the assumption of differences in capital intensity between sectors for ease of exposition), like point B in Figure 3.2, we move downwards, making skilled households capital-poor and generating an opposition towards immigration since they are assumed to be the majority.

How are these results affected when immigrants also own capital? The basic difference from the previous analysis is that national factor rewards react both to the change in labor endowment and to the change in the capital stock. As both effects work in opposite directions, there is scope for a capital "compensation effect" on the immigrants' side, which might lead to a reversal of the net impact of immigration on factor rewards.

It can be shown that the critical capital ownership level of immigrants is exactly the same as that of the native unskilled in the benchmark case. If immigrants own more capital than this critical level, they become "capital-rich" and attitudes towards immigration are reversed. This may explain why capital requirements are a critical factor in the immigration policy of certain countries.

In sum, the Ricardo–Viner model provides a useful framework to analyze the changing pattern of attitudes towards legal immigration identified in industrialised countries. On the one hand, the loss of majority by unskilled natives is likely to have led to a reversal of national attitude from one of acceptance to one of opposition towards immigration. On the other hand, this stiffening of attitudes towards immigrants may have been exacerbated by globalization or by an increasing inequality of capital distribution among natives. At the same time, a relaxation of this anti-immigrants stance can be obtained by imposing capital requirements on immigrants, which, by the way, is being increasingly observed across receiving countries. Moreover, opposition towards skilled immigrants is less strong, particularly if the "immigration surplus" is large. In the next section, we show how a slight modification to the model makes it useful to examine the political economy of illegal immigration.

Why illegal migrants?

The Ricardo–Viner framework can be extended to the analysis of illegal immigration. Following Hillman and Weiss (1999a), we assume now that there is only one type of labor (L), which is the mobile factor, and two types of sector-specific capital (K_X, K_Y). There are two classes of households, "workers" each owning one unit of labor, and "capitalists" each owning one unit of either type of capital. Immigrants do not bring any capital with them. There are more workers than capitalists so the median voter is a worker.

Traded goods only

Start with the case where both goods are traded, and illegal immigrants are confined to one sector (illegal Mexicans in California employed in the garment and citrus fruit industries). Immigration, which brings down real wages, should never be observed, as it will be opposed by a majority of voters. However, illegal immigration may occur, and will be welcomed by capitalists. Suppose illegal immigration took place in the past, so that we start from an initial situation where there is already a substantial number of illegal immigrants in the country.[16] Moreover we assume that all illegal immigrants have been confined in sector X by an exogenous segregation process, which has displaced all native workers to sector Y.

This situation is depicted by Figure 3.7, where the number of illegal immigrants (M) is larger than the critical amount of immigrants that displaces the last native worker from sector X to sector Y ($M > M^*$). This means that native labor has become specific to sector Y and that the wage

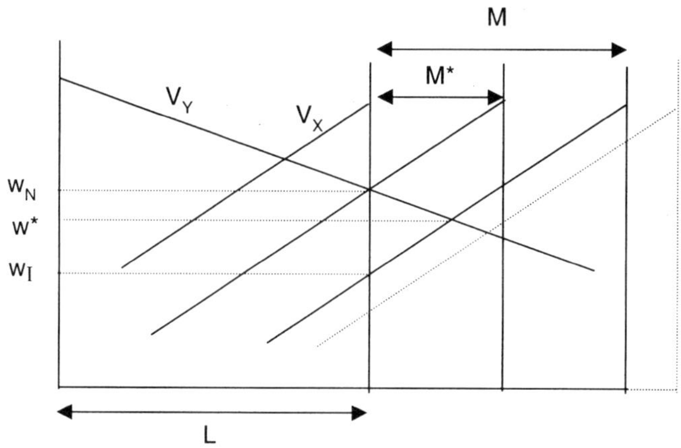

V_X: marginal product of labor in sector X
V_Y: marginal product of labor in sector Y
L: number of native workers
M: number of immigrants
M*: number of immigrants such that all natives are excluded from sector X.

Figure 3.7 Illegal immigration (labour is the mobile factor).

rate of natives (w_N) is higher than the wage rate of immigrants (w_I). In this case, as in a similar situation analyzed by Djajić (1997), native workers are "immunized" against additional illegal immigration. Indeed, any additional increase of the immigrant population (represented by the dotted lines in Figure 3.7) is Pareto improving for natives as it will depress the immigrants' wage while increasing the real return to K_Y and leaving unchanged both w_N and the real return to K_X.

What if immigration policy is now put up to a vote? If mass expulsion is not an option, the median voter will prefer to keep immigrants illegal rather than opt for an amnesty that would allow immigrants to enter sector Y and would bring down his or her wage to w^*. Moreover, a vote on additional illegal immigration would be positive as it would increase capital remuneration in sector Y while leaving indifferent native workers and sector X capitalists.

Non-traded sector

This illustrates the case where immigrants are confined to the lodging, restaurant and domestic help activities, as is the case in European countries with guest-worker systems. Provided that preferences are the same across household groups, the previous conclusion is reinforced if one of the two sectors produces non-traded goods. Suppose it is sector X, where illegal immigration is frequently observed, and start again from an initial situation where all natives are employed in sector Y (now the composite traded good). With respect to the analysis of Figure 3.7, the additional consequence of allowing more illegal immigration would be a decrease in the relative price of non-traded goods (there is an increase in the relative supply of non-traded goods while the relative demand is unchanged provided immigrants share a common consumption pattern with natives). This leaves every household better off than in the traded-goods case, generating a clear majority in favor of additional illegal immigration.[17]

The predictions here, according to which one would not vote to legalize illegal immigrants and where illegality permits the selective enforcement of restrictive immigration laws which confine immigrants to sectors where the median voter benefits from their presence, are supported by recent evidence. Hanson and Spilimbergo (1999a) show that illegal immigration between Mexico and the US responds to wage differences. In further work (Hanson and Spillimbergo, 1999b), they show that border enforcement efforts can be explained by the clashes in lobbying activities between sectors that use illegals intensively (apparel, fruits, lodging and restaurants) and hence lobby for lax enforcement, and labor unions that oppose lax enforcement. They also point out that an inefficient enforcement mix (at the border rather than the interior) is chosen for political economy reasons, though officially it is to avoid directly injuring the parties involved.

Dual labor markets and "guest-worker" migration

Segregation appears not only in the context of illegal immigration, but is observed in many countries even in the case of legal migration. The extent of segregation seems to depend on migration policy: it is more pronounced in countries with a "guest-worker" system than in countries favoring permanent immigration ("melting-pot").[18] Furthermore, Table 3.1 shows that among European countries, those with a "guest-worker" system (Germany, Austria, Switzerland) have experienced the greatest increases in the share of foreigners. From the viewpoint of political economy, one might therefore conjecture that the probability that immigration is accepted by natives depends on the type of immigration policy and thus on the extent of segregation it generates.

In the preceding section, we assumed complete sectoral segregation between natives and illegal immigrants. Here we investigate further the link between migration policy, (incomplete) sectoral segregation, and the political economy of immigration. To analyze this issue, we use an efficiency-wage model of a dual labor market with "good" and "bad" jobs. In this model, segregation and discrimination against immigrants are a consequence of the fact that migrants face different incentives and legal constraints than natives. On the one hand, migrants are likely to return to their home country (voluntarily or forced by limited work permits). On the other hand, preferential hiring regulations lead to discrimination against immigrants if good jobs are rationed.

We continue with the Ricardo–Viner small-country model with both goods traded, capital being the specific factor. Each native worker owns some quantity of capital, which is paid at the average return of the two sectors. The dual labor market is modelled in a standard efficiency-wage framework following Shapiro and Stiglitz (1984) and Bulow and Summers (1986). Work conditions in the primary and the secondary sectors are not identical. The primary sector, Y, offers good working conditions. By assumption, workers in this sector cannot be perfectly monitored. Thus firms prefer to pay wages above market-clearing levels in order to induce workers to supply effort. As a consequence, jobs are rationed in the primary sector and workers are queuing up for them. However, they can always find jobs in the secondary sector, X. These jobs are much less attractive and consist of repetitive tasks that can be easily monitored at negligible cost. The wage rate is set competitively in this sector. There is no unemployment.[19] First, we develop the model to show how the equilibrium is affected by an inflow of migrants, and second, we ask what type of system ("melting-pot" or "guest-worker") will be preferred by natives.

Segregation and discrimination in the efficiency wage model

Workers are assumed to be risk-neutral and to have identical instantaneous utility functions. Worker i holds a certain amount of capital k_i, and his indirect utility function is given by:

$$U = w + r_K\, k_i - e \qquad (2)$$

where w is the wage, r_K is the average return to capital in the two sectors and e denotes effort. The variable e can take two values: 0 if the worker does not make any effort (i.e. if he "shirks"), and $e>0$ if he does not shirk. Workers are assumed to maximize expected utility over their infinite life horizon, using discount rate r.

Consider first the situation of natives. The problem of a worker in the primary sector who has to decide whether to shirk or not, can be analyzed by relating the utility levels that he can attain in the two cases. Let U_Y^s (U_Y^n) denote the expected present value of utility of a shirking (non-shirking) worker holding a primary-sector job. Let V_X denote the expected utility of a secondary-sector job. To relate these situations, the asset-equation approach introduced by Shapiro and Stiglitz (1984) is followed. A worker who shirks faces a probability d per unit time of being discovered and fired. Moreover, there is an exogenous probability q per unit time for each primary-sector job to end; in that case the worker takes up a job in the secondary sector. If a worker has a job in the primary sector, he receives wage w_Y. He earns the following return, according to whether he shirks or not:

$$rU_Y^n = w_Y + r_K k_i - e - q(U_Y^n - U_X) \tag{3}$$

$$rU_Y^s = w_Y + r_K k_i - (q+d)(U_Y^s - U_X) \tag{4}$$

A worker in the primary-sector does not shirk if $U_Y^n \geq U_Y^s$. At equilibrium, there is no shirking and this condition holds with equality since there is no reason for a primary-sector firm to pay a higher wage. Using equations (3) and (4), the no-shirking condition can be rewritten as follows:

$$d(U_Y^n - U_X) = e \tag{5}$$

The return to a job in the secondary sector is equal to:

$$rU_X = w_X + r_K k_i - e + \alpha(U_Y - U_X) \tag{6}$$

where α is the probability of moving from a secondary-sector job to a primary-sector job.

In a steady-state equilibrium, the flow out of the primary sector is qL_Y, where L_Y is native employment in the primary sector. The flow into the primary sector is $\alpha(L\text{-}L_Y)$, where L is total native employment. At equilibrium, these two must be equal. Thus, for natives α is given by $qL_Y/(L-L_Y)$. Using (3) and (6), the no-shirking condition (5) becomes:

$$w_Y - w_x = \frac{e}{d}\left(r + \frac{qL}{L - L_Y}\right) \tag{7}$$

At equilibrium, the wage rate is equal to the marginal product of labor in each sector. Labor market equilibrium is depicted in Figure 3.8. The upward-sloping curve is the natives' no-shirking condition (7), and the downward-sloping curve represents the difference between marginal products of labor in the two sectors. The intersection determines the equilibrium wage differential and native employment in both sectors. Note that the employment of immigrants is considered exogenous in this figure, and that the equilibrium in the dual labor-market is inefficient. The distortion could be corrected by subsidising primary-sector (high-income) employment. Since such a measure would meet with strong political opposition, because of its anti-egalitarian implications, we assume that it is not realized.

The welfare outcome of immigration obviously depends on the migrants' incentives and on migration policy. Indeed, a distinctive characteristic of immigrants is their probability of return.[20] Therefore, even if migrants are identical to natives in all other respects, their incentive not to shirk is influenced by the probability of return to their home country. Moreover, the return probability is influenced by various aspects of migration policy, such as the existence of temporary work permits, or the government's attitude towards social and economic integration of immigrants. Other

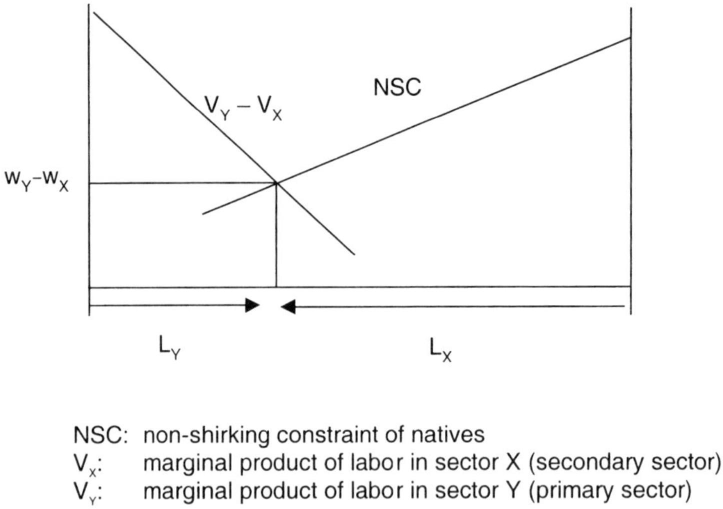

Figure 3.8 Equilibrium in the dual labor market.

legal dimensions of migration policy are equally important. In most countries, migrants are granted equal rights in the host country's labor market only after a certain period of stay. Firms are compelled to prefer natives and "old" migrants over "new" migrants in their hiring decision.

All these factors contribute to segregation and thus discrimination against migrants. Since competition ensures that natives and migrants are paid the same wages, discrimination is of the type "equal pay for equal work, but not equal work." Hence migrants have smaller chances of finding "good" jobs than natives and suffer from sectoral segregation. The extent of segregation which results from these differences in incentives can be summarized by the following equation relating the migrants' chances of being employed in the primary sector to that of the natives:[21]

$$\frac{L^*_Y}{L^*} = (1-\zeta)\frac{L_Y}{L}; 0 < \zeta \leq 1 \tag{8}$$

where an asterisk on a variable denotes an immigrant and ζ measures the extent of segregation.

The choice of migration policy

Is it more likely that natives will vote in favor of immigration if the government applies a "guest-worker" system rather than a "melting-pot" policy? To analyze this issue, assume that capital is distributed unequally among native workers. Consider a worker (indexed by i) holding k_i units of capital. Immigration entails an identical change in his steady-state utility, whether he works in the primary or the secondary sector. Indeed, differentiating equations (3) and (5) yields:

$$dU_Y = dU_X = (l/r)(dw_Y + k_i dr_K) \qquad (9)$$

How does the critical level of capital, k_i^c (at which a native is indifferent towards immigration, i.e. $dU_X = dU_Y = 0$), depend on migration policy? Consider first, as a benchmark case, the standard Ricardo–Viner model without dual labor markets. Here the critical level of capital is given by the total per capita stock of capital, $(K_X + K_Y)/L$. By contrast, the "zero-sum" property of (infinitesimal) immigration is not preserved in the dual-labor-market model, as the equilibrium is inefficient. Immigration has a positive (negative) first-order effect on the natives' aggregate welfare if native employment in the primary-sector, L_Y, increases (decreases).[22] As a consequence, the critical level of capital is inferior (superior) to the per capita average capital stock, if native primary-sector employment increases (decreases) with immigration.

Thus the reaction of native primary-sector employment is crucial for the political economy of immigration. Immigration does not shift the natives' no-shirking constraint (NSC). Therefore the question whether L_Y increases with immigration reduces to whether the marginal-labor-product curve shifts upwards in Figure 3.8. In Müller (forthcoming), it is shown that this is more likely to happen if migration policy leads to a high degree of segregation, ζ.

It is instructive to consider the special case of a "guest-worker" system where segregation is maximized ($\zeta = 1$). As immigrants "push" natives towards the primary sector, the marginal-labor-product curve shifts to the right, and L_Y increases unambiguously with immigration. The critical level of capital is equal to:

$$k_i^c = \frac{K_X + K_Y}{L_Y + L_X[1 + \eta_Y / \varepsilon_Y]} \qquad (10)$$

where η_Y is the absolute value of the inverse labor demand elasticity in the primary sector and ε_Y is the elasticity of the wage with respect to the primary-sector employment along the no-shirking constraint. Thus the "guest-worker" system implies a critical level of capital which is lower than the average capital per capita, since $k_i^c < (K_X + K_Y)/L$. If the distribution of capital is symmetric (or if the median capital level is not too far below the average), the median voter will therefore be in favor of immigration.

By contrast, with a non-discriminatory "melting-pot" policy ($\zeta = 0$), it is likely that the critical capital level exceeds the average per capita capital stock. In that case (and if the median capital level is not greater than the average), the majority of natives will vote against immigration.

Conclusions

This chapter has presented an overview of the determinants of migration policies in industrial countries. It has argued that overall, migration probably yields efficiency gains for natives (i.e. an immigration surplus), and an overall welfare gain, if compensation policies can be put in place. We have argued that it is a useful way to view immigration policies as largely determined by the electorate at large in representative democracies, as would be the case in a direct democracy, because of the strong positions taken by politicians and the electorate at large.

Using the direct-democracy framework in several variants of a specific-factors model, we have shown how it can help interpret several stylized facts about recent immigration policies: a stiffened stance towards immigration of the unskilled; coexistence of legals and illegals; lax enforcement towards illegals; a preference for 'guest-worker' programs; and a shift towards eligibility criteria included in immigration decisions.

While going beyond the framework of market-determined outcomes, and of policies determined by benevolent policymakers, the approach has remained grounded in the standard trade models. This has enabled us to relate trade and migration policies, as they are in policy and political debates. As a result, several aspects of migration policies, such as the determination of refugee policies towards asylum claims, have been left out. Neither have the links between foreign direct investment, trade policy and migration policy been examined.

Notes

1 See Zimmermann (1995) for a discussion of the phases of European migration and The Economist, May 6–12, 2000, for recent characteristics of immigration in the EU. For the US see Borjas (1994) and Trefler (1998).

2 A poll conducted on behalf of the European Commission shows that a significant majority of those interviewed believe that "immigrants are too many." This is particularly true in the four largest European countries, with 54 percent of Frenchmen, 57 percent of Germans, 51 percent of Britons, and 64 percent of Italians believing the number of migrants to be excessive. And in the US, results of the US National Elections Survey of 1992, in which respondents were asked to reveal their preference over immigration policy on a scale of 1 (increase a lot), to 5 (decrease a lot) produced a mean of 3.6 and a standard deviation of 1.0 (Scheve and Slaughter, 1998).

3 The stiffening in attitude towards immigrants in the EU, especially towards low-skill ones, is all the more remarkable since according to the United Nations' Population Division projections based on current trends, the current flow of immigrants in the EU as a whole would have to reach 1.6 million a year to keep its working population stable, and 13.5 million a year to keep the ratio of pensioners to workers steady.

4 Wong (1995) explores systematically trade models in the presence of factor mobility. Venables (1999) explores the links between trade liberalization and factor mobility in a family of models. Faini and Grether (1997) and Grether et al. (1999) present models that accommodate the observed asymmetry between trade and migration policies.

5 Leamer and Levinsohn (1995) refer to this result as the Factor-Price-Insensitivity (FPI) theorem. However, with more tradable products than factors, we are in the multi-cone setting, so that with sufficiently large immigration shocks, the diversification cone will be altered and factor prices will change. Also, if both countries are in different cones, different goods are produced and trade will not eliminate incentives for factors to migrate.

6 Kenen (1971) analyzes the terms-of-trade effects of migration in an H–O model, but from the standpoint of the source country.

7 Though in a different context, this result is reminiscent of the discussion on the optimal population size where there are advantages (increasing returns to scale, sharing of public goods) and disadvantages (diminishing factor productivity, congestion effects). See Razin and Sadka (1997).

8 Scheve and Slaughter (1999) find that less-skilled workers are significantly more likely to prefer limiting immigrant inflows into the US, and that individuals form their opinions in accord with their interests as labor-force participants. This justifies the approach taken here. Their results also reject the "area analysis" framework used by labor economists according to which immigrants pressure the wages of similarly-skilled natives who reside in gateway communities where immigrants settle, but are in accordance with the "factor proportion analysis" where the pressure on wages is nationwide, as in the multi-cone H–O and Ricardo–Viner trade models.

9 For examples of the pressure-group approach, see Buckley (1996) and Mezza and Winden (1996).

10 Hillman and Weiss (1999b) suggest that voters probably find the H–O model appealing when formulating trade policy since it captures the indirect effect of labor (via embodiment in imports), and the Ricardo–Viner model when formulating immigration policy since immigrants compete directly with domestic labor. Bilal et al. (2000) provide an algebraic treatment of the long-run version of the model presented here with the same two goods and the assumption that the three factors, capital, unskilled labor and skilled labor, are mobile across sectors. Benhabib (1996) uses a similar approach in a one-sector economy.

11 An alternative would be to consider that skilled labor is the mobile factor; however, besides being less realistic in a two-sector context, this case is less interesting as the pattern of attitudes that emerge is independent of capital distribution (see Bilal et al., 2000).

12 Should the unskilled be the majority, then the economy is to the right of the "majority" line, and, since the economy is below the diagonal, the median voter would be favorable to unskilled immigration. And if Y were labor intensive, the economy would be above the diagonal, so that the results would, once again, be reversed.

13 This case also depicts the impact of an infinitesimal increase of unskilled migrants starting from an initial situation (like point B in Figure 3.4) where there are already immigrants in the country.

14 If migrants get progressively "assimilated" and vote, then the critical line in figure 3.5 rotates back to the diagonal, but the changes in attitudes would still be observed if the unskilled changed from majority to minority.

15 The case where capital is unevenly distributed within groups but the average capital per capita is identical between groups (within inequality) is treated in Grether et al. (2000) who also use a Beta distribution to examine numerically the case where capital ownership distribution is skewed to the left within each household group. The simulations reveal an "opposition cone" along the diagonal of Figure 3.3c, whose width depends on the skewness of the capital within each group.

16 This corresponds to the case analyzed by Hillman and Weiss, who also assume that undesired (from the point of view of the median voter) illegal immigration has taken place. It is a shortcoming of the median voter framework that it is unsuitable to explain why illegal immigrants would have entered in the first place. A more appropriate framework is the pressure group model (see Hanson and Spilimbergo, 1999b), where industries that benefit from illegals make contributions in return for lower levels of enforcement while groups that oppose immigration, say unions (and perhaps other groups) make contributions for higher enforcement levels.

17 See Djajić (1997). This is all the more likely if one makes the assumption, as do Hillman and Weiss (1999a), that domestic (and legal immigrant) households have stronger preferences for non-traded goods than illegal immigrant households.

18 Zimmermann (1994) shows that in "guest-worker" countries like Germany and Switzerland, immigrants are heavily represented in construction and manufacturing, as opposed to the United States, where the sectoral distributions of natives and immigrants are very similar.

19 For the effects of immigration in efficiency-wage models with unemployment, see Müller (2000) and Epstein and Hillman (2000), where the natives' willingness to exert effort increases with the number of immigrants.

20 In 1995, average return rates ranged from 1.5 percent for Netherlands to 7.8 percent for Germany, though much higher return rates are attained for particular groups (25.6 percent return rates for Polish immigrants in Germany) of for certain legal categories (10.3 percent for holders of annual work permits in Switzerland).

21 Equation (8) can be considered as a reduced form. The exact relation between segregation, discrimination and structural parameters (such as the return probability) is derived in Müller (forthcoming).

22 To see this, consider the variation of aggregate native welfare: $L_X\, dU_X + L_Y\, dU_Y = (1/r)\, L_X\, (dw_Y - dw_X) = [(1/r)\, (w_Y - w_X) - (e/d)]\, dL_Y$, where the expression between brackets is positive. Including the gain of secondary-sector workers, $(U_Y - U_X)\, dL_Y = (e/d)\, dL_Y$, does not change this qualitative result.

References

Benhabib, J. (1996) "On the Political Economy of Immigration," *European Economic Review*, 40: 1737–1743.

Berry, R.A. and R. Soligo (1969) "Some Welfare Aspects of International Migration," *Journal of Political Economy,* 77 (5): 778–794.

Bhagwati, J. (1991) "Free Traders and Free Immigrationists: Strangers or Friends," Working Paper 20, Russell Sage Foundation.

Bilal, S., J.M. Grether and J. de Melo (2000) "Attitudes Towards Immigration in a Direct Democracy: A Trade-Theoretic Approach," mimeo, University of Geneva.

Borjas, G. (1994) "Immigration and Welfare: 1970–90," Working Paper 4872, Cambridge, Mass.: National Bureau of Economic Research.

Borjas, G. (1995) "The Economic Benefits of Immigration," *Journal of Economic Perspectives*, 9 (2): 3–22.

Buckley, F.H. (1996) "The Political Economy of Immigration Policies," *International Review of Law and Economics,* 16: 81–99.

Bulow, J. and L. Summers (1986) "A Theory of Dual Labor Markets with Application to Industrial Policy, Discrimination, and Keynesian Unemployment," *Journal of Labor Economics,* 4 (3): 376–414.

Djajić, S. (1997) "Illegal Immigration and Resource Allocation," *International Economic Review*, 38 (1): 97–117.

Epstein, G. and A. Hillman (2000) "Social Harmony at the Boundaries of the Welfare State: Immigrants and Social Transfers", Working Paper 2414, London: Centre for Economic Policy Research.

Faini, R. and J.M. Grether (1997) "L'Ouverture au Commerce peut-elle réduire la Migration Nord-Sud," in J. de Melo and P. Guillaumont (eds), *Commerce Nord–Sud: Migration et Délocalisation*, Paris: Economica.

Findlay, R. (1982) "International Distributive Justice: A Trade Theoretic Approach," *Journal of International Economics*, 13: 1–14.

Grether, J.M., J. de Melo and T. Müller, (1999) "Réflexions sur la non-équivalence entre politiques migratoires et politiques commerciales," in A. Bouët and J. le Cacheux (eds), *Globalisation et Politiques Economiques*, Paris: Economica.

Grether, J.M., J. de Melo and T. Müller (2000) "Why Have Attitudes Towards Immigration Changed?," in progress, University of Geneva.

Hanson, G. and A. Spilimbergo (1999a) "Illegal Immigration, Border Enforcement, and Relative Wages: Evidence from Apprehensions at the US–Mexico Border," *American Economic Review*, 89 (5): 1337–1357.

Hanson, G. and A. Spilimbergo (1999b) "Political Economy, Sectoral Shocks, and Border Enforcement," Working Paper 7315, Cambridge, Mass.: National Bureau of Economic Research.

Hillman, A. and A. Weiss (1999a) "A Theory of Permissible Immigration," *European Journal of Political Economy*, 15: 585–604.

Hillman, A. and A. Weiss (1999b) "Beyond International Factor Movements: Cultural Preferences, Endogenous Preferences, Endogenous Policies and the Migration of People: An Overview," in R. Faini, J. de Melo and K. Zimmermann (eds), *Migration: The Controversies and the Evidence*, Cambridge: Cambridge University Press, 76–90.

Kenen, P. (1971) "Migration, the Terms of Trade and Economic Welfare in the Source Country," in J.N. Bhagwati et al. (eds), *Trade Balance of Payments and Growth: Essays in Honour of Charles Kindleberger*, Amsterdam: North-Holland.

Krugman, P. (1991) "Increasing Returns and Geography," *Journal of Political Economy*, 99: 483–99.

Leamer, E.E. and J. Levinsohn (1995) "International Trade Theory: The Evidence," in G. Grossman and K. Rogoff (eds), *Handbook of International Economics, Vol. III*, Amsterdam: North-Holland.

Ludema, R. and I. Wooton (1999) "Regional Integration, Trade and Migration: Are Demand Linkages Relevant in Europe?," in R. Faini, J. de Melo and K. Zimmermann (eds), *Migration: The Controversies and the Evidence*, Cambridge: Cambridge University Press.

Mezza, I. and F. Winden (1996) "A Political Economic Analysis of Labor Migration and Income Redistribution," *Public Choice*, 88: 333–63.

Müller, T. (2000) "Migration, Unemployment and Discrimination," Cahier du département d'économetrie No. 2000.03, University of Geneva.

Müller, T. (forthcoming) "Migration Policy in a Small Open Economy with a Dual Labor Market," *Review of International Economics*.

Mundell, R.M. (1957) "International Trade and Factor Mobility," *American Economic Review*, 47: 321–335.

Razin, A. and E. Sadka (1995) "Resisting Migration: Wage Rigidity and Income Distribution," *American Economic Review*, Papers and Proceedings, 85 (2): 312– 316.

Razin, A. and E. Sadka (1997) "International Migration and International Trade," in M. Rosenzweig and O. Stark (eds), *Handbook of Population and Family Economics*, Amsterdam: North-Holland.

Razin, A. and E. Sadka (1999a) "Migration and Pension with International Capital Mobility," *Journal of Public Economics*, 74 (2): 141–150.

Razin, A. and E. Sadka (1999b) "Unskilled Migration: A Burden or a Boon for the Welfare State," Working Paper 7013, Cambridge, Mass.: National Bureau of Economic Research.

Razin, A., E. Sadka and P. Swagel (1998) "Tax Burden and Migration: A Political Economy Theory and Evidence," Working Paper 6734, Cambridge, Mass.: National Bureau of Economic Research.

Scheve, K. and M. Slaughter (1998) "What Determines Individual Trade-Policy Preferences," Working Paper 6531, Cambridge, Mass.: National Bureau of Economic Research.

Scheve, K. and M. Slaughter (1999) "Labor-Market Competition, and Individual Preferences over Immigration Policy," Working Paper 6946, Cambridge, Mass.: National Bureau of Economic Research.

Schiff, M.S. (1998) "Social Capital, Trade, and Optimal Migration Policy," Policy Research Working Paper 2044, World Bank.

Schiff, M.S. (1999) "Labor Market Integration in the Presence of Social Capital," Policy Research Working Paper 2222, World Bank.

Shapiro, C. and J. Stiglitz (1984) "Equilibrium Unemployment as a Worker-discipline Device," *American Economic Review*, 74: 433–444.

SOPEMI (1999) *Trends in International Migration: Annual Report*, Paris: OECD.

Trefler, D. (1993) "International Factor Prices Differences: Leontief Was Right!," *Journal of Political Economy*, 101: 961–987.

Trefler, D. (1998), "Immigrants and Natives in General Equilibrium Trade Models," in J.P. Smith (ed), *The Immigration Debate: Studies on the Economic, Demographic, and Fiscal Effects of Immigration*, Washington, D.C.: National Academy Press.

Venables, A. (1999) "Trade Liberalisation and Factor Mobility: an Overview," in R. Faini, J. de Melo and K. Zimmermann (eds), *Migration: The Controversies and the Evidence*, Cambridge: Cambridge University Press.

Wildasin, D. (1992) "Relaxation to Factor Mobility and Income Distribution," in P. Pestieau (ed.), *Public Finance in a World of Transition, Public Finance*, 47: 216–32.

Wildasin, D. (1994) "Income Distribution and Migration," *Canadian Journal of Economics*, 27 (3): 637–656.

Wong, K. (1995) *International Trade in Goods and Factor Mobility*, Cambridge, Mass.: MIT Press.

Zimmermann, K. (1994) "European Migration: Push and Pull," Proceedings of the World Bank Annual Conference on Development Economics, The World Bank.

Zimmermann, K. (1995) "Tackling the European Migration Problem," *Journal of Economic Perspectives*, 9(2): 45–62.

4 Interactions between international migration and the welfare state

Assaf Razin and Efraim Sadka

The intertemporal and intratemporal redistribution features of the welfare state make it an attractive destination for immigrants, particularly for low-skill immigrants. George Borjas (1994) reports that foreign-born households in the United States accounted for 10 percent of households receiving public assistance in 1990, and for 13 percent of total cash assistance distributed, even though they constituted only 8 percent of all households in the United States. In this chapter we explore the implications of various redistribution policies for the attitude of the native-born towards migrants. We analyze the effect of migration on the shape and magnitude of redistribution policies that are determined in a political economy equilibrium; at the same time, we address the question of whether the level of migration, when not restricted, is higher or lower in this welfare state than in the *laissez-faire* (no-redistribution) economy.

A general equilibrium model of migration and a welfare state

There is a continuum of individuals. Each individual is characterized by an innate ability parameter e which is the time cost needed to acquire skill. The c.d.f. of e is given by $G(\cdot)$, *so* that $G(1)=1$. (The number of individuals is normalized to one.) All individuals live for one period. They are born unskilled, each with a unit of labor time and K units of capital. By investing e units of labor time in education, an individual becomes skilled, which means that each unit of her remaining labor time (that is, $1-e$) is worth one unit of effective labor. If, however, she does not acquire skill (that is, she remains unskilled) her labor time is worth only $q(<1)$ units of effective labor.

The government can only employ an income tax in order to redistribute income. Many studies (for instance, Mirrlees, 1971) suggest that the best egalitarian income tax may be approximated by a linear tax which consists of a flat rate (τ) and a lump-sum cash demogrant (b). Since all families are of similar size and age structure, the uniform demogrant may capture also free provisions of public services such as health care, education, etc.

Consider the schooling decision of an individual. If she acquires a skill by investing e units of her time, she will earn an after-tax income $(1-e)\,w\,(1-\tau)$, where w is the wage per unit of effective labor. If she does not acquire a skill, she earns an after-tax income of $qw\,(1-\tau)$. In this set-up the tax has no effect on the decision to acquire skill. The cut-off ability level (e^*) between acquiring and not acquiring skill is given by the following equation:

$$e^* = 1 - q \tag{1}$$

Denote the consumption of an e-individual by $c(e)$. It is equal to disposable income: Hence:

$$c(e) = \begin{cases} (1-\tau)w(1-e) + [1+(1-\tau)r]K + b \text{ for } e \leqq e^* \\ (1-\tau)qw + [1+(1-\tau)r]K + b \text{ for } e \geqq e^* \end{cases} \tag{2}$$

where w is the wage per unit of effective labor, and $(1+r)$ is the gross rental price of capital. With no loss of generality, it is assumed that capital fully depreciates at the end of the production process; the income tax (τ) applies to the net rental price of capital (r).

Note that the disposable income (namely, consumption) distribution curve is piece-wise linear in the ability parameter e. This refers to the native-born population. For individuals who do not acquire skill (i.e. those with an ability parameter e above the cut-off parameter e^*), the ability parameter is irrelevant and they have the same income. Naturally, within the group of individuals who do decide to become skilled (i.e. for $e \leqq e^*$) the more able is the individual (i.e. the lower is e), then the higher is her disposable income. As can be seen from (2), this relationship is linear. The income distribution curve is depicted in Figure 4.1. Note that the slope of the downward sloping segment is $-(1-\tau)w$. Also, notice that e^* is unaffected by the income distribution policy (namely, τ and b). We assume that the migrants (whose number is m) are all unskilled and possess no physical capital. Their disposable income is only $(1-\tau)qw+b$, which is below that of the unskilled native-born individuals.

We assume a standard (concave, constant-returns-to-scale) production function:

$$Y = F(K,L) \tag{3}$$

where Y is gross output, K is the total stock of capital (recall that each individual possesses K units of capital and the number of individuals is normalized to one), and L is the supply of labor which is given by:

$$L = \int_0^{e^*} (1-e)\, dG + q\,[1 - G(e^*)] + qm \tag{4}$$

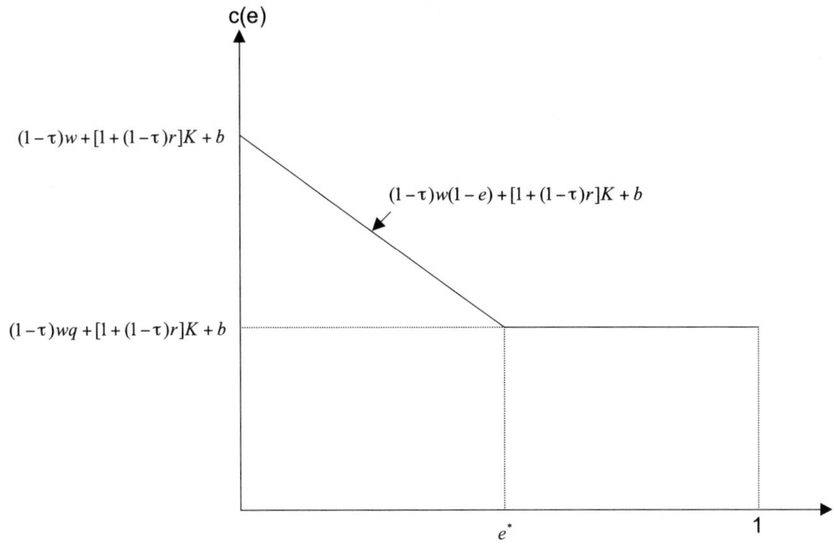

Figure 4.1 The income distribution curve.

The wage rate and the gross rental price of capital are given in a competitive equilibrium by the marginal productivity conditions:

$$w = F_L(K,L) \tag{5}$$

and

$$1 + r = F_K(K,L) \tag{6}$$

The income tax parameters τ and b are related to each other by the government budget constraint:

$$b(1+m) = \tau(Y-K) \tag{7}$$

Note that the base for the flat income tax rate is net domestic product $(Y-K)$, including labor income of migrants which is subject to the income tax. Also, migrants qualify to the uniform demogrant b.

Finally, there are no barriers to migration so that m is determined endogeneously by:

$$(1-\tau)qw + b = w^* \tag{8}$$

where w^* is the opportunity income of the migrants in the source countries.

This model is employed in the next sections in order to investigate two issues: (i) how the welfare state attracts migration of various skill levels; (ii) more importantly, the effects of migration on the income distribution among the native-born which in turn shape their attitude towards migrants.

Attractiveness of the welfare state to migrants

Within this framework we address the first issue of whether the welfare state indeed attracts migrants. More generally, is it true that more taxes and more transfers attract more migrants in the context of our stylized model? Specifically, we study the sign of $dm/d\tau$.

To simplify the analysis we assume a uniform distribution of the ability parameter e over the interval [0,1]. This assumption yields a simple labor supply function as follows:

$$L = \frac{1}{2}(1-q)^2 + q\,(1+m) \tag{4'}$$

where use is made of (1).

Substituting (3), (4′), (5) (6) and (8) into (7) and rearranging terms yields:

$$\left\{w^* - (1-\tau)qF_L\left[K, \frac{1}{2}(1-q)^2 + q\,(1+m)\right]\right\}(1+m)$$
$$= \tau\left\{F\left[K, \frac{1}{2}(1-q)^2 + q\,(1+m)\right] - K\right\} \tag{9}$$

Total differentiation of the latter equation with respect to τ yields:

$$[w^* - qF_L - (1+m)\,(1-\tau)\,q^2F_{LL}]\frac{dm}{d\tau} = F - K - (1+m)\,qF_L \tag{10}$$

By substituting (5), (8), $F=(1+r)K+wL$ (Euler's equation) and (4′) into (10) we conclude that:

$$[b - q\tau w - (1+m)\,(1-\tau)\,q^2F_{LL}]\frac{dm}{d\tau} = rK + \frac{1}{2}(1-q)^2 w \tag{11}$$

It is straightforward to see from the government budget constraint (namely, equation (7)) that the tax on labor income paid by an unskilled individual (namely, τqw) must fall short of her demogrant (namely, b), that is $b > \tau qw$. Since $F_{LL} < 0$, it follows from (11) that:

$$\frac{dm}{d\tau} > 0 \tag{12}$$

Thus, more taxes and transfers attract more unskilled migrants.

This unambiguous conclusion that the more intensive is the welfare state, the more attractive it becomes to migrants, is restricted naturally to the case of low-skill migration. If we allow for high-skill migrants as well, we can see in a natural extension of our stylized model that the welfare state attracts more low-skill migrants but fewer high-skill migrants, as long as "supply-side economics" does not prevail (that is, as long as raising taxes does not yield less revenues). This is shown in Appendix 1.

The attitude of the native-born towards migration

Migration changes the income distribution among the native-born, and the attitude of native-born towards migrants is shaped accordingly.

A benchmark case: no redistribution policies

Let us start with a benchmark case where the government does not engage in redistributing income. This benchmark case highlights the gains-from-trade effect of labor mobility. In this case we set the tax-transfer parameters at zero (i.e. $\tau=b=0$) and drop out the government budget constraint (7).

Suppose initially that there is no migration, so that m is set equal to zero and the migration equilibrium condition (8) is dropped out. The resulting

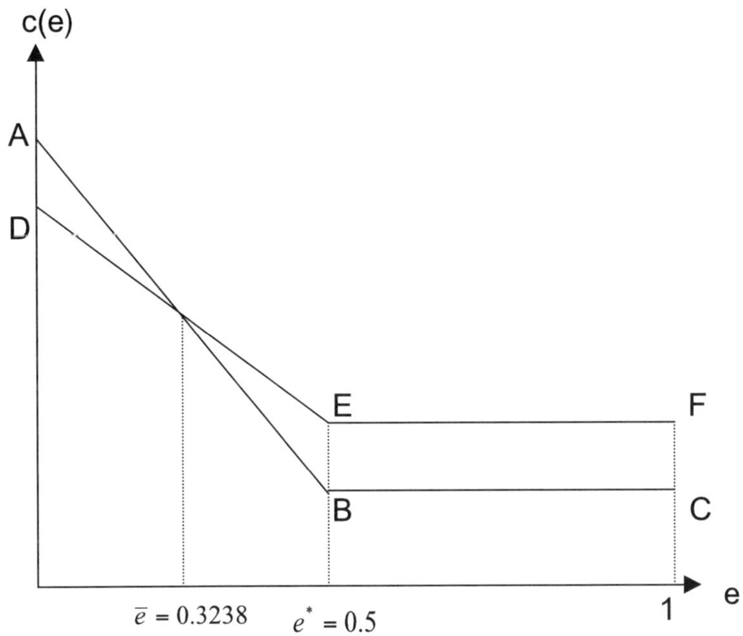

Figure 4.2 The effect of migration on the income distribution, among the native-born, with no income redistribution policy.

Notes: The parameter values are: $q=0.5$; $K=1$, $w^*=0.95qw$ where w is the wage rate in the no-tax-transfer-no-migration case; e is uniformly distributed over [0,1]; and the production function is Cobb-Douglas, $F(K,L)=AK^{\alpha}L^{1-\alpha}$, with alpha=0.35 and $A=4.5$.

income distribution among the native-born is depicted by the curve *ABC* in Figure 4.2, which is based on numerical simulations. Assuming that *e* is uniformly distributed, the area under the income distribution curve is equal to net output (*i.e.* $Y-K$), less payments to migrants (i.e. w^*m) which is initially zero.

Now we allow free migration. That is, we reinstate the migration equilibrium condition (8) and reintroduce *m* as an endogenous variable. The ensuing income distribution among the native-born is described by the curve *DEF* in Figure 4.2. As expected, the gains-from-trade effect is impeccable in the absence of any costly redistribution: *total* income of the native-born (i.e. the area under the income distribution curve) rises as a result of the influx of migrants.

The determination of the free-migration number of immigrants is neatly described in Figure 4.3. The aggregate labor supply of the native-born is perfectly inelastic. (Capital is also fixed.) Thus, the labor supply of migrants changes the total domestic labor supply one-to-one. The downward-sloping curve describes the marginal product of low-skilled migrants (namely, *qw*) as a function of the number of migrants. The equilibrium level of *m* occurs at point *A*, where *qw* is equated to w^*. The standard gains from trade (to the native-born) is measured by the triangle-like area *ABC*, which consists of the total output produced by the migrants (*OCAm*), less the amount of wages paid to them (*OBAm*).

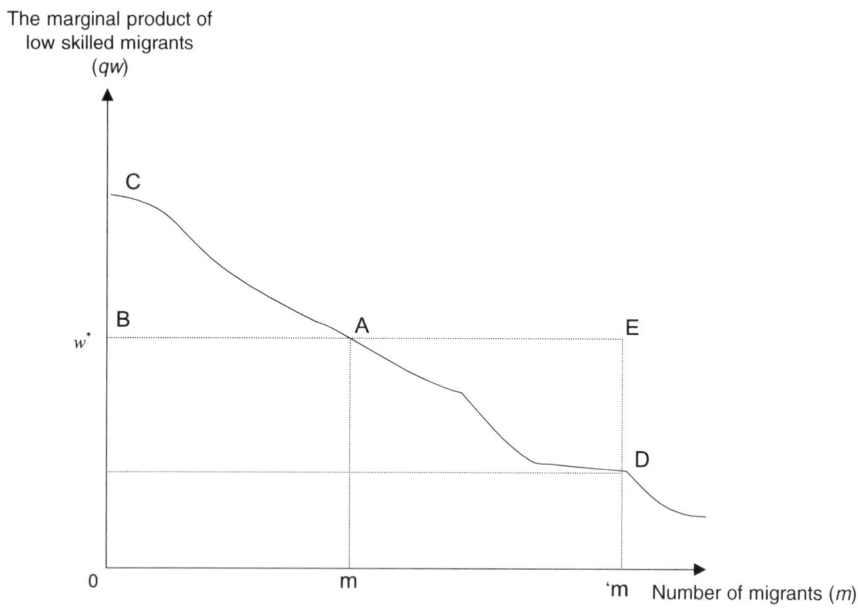

Figure 4.3 Free migration: the income gain to the native-born.

However, the distributional effects of migration are in general not clear: some must always gain, but others may lose. In our particular model and for our specific parameter values, it so happens that some individuals (those with an ability parameter above $\bar{e}$; see Figure 4.2) gain, but other individuals (those with $e < \bar{e}$) lose. Nevertheless, with an active redistribution policy *all* may lose as we shall see below.

Redistribution policy

Now, consider a typical welfare state which redistributes income from the rich to the poor. That is, it levies a positive flat tax ($\tau > 0$) on income (labor and capital) and uses the proceeds to finance a positive demogrant ($b > 0$). The immigrants are typically not only subject to the income tax, but also eligible for the benefits of the welfare state, in contrast to guest-workers.

We perform the following exercise. Suppose first that there is no migration. The closed-economy equations described above (that is, (1), (3)–(7)), allow the government one degree of freedom in designing its redistribution policy (that is, the τ and b parameters). Thus, for each τ there is a corresponding equilibrium b. Consider a certain configuration of the equilibrium pair (τ, b). For this pair we find the income distribution curve given by (2). We then allow free migration, that is, we endogenize m and reinstate the free migration equilibrium equation (8). We next redesign the tax-transfer pair (τ, b) in such a way so as to maintain the income of the native-born unskilled individuals at its pre-migration level, and ask what happens to the income of the skilled individuals. The above exercise is carried out for various (pre-migration) tax-transfer configurations, starting from a very low level of redistribution up to a very high level.

Notice that in the absence of migration, the redistribution is not distortionary: in the absence of a pecuniary cost of acquiring education, the redistribution policy affects neither the individual decision whether to become skilled or remain unskilled (that is, the determination of e^*), nor the supply of labor and capital. A dollar taxed away from some individuals ends up *entirely*, with no deadweight loss whatsoever, at the hands of some other or the same individuals. With migration, there is still no deadweight loss in the common use of this term: it is still the case that a dollar taxed away from some individuals ends up entirely at the hands of some other or the same individuals. But there is a loss from the point of view of the native-born individuals because the low-skilled migrants are typically net beneficiaries of the welfare state in the sense that their tax payments (namely, τqwm) fall short of their gross benefits (namely, bm); thus, a dollar of revenues collected from the native-born does not end up entirely at the hands of the native-born, as a portion of it "leaks" to the migrants.

Furthermore, note that with a redistribution policy the gains from trade (to the native-born) may disappear altogether: total income of the native-born may actually decline as a result of migration. To see this, refer again to Figure 4.3. The migrants who are low-skilled and do not own any capital are net beneficiaries of the welfare state. That is, $\tau qw<b$, which means that their net income (namely, $(1-\tau)qw+b$) is above their net marginal product (namely, qw). Since their net income is equal to their reservation income w^* it follows that free-migration equilibrium occurs at a point such as *D*, where $qw<w^*$. In this case the net gain to the native-born is measured by the area *ABC*, less the triangular-like area *AED*. This "gain" from trade could well become negative when τ (and b) are sufficiently high. When this happens, it may also be the case that *all* (skilled and unskilled) native-born individuals lose from free migration.

Our simulations show (see Table 4.1) that when the flat tax rate (τ) in the absence of migration is between 35 percent and 55 percent (and the corresponding demogrant (b) is between 17.7 percent and 25.7 percent of GDP), indeed the skilled individuals all strictly lose from migration, if the redistribution policy is adjusted in order to maintain the disposable income of low-skill native-born at its pre-migration level. The aggregate gains (losses) to the skilled individuals are presented in the last column of Table 4.1. These gains (losses) to the skilled individuals are also the aggregate gains (losses) to the entire native-born population, as the redistribution policy is geared at leaving the unskilled individuals intact. Thus, migration cannot be a Pareto-improving shock for the native-born population, when τ originally (before any migration takes place) exceeds 35 percent.

As was already mentioned, when the income distribution policy is geared to maintaining the income of the native-born unskilled individuals intact, then the net gain (or loss) to the native-born skilled individuals measures

Table 4.1 Free migration and income distribution policy: taxes, transfers and the gains from trade

Pre-migration (1)		*Post-migration (2)*			*Gains from trade*
τ	b/Y	τ	b/Y	m	
0.35	0.2434	0.4024	0.1687	0.8748	(0.0646)
0.40	0.2782	0.3921	0.1648	0.8771	(0.0478)
0.45	0.3130	0.3902	0.1628	0.9009	(0.0341)
0.50	0.3478	0.3798	0.1587	0.9062	(0.0167)
0.55	0.3825	0.3737	0.1552	0.9261	(0.0011)
0.60	0.4173	0.3737	0.1539	0.9517	(0.0116)

Notes:
τ=tax rate.
b=demogrant.
m=ratio of migrants to native-born individuals.
Y=GDP
(l) exogenously given tax rate.
(2) endogenous tax rate: tax rate is determined so as to restore post-migration disposable income of low-skilled individuals to its pre-migration level, for each tax rate shown in the pre-migration cell. For example, τ=0.4024 is the endogenously determined tax rate corresponding to a post-migration disposable income of low skilled, which is equal to its pre-migration level at a pre-migration level at a pre-migration tax rate of 0.35.

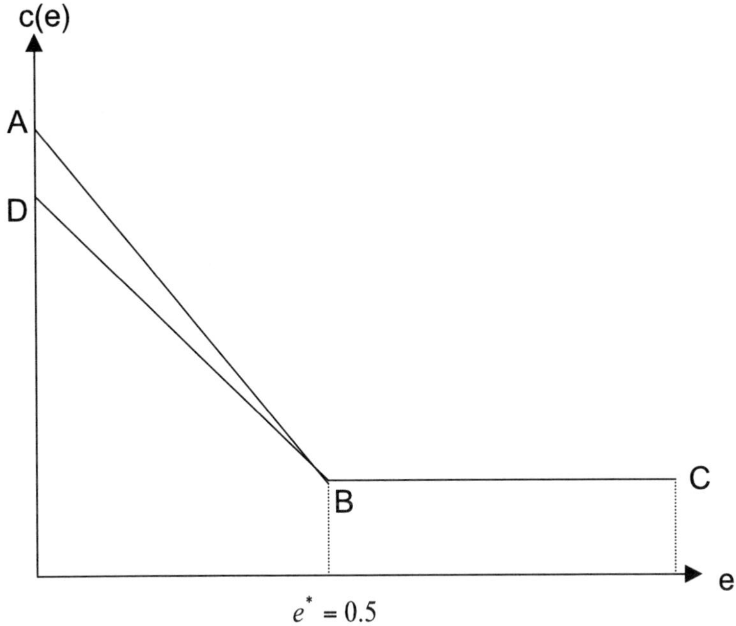

Figure 4.4 The effect of migration on the income distribution, among the native-born, with an income redistribution policy.

the standard gain (or loss) from trade to the native-born population. For instance, when pre-migration τ is between 35 percent and 55 percent (and the corresponding b is between 17.7 percent and 25.7 percent of GDP), then the curves describing the disposable income distribution among the native-born look like the curve *ABC* in Figure 4.4. Now, if we allow free migration and adjust the tax-transfer parameters so as to maintain the disposable income of the native-born unskilled intact, then the new disposable income distribution curves look like the curve *DBC*. (Note that among the native-born the triangle-like area *ADB* in Figure 4.4 measures the total net loss to the native-born and is therefore equal to the area *AED*, less the area *ABC* in Figure 4.3.)

Political-economy effects on the host country

The preceding section analyzed the attitude of the native-born towards migration. We examined the effects of migration on the aggregate income of the native-born people and its distribution among them. The scope of the welfare state itself was not the focus of analysis as the tax-transfer parameters were assumed exogenous (though, of course, constrained by the government budget constraint).

In this section we examine how the redistribution policy is determined in a political economy equilibrium. We then address the following issues in this setup. Does migration necessarily tilt the political power balance in favor of heavier taxation and more intensive redistribution? Relatedly, how does migration affect income ineqality among the native-born?

The extent of taxation and redistribution policy in our analytical framework is determined by a direct-democracy voting. The political economy equilibrium is then determined by a balance between those who gain and those who lose from a more extensive tax-transfer policy. The model captures two conflicting effects of migration on taxation and redistribution. On the one hand, the low-skill, low-income migrants who are net beneficiaries from the tax-transfer system will join forces with the native-born low-income voters in favor of higher taxes and transfers. On the other hand, redistribution becomes more costly to the native-born population, as the migrants share some of the benefits at their expense.

Redistribution policy in a direct democracy

We continue to employ the basic intratemporal model of an economy with migration and redistribution which was described earlier with two modifications. As explained, the tax-transfer policy is not distortionary in the absence of migration. With no migration, there is also no "leakage" of tax revenues to migrants (through the demogrant) and, as a result, there need not be an interior solution for the equilibrium tax rate: it may go all the way either to zero or to 100 percent. We therefore introduce a positive pecuniary cost of acquiring skill which is not tax deductible; thus, e^* is now determined by:

$$(1-\tau)w(1-e^*)-\gamma=(1-\tau)wq$$

and, by rearranging terms:

$$e^* = 1 - q - \frac{\gamma}{(1-\tau)w} \tag{13}$$

The second modification is done for the sake of simplicity: We consider the case where migration is restricted by quotas. Formally, it means that m is exogenously given, so that equation (8) which specifies the equilibrium level of free migration is dropped out. It turns out that in this case of exogenous m, one can analytically derive the results when factor prices are not variable. Thus, for analytical tractability in this section we assume a linear production function:

$$Y=wL+(1+r)\mathrm{K} \tag{14}$$

where the marginal productivity conditions for setting up factor prices (namely, equations (5)–(6)) were already substituted into the production function. We continue to assume that e is distributed uniformly over [0,1], so that the labor supply equation (4) becomes:

$$L = e^* - \frac{1}{2}(e^*)^2 + (1 - e^* + m)q \tag{15}$$

Finally, the government's budget constraint (7) implies that:

$$b = \frac{\tau\,(wL + rK)}{1 + m} \tag{16}$$

For any exogenously given migration quota m, equations (13), (15) and (16) determine e^*, L and b as functions of τ and m:$e^* = e^*(\tau, m)$, $L = L(\tau, m)$ and $b = b(\tau, m)$. The number of migrants (m) is exogenous, but we nevertheless write e^*, L and b as functions also of m, because we wish to explore in this section the effect of m on these variables. Recall that consumption is a strictly decreasing function of the innate ability parameter (e) for the native-born skilled, then constant for the native-born unskilled. It is also constant for the migrants, but at a lower level than for the native-born unskilled since the migrants do not own any capital. This function is given by:

$$c(e, \tau, m) = \begin{cases} (1-\tau)w(1-e) - \gamma + [1 + (1-\tau)r]\,K + b\,(\tau, m) & \text{for } 0 \leqq e \leqq e^*(\tau, m) \\ (1-\tau)wq + [1 + (1-\tau)r]\,K + b\,(\tau, m) & \text{for } e \geqq e^*(\tau, m) \\ (1-\tau)wq + b\,(\tau, m) & \text{for } 1 \leqq e \leqq 1 + m \end{cases} \tag{17}$$

where for ease of exposition we artificially attribute a parameter e between 1 and $1+m$ to the migrants, simply in order to indicate that their consumption is below that of native-born unskilled. For a given tax rate (τ_0), consumption as a function of e is depicted in Figure 4.5. by the curve *ABCDEF* (m is supressed).

The political economy τ is then determined by majority voting. By twice differentiating $c(e, \tau, m)$ with respect to e and to τ we find that:

$$\frac{\partial^2 c(e, \tau, m)}{\partial e \partial \tau)} = \begin{Bmatrix} w \text{ for } 0 \leqq e \leqq e^*(\tau) \\ 0 \text{ for } e^*(\tau) < e < 1 \\ 0 \text{ for } 1 + m \geqq e > 1 \end{Bmatrix} \tag{18}$$

Thus, $\partial^2 c/\partial e \partial \tau \geqq 0$. Therefore, if $\partial c/\partial \tau > 0$ for some e_o, then $\partial c/\partial \tau > 0$ for all $e \geq e_o$. Similarly, if $\partial c/\partial \tau < 0$ for some e_o, then $\partial c/\partial \tau < 0$ for all $e \leq e_o$. This implies that if an increase in the income tax rate (τ) benefits a certain individual (because the higher tax rate can support a higher transfer b), then

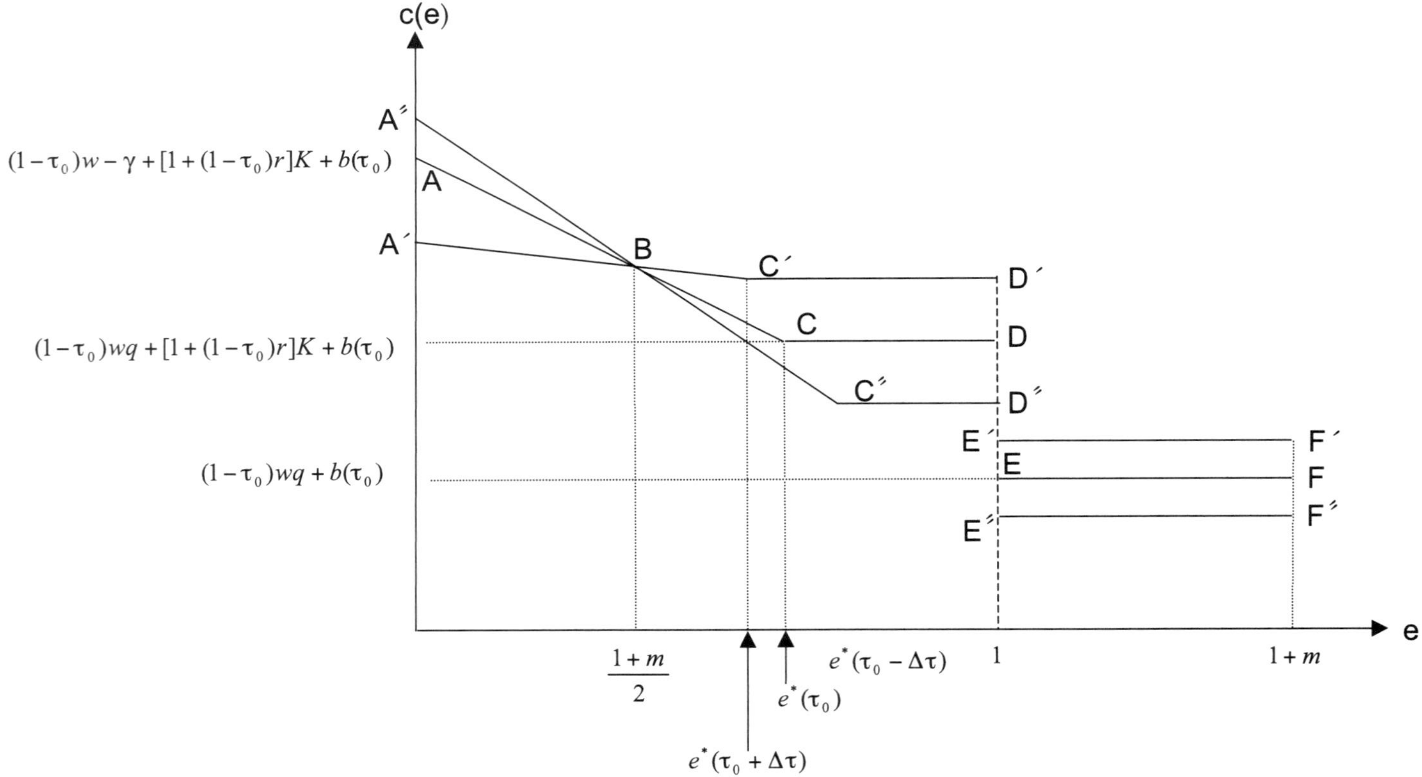

Figure 4.5 Income distribution and a political economy equilibrium.

all individuals who are less able (that is, those who have a higher innate ability parameter e), including the migrants, must also gain from this tax increase. Similarly, if an income tax increase hurts a certain individual (because the increased transfer does not fully compensate her for the tax hike), then it must also hurt all individuals who are more able (that is, those who have a lower innate ability parameter e). These considerations imply that the median voter is a pivot in determining the outcome of majority voting. That is, the political equilibrium tax rate maximizes the consumption of the median voter.

Denote the innate ability parameter of the median voter by e_M. Assuming that migrants are allowed to vote, then:

$$e_M(m) = (1+m)/2 \tag{19}$$

(Recall that the size of the native-born population was normalized to one and the ability parameter is uniformly distributed.) Diagramatically, suppose that τ_o in Figure 4.5 is a political equilibrium tax rate. Suppose further for the sake of concreteness that the median voter is skilled, that is $(1+m)/2 < e^*(\tau_o)$. An increase of $\Delta\tau > 0$ in the tax rate must tilt the income distribution curve from $ABCDEF$ to $A'BC'D'E'F'$, so that all individuals who are more able than the median voter lose and all the rest gain. Similarly, if the tax rate is lowered to $\tau_o - \Delta\tau_o$, then the income distribution curve tilts from $ABCDEF$ to $A''BC''D''E''F''$, so that all individuals who are more able than the median voter gain and all the rest lose.

As noted, the political equilibrium τ (denoted by $\tau_o(m)$) maximizes the consumption of the median voter, that is:

$$\tau_0(m) = \underset{\{\tau\}}{\arg\max}\, c(e_M(m), \tau, m) \tag{20}$$

Therefore, $\tau_o(m)$) is implicitly defined by:

$$\frac{\partial c(e_M(m), \tau, m)}{\partial \tau} \equiv B(\tau, m) = 0 \tag{21}$$

where, by (17):

$$B(\tau, m) = \begin{cases} -w(1-m)/2 - rK + b_\tau(\tau, m) & \text{if } 0 < e_M(m) < e^*(\tau, m) \\ -wq - rK + b_\tau(\tau, m) & \text{if } e^*(\tau, m) < e_M(m) < 1 \\ -wq + b_\tau(\tau, m) & \text{if } e_M(m) > 1 \end{cases} \tag{22}$$

As a second-order condition for maximization we have:

$$\frac{\partial^2 c(e_M(m), \tau_0(m), m)}{\partial \tau^2} = B_\tau(\tau_0(m), m) \leqq 0 \tag{23}$$

where subscripts stand for partial derivatives.

Note that the equation $B(m,\tau)=0$ which determines the political equilibrium tax rate ($\tau_o(m)$) depends, among other things, on the median income versus the average income. For instance, consider the case where the median voter is an unskilled native-born person, that is: $e^*(\tau,m)<e_M(m)<1$. Since equation (16) implies that b is equal to $\tau(wL+rK)/(1+\text{m})$, it follows that the equation $B(\tau, m)=0$ implies that:

$$I_M = \frac{\partial(\tau \bar{I})}{\partial \tau} \Rightarrow I_M - I = \tau \frac{\partial I}{\partial \tau}$$

where $I_M = wq+rK$ is pre-tax median income (net of depreciation) and $\bar{I}= (wL+rK)/(1+m)$ is pre-tax mean income.

The effects of migration on redistribution

Having described the political economy equilibrium, we now turn to the question of how this equilibrium is affected by migration.

Total differentiation of (21) with respect to m implies that:

$$\frac{d\tau_0(m)}{dm} = \frac{B_m(\tau_0(m),m)}{B_\tau(\tau_0(m),m)} \tag{24}$$

Since $B_\tau \leqq 0$ (see (23)), it follows that the direction of the effect of migration (m) on the equilibrium tax rate (τ_o) is determined by the sign of $B_m(\tau_o(m),m)$.

By differentiating equation (22) with respect to m and evaluating it at $\tau = \tau_o(m)$ we conclude that:

$$B_m(\tau_0(m),m) = \begin{cases} \dfrac{w(q+m)}{1+m} - \dfrac{rK}{1+m} & \text{if } e_M < e^* \\ \dfrac{-rK}{1+m} & \text{if } e^* < e_M < 1 \\ 0 & \text{if } e_M > 1 \end{cases} \tag{25}$$

See Appendix 2 for the derivation of the latter equation.

As noted, if the sign of $B_m(\tau_o(m),m)$ is negative, then an increase in the number of migrants lowers the political equilibrium tax rate (τ_o) and, consequently, the demogrant b. Whether this is what actually happens depends on whether the median voter is skilled or unskilled. Consider first the case where the median voter is skilled, that is, $e_M<e^*$. As can be seen from equation (25), the sign of B_m is *a priori* not determined. In this case, an increase in the number of migrants can either raise or lower the political equilibrium tax rate and demogrant. Consider next the case where the median voter is a native-born unskilled individual, that is $e^*<e_M<1$. In this case, an increase in the number of migrants unambiguously lowers the political equilibrium tax rate and demogrant. In the extreme case where the median voter is an (unskilled) migrant, an increase in the number of migrants has no effect on the tax rate and the demogrant.

The rationale for this result is as follows. It is most instructive to begin with the case where the median voter is a native-born unskilled individual (that is, $e^* < e_M < 1$). In this case, the majority of the voters are unskilled and they are certainly pro-tax. This majority has already pushed upward the tax rate to the limit (constrained by the efficiency loss of taxation). A further increase in the number of migrants who join the pro-tax group does not change the political power balance which is already dominated by the pro-tax group. However, the median voter who is a native-born member of this group (and, in fact, all the unskilled native-born individuals) would now lose from the "last" (marginal) percentage point of the tax rate because a larger share of the revenues generated by it would "leak" to the migrants whose number has increased. (Recall that before more migrants arrived, this median voter was indifferent with respect to the marginal percentage point of the tax rate.) Therefore, the median voter and all unskilled native-born individuals support now a lower tax rate. Indeed, B_m which is equal to $-rK/(1+m)$ in this case reflects the marginal increase in tax revenues that are collected from the median voters (but not the migrants who own no capital) and "leak" to the migrants. This is also why $B_m=0$ in the case in which the median voter is an unskilled migrant (that is, $e_M>1$) because the "leakage" element does not exist. In this case, an increase in the number of migrants does not change the political equilibrium tax rate and demogrant.

Turn now to the case where the median voter is a native-born skilled individual. The "leakage" elements, as in the case where the median voter was a native-born unskilled individual, works for lowering the tax rate when m increases. However, now an increase in m tilts the political power balance towards a median-voter who is less able and has a lower income; she benefits more from a tax hike than the original median voter. Thus, an increase in m generates two conflicting effects on the political equilibrium tax rate. Therefore, one cannot unambiguously determine the effect of m on τ and b.

A further insight into these conflicting effects can be gained when the second effect (that is, the shift in the political power balance) is eliminated by assuming that migrants are not entitled (or choose not) to vote. In this case (see Appendix 2) one can show that:

$$B_m(\tau_0(m),m)=\begin{cases}\dfrac{w}{1+m}\left(-\dfrac{1}{2}+q\right)-\dfrac{rK}{1+m} & \text{if } e_M<e^* \\ \dfrac{-rK}{1+m} & \text{if } e^*<e_M<1 \\ 0 & \text{if } e_M>1\end{cases} \qquad (25')$$

As noted before, when the median voter is either a native-born unskilled individual or an unskilled migrant, then even if the migrants were to exercise their voting rights, they do not effectively tilt the political balance of power; and indeed equations (25) and (25′) are identical when $e_M > e^*$. However, when the median voter is a native-born skilled individual, it does matter whether the migrants do or do not vote. If they do not vote, then B_m is unambiguously negative (see Appendix 2 for the proof). When migrants do not vote, the tilting power-balance effect vanishes and only the "leakage" effect is at play and an increase in m lowers τ and b.

We conclude this chapter by noting that the effect of m on τ and b has an interesting implication for the income distribution among the native-born. Recall that we showed that more migration leads or can lead to lower taxation and redistribution. For instance, this is always the case when migrants do not participate in the political process (namely, they do not vote), or when the median voter is an unskilled native-born individual. Then more migration which leads the native-born to vote for a lower tax rate and a lower demogrant has the unintended consequence of a greater inequality of the income distribution among the native-born.

Appendix 1: the welfare state and the skill mix of migration

Let us allow for high-skill migrants as well as low-skill migrants. Denote the number of low-skill migrants and high-skill migrants by m_l and m_h, respectively. Suppose that their reservation wages in their home countries are w_l^* and w_h^*, respectively. Then equation (8) is replaced by two equations, one for each skill type:

$$(1-\tau)qw+b=w_l^* \tag{A1.8a}$$

and

$$(1-\tau)w+b=w_h^* \tag{A1.8b}$$

The labor supply equation (4′) becomes now

$$L=\frac{1}{2}(1-q)^2+q(1+m_\ell)+m_h=\frac{1}{2}(1-q)^2+q+m_1 \tag{A1.4′}$$

where $m_1=qm_l+m_h$ is the labor supply of the migrants in efficiency units. The government's budget constraint (namely, equation (7)) becomes now:

$$b(1+m_2)=\tau(Y-K) \tag{A1.7}$$

where $m_2=m_l+m_h$ is the total number of low- and high-skill migrants. Finally, the other equations of the model, namely (1), (3), (5) and (6), remain intact. We can solve equations (A1.8a) and (A1.8b) for b and w:[2]

$$b = \frac{w_\ell^* - qw_h^*}{1-q} \tag{A1.1}$$

and

$$w = \frac{w_h^* - w_\ell^*}{(1-\tau)(1-q)} \tag{A1.2}$$

Substituting (A1.4′) and (A1.1) into (A1.7) we get:

$$\left(\frac{w_\ell^* - qw_h^*}{1-q}\right)(1+m_2) \tag{A1.3}$$
$$= \tau\left\{F\left[K, \frac{1}{2}(1-q)^2 + q + m_1\right] - K\right\} \equiv R(\tau, m_1)$$

where $R(\tau, m_1)$ is tax revenues. Substituting (A1.2) and (A1.4′) into equation (5) yields:

$$w_h^* - w_\ell^* = (l-\tau)(1-q)\,F_L\left[K, \frac{1}{2}(1-q)^2 + q + m_1\right] \tag{A1.5}$$

The latter two equations (namely, (A1.3) and (A1.5)) can be solved for the labor supply (m_1) and the number (m_2) of the migrants as functions of the tax rate (τ). Total differentiation of (A1.5) with respect to τ yields:

$$\frac{dm_1}{d\tau} = F_L\,[(1-\tau)F_{LL}]^{-1} < 0$$

because we assume that the marginal product of labor is diminishing (that is, F is concave). Upon inspection of (A1.3) we can see that:

$$sign\left(\frac{dm_2}{d\tau}\right) = sign\left(\frac{dR}{d\tau}\right)$$

where $dR/d\tau = \partial R/\partial\tau + (\partial R/\theta m_1)(dm_1/d\tau)$. Suppose that "supply-side economics" does not prevail, that is $dR/d\tau > 0$. (This is always true for small τ´s.) Then, $dm_2/d\tau > 0$.

Thus, we have established that the labor supply of the migrants (m_1) falls while their number (m_2) rises, when the tax rate τ is raised. That is:

$$\frac{dm_1}{d\tau} \equiv q\frac{dm_\ell}{d\tau} + \frac{dm_h}{d\tau} < 0$$

while

$$\frac{dm_2}{d\tau} \equiv q\frac{dm_\ell}{d\tau} + \frac{dm_h}{d\tau} > 0$$

This can happen, if, and only if, $dm\tau/dr > 0$ and $dm_h/d\tau < 0$. Thus, more taxes and transfers attract more low-skill migrants but fewer high-skill migrants.

Appendix 2: migrants vote vs. migrants do not vote

In this appendix we prove equation (25) and (25′). Differentiating equation (22) with respect to m implies that:

$$B_m(\tau,m) = \begin{cases} \frac{w}{2} + b_{\tau m}(\tau,m) & \text{if } e_M < e^* \\ b_{\tau m}(\tau,m) & \text{if } e^* < e_M < 1 \\ b_{\tau m}(\tau,m) & \text{if } e_M > 1 \end{cases} \tag{A2.1}$$

Using equation (16), we conclude that:

$$b_\tau(\tau,m) = \frac{wL + rK}{1+m} + \frac{\tau w}{1+m}\frac{\partial L}{\partial \tau} \tag{A2.2}$$

Differentiating equation (15) with respect to τ implies that:

$$\frac{\partial L}{\partial \tau} = (1 - e^* - q)\frac{\partial e^*}{\partial \tau} \tag{A2.3}$$

where $\frac{\partial e^*}{\partial \tau}$ is derived from equation (1).

Substituting equation (A2.3) into equation (A2.2) yields:

$$b_\tau(\tau,m) = \frac{wL + rK}{1+m} - \frac{\gamma\tau(1 - e^* - q)}{(1+m)(1-\tau)^2} \tag{A2.4}$$

Differentiate b_τ in equation (A2.4) with respect to m to obtain:

$$b_{\tau m}(\tau,m) = -\frac{b_\tau(\tau,m)}{1+m} + \frac{wq}{1+m} \tag{A2.5}$$

where use is made of equation (15) in order to obtain $\partial L/\partial m = q$.

Since $B(\tau_o(m), m) = 0$, we conclude from equation (22) that:

$$b_\tau(\tau_0(m), m) = \begin{cases} \dfrac{w(1-m)}{2} + rK & \text{if } e_M < e^* \\ wq + rK & \text{if } e^* < e_M < 1 \\ wq & \text{if } e_M > 1 \end{cases} \tag{A2.6}$$

Substituting equation (A2.6) into equation (A2.5) yields:

$$b_{\tau m}(\tau_0(m), m) = \begin{cases} \dfrac{w}{1+m}(-\dfrac{1-m}{2} + q) - \dfrac{rK}{1+m} & \text{if } e_M < e^* \\ \dfrac{rK}{1+m} & \text{if } e^* < e_M < 1 \\ 0 & \text{if } e_M > 1 \end{cases} \tag{A2.7}$$

Finally, combining equation (A2.7) with equation (A2.1), we conclude that:

$$b_m(\tau_0(m), m) = \begin{cases} \dfrac{w(q+m)}{1+m} - \dfrac{rK}{1+m} & \text{if } e_M < e^* \\ -\dfrac{rK}{1+m} & \text{if } e^* < e_M < 1 \\ 0 & \text{if } e_M > 1 \end{cases} \tag{A2.8}$$

This completes the derivation of (25).

Consider now the case where migrants are not entitled (or choose not) to vote. Then the ability index of the median voter is $e_M = \frac{1}{2}$ independently of m. In this case, a straightforward application of the same procedure yields:

$$b_m(\tau_0(m), m) = \begin{cases} \dfrac{w}{1+m}(-\dfrac{1}{2} + q) - \dfrac{rK}{1+m} & \text{if } e_M < e^* \\ \dfrac{rK}{1+m} & \text{if } e^* < e_M < 1 \\ 0 & \text{if } e_M > 1 \end{cases} \tag{A2.9}$$

This completes the derivation of (25′).

Note also that when $e_M = \frac{1}{2} < e^*$, then $q < \frac{1}{2}$ (see equation (13)), which implies that $B_m < 0$ in this case.

Notes

1 This paper draws on Chapters 4 and 5 in A. Razin and E. Sadka, *Labor, Capital and Finance: International Flows,* Cambridge: Cambridge University Press, forthcoming.

2 Note from equation (A1.7) that positive b and τ are possible in this case of migration of both low- and high-skill migrants only when the wage differential at the source country (that is, w_h^*/w_ℓ^*) is lower than the wage differential at the destination country which is q.

References

Borjas, George (1994) "Immigration and Welfare, 1970–1990," Working Paper 4872, Cambridge, Mass.: National Bureau of Economic Research.

Mirrlees, James, A. (1971) "An Exploration in the Theory of Optimum Income Taxation," *Review of Economic Studies*, 38 (114): 175–208.

5 Trade and migration

The Mexico–US case

Philip L. Martin

Introduction

Most regional and international regimes – systems in which national governments yield at least some power to a supranational authority that grants member nations rights and impose obligations on them – emerge from crisis (Massey et al., 1998). For example, after wars end, security regimes are often created to which nations pledge troops and mutual support to head off future armed conflicts; after economic crises trade regimes may be established that require member states to lower barriers to goods from other member nations.[1] Financial regimes set out rules for protecting investments and disclosing financial data in order to encourage the citizens of one country to invest in another.

This chapter explores the migration consequences of one trade regime. About 7 percent of the 107 million persons alive today who were born in Mexico live in the US, and another 1–2 percent of Mexican-born persons work seasonally in the US. The Mexican-born population of the US, about 8 million in 2000, is increasing by about 300,000 a year. In 1999, some 4 to 5 million Mexican-born workers were employed in the US labor market, equivalent to about one-third of the 12 million Mexicans employed in formal sector jobs in Mexico (enrolled in the pension system IMSS).

The major relationship between Mexico and the US for most of the twentieth century was a migration relationship that moved primarily unskilled Mexicans into US jobs (Martin, 1993; Massey et al., 1987). This migration relationship has been rife with problems. Mexico complained frequently about the poor treatment of Mexican citizens in the US, but there were few mechanisms to enable the two governments to work cooperatively to improve conditions for legal or unauthorized Mexican migrants. On the US side of the border, several thousand farm employers set the terms for most Mexico–US migration, as US farmers were allowed to recruit Mexican workers for temporary US employment between 1917 and 1921 and again between 1922 and 1964. On the Mexican side, anger over the treatment of legal and unauthorized migrants and fears of being overwhelmed by the US supported a nationalistic stance that made cooperation difficult.

The networks created by the Bracero programs and illegal migration meant that Mexico-US migration was increasing in the mid-1980s, when Mexico changed its economic policies, joining the General Agreement on Tariffs and Trade (GATT) in 1987, proposing the North America Free Trade Agreement (NAFTA) in 1990, and then joining the Organisation for Economic Cooperation and Development (OECD). Increasing economic integration and increased migration went together in North America, producing an immigration backlash in California just as NAFTA went into effect in 1994. Leaders in both Mexico and the US urged the approval of NAFTA under the theory that, in the medium to long term, trade would act as a substitute for migration. After a rough start in 1994–95, NAFTA is having its expected effects on Mexico–US migration, spurring economic and job growth in parts of Mexico, but some Mexican regions lag economically, and US farmers would like to have once again a large-scale guest-worker program.

Evolution of Mexico–US migration

Mexico–US migration has a long history. Between 1769 and 1833, for example, the 21 Spanish missions established along the El Camino Real in California (today's Highway 101) employed local Indians to work on surrounding farmland as a means of exercising control over them. The Spanish priests soon complained of labor shortages and, at the behest of Franciscan Father Junipero Serra in 1773, the Spanish viceroy in Mexico City agreed to permit the California missions to "recruit" workers in what is today the Mexican state of Baja California. The rights of these "first Braceros" were laid out in a 1773 Reglamento (Steven Street, 1996/97: 316).

There has been significant Mexico–US migration in every decade of the twentieth century, but during only two periods, 1917–21 and 1942–64, did formal bilateral agreements regulate the employment of Mexican workers who were temporarily employed in the US. In both cases, large numbers of Mexican workers were recruited to work in US agriculture because of wartime emergencies, these guest-worker programs expanded after the war ended, and labor and civil rights arguments were used in the US to end the programs unilaterally. To obtain permission to employ Mexican workers in 1917, US farmers used the motto "Food to Win the War" to persuade the US Department of Labor (DOL) to suspend the head tax and the literacy test in order to admit temporary Mexican farm workers. The US Border Patrol was established in 1924, but it did little to impede the movement of Mexicans migrating north to be seasonal farm workers even after this first Bracero program ended in 1921. Instead, the 1920s wave of Mexico–US migration was stopped by repatriations: between 1929 and 1933 some 400,000 Mexicans (including their US-born and US-citizen children) were returned to Mexico in an effort to free up jobs for Americans.

The US and Mexico signed a "farm labor supply agreement" on July 23, 1942 (Scruggs, 1960). Throughout the 1930s, farm labor reformers argued that large farms in the western US were really "factories in the fields" that should be covered by the same labor laws as nonfarm factories or broken up into family-sized parcels; if there were land reform, this argument ran, there would be no need for hundreds of thousands of seasonal farm workers. The reformers appeared to be on the verge of changing government policy in 1939–40, when a series of academic and government reports demonstrated convincingly that (i) low farm wages were capitalized into higher land prices and (ii) large landowners invested in the political process to ensure that they had a flexible workforce willing to accommodate to seasonality and thereby preserved the land wealth acquired in part from previous immigration (Martin, 1996: Chapter 2).

John Steinbeck's 1940 book *The Grapes of Wrath* provided the emotional impetus for farm labor reforms. However, before any farm labor reforms could be enacted or implemented, World War II broke out, and the US young men who may have formed the core of a farm worker union exited the seasonal farm workforce for the armed forces or factory jobs. Some were replaced by Braceros. Braceros were less than 2 percent of US hired farm workers during World War II, but their presence, along with prisoners of war, interned Japanese, and US prisoners, sent an unmistakable signal to US farm workers – economic mobility would require geographic mobility, or getting ahead in the US labor market would require getting out of the farm workforce.

The Mexican government, remembering the humiliation of early 1930s repatriations, insisted that the US government guarantee the contracts that farmers were required to provide to Mexican Braceros, including round-trip transportation and the payment of wages equal to those of similar American workers. While the US–Mexican government agreement contained many safeguards for workers, it also required many workers to pay bribes to get on the list to be hired by US farmers, and required farmers to pay transportation and housing costs. It took little encouragement for Mexican workers and US farmers to go outside the program, and the number of so-called "wetbacks" increased significantly in the late 1940s and early 1950s.[2]

The Bracero program in the early 1950s became a kind of rolling quasi-amnesty program for seasonal workers from Mexico, many of whom arrived illegally. Newspaper headlines that read "Wetbacks swarm in" led to the perception that Mexico–US migration was out of control. A retired army general was appointed head of the Immigration and Naturalization Service (INS). He launched Operation Wetback in 1954, a massive border control and interior enforcement operation that removed from the US over one million Mexicans. Simultaneously, the US government relaxed rules for employing Mexicans as legal Bracero workers, with the result that the number of Braceros admitted peaked at 550,000 in 1955–56. One result of the expansion of the Bracero program was that US workers, especially

Mexican-Americans who faced competition from Braceros in the fields, responded by moving to cities such as Los Angeles and San Jose.[3]

The Bracero program was ended unilaterally by the US in 1964, amid predictions that US labor-intensive agriculture would collapse and that tomatoes and other commodities would have to be imported from Mexico. These predictions – by farmers and agricultural officials – proved to be false. Farm wages rose sharply in the mid-1960s, when the combination of the Vietnam-war economy and a smaller excess supply of farm workers permitted Cesar Chavez and the United Farm Workers (UFW) to win a 40 percent wage increase for grape pickers, increasing their wages from $1.25 to $1.75 an hour in the UFW's first contract in 1966. During the late 1960s, farm wages rose faster than other US wages, especially in California, and there were expectations that the career of farm worker would become very similar to that of construction worker, offering high hourly wages when seasonal work was available, and then maximum unemployment insurance benefits (Martin and Olmstead, 1985).

After the Bracero program ended, there was a golden era for US farm workers. There were relatively few newly arrived foreigners in the farm workforce, and farm wages rose relatively fast, closing the gap with non-farm wages. However, in the late 1960s, many ex-Braceros became US immigrants because their US employers sponsored them as "needed workers." There was illegal immigration as well – the UFW complained about farmers using unauthorized workers to break strikes, and the UFW was a major force behind the passage of employer sanctions in the US House of Representatives in the 1970s – but illegal immigration was relatively modest until the early 1980s. Some 110,000 deportable aliens were located in FY65, 212,000 in FY68, 420,000 in FY71, and 788,000 in FY74. The number first jumped over one million in FY83, after Mexico devalued the peso, and then rose to a peak 1.8 million in FY86 (INS, *Statistical Yearbook*).

There was a clear link between Braceros, legal immigration, and illegal immigration. Most Braceros were young men. Those sponsored by US employers in the 1960s tended to be in their thirties. As they reached 40 and aged out of seasonal harvest work in the 1970s, some of their US farm employers made them foremen, and asked their foremen to recruit seasonal workers. The foremen, who typically visited Mexico during the winter months, recruited workers there, and they arrived illegally the next summer. This process of network recruitment soon linked particular Mexican villages and regional US labor markets.

The UFW's fortunes rose when there was little illegal immigration, and fell when immigration surged. The high water mark for the UFW came in 1978–79, when the union represented about 70,000 farm workers in California, 10 percent of the individuals who worked for wages sometime during the year on the state's farms. As UFW contracts expired in 1978–79, the UFW demanded 50 to 60 percent wage increases at a time when President Carter asked US employers not to grant wage increases in excess of 7 percent. The UFW called a strike against major lettuce growers and eventually won a 42 percent wage increase, raising entry level wages in 1979 from $3.75 to $5.26 per hour, but most of the companies that signed agreements increasing wages to these levels went out of business in the early 1980s, or became only non-farm marketers of lettuce, or adapted in some other way so that they employed no farm workers.

Farm worker wages and benefits were eroding in the mid-1980s when what became the Immigration Reform and Control Act (IRCA) began moving through Congress. IRCA was a "Grand Bargain," requiring control-minded politicians to accept an amnesty for some unauthorized migrants in the US and admissionist-oriented legislators to accept sanctions on employers who knowingly hired illegal workers – many Hispanic legislators believed that sanctions would increase discrimination against Latinos, and thus increase their unemployment rates. However, the major actor in resolving the sanctions–amnesty grand bargain were farm employers. They insisted that, in exchange for agreeing to sanctions, US farmers would have to have easy access to legal Mexican workers under a guest-worker program that did not require growers to obtain certification from the US Department of Labor before employing foreign workers. However, control-minded Republicans and worker-advocate Democrats prevented the approval of a farmer-friendly guest-worker program, and the compromise was one of strangest amnesty programs ever: the Special Agricultural Worker (SAW) program.

The SAW program permitted unauthorized foreigners who did at least 90 days of farm work in 1985–86 to apply for US immigrant status. Because it was widely asserted that many US farm employers paid their workers in cash, the regulations implementing the SAW program were written in a manner that enabled a foreigner, once he applied for legalization and asserted that he qualified, to shift the burden of disproving his claim to the US government. The government had no mechanism to cope with the flood of applications, over 1.2 million rather than the expected 400,000, and no means of disproving what were in many cases false assertions. As a result, over 1.1 million foreigners were legalized, including one million Mexicans, the equivalent of one in six adult men in rural Mexico.

The theory of SAW legalization was that it would reverse the early 1980s slide in farm worker wages and working conditions by enabling now legal workers to join unions and press for wage increases. Instead, more Mexicans migrated to the US, as SAW legalization documents were widely forged or borrowed. The US farm workforce in the early 1980s was estimated to be 20 to 25 percent unauthorized, and was 20 to 25 percent SAW workers in the early 1990s. But legal SAWs got out of agriculture as wages stayed low – a result of workers continuing to arrive illegally – and SAWs were replaced by illegal workers. As a result, by 2000, over half of US farm workers are believed to be unauthorized.

Mexico–US migration during the twentieth century has not been a managed flow of temporary workers. There were 100 years of migration, and 26 years of managed labor migration. Managed labor migration in the North American case showed that the programs tended to be largest after the wartime emergencies that justified them had passed; the availability and presence of Mexican guest-workers in US labor markets encouraged US workers with other options to get out of the farm labor force, and the US safety valve permitted Mexico to neglect West Central Mexico, the area from which many migrants came, so that emigration and remittances became pillars of local economies there.

Maquiladoras: substitute for guest-workers?

The Bracero program ended in 1964, and one result was an unemployment crisis in Mexican border cities. US employers were required to pay transportation costs from the worker's home to the US work place, and many Mexicans moved with their families to the border area to reduce US employers' transportation costs and thus increase the probability of being selected. This meant that, in the mid-1960s, there were thousands of families living along the Mexico–US border who were dependent on the US labor market.

To create jobs for these workers in Mexico, Mexico and the US launched the Border Industrialization Program in 1965. Both countries modified their trade and investment laws so that foreign (US) investors could create jobs in maquiladoras or factories in Mexico border areas. Mexico allowed foreign ownership of the maquiladoras, and permitted the duty-free importation of components and any machinery needed to produce and assemble maquiladora goods. Maquiladora goods had to be exported from Mexico and, as they entered the US, the US tariff schedule was modified to limit the duty on maquiladora products to the value that was added by Mexican assembly operations (wages and Mexican inputs usually account for 10 to 20 percent to the value of maquiladora products entering the US).[4]

The maquiladora program expanded slowly. There were 12 maquiladoras employing 3,000 workers in 1965, 600 maquiladoras employing nearly 120,000 workers in 1980, 2,000 maquiladoras employing 472,000 workers in 1990, and 4,000 maquiladoras employing 1.1 million workers in February 1999.[5] Foreign direct investment in Mexico averaged $11 billion a year between 1994 and 1997, and much of it went into maquiladoras. By 1999, maquiladoras provided almost 10 percent of the formal sector jobs in Mexico, about 30 percent of the manufacturing jobs, and accounted for 44 percent of all Mexican exports – in 1998, maquiladora exports of $53 billion surpassed oil as Mexico's leading source of foreign exchange.[6]

Maquiladoras have been a major job-creating success, creating 1.1 million jobs that pay wages at least twice Mexico's minimum wage and provide fringe benefits; maquiladora job growth has been averaging 125,000 a year. However, maquiladoras did not create jobs for ex-Braceros. The Braceros were young men; the workers employed in maquiladoras were young women – even though the percentage of women is falling, it is still almost 60 percent in 1999. Instead of hiring men who had moved to the border to be closer to US farm jobs, the assembly plants recruited young women from the interior of Mexico; they were believed more willing to work for low wages, have more dexterity, and not complain about repetitive assembly line work. Young women have remarkably high labor force participation rates in border cities – 60 to 80 percent of the 20 to 24-year-old women are in the workforce.

Wages and benefits in the maquiladoras are remarkably similar – averaging about 702 pesos ($75) a month in 1999. Turnover is high, since maquiladoras are constantly hiring new workers, so that disputes with a supervisor, or the opportunity to commute to work with a neighbor, may cause a woman to switch from one assembly plant to another. Maquiladora wages in real terms fell about 11 percent between 1994 and 1998.

The young women who are the core of the maquiladora workforce tend not to migrate on to the US, but their husbands and the men who often accompany them do. Thus, maquiladoras can serve as indirect stepping stones for Mexico–US migration, as younger brothers follow sisters to the border area in search of jobs and then continue across the border. It is thus clear that:

1 Maquiladoras did not achieve their original goal of providing jobs for ex-Bracero men who had become dependent on the US labor market.
2 Maquiladoras stimulated population and economic growth along the US–Mexican border. About 8 million people live within 50 miles of the US–Mexican border, one of the richest parts of Mexico and one of the poorest parts of the United States.
3 Most maquiladoras pay more than the Mexican minimum wage, although critics note labor and environmental practices are sometimes poor. Employee turnover is very high.

Much of the criticism of maquiladoras centers on their alleged labor and environmental shortcomings. The major Mexican union federation, the CTM, is closely associated with the ruling party, allegedly fails to represent maquiladora workers effectively and impedes the formation of "independent" unions. The struggle between the CTM and independent unions has been played out over the past two years at the Han Young maquiladora in Tijuana, which makes truck chassis for Hyundai. Workers there trying to form an independent union contend that the CTM and local politicians have unlawfully blocked their effort.

It has been very hard to show that maquiladoras increase Mexico–US migration, but that is not the case for Mexico's export-oriented vegetable industry. This industry, symbolized by fresh tomatoes, is centered in Sinaloa, about 600 miles south of the US border. Mexican fresh tomato exports almost doubled between 1989–93 and 1994–98, from $256 million a year to $477 million a year.

Both Mexican tomatoes and competing tomatoes in Florida are harvested by Mexican migrants. In Mexico, large farms in Sinaloa and Baja California employ about 170,000 Mexican workers – mostly migrants from southern Mexico – for four to five months between December and April. In 1996, typical wages for tomato picking in Sinaloa were reported to be about $3 to $5 per day, and children often join their parents in the fields.[7]

Seasonal work ends in Sinaloa just as US growers begin to hire farm workers. Most of the family migrants return to small farms in southern Mexico in April to tend to their own farms, but landless workers tend to migrate onward to the US if they have network connections that can help them to find jobs. One survey of Mixtec workers in the US reported that two-thirds had worked in northern Mexican export-oriented agriculture, and were encouraged to migrate to the US by US-based friends and relatives (Zabin et al., 1993).

NAFTA's migration effects

In 1990, Mexico's President Salinas proposed a free trade agreement with the US. Canada, which had entered into a free trade agreement with the US in 1989, joined the negotiations for what became the North American Free Trade Agreement (NAFTA). NAFTA went into effect on January 1, 1994,[8] with the goal of lowering barriers to trade and investment and thus spurring job and wage growth in the three member countries. Although general agreements on migration were explicitly not part of the NAFTA, the hope that NAFTA-led economic development would reduce the volume of undesired, illegal migration was a reason why some wavering Congressional representatives in the end voted for NAFTA.

The NAFTA debate highlights the larger question of whether trade liberalization is an effective means for reducing "unwanted" south–north migration.[9] The answer of most economists is of course that the standard comparative statics analysis highlights the fact that the migration of labor tends to be self-stopping because of the adjustment processes that migration sets in motion, speeding the growth of wages in the sending area and slowing the growth of wages in the receiving area. The conclusion of the standard trade model is that migration and trade are substitutes in both the short and long run (Heckscher, 1949; Ohlin, 1933; Mundell, 1957; Stolper and Samuelson, 1941; Krauss, 1976).

The major policy-relevant question was not what would happen in the long run, after the North American economies reach a new equilibrium, but what would happen during the adjustment period. The US Commission for the Study of International Migration and Cooperative Economic Development, which embraced free trade as the best long-term solution for unwanted economically motivated migration – "expanded trade between the sending countries and the United States is the single most important remedy" – nonetheless concluded that "the economic development process itself tends in the short to medium term to stimulate migration" (US Commission, 1990: xv). In other words, the same policies that reduce migration in the long run can increase migration in the short run, creating "a very real short-term versus long-term dilemma" for a country such as the United States considering a free trade agreement as a means to curb unauthorized immigration from Mexico (US Commission, 1990, p. xvi).

The Commission embraced the hypothesis that economic integration can produce a "migration hump," meaning that, when migration flows are charted over time, migration first increases with closer economic integration and then decreases – in economic terms, migration and trade are complements in the short run and substitutes in the long run (Martin, 1993). The Commission concluded that the migration hump was a worthwhile price to pay for the adoption of policies in both Mexico and the US that would reduce unwanted migration in the long run.

The solid line in Figure 5.1 represents the status quo of unwanted international migration between sending and receiving areas without trade

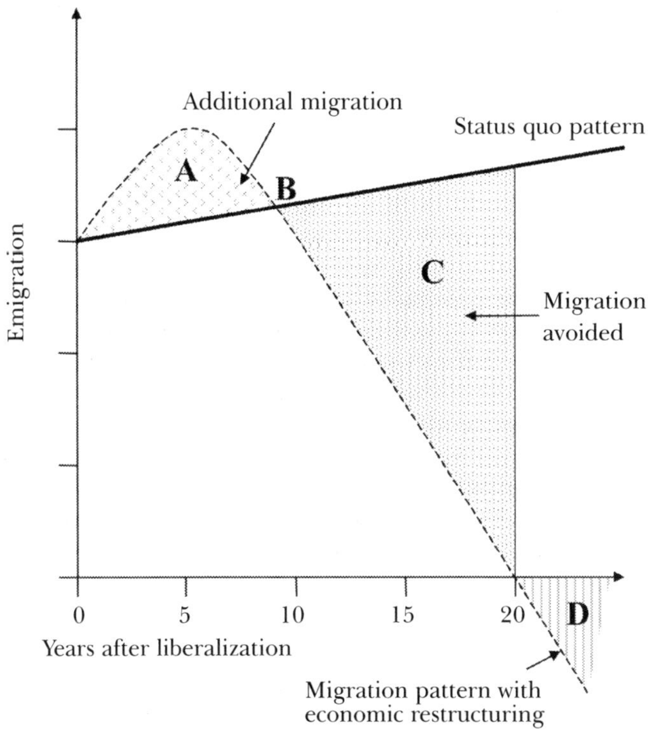

Figure 5.1 The migration hump with trade liberalization.
Source: Martin (1993: Figure 9).

and economic reform. The status quo trajectory reflects demographic-driven emigration; it is based on the assumption that, without trade reforms, migration would continue rising because labor force growth would exceed job growth.

The broken line depicts a migration hump. There is trade reform depicted by year 0, and then the dashed line shows the short-run complementarity of trade and migration in region A, as migration rises above the status quo trajectory. However, migration peaks after 5 years, when trade liberalization begins to speed up economic and job growth. At B, after 10 years, there is as much migration as there would have been without trade liberalization. As a result of trade liberalization, migration continues falling, with the migration avoided represented by area C. Finally, after 20 years, the country may turn from a labor exporter to a labor importer, with immigration represented by area D.

The critical policy parameters in the migration hump are A, B, and C. Given a status quo trajectory, how much does emigration increase as a result of trade liberalization (A), how soon does this hump disappear at B, and then how much migration is "saved" by faster economic and job growth (C)? The size of A and C, and the time at which B is reached, depend on how trade, economic and job growth, and migration interact.

Trade theory and migration

Generally, three factors must be present to produce a migration hump: a continued demand pull for migrant labor in the destination country despite economic integration, an increased supply push in the origin country as a result of economic integration, and pre-existing migration networks that can move workers across borders. Most economic analyzes ignore the possibility of a migration hump because they tend to emphasize comparative statics – comparing before and after equilibrium points, thereby ignoring the *process* of adjustment to free trade. In neoclassical trade models, the prediction that free trade in goods offers a substitute for migration, or trade in people, is an example of a longrun comparative statics prediction. The migration hump, by contrast, is a shortrun relationship between migration and economic adjustment to free trade.

The standard trade model rests on five major assumptions – identical production technologies; factor homogeneity; constant returns to scale; instantaneous adjustment; and perfect competition, full employment, and complete markets. When any or all of these assumptions do not hold, trade and migration can be complements, that is, increased trade can be associated with more migration, or there can be a migration hump when migration flows are plotted against time.

Consider two countries with different factor endowments. A country in the north (Country N) is capital rich, and a country in the south (Country S) is capital poor. Assume that the two countries share the same technologies or production functions, and that the same two factors of production, capital and labor, are used in each country to produce two goods. If the two countries engage in free trade, each country will export the good that is more intensive in the factor that is relatively more abundant in it. That is, Country N will import labor-intensive goods from Country S, and Country S will import capital-intensive goods from Country N.

Stolper and Samuelson considered the effect on factor prices (wages and the return on capital) of an import tariff that increases the domestic price of the import competing good relative to that of the export good. Under the Heckscher–Ohlin assumptions, and the assumption that the underlying trade pattern is not altered by the tariff, an import tariff increases the real reward of the relatively scarce factor and lowers the real reward of the other factor. Thus, a tariff levied against labor-intensive imports in Country N will increase Country N wages relative to the return to capital compared with the freetrade case.

Both Stolper–Samuelson and the Heckscher–Ohlin theorem on which it is based assume that there is no international migration. If migration responds positively to international wage differentials, then (i) protectionism in the north (Country N) should increase migration from the south, or (ii) the protection of capital-intensive industries in the south should spur emigration. Conversely, trade liberalization shifts the production of labor-intensive goods to Country S and capital-intensive goods to Country N, which in turn puts upward pressure on Country S wages, discouraging emigration.

The standard trade model can produce a migration hump by altering some of its key underlying assumptions. The critical assumptions fall into five main categories:

1 The two countries share identical production technologies;
2 The two countries use the same factors of production (factor homogeneity);
3 Technologies exhibit constant returns to scale in production (there are no scale economies);
4 Adjustment to changes in international markets is instantaneous;
5 There is perfect competition, with full employment and complete markets in both countries.

Technology differences

Suppose a labor-intensive good is produced in the emigration country behind tariff and other trade barriers, as corn was in Mexico. If herbicides and other capital inputs give the US a comparative advantage in corn production, then freer trade should permit the US to produce and export more corn. This has in fact happened under NAFTA: the US produces about ten times more corn than Mexico, and the US can export corn to Mexico for less than Mexican farmers can produce corn with labor-intensive technologies. However, half of the man-days worked in Mexican agriculture in the mid-1990s were used to produce corn. Freeing up trade in corn thus eliminated millions of man-days of work for the three million Mexican farmers and workers employed in corn production, putting downward pressure on wages in rural areas and encouraging emigration.

The Mexican corn example illustrates the fact that, if the basis for trade is differences in technology, trade and migration may be complements, as for example, trade in computers and software is accompanied by the migration of computer specialists.

Productivity differences

Differences in factor productivity between countries are implicit in the standard trade model, and the reasons for the productivity differences can help to explain migration behavior. If the differences in factor productivity are due to the presence of complementary public and private inputs, such as education systems, public services, and transportation and communications systems, then the same worker may be more productive in the US than in Mexico, encouraging migration. This is sometimes referred to as the "Third World labor force with First World infrastructure" productivity difference, and is used to explain, for example, why some of the Mexican shoe industry moved from Leon in Mexico to Los Angeles in the US in the 1980s, and shoes produced with Mexican workers and US capital were exported to Mexico.

Similarly, when NAFTA came into effect on January 1, 1994, Mexico lowered some of its tariff and non-tariff barriers on agricultural commodities, including fresh and processed fruits and vegetables. US exports of lettuce and grapes jumped sharply, as the US grower-shippers who dominate North American production learned that it was cheaper to produce many fruits and vegetables with Mexican workers in the US for Mexico because of better US infrastructure. After five years in Mexico, the second largest US vegetable grower ceased operations there with the observation that "we can even produce more efficiently for the Mexican market from the US" (*Ag Alert*, July 14, 1993, 28).[10] Migration, by converting Mexican workers into US workers, in this case discouraged the production of some laborintensive goods in Mexico, and thus encouraged more migration to the US.

Economies of scale

The third assumption of the standard trade model is that (identical) production functions in the two countries exhibit constant returns to scale, which means that increasing all inputs by 10 percent will increase output by 10 percent, whether a country produces 10 or 90 percent of the world's supply of the good. However, if costs fall as production increases in the US in industries that employ migrant workers, trade liberalization may lead to expanded production in the US, and thereby increase the demand-pull of jobs that attract migrant workers. When trade is due to economies of scale, migration and trade are complements.

Slow adjustments

The fourth assumption of the standard trade model is that adjustments to changing prices and wages are instantaneous, and the process of adjustment does not affect the comparative static outcome. In many cases, prices drop and workers are displaced when freer trade is implemented, but finding a new job takes time. For example, Mexican farmers can be displaced or have their incomes lowered with free trade in corn, but it may take several years for foreign and domestic investment to create jobs in manufacturing, where Mexico may have a true comparative advantage, and manufacturing jobs may not be created in the rural areas where farmers are being displaced.

NAFTA provides for a 15-year phase-in of free trade in corn, i.e. by 2009, but Mexico in the early 1990s phased out input subsidies, permitted ejido farmers[11] to sell or rent their land, and "decoupled" farm production from government supports. New job growth in Mexico is concentrated in the northern regions – about 40 percent of Mexico's 2.5 million manufacturing jobs are in the 3,000 maquiladoras that are usually located in border cities and tend to hire young women. The adjustment to free trade in agricultural commodities is complicated by factor specificity – many of those displaced from Mexican agriculture are men, and the maquiladoras tend to hire women. For this reason, many of the Mexican men migrate across the border, to seek work in US farm fields.

Guanajuato, an agricultural state in west central Mexico, estimates that 20 percent of the 250,000 farm families in the state left the land between 1990 and 1999. There are 4.4 million residents of Guanajuato, and another two million adults and their US-born children – equal to 45 percent of Guanajuato's population – living in or migrating regularly to the United States, legally or illegally. Remittances to Guanajuato are estimated to be $1 billion a year, the mainstay of the economy. The removal of farm subsidies and freer trade in farm commodities has spawned many protest movements, including one group, El Barzon, demanding a moratorium on debt repayments. On November 28, 1999, El Barzon retraced the 1,000-mile December 1914 march of Pancho Villa from the border city of Juarez to Mexico City, demonstrating the depth of problems in Mexican agriculture.

Imperfect markets

The fifth assumption of standard trade theory is perfect markets, including full information, no risk, and no transactions costs. This assumption is rarely fulfilled, giving rise to insights that have been collected under the rubric of the new economics of labor migration. For example, suppose that the benefits of migration are significant, but that there are no legal means to cross borders to take advantage of wage differences, so that the migrant must utilize the services of a smuggler who demands an up-front fee. In such situations, freer trade that speeds job and economic growth may also increase migration, as rising incomes mean that more migrants can afford smugglers' fees (Schiff, 1996). This seems to have happened in the south-western Chinese province of Fujian.

Families in the rural areas of sending countries dependent on agriculture may treat family members as a portfolio of income earners, and deploy sons and daughters in a manner that maximizes earnings and minimizes risks. This means that Mexican families may send daughters to border-area maquiladoras and sons to the US: if both succeed in getting jobs, the family can be much better off. However, even if the son is apprehended, the daughter's near 100 percent probability of getting a maquiladora job acts as insurance for the son's attempted illegal entry.

NAFTA and migration: 1994–2010

Proponents of NAFTA knew that Mexico would obtain (i) the greatest benefits from NAFTA in the form of more jobs and higher wages and (ii) Mexico would experience the greatest adjustments to free trade as well. No one knew how quickly Mexico–US migration flows would be affected by adjustments and job creation. However, political arguments in support of NAFTA often assumed that reductions in migration would be immediate, or noticeable after a relative short period of adjustment. US Attorney General Janet Reno in 1993 said: "If NAFTA passes, my job guarding the border will be easier. If NAFTA fails, my job stopping the flow of illegal immigrants will become even more difficult." Mexican President Carlos Salinas similarly asserted that "We want NAFTA because we want to export goods, not people."

Many of the predictions about NAFTA's effects on wages and jobs were derived from computable general equilibrium (CGE) models. The US International Trade Commission summarized the results of ten models, and reported that Mexico's real GDP was projected to rise because of NAFTA from 0.1 to 11.4 percent, Mexican employment was expected to be at least 7 percent higher due to NAFTA, and real wages would be 0.7 to 16.2 percent higher because of NAFTA. The primary mechanism by which these results were to be achieved was through foreign investment – foreign capital would flow to Mexico, the argument ran, bringing new technology and new management and creating jobs. As a Latin American tiger, Mexico could run a trade deficit for years as foreign investors built up Mexico's productive capacity and infrastructure, much as South Korea did during a similar phase of development in the 1960s and 1970s. However, aggregate models predicted that, in the mean time, agricultural liberalization policies in Mexico, including the removal of price supports for corn, would stimulate migration from rural areas, with many migrants heading to the US.

NAFTA got off to a rocky start. Foreign capital had flowed into Mexico in anticipation of NAFTA in the early 1990s, and Mexico permitted the peso to become overvalued in 1993–94, making imports of both capital and consumer goods cheap. US and other foreign investors lent billions of dollars to Mexico, and Mexicans used many of these foreign savings to buy US and other foreign goods, not to build factories and create jobs. In 1994 a series of events dampened investor enthusiasm. Zapatista rebels launched an armed campaign in the state of Chiapas on January 1, 1994; the leading presidential candidate was assassinated in March 1994; and the Mexican money supply was increased sharply in summer 1994 in support of the ruling party's candidates in July elections. President Salinas resisted an "orderly" devaluation of the peso in the fall of 1994, but in December 1994, just after Salinas left office, Mexican and foreign investors began converting pesos into dollars at the fixed 3.45 to $1 rate. Mexico ran out of reserves to support the peso, and the peso was devalued in December 1994.

The economic crisis in Mexico sharply increased unemployment. Mexico, a country with about 10 million formal sector private jobs for a paid labor force of 30 million, experienced almost one million layoffs from formal sector jobs in 1995. In the villages from which many migrants come, economic models projected a migration elasticity with respect to peso devaluations of 0.7 – that is, a 7 percent increase in emigration for every 10 percent devaluation of the Mexican peso – which fell almost 60 percent between November 1994 and November 1995. Many Mexicans responded to the 1994–95 crisis by migrating to the US despite stepped up border controls. The US apprehended 1.1 million foreigners, over 95 percent Mexicans, in FY94; 1.4 million in FY95; 1.6 million in FY96; 1.5 million in FY97; 1.7 million in FY98; and 1.5 million in FY99.

Mexico's economy recovered after 1997, and the migration hump associated with gradual economic integration may be coming into view. GDP growth was 6 percent in recent years and long-term foreign investment has returned to Mexico.[12] Employment has rebounded: the number of Mexican workers in formal private sector jobs rose by 400,000 in 1998. Mexican exports have surged, foreign investment is expected to total $13 billion in 2000, and Mexico has become the second largest trading partner of the US.

Interior Mexican cities and states are aggressively seeking maquiladoras and other foreign investment to create jobs, and foreign firms are responding to the overtures of interior states because of high wages and living costs along the border. For example, Hermisillo, the capital of the Mexican state of Sonora, had 326 maquiladoras employing 96,000 workers in summer 1999 at an average weekly labor cost of $28, half of the weekly wage on the border. Sonora, once known as an exporter of beef and shrimp, is rapidly becoming a manufacturing center via maquiladoras – Ford has an auto assembly plant in Hermisillo.

Guadalajara, the capital of the major state of emigration, Jalisco, is becoming a center for electronics exports. It is more expensive to manufacture components in Guadalajara than in Asia, but Guadalajara is closer to the US, which allows components to be assembled and shipped by truck to the US border area, 600 miles north, to maquiladoras for final assembly. IBM, Motorola, Eastman Kodak and Hewlett-Packard have set up plants in Guadalajara and the electronics industry in 2000 employed 60,000 workers in Guadalajara, up from 5,000 in 1995 – companies note that both wages and employee turnover are lower away from the border.

Mexico–US migration may fall much faster than many pessimists in both countries expect for demographic and economic reasons, which may result in the curious effect of the US constructing an elaborate system of border controls just as Mexico–US migration falls. Mexico's population of almost 100 million is growing by 2 percent a year. About 300,000 Mexicans migrate to the US each year, equivalent to 15 percent of Mexico's population growth. US efforts to prevent such migration have made the Immigration and Naturalization Service one of the fastest-growing federal agencies, with a 2000 year budget of $4.3 billion.

The Mexican population growth rate peaked at 3.3 percent in 1970, when 45 percent of Mexican residents were under 15 years of age. In 1974, the Mexican government launched an enterprising program to persuade families to have fewer children, and birth rates fell sharply in the 1980s and 1990s – fertility dropped from seven children per woman in 1965 to 2.5 in 1998 – so that the number of new job seekers will be 500,000 to 550,000 per year by 2010. Mexico's population is expected to stabilize at about 141 million in 2025, when the US population is projected to be 335 million. The number of persons turning 15 is projected to drop by 50 percent between 1996 and 2010, from about 1 million a year to 500,000 a year. Declining fertility reduces migration directly, with fewer people, and indirectly, because households with fewer children tend to keep them in school longer, reducing the need for jobs for young people entering the labor market, and reducing the probability of emigration.

Second, each 1.35 percent increment to economic growth was associated with 1 percent job growth in Mexico between 1988 and 1995. If this ratio persists, then 5 percent economic growth can generate 3.7 percent job growth, or 1.1 million new jobs each year, enough to employ new job seekers and begin to reduce un- and underemployment. Mexico had 14 million workers in formal sector jobs enrolled in the social security system IMSS in March 1999, up from 13 million a year earlier.

This combination of declining fertility and faster job creation create an X in the Mexican fertility/jobs figure – a point in time when enough new jobs are created to employ fully new workforce entrants. Figure 5.2 highlights two such points – the optimistic one already occurred in 1998, and the more pessimistic one will occur in 2006. If job growth persists as fewer teens seek first jobs, Mexico can begin to reduce unemployment and underemployment.

Mexican leaders have begun to talk about the end of the migration hump. Francisco Labastida, the presidential candidate of Mexico's governing party, the PRI, said in a January 30, 2000 interview that "If the economy grows at a six percent annual rate, and we can create 1.25 million jobs a year, and these jobs pay about five points above inflation, then we could see a significant reduction in the immigration of Mexicans to the US."

Conclusions

International migration has great potential for disrupting orderly relations between nations, despite the fact that the number of migrants is relatively small. In a world of six billion, the number of international migrants – persons living outside their country of birth or citizenship for 12 months or more – approached 150 million in 2000, meaning that just about 2.5 percent of the world's residents were legal or unauthorized immigrants, non-immigrant guest-workers, students, business people, or refugees or asylum seekers.

However, the number and type of migrants has increased faster than the capacity of national governments, regional bodies, or international organizations and agreements to deal with international migration. Several responses are apparent: increased expenditures on immigration control and new regional forums to discuss migration issues.

NAFTA represents a test of using trade to reduce migration. Freer trade and investment regimes accelerate economic growth in both emigration and immigration countries, and thus they are desirable for their own sake. However, the transition to freer trade in relatively closed emigration economies such as Mexico's is disruptive, altering relative prices and thus wages, incomes, and job opportunities. If migration networks link those adversely affected by restructuring to the international labor market, and if the labor markets in which migrants seek jobs abroad do not shrink, than increased trade is likely to be accompanied by increased migration.

Over time, freer trade and investment should increase the rate of income and job growth in the emigration country, thus diminishing migration pressures. When viewed over a decade or two, the number of migrants first increases and then decreases, producing a migration hump, which can be relatively small and short. In southern Europe and Asia, when wage differences decreased to 4 or 5 to 1 and economic and wage growth seemed assured in the emigration country, economically-motivated migration dropped dramatically, as in the case of Italy after 1968 or Korea in the 1980s. This offers a powerful argument for freer trade and investment.

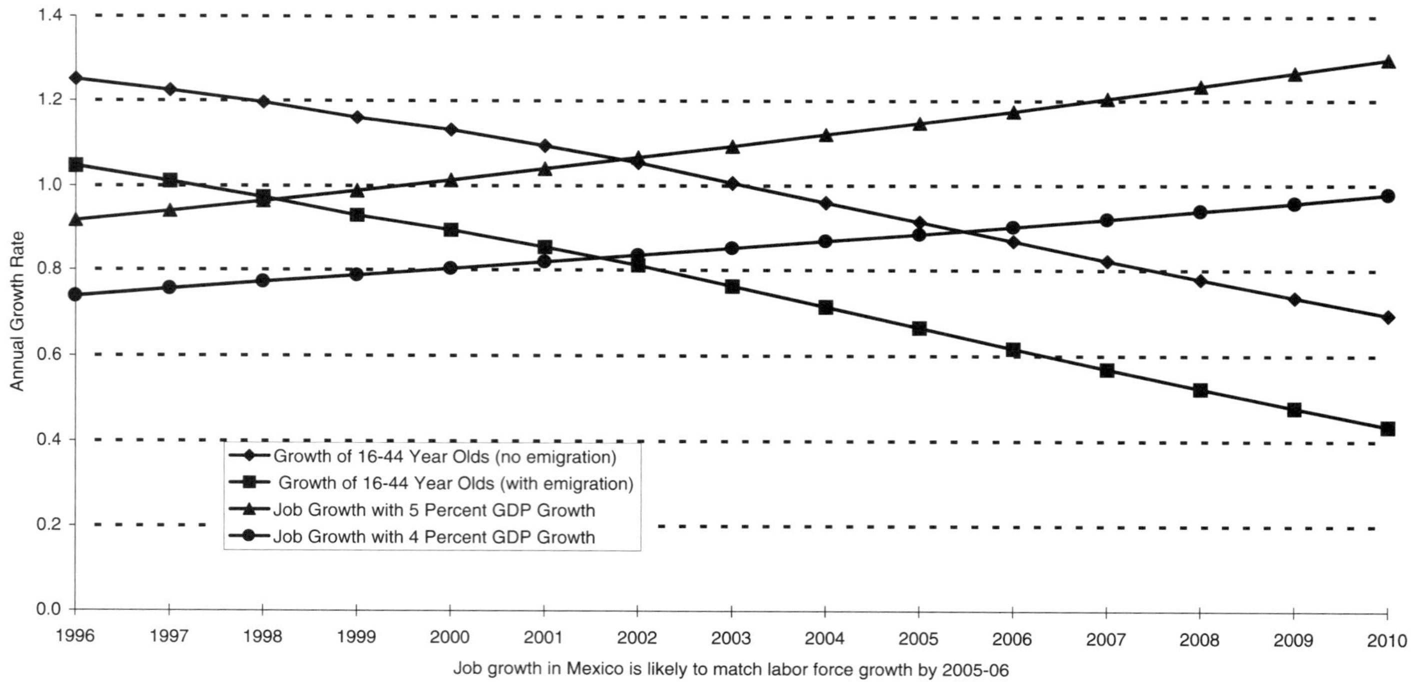

Figure 5.2 Labor force and job growth in Mexico: 1996–2010.

The possibility of a migration hump accompanying freer trade regimes has three major policy implications. First, freer trade and investment should be advocated as the best longrun policies to promote what has been called "stayathome" development, but they should not be sold as a short-term cure for unwanted migration. Second, we need a better understanding of adjustment costs and migration networks and other factors that motivate and sustain migration. The obvious example in the case of NAFTA was how to deal with the 3 million Mexican farmers growing corn, particularly in the light of market imperfections characterizing the rural Mexican economy.

Third, the emigration countries that benefit from freer trade and investment should be expected to help immigration countries manage migration, especially the unwanted or unauthorized migration that freer trade is expected eventually to reduce. Given the resistance to free trade in many aging industrial democracies worried about unwanted immigration, it seems naive to suggest that migration can continue to be excluded from trade negotiations.

Notes

1 The international trade regime is bolstered by an economic theory that concludes that freer trade means faster economic and job growth, i.e. countries that refuse to participate pay a price in the form of slower economic growth. To prevent national governments from giving in to special interests, the 143–member World Trade Organization sets and enforces rules that seek to promote free trade.

2 The usual practice was for a Mexican worker to enter the US illegally, find a US farm job, and go to work, usually under prevailing wages, but without, e.g., government-inspected free housing or other protections specified in the contracts that each Bracero worker received. If apprehended inside the US, the Mexican worker was usually taken to the Mexican border, issued work documents, and returned to his US employer, a process termed, even in official government reports, "drying out wetbacks." The fact that there was no enforcement penalty on workers or employers for being outside the program encouraged illegal immigration, leading one researcher to conclude that "the Bracero program, instead of diverting the flow of wetbacks into legal channels ... actually stimulated unlawful emigration" (Scruggs, 1960: 151).

3 California vegetable production rose 50 percent, as the state replaced New Jersey, the "Garden state." According to the US Department of Agriculture (USDA), farm worker wages rose 41 percent, from $0.85 in 1950 to $1.20 in 1960, while factory workers wages rose 63 percent during the 1950s.

4 The value-added in Mexican maquiladoras remains low. In the first six months of 1997 maquiladoras exported goods worth $20 billion, but imported goods worth $16 billion, so Mexico's value-added was only about $4 billion

5 About 30 percent of maquiladora jobs are in Juarez, across the border from El Paso, and 20 percent are in Tijuana, south of San Diego.

6 About 81 percent of Mexican manufactured products exported to the US in 1998 were products assembled in maquiladoras.

7 The schools in the camps teach from 5 p.m. to 8 p.m., so that children can help their parents in the fields.

8 In 2001, the maquiladora will be incorporated into the Mexican economy and, under NAFTA, restrictions on Mexican sales and temporary imports from the US and Canada will be no more. New Mexican laws passed in the last decade also stand to stimulate joint ventures and manufacturing employment.

9 We use "unwanted" rather than illegal to describe the migration industrial countries are trying to reduce because much of the migration most amenable to being reduced with trade and other economic development measures involves legal but not necessarily wanted foreigners, such as "economic refugees" in Western Europe, and Salvadorans with a "Temporary Protected Status" in the US. In both cases, the host countries would like to reduce the number of such aliens, but their presence is not unlawful.

10 Mexican tomato pickers pick tomatoes into buckets about twice as fast in the US as in Mexico, in part because piecerate wages in the US tend to attract Mexican workers who prefer to be paid by how much work they accomplish, while many farm workers in Mexico are paid by the day.

11 Ejidos were created from plantations or haciendas seized during and after the Mexican revolution. Ejido members were able to farm their land and pass it on to their heirs, but could not sell, rent, or use it for security for loans until 1992.

12 Between 1994 and 1998, foreigners invested $57 billion for long-term projects, making Mexico second only to China in the receipt of foreign investment dollars.

Bibliography

Heckscher, E.F. (1949) "The Effects of Foreign Trade on the Distribution of Income," in H.S. Ellis and L.A. Metzler (eds), *Readings in the Theory of International Trade*, Philadelphia: Blakiston.

INS (Immigration and Naturalization Service) (Annual) *Statistical Yearbook*, Washington, D.C.: INS.

Krauss, M.B. (1976) "The Economics of the 'Guest Worker' Problem: A Neo-Heckscher–Ohlin Approach," *Scandinavian Journal of Economics*, 78: 470–476.

Martin, P.L. (1993) *Trade and Migration: NAFTA and Agriculture*, Washington, D.C.: Institute for International Economics.

Martin, Philip (1996) *Promises to Keep: Collective Bargaining in California Agriculture*, Ames, Iowa: Iowa State University Press.

Martin, Philip L. and Alan L. Olmstead (1985) The Agricultural Mechanization Controversy," *Science* 227, (4687). 601–606.

Massey, D.S., R. Alarcon, J. Durand and H. Gonzalez (1987) *Return to Aztlan: The Social Process of International Migration from Western Mexico*, Berkeley and Los Angeles: University of California Press.

Massey, D.S., J. Arango, G. Hugo, A. Kouaouci, A. Pellegrino and J.E. Taylor (1998) *Worlds in Motion: Understanding International Migration at the End of the Millennium*, Oxford: Oxford University Press.

Mundell, R.A. (1957) "International Trade and Factor Mobility," *American Economic Review*, 47: 321–335.

Ohlin, B. (1933) *Interregional and International Trade*, Cambridge, Mass.: Harvard University Press.

Schiff, M. (1996) "Trade Policy and International Migration: Substitutes or Complements?," in J.E. Taylor (ed.), *Development Strategy, Employment and Migration: Insights from Models*, Paris: OECD Development Centre.

Scruggs, Otey. (1960) "Evolution of the Mexican Farm Labor Agreement of 1942," *Agricultural History*, 34: 140–149.

Steven Street, Richard (1996/97) "First Farmworkers, First Braceros: Baja California Field Hands and the Origins of Farm Labor Importation in California Agriculture, 1769–1790," *California History*, 75 (4): 306–321.

Stolper, W.F. and P.A. Samuelson. (1941) "Protection and Real Wages," *Review of Economic Studies,* IX (November): 58–73.

US Commission for the Study of International Migration and Cooperative Economic Development (1990) *Unauthorized Migration: An Economic Development Response*, Washington, D.C.

Zabin, Carol, Michael Kearney, David Runsten and Ana Garcia (1993). *A New Cycle of Rural Poverty: Mixtec Migrants in California Agriculture*, Davis: California Institute for Rural Studies.

6 Aggregate-level migration studies as a tool for forecasting future migration streams

Michael Fertig and Christoph M. Schmidt

Introduction

From the vantage point of economic policy, assessing migration potential and predicting future migration streams are among the most relevant, yet least well understood topics of migration research. Most theoretical models and a large range of econometric studies successfully address heterogeneity at the individual level, with an emphasis on the detection of demographic and socioeconomic determinants of the individual migration decision, or on the identification of the appropriate decision unit. In the aggregate, though, many important explanatory factors are shared within the regions of origin and destination, rendering the individual-level results inappropriate as a predictive tool, and necessitating an analysis over time and space. The usual approach taken to address aggregate-level prediction problems is to fit *ad hoc* specifications to historical data, and to extrapolate from these estimates on the basis of conditioning information that is assumed to be known with certainty.[1]

This strategy faces formidable problems that exceed the usual difficulties in predicting economic variables. One reason for these deficiencies is the paucity of the data material, making precise estimation of historical relationships both between demographic and economic determinants and the resulting migration streams, and the univariate prediction of those economic variables very difficult. This concern is already relevant for demographic variables, although one might reasonably well predict future population size and age structure. It applies even more to the prediction of economic developments, such as changes in wages, income and employment. Typically, forecasts in the literature do not address this problem of precision systematically.

The second, and conceptually more severe problem is the identification problem that has to be solved satisfactorily for any valid extrapolation, irrespective of the available data points. In the particular case at hand, it is not only the usual temporal invariance that would have to be imposed directly or via the parameterization of trends in variables or relationships, but also the additional invariance across space: often future migration is likely to take place between origin and destination regions that do not share a common history of migration. Moreover, the intertemporal pattern of regulations and institutions relevant for migration streams, albeit endogenous to social and economic changes, is often taken as exogenously given.

This chapter will formally address this double extrapolation problem, with an application to the case of EU enlargement and the ensuing expected migration streams from Eastern Europe after the associated changes in the regulations concerning migration. The chapter thus intends to contribute to the clarification of three important issues:

1 Specific *identification assumptions* have to be invoked by every aggregate migration study. These assumptions might appear particularly restrictive in studies being motivated by microeconomic considerations; basing the analysis on theoretical reasoning is necessary, though, if we want to improve upon mechanical curve fitting.
2 The role of *demographic factors* in the migration decision is widely neglected; evaluating the size and impact of migration flows has to take into account this major supply side factor. This holds particularly within the EU, which erects fairly low institutional barriers to migratory movements of citizens.
3 Imposing more and more structure on the estimation of the determinants of aggregate migration flows has important consequences for the forecasting of future migration flows; more structure typically reduces uncertainty *within* sample if the invoked assumptions are correct, but may not necessarily lead to better forecasts.

The chapter is structured into two major parts. The following section provides a selective survey of existing aggregate-level migration studies. The first half of this is devoted to technical issues, emphasizing the characterization of the particular empirical strategy chosen in each paper to identify the impact of explanatory demographic and economic factors on the magnitude of migration flows. Here we aim at clarifying the implicit and explicit identification and invariance assumptions invoked by the migration literature. In this context, the role of structural economic models as opposed to reduced-form models as predictive tools is also discussed. Recent developments link the migration literature to the macroeconomic literature on convergence by introducing political variables such as freedom and rule-of-law indices; the predictive potential and the additional problems arising from such variables are explored. The second half of the section provides a synoptic discussion of the results of existing studies of aggregate migration flows to Germany, in the light of these technical arguments; specific emphasis is on the explanation of agreement and disagreement between existing studies as results of the chosen identification strategies.

The second part of the chapter will develop our own approach to the particular problem of predicting future migration streams from Central and Eastern Europe to the West within a unified Europe. This topic has received increased attention in recent years, with the answers varying substantially across studies (cf., e.g., Bauer and Zimmermann, 1999; Fertig, 1999; and Sinn, 1999, 2000). First of all, we prepare this empirical application by formulating a generic theoretical model as a frame of reference, and then discussing alternative identification assumptions. On the basis of our Western data for the post-World War II period, we proceed to estimate the historical relationship between migration to Germany and its aggregate-level determinants. We then use these estimates to generate concrete predictions of the immigration flows from Eastern Europe following EU enlargement, with a focus on the impact of varying identification strategies on these results.

Finally, we summarize our results, both on the methodological lessons to be drawn and the concrete results of our empirical application, and provide an agenda for further research on this issue.

The state of discussion

In this section, we will provide a selective survey of existing aggregate-level studies of international migration. Our review emphasizes the particular empirical strategy chosen by each paper to identify the impact of explanatory demographic and economic factors on the magnitude of migration flows. The aim of this focus is the clarification of the implicit and explicit identification and invariance assumptions invoked by the migration literature. In this context, the role of structural economic models as opposed to reduced-form models as predictive tools will also be discussed.

Empirical strategies and identification assumptions

Empirical analyzes of international migration typically rests on aggregate data. In the particular case of (gross or net) emigration from a set of origin countries to a single destination these models take the generic form:

$$m_{s,t}=\mu_s+X_{s,t}\,\beta_s+\delta m_{s,t-1}+\varepsilon_{s,t} \qquad (1)$$

where $m_{s,t}$ typically denotes an appropriate measure of the aggregate migration rate (i.e. the actual migration as a proportion of potential migrants at the origin) from sending country s in year t. The parameter μ_s captures all unobservable aspects of the process which are specific to country s but constant over time, while the k-dimensional matrix $X_{s,t}$ denotes the observable time-varying characteristics of country s at time t (relative to the destination), and β_s and δ are (vectors of) unknown parameters to be estimated. Since the lagged dependent variable introduces dynamics into expression (1), $\delta<1$ is a necessary condition for the stationarity of the process. Finally, $\varepsilon_{s,t}$ is the error term reflecting all unsystematic influences on the process.

Variations of this generic form are typically more restrictive, either by expressing country-specific intercepts as a linear combination of time-constant observable characteristics, by restricting slope coefficients to be equal across countries, $\beta_s = \beta \forall s$ by omitting the lagged dependent variable, or by a combination of these restrictions. Usually, this model specification and the concrete choice of explanatory factors included in X is more or less based on microeconomic considerations relating the individual decision to migrate or not to rational economic behavior in the context of utility or income maximization.

Building on a long-standing tradition of economic reasoning about the determinants of migration, at the center of attention in such models are usually the economic variables collected in X. When social scientists first started thinking about the determinants of aggregate migration flows (a prominent early contribution is Ravenstein, 1889), they did this in the demographically relatively homogenous context of internal migration. The large variety of possible driving forces offered by these contributions is a tribute to the ingenuity of the social sciences in modeling human motivation and behavior. Current studies typically follow the seminal paper by Sjastaad (1962) and understand migration as an investment in human capital. This approach assumes that in their individual decision agents weigh current cost of migration, direct as well as opportunity cost, against the stream of benefits to be expected after the move, most prominently increased wages.

Yet, both historical data as well as current accounts of the problem (see, for instance, Plakans and Wetherell, 1995; and Rogers and Castro, 1986) demonstrate clearly that migration typically happens in a narrow band of the life-cycle, ranging from early adulthood to, at most, the prime of the working career. Since the demographic structure usually varies much more across countries than within regions of the same country – as a manifestation of differences in fertility, mortality, and migration[2] – one would certainly expect deviations in this structure to be prime determinants of migration flows. Specifically, the first question should be about the size of the population in the core migration age band – after all, it is not the individual migration decision that an aggregate study wants to explain, but the convolution of individual decisions, motivated economically or otherwise, with demographic structure.

Thus, in the context of international migration it seems rather unfortunate that current analysts often think first and foremost about the economic differences when they attempt to assess migration potential (see, for instance, Sinn, 1999). Conceptually, it is the very idea of migration as an investment in human capital that makes the ample supply of core age individuals in the population of the origin countries a necessary prerequisite for economic discrepancies to have an effect on migration flows. Even in the presence of substantial disadvantages in the standard of living, compared with the destination countries, it would be very unlikely that a demographically mature society would produce substantial emigration flows.

In consequence, we would expect a complex interaction of indicators of demographic structure with economic variables to yield superior explanatory power for understanding emigration activity. That is, demographic characteristics such as the fraction of core age individuals in the sending country do not simply appear as additional regressors, since this would assume that all other regressors are taken to impact on aggregate migration rates (i.e. actual migration relative to the population at the origin, irrespective of the age composition of numerator or denominator) *identically*, whether the origin country is relatively old or relatively young. In our own empirical approach, we will deviate from the reviewed literature and move emigration rates from within the core age group into the center of attention. Specifically, we will argue that for purposes of prediction the modeling strategy of choice should be to start from a simple model of emigration rates among individuals of core age. There are good reasons to be reluctant to augmenting this model by notoriously difficult to predict economic information.[3]

In the received literature on international migration wages and employment or unemployment rates play a major role as regressors. Mostly, per-capita incomes or the growth rate of income in sending and destination countries are taken as proxies for wages. Following Sjaastad (1962) and Harris and Todaro (1970) it is *expected* income which is the relevant income measure for the migration decision. Expected income is typically defined by the wage times the probability of finding a job, where these variables are approximated by per capita income and the (un-)employment rate, respectively. In the empirical application, both variables are then typically either entered separately into the regression, or parameter restrictions are imposed *a priori* and, perhaps, tested statistically.

In addition, there are several other variables which are often employed in empirical studies. For example, following the literature on international trade relations, some papers set up a "gravity model" which includes the geographical *distance* in addition to the economic variables.[4] Another strand of the literature focuses on potential network effects in the migration decision proxied by the *stock of migrants* in the destination country (an alternative interpretation of this stock variable is given below). In addition, most empirical studies employ a set of dummy variables to capture (often quite persistent) institutional and/or legal aspects, for example, EU membership, a common border or language. A more recent approach focuses on supply-side non-linearities à la Kuznets and includes various measures for the level of development and the political and human rights situation (cf. Vogler and Rotte, 2000) in this equation. Alternatively, health measures or life expectancy could be included. It has to be understood that while their inclusion is based on underlying theoretical reasoning, the way these variables enter the specification is still completely *ad hoc*.

The *counterfactual* question implicitly asked by such a model is what would have happened to immigration flows from a specific country if one or several of the explanatory factors were different. Unfortunately, one only observes a country at any point in time with a single specific configuration of explanatory variables, making the decision to use a regression model such as (1) a method of choice. This decision is not innocuous. Any particular specification of this model necessarily invokes a set of *a priori* identification assumptions beyond the (log-)linearity of migration rates, enabling the analyst to construct this unobserved counterfactual situation. These identification assumptions are *assumed* to be true for the purposes of the analysis and their validity is not reflected in the usual measures of sampling variability (Schmidt, 1999). Moreover, more restrictive assumptions will generally reduce the remaining uncertainty within sample if these assumptions were correct. However, the reduction of uncertainty *within* sample need *not* necessarily be accompanied by a smaller uncertainty *out-of-sample*, a principle evidenced by the prominence of univariate prediction models in the analysis of financial markets.

Several different and non-exclusive identification assumptions are listed below. They concern the level of aggregation (1 and 2), the loss of information from focusing on selected origins and destinations (3), restrictions on the parameters (4), and restrictions on the disturbance process (5).

1 "*Population homogeneity*": Using the aggregate migration rate requires the assumption that this rate accurately reflects the average individual probability of migration for individuals from origin country s. The implicit assumption of no positive or negative selection due to unobservables is particularly severe, since nearly every individual characteristic, like education, marital status etc., is unobservable on the aggregate level. If this assumption is violated, using aggregate figures like the per capita income or unemployment rates in the explanation of the migration decision is misleading since these figures do not describe the economic opportunities of the migrants correctly.
2 "*Participation assumption*": Using aggregate (un-)employment rates as proxy for individual probabilities to find a job requires the assumption that participation issues play no substantial role (Dustmann and Schmidt, 2000), particularly since empirical studies usually do not distinguish between male and female immigrants.
3 "*Stability of alternative destinations*": Focusing the analysis on permanent immigration from different origin countries into one destination country requires the assumption that immigration into other potential destination countries varied proportionally to observed migration flows over the considered time horizon. For instance, if a substantial increase in immigration figures to Germany from, say, Turkey is accompanied by a moderate increase in the income differential between Turkey and Germany, one would conclude that this moderate increase has led to

the greater inflow. But if, at the same time, economic prospects in other potential destination countries deteriorated considerably, the great increase in immigration to Germany might simply stem from a redirection of flows. This argument naturally extends to the implied stability of the political and institutional environment.

4 "*No country-specific effects*": Using an overall constant, i.e. $\mu_s = \mu \forall s$, instead of country-specific intercepts requires that there be no persistent country-specific determinants of aggregate migration streams.[5] With the inclusion of country-specific intercepts, the identification of the β_s exclusively stems from the time-varying components of the $X_{s,t}$ matrix. The latter, however, are typically restricted to equality, i.e. $\beta_s = \beta \forall s$, if one intends to allow for country-specific intercepts.

5 "*Spherical disturbances*": In the case of pooled data sets, parameter estimation by pooled OLS invokes a set of severe covariance restrictions. Specifically, this estimation procedure requires the assumptions of *homoscedasticity* across regions and time, no correlation across regions, and no *autocorrelation* across time. For a sufficiently heterogenous sample of sending countries this seems to be very implausible. For example, if there are unobserved shocks which affect migration streams from different countries in a similar manner, observed migration figures may be correlated across groups. Also, it is quite plausible that there may be shocks which will lead to a correlation across time. Finally, the sheer difference in magnitude of inflows from different countries of origin may lead to a non-constant variance across countries.

Our selective review of studies of aggregate international migration flows will demonstrate that assumptions (1) to (3) are typically not questioned, while some studies introduce country-specific effects μ_s at the expense of (4), and others model their error process more carefully in a weakening of (5). Naturally, none of the studies works without identification restrictions.

Results of existing studies

This section will synoptically discuss the results of selected existing studies of aggregate immigration flows to Germany in the light of these identification assumptions. Specific emphasis will be on the explanation of agreements and disagreements between existing studies as results of the chosen identification strategies.

The literature on empirical investigations of aggregate immigration flows to Germany is quite scarce. An early contribution is the analysis of migrant flows from Greece to Germany by Katseli and Glytsos (1986). In terms of the generic expression (1), we necessarily have $s=1$ in this paper. Overall, the employment rates in both countries are statistically significant in almost all variants of the basic specification, whereas for the most part

Table 6.1 Existing aggregate-level studies of migration to Germany

	Katseli and Glytsos (1986)	*Karras and Chiswick (1999)*	*Fertig (1999)*	*Vogler and Rotte (2000)*
Dependent variable	Gross migration rate	Net migration rate	Change in net migration rate	Log of gross rates and asylum seeker rates
PCI in origin country	0			+ (level), − squared level
PCI in Germany	0			
Relative PCI		0	+ (Level and change)	+
Growth of GDP in Germany		+		+
Growth of GDP in origin country		−		
Unemployment rate in origin country	+		+ (Level and change)	
Unemployment rate in Germany	−		− (Level and change)	
Lagged dependent variable	0	+	− (Level)	
Stock of migrants in Germany			0	
Other variables	0 Remittances	+ Mean schooling	+ (EU dummy); 0 (guest-worker dummy)	0 Political Terror Scale; − Civil rights; + Share of urban population
Dataset	Time series for Greek-German migration (1961–83)	Pooled cross-section/time-series mainly for European countries (1960–88)	Pooled cross-section/time-series mainly for European countries (1960–94)	Pooled cross-section/time-series for Asian and African countries (1981–95)
Estimation procedure	OLS	Pooled OLS	ML by iterated GLS	Fixed (preferred) and random effects panel estimator
Identification assumptions	(1), (2), (3), (5)	(1), (2), (3), (4), (5)	(1), (2), (3)	(1), (2), (3), (5)
Forecasting	None	None	Double out of sample for 10 CEEC's	None
Identification assumptions	(1), (2), (3), (5)	(1), (2), (3), (4), (5)	(1), (2), (3)	(1), (2), (3), (5)
Forecasting	None	None	Double out of sample for 10 CEEC's	None

Note: +denotes a significant positive impact on the dependent variable, −a significant negative, and 0 an insignificant effect.

the real income variables, the lagged dependent variable as well as the additional variables, are not.

Karras and Chiswick (1999) utilize pooled cross section-time series data, that is $\beta_s=\beta$, to analyze aggregate migration flows to Germany for a sample of 17 countries of origin and a time period covering 1964–88. The authors perform two pooled OLS regressions of the net migration rate on different sets of explanatory variables. One regression uses a common constant, i.e. $\mu_s=\mu$, and another employs country-specific intercepts. The different sets of explanatory variables include the lagged migration rate, the per capita income ratio between Germany and the origin countries as well as the growth rates of per capita income and lags of these variables, a measure of average schooling in the sending country, a dummy variable for EU membership and different interaction terms of this dummy variable with all other variables. The sample was split into the two sub-periods 1964–73 and 1974–88. The fixed-effects specification was rejected; the results of the specification with a common intercept indicate no statistically significant effect of the income ratio and the schooling measure for the first sub-sample. The lagged net migration rate and the income growth rate in Germany were statistically significant in both sub-samples.

A similar approach is used by Fertig (1999). The author also uses a pooled cross section-time series dataset for 17 countries of origin and a period covering 1960–94. The estimation equation specifies the first difference of the net migration rate in terms of the changes and the levels of the per capita income ratio (in PPP) between Germany and the sending countries, as well as the changes and levels of the employment rates of the respective countries. In addition the stock of migrants, the lagged level of the net migration rate and two dummy variables for EU membership and the German guest worker system of the 1960s and 1970s are included. The model is specified with country-specific intercepts, i.e. $\mu=\mu_s$, and estimated by iterative GLS.

The restrictions on the disturbance matrix are relaxed in a stepwise process leading to groupwise heteroscedastic and correlated disturbances. The estimation results suggest a statistically significant positive impact of the income differential, the employment rate in Germany and the dummy variable reflecting EU membership, as well as a statistically significant negative effect of the employment rate in the sending countries and the lagged level of the migration rate on observed immigration flows. The stock of migrant measure and the dummy variable for the guest-worker years were statistically insignificant. The author also performed forecasting scenarios for future migration streams from Eastern Europe which support the view of positive albeit moderate future inflows from those countries. The predicted figures for the first-round candidates varied between 32,900 and 36,300 immigrants per year between 1995 and 2015.

On the basis of a substantially wider set of origin countries Vogler and Rotte (2000) address the complex set of issues associated with the relation of migration and economic development, political freedom, rule of law, and democracy. Specifically, their dataset contains immgration flows by asylum seekers for a sample of 86 Asian and African countries between 1981 and 1995 as well as indices of political participation opportunities (Freedom House Index) and political violence (Political Terror Scale) in the respective sending country. In addition, these authors try to account for changing emigration activity in the course of development, similar to the argument raised in Faini and Venturini (1994). The random-effects panel data estimates of Vogler and Rotte (2000) suggest a positive impact of economic differences between Germany and the countries of origin which declines in magnitude over time. The results also suggest an important role for financial restrictions and migrant networks in explaining the migration decision.

Overall, these previous studies provide an interesting, albeit not completely satisfying account of aggregate migration flows to Germany during the past decades. Specifically, the most prominent factors which are accounted for, such as wages or unemployment rates, do not yield stable results. Conceptually, in our view, most problematic in the explanation of emigration flows is the omission of source country-specific heterogeneity, accounting for which requires access to panel data. That is, studies which impose a common intercept term either follow an implicit assumption that no important persistent differences in migration activity exist across source countries, or that this variation across countries is orthogonal to the other determinants included in the specification. Yet, even under this latter, quite restrictive implicit assumption, most studies tend not to provide the most efficient (GLS) estimator but rather LS estimates (an exception is Fertig, 1999).

We have argued here that discrepancies in the demographic structure of source and destination countries might be an important, perhaps the crucial driving force behind migration. Yet, demographic characteristics of the source countries are hardly a prominent factor in the existing studies. If demographic and economic factors are highly correlated, using economic predictors might alleviate this problem somewhat – but in terms of *explaining* migration flows, accepting this argument raises a critical shadow of doubt on existing estimates. The existing evidence also suggests that there is considerable temporal persistence in the process, although none of these studies (except Fertig, 1999) modeled cyclical variation in migration activity which affected origin countries together.

Moreover, since prediction was not the major objective of most of these studies, their potential as the basis of such predictions is in doubt. Specifically, it was the declared aim to provide a maximal fit to the historical data, leading to a relatively large set of conditioning variables. Not only will a good within-sample fit not necessarily guarantee a satisfactory predictive performance out-of-sample, but predictions of migration rates will require predictions of the conditioning variables. The large set of controls included in these studies will make this task extremely difficult. This problem will be relatively moderate, though, if the set of conditioning variables is exclusively demographic – demographic developments can usually be predicted relatively well, since most people present tomorrow have typically been born in this country already today.

Prediction of future migration flows to Germany

This section develops our own approach to the problem of predicting future migration streams from Eastern Europe to the West within a unified Europe, including the first-round accession candidates, i.e. Czech Republic, Estonia, Hungary, and Poland. The first subsection briefly describes the Eastern European countries with a special emphasis on demographic developments. Finally, the following subsection outlines the utilized model and describes the employed estimation technique.

The crucial role of demographics

In a legal framework like that of the European Union with only small institutional barriers to internal migration, demographics are a major determinant of immigration streams. For a discussion of the potential size as well as the ensuing impact of immigration, it is therefore necessary to take into account demographic factors. Germany, for instance, experienced a substantial inflow in the post-1950 era (e.g. Schmidt and Zimmermann, 1992). Gross immigration amounted to 25.5 million up to 1990, and net migration was around 10 million people. In addition, after 1990 with the demise of communism in Eastern Europe and the civil wars in former Yugoslavia, a remarkable inflow of "ethnic Germans" (*Aussiedler*) and war refugees was added. Demographic aspects have played an important role in this impressive immigration record for two reasons.

First, there has been a remarkable life-cycle pattern in the influx of immigrants to Germany (cf. Schmidt, 2000); many immigrants have been young adults. In addition, during the first years of the post-1950 era most of the net migration comprised males, thereby confirming the view of the typical migrant being a young male worker. This observation is a direct reflection of the fact that Germany actively recruited so-called guest workers, who were typically young males. While the age structure of the influx has changed over time, particularly after the halt in active recruitment in 1974, this observation nevertheless emphasizes that migration activity is crucially determined by the size of young cohorts at the origin. This general conclusion is unlikely to change when considering future migration potential from the EU accession candidates. Thus, in our own approach to its prediction, we concentrate on the characterization of the size of the population at these origins, specifically among more recent cohorts.

Second, these relatively young immigrants displayed a higher survival rate than the relatively old indigenous population. Moreover, even if one assumes that fertility rates are not higher for migrants than for natives of the same birth cohort, the fact that the largest part of the migrant population is in prime childbearing age has contributed substantially to the growth of the migrant population over time (cf. Schmidt, 2000). Potentially, there might be an important dynamic impact of this migrant stock on future immigration to be expected. However, as the following discussion demonstrates, its direction is indeterminate, suggesting that one should start the prediction exercise with a static model of migration.

Past immigration flows and the resulting *stock of immigrants* in a specific destination country may have several implications for the individual migration decision and, therefore, current migration flows. A part of the literature on the migration decision tries to take into account so called *network* effects. If people already living in a foreign country help their friends and relatives to get started, e.g. in finding accommodation or jobs, this effect would induce *chain migration*. This hypothesis might be captured empirically by the stock of previous immigrants to a country. Several empirical papers indeed suggest that there has been a positive effect of previous migration on contemporary migration. However, network effects are not the only possible interpretation for this pattern. For instance, as already pointed out by Greenwood (1975), the stock of migrants could also be seen as a proxy for an informal information flow between the sending country and the potential destination countries.

One could imagine that for a potential migrant there are two principal channels of information flows concerning the economic opportunities at the destination. One channel is the publicly available statistics on official unemployment rates and per-capita income provided by the statistical offices or the media, while the second comprises informal information by compatriots already living in the possible target country. While the official statistics are certainly a good starting point for the formation of expectations on the economic prospects at the destination, they rarely reflect the relevant opportunities accurately, especially if skills acquired at the origin are not fully transferable to the destination country. In Germany, for instance, new immigrants are competing with low-skilled native workers and previous immigrants in a small range of occupations where unemployment is higher than the national average (cf., e.g., Schmidt, 1997). This implies that their employment prospects would be overestimated by the average unemployment rate and that informal information flows could very well lead to a reduced migrant influx as the population of compatriots accumulates over time.

Thus, the relationship between size and structure of the immigrant population at the destination and prospective migrant influx is intricate. Moreover, a closer look at *cohort specific* emigration rates (cf. Baevre et al., 2000 for the case of Norwegian emigration) suggests that there is a negative effect of emigration of members of one cohort on future emigration from the *same* cohort. This observation is in line with the hypothesis that the propensity to migrate may be heterogenous and the individuals with the highest propensity are migrating first. Alternatively, the emigration of a part of a cohort reduces the labor market competition for the stayers and reduces their incentives to migrate.[6] On balance, these arguments suggest a conservative approach to the prediction of future migration flows which de-emphasizes the dynamic impact of previous on current immigration.

Both the general historical evidence (cf. Plakans and Wetherell, 1995) and these observations on the specific case of post-World War II Germany have induced us to pursue a modeling strategy emphasizing demographics while absorbing the – slowly changing over time and difficult to predict – economic differences between origin and destination regions into region-specific factors, and an autocorrelated error-component common to all origins. Most importantly, following the received literature in trying to explain observed aggregate migration flows mainly by economic variables, like differences in per capita incomes, while omitting demographics, might not be very promising. These variables typically reflect economic opportunities of average natives at the origin and at the destination, not of those individuals facing the migration decision.

Moreover, differences in economic opportunities are relevant only to a fraction of the population, that in the core age-group of migration. In the extreme, very large cross-country differences in economic opportunities might not induce any migration worth mentioning, if the population in the origin region mostly comprises old men and women. What we therefore suggest using instead of the usual migration rates are *core age migration rates*, describing migration activity only among the young. Alternatively, we will use age structure as a regressor in the empirical model, thereby probing the robustness of our predictions. Before we proceed to develop our parsimonious model of migration, we will briefly characterize the demographic structure of the prospective EU accession countries.

The most likely candidate countries for the first round of EU enlargement towards Central and Eastern Europe are the three Eastern European NATO members the Czech Republic, Hungary and Poland, as well as one Baltic country, Estonia. These four countries (henceforth denoted as CEEC-4) currently comprise some 60 million inhabitants and are quite heterogeneous in their economic and demographic characteristics. They also exhibit remarkable differences compared to Germany. Most importantly, post-World War II population dynamics as well as World War II itself have left their imprint on the population age structure of these countries (cf. also Schmidt, 1996).

Whereas Germany experienced a decade of high birth rates in the late 1950s and early 1960s, the CEEC-4 experienced such a *baby-boom* directly after the end of World War II. Therefore, at the end of the twentieth century the population age distribution varies considerably between possible origin countries and the potential destination of migrant flows. For 1993 (1990 for Germany) Figure 6.1 documents a relatively high proportion of people in the age group [20–29] for Germany, while the CEEC-4 display substantially higher population shares among the very young [<20]. These cohorts and their children will be the prime candidates for the migration to the West that might be expected after EU enlargement.

Moreover, whereas mortality rates remained relatively stable during the 1990s (cf. United Nations, 1996), there was a remarkable decline in birth rates in the beginning of the 1990s for all of the CEEC-4, thereby moderating future migration pressure. In our predictions we will try to defend ourselves against a downward bias in predicted migration flows and predict the CEEC-4 population into the future using relatively high fertility rates (see below). It is the predicted (young) population at the origin that, together with our estimates of migration rates will then lead to predicted migration flows.

The considerable differences in economic indicators between the four accession candidate countries and Germany, as well as among the CEEC-4 themselves, have led some economists to conclude that there is a vast migration potential in the CEEC-4 just waiting for the starting signal to launch their march to the West and especially to Germany (cf. the controversial views in Bauer and Zimmermann, 1999; Fertig, 1999; and Sinn, 1999, 2000). By contrast, economic differences and their certainly imprecise predictions into the future are not discussed at length in this contribution, relieving us from the requirement to construct convergence scenarios between East and West.

Rather, we utilize our arguments on the crucial role of demographic factors for our predictions, which enables us to assess the migration potential without a large range of daring assumptions on the evolution of conditioning variables. Implicitly, this presumes that economic differences are either persistent enough in the short- and medium-term to be absorbed in the country-specific intercept of the migration rate equations or are correlated enough to be absorbed by the time varying error component. The convincing choice of the country-specific intercept for countries for which no previous migration record exists is therefore the principal conceptual challenge for the prediction – yet, this has not been addressed formally in any of the previous papers on this topic.

Theoretical model and alternative identification assumptions

We will prepare the empirical application by the formulation of a generic model of aggregate migration flows to a single destination as a frame of reference. Within this framework we are then able to discuss a variety of identification assumptions and corresponding specifications of the model. The simplest conceivable model of aggregate migration rates would be in

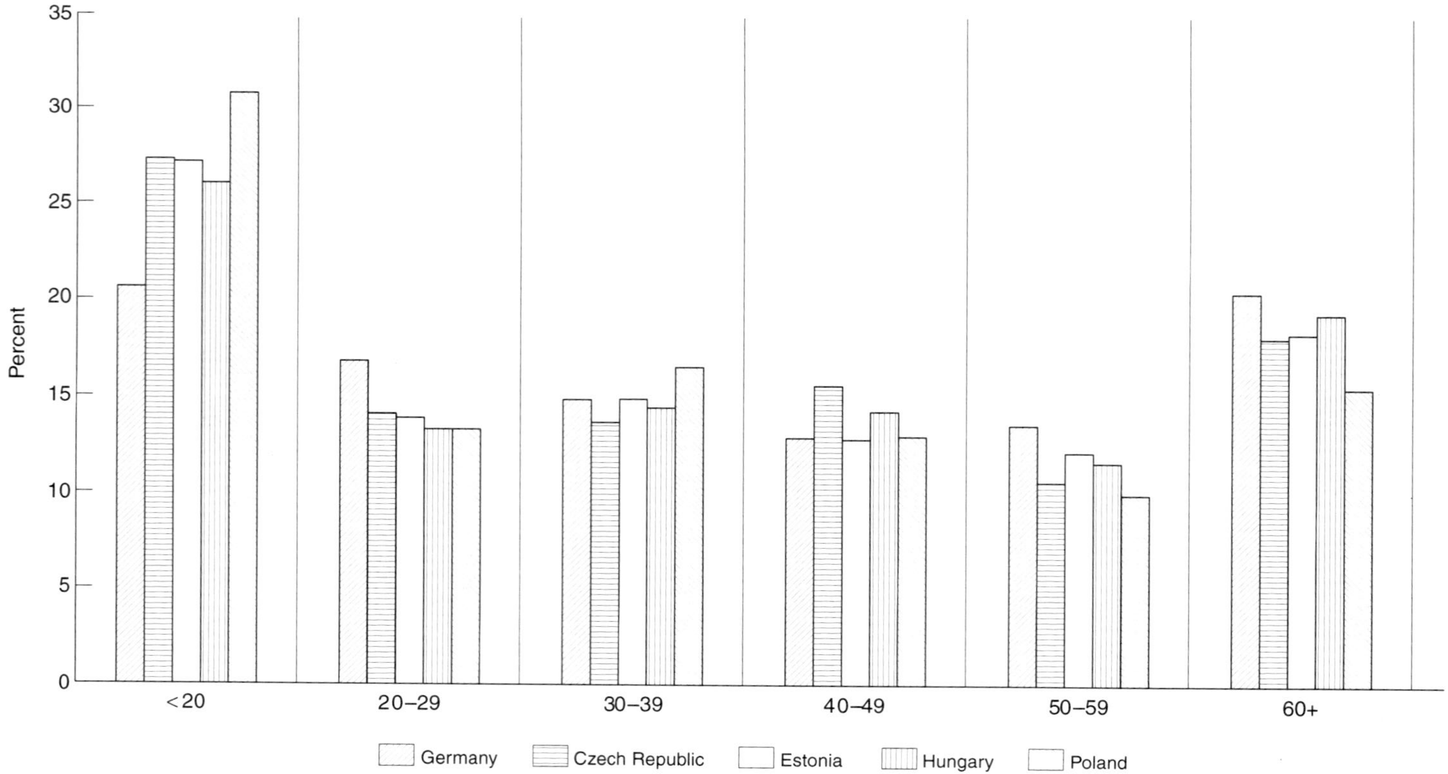

Figure 6.1 Population by age groups – CEEC-4 vs. Germany.
Source: United Nations (1996); own calculations.

terms of orthogonal country- and time-specific components, drawn from a common distribution of effects, respectively. In such a variance-components model (in a different context, a similar model is employed by Ashenfelter and Card, 1985) the migration rate $m_{s,t}$ in the relevant age range for origin country $s=1, \ldots, S$ and period $t=1, \ldots, T$ consists of an overall intercept term μ, a random component specific to country s but persistent over time ε_s, a component specific to time periods but relevant for all countries at this point in time ε_t, and an unpredictable white noise error term $\varepsilon_{s,t}$.

In effect, we have

$$m_{s,t}=\mu+\varepsilon_s+\varepsilon_t+\varepsilon_{s,t} \tag{2}$$

The country-specific component ε_s captures all aspects of the process determining migration from s to the destination country which tend to persist over time, such as a common (colonial) history, climate and distance, a common language or border but also persistent economic differences. This formulation enables us to characterize the distribution from which the country-specific intercept term of those future migration countries is chosen for which no previous immigration record is available.

The period-specific component ε_t reflects all determinants of migration activity which vary over time but operate in all countries identically during the same period. A case in point could be any fluctuations in economic activity in the destination country, for instance in aggregate labor demand. Even in this basic model we would be very hesitant to exclude correlation of this factor across periods. Modeling the autocorrelation of this factor will therefore be central to our application. Specifically, we will model this process as an autoregressive process of first order. In brief, the stochastic structure of the process (there are naturally no correlations across the variance components) is:

$$\varepsilon_s \sim (0,\sigma_s^2),\ \varepsilon_t \sim (0,\sigma_t^2,\ \rho),\ \varepsilon_{s,t} \sim (0,\sigma_{s,t}^2) \tag{3}$$

In our empirical work we will solve the estimation problem by using Method of Moments techniques. Intuitively, the idea behind Method of Moments is estimating the unknown parameters by matching the theoretical population moments, which are functions of the unknown parameters, with the appropriate sample moments (Harris and Matyas, 1998). Formally, the first step in this endeavour is to define the moment conditions. We want to estimate from our observed sample $(m_{s,t};\ s=1,\ldots, S; t=1,\ldots, T)$ a $p\times 1$ vector θ of unknown parameters with true value θ_o. If $f(m_{s,t},m_{s',t'};\theta)$, denotes a continuous $q\times 1$ vector function of θ and $E(f(m_{s,t},m_{s',t'};\theta))$ exists and is finite for all s,s',t,t', and θ, then $E(f(m_{s,t},m_{s',t'};\theta_o))=0$ are the *moment conditions*.

In our application the vector of unknown parameters is $\theta=(\mu\ \sigma_s^2\ \sigma_t^2\ \rho\ \sigma_{s,t}^2)'$ and the moment conditions are:

$$
\begin{aligned}
g_0 &\equiv E(m_{s,t}) &&= \mu \\
g_1 &\equiv Var(m_{s,t}) &&= \sigma_t^2 + \sigma_s^2 + \sigma_{s,t}^2 \\
g_2 &\equiv Cov(m_{s,t}, m_{s',t}) &&= \sigma_t^2 && for \quad s \neq s' \\
g_3 &\equiv Cov(m_{s,t}, m_{s,\tau}) &&= \rho^{|t-\tau|}\sigma_t^2 + \sigma_s^2 \\
g_4 &\equiv Cov(m_{s,t}, m_{s',\tau}) &&= \rho^{|t-\tau|}\sigma_t^2 && for \quad s \neq s'
\end{aligned} \tag{4}
$$

The moment conditions g_3 and g_4 imply that the covariance of migration rates over time jointly reflects country-specific variation and persistence of the process. If one restricted ρ to zero, all this covariance would be attributed to country-specific effects.

Let $u_{s,t}=f(m_{s,t},m_{s',t'};\theta_0)$ denote the Method of Moments disturbance and assume that $\{m_{s,t}\}$ is a stationary process. Let $f_{S,T}(\theta)=(ST)^{-1}\Sigma_{s=1}^{S}\ \Sigma_{t=1}^{T}\ f(m_{s,t},m_{s',t'};\theta)$ denote the sample moments corresponding to the moment conditions and define the criterion function $Q_{S,T}(\theta)=f_{S,T}(\theta)'Af_{S,T}(\theta)$, where A is a stochastic positive definite matrix. Then the Generalized Method of Moments (GMM) estimator of θ is

$$
\hat{\theta}_{S,T}=argmin_{\theta}Q_{S,T}(\theta) \tag{5}
$$

Given a number of assumptions (Harris and Matyas, 1998: 11–21), the GMM estimator is weakly consistent and asymptotically normally distributed.

If the number of moment conditions is equal to the number of parameters to be estimated, the above system is exactly identified. Then the GMM estimator does not depend on the choice of the distance matrix A and collapses to the Method of Moment estimator. However, if the system is overidentified, i.e. if $q>p$, different GMM estimators are obtained for different distance matrices. The choice of the distance matrix that results in an asymptotically efficient GMM estimator is the long-run covariance matrix V of the GMM disturbance $u_{s,t}$. Given this choice of the distance matrix $\sqrt{ST}(\theta_{S,T} - \theta_0)$ has an asymptotic normal distribution with mean zero and covariance matrix $(F'V^{-1}F)^{-1}$, where F denotes the matrix of derivatives of the moment conditions with respect to the parameters.

With a consistent estimator $\hat{V}$ for V in hand one will be able to obtain $\theta_{S,T}$ by setting $A=\hat{V}^{-1}$. The resulting estimator is called the optimal or efficient GMM estimator given $f(m_{s,t},m_{s',t'};\theta)$. The estimated standard errors of this optimal GMM estimator are then obtained as the square roots of the diagonal elements of $(ST)^{-1}\{F'_{ST}\hat{V}^{-1}F_{ST}\}^{-1}$. Furthermore, given the optimal choice of the weighting matrix, the resulting value of the criterion function can be used as a test statistic for the detection of mis-specification, since $(ST)^{-1}Q_{S,T}(\hat{\theta})$ is asymptotically distributed as χ^2 with the number of overidentifying restrictions as the appropriate degrees of freedom. In our application, we estimate the long-run covariance matrix V as a diagonal matrix using the empirical moments in the sample.

Estimation results and forecasting scenarios

On the basis of our Western data for the post-World War II period, we will now estimate the historical relationship between migration to Germany and its aggregate-level demographic determinants, and use these estimates to generate concrete predictions of the immigration flows from Eastern Europe following EU enlargement. To explore the robustness of our predictions we will contrast three different specifications of our model. In a first specification, we model the overall migration rate (the migrant flow relative to the population at the origin) using our most parsimonious variance-components formulation.

A second specification concentrates on the population of core age (less than 39 years of age), retaining the parsimonious empirical specification. This strategy requires that we prepare the estimation by a careful transformation of the available data. Finally, the time-varying age structure in the various origin countries is used as a regressor parameterizing the mean migration rate μ. In all variants of the model we contrast exactly identified and overidentified specifications. Before we proceed to reporting our estimation results, we briefly introduce the data material and the preliminary data transformations necessitated by our approach.

Data and variable construction

Our sample consists of observed migration streams from 17 countries of origin (Austria, Belgium, Switzerland, Denmark, Spain, Finland, France, Greece, Italy, Yugoslavia, Netherlands, Norway, Portugal, Sweden, Turkey, United Kingdom, and USA) for the time period covering 1960 to 1997. Therefore, the number of observations is 646. Immigration figures comprise inflows and outflows of foreigners only, while the flows from and to the numerically negligible CEEC-4 were excluded from the sample. In effect, we have to predict the net migration from the CEEC-4 not only out of the temporal sample experience, but also out of the realm of the observed origin countries. Since the data only comprises foreigners, for the years after 1990 the substantial inflow of ethnic Germans (*Aussiedler*) is not taken into account. The migration data stems from the German Federal Statistical Office (*Statistisches Bundesamt*), which also provides information on the population by birth cohorts in Germany. Population data for the sample countries as well as the CEEC-4 is reported in the *Demographic Yearbook* published annually by the United Nations.

In our estimations we utilize two different dependent variables. In a first variant we use the standard net migration rate, i.e. net migration from country s in year t divided by the stock of population in the respective country and year, as dependent variable. In a second variant, following our reasoning outlined above, the dependent variable is the "age adjusted" net migration rate, i.e. the flow of migrants from s at time t in the core age group (0 to 39 years of age) divided by the population in s and t in this age group. These migration rates, however, are neither observable directly nor can they be constructed from the available official statistics. Therefore, we employ a simple population accounting approach which enables us to construct such rates.

Specifically, immigration figures have generally been recorded as an aggregate over all ages. To calculate the number of immigrants from any particular country of origin, we would like to correct observed overall influx from that source country by an appropriate correction factor lying between 0 and 1 and varying over time. While we are not be able to construct separately such a correction factor for each origin country, we are able to offer an estimate of the aggregate net influx by age for each individual year of the sample period (cf. Schmidt, 2000 for details). The desired time-varying correction factor is derived by tracking individual birth cohorts through time in a variant of the *life-table survival method*. Abstaining from distinguishing natives and migrants along any other dimension than age and gender, this method applies a life-table to a census count to project survivors at either past or future time points.

The difference between the projected number of survivors and the enumerated population at that time is then taken as the estimated net migration, with an estimated migration figure for each individual year of age. The net immigration measured for each individual birth cohort in the sample range can then be accumulated appropriately for each year t to estimate the net immigration in a certain age range. Since mortality only changes slowly over time, the survival probabilities are taken from the 1970/72 lifetable for Germany and, thus, describe most accurately the middle of the observation period. In the calculations, identical conditional survival probabilities are applied to natives and migrants already present in the destination country. The primary basis for the population data employed here are the census waves of 1950, 1961, 1970, and 1987. Annual data are updates based on community registers of births, deaths and relocation.

For both dependent variables the variance components-model is estimated by the Generalized Method of Moments. In addition, in the model for the standard migration rate, the constant overall intercept is parameterized in a third variation of the model as a linear function of the share of young inhabitants (0–39 years) in the various origin countries yielding a sixth parameter β to be estimated. In all three cases, the estimation procedure comprises two different specifications. Firstly, we estimate an exactly identified system, where we chose five (six) moment restrictions in order to estimate the five (six) unknown parameters of the model. Secondly, we overidentify the system by imposing two (one) additional moment restrictions, thus yielding seven moment restrictions for the estimation of five (six) parameters. Obviously, the criterion function evaluated at the final estimates need not necessarily yield a value of zero.

Therefore, one has to test whether these additional overidentifying restrictions hold in the data.

Parameter estimates

GMM estimation results for the standard migration rates as dependent variables are reported in Table 6.2. The first column shows the results for the *exactly* identified system whereas results for the overidentified system are reported in the last column. Our interpretation and our simulations (see below) will focus on the overidentified model.

The average migration rate for the typical origin country during the sample period was approximately 0.03 percent of its population. Around this average value, we observe a substantial fluctuation across space and time with all variance components being estimated quite precisely. The country-specific variance component is estimated to account for more than a third of the overall variation, despite allowing for persistence in the temporal error component.

By contrast, this variance component being common to all countries is estimated to be relatively small in magnitude, although the large value of the autoregressive parameter indicates that any shock to aggregate migration activity typically has a long-lasting impact. Close inspection of the predicted values of the time-specific component over the sample period indicates that migration activity to Germany was relatively low at the end of the 1990s. Finally, the computed value 4.22 of the test statistic implies that the null hypothesis that the overidentifying restrictions hold is not rejected at any reasonable level of significance.

The results of the GMM estimation with the "age adjusted" net migration rates as dependent variable are reported in Table 6.3. Again, the first

Table 6.2 GMM results – standard migration rates (×100)

	Exactly identified model	*Overidentified model*
Common intercept	0.029	0.029
	(0.0045)	(0.0045)
Variance of		
Country-specific component	0.008	0.005
	(0.0018)	(0.0012)
Time-specific component	0.0022	0.0024
	(0.0006)	(0.0006)
Unsystematic component	0.003	0.006
	(0.003)	(0.003)
Persistence parameter	0.645	0.645
	(0.224)	(0.186)
Overidentification test	–	4.23

Note: Standard errors are reported in parentheses.

Table 6.3 GMM results – "age adjusted" migration rates (×100)

	Exactly identified model	*Overidentified model*
Common intercept	0.041	0.041
	(0.0062)	(0.0062)
Variance of		
Country-specific component	0.015	0.009
	(0.004)	(0.0023)
Time-specific component	0.005	0.005
	(0.001)	(0.001)
Unsystematic component	0.006	0.011
	(0.006)	(0.005)
Persistence parameter	0.642	0.633
	(0.214)	(0.183)
Overidentification test	–	3.59

Note: Standard errors are reported in parentheses.

column contains the exactly identified and column two the overidentified model. As was to be expected, the overall average of the migration rate among the young is relatively high, approximately 0.04 percent. Estimation results for the variance components are qualitatively very similar to those reported in the previous table, and are again estimated quite precisely. The country-specific component accounts for approximately one-third of the overall variance; the time-specific component is of relatively minor magnitude but of remarkable persistence. Again the overidentification test indicates a satisfactory performance of the model specification.

Finally, Table 6.4 reports the results of fitting a third specification to the data which parametrizes the overall constant to be a linear function of the share of young individuals (0–39 years of age) in the population. Of course, the average migration rate is again estimated to be 0.03 percent for a country with the typical age-structure (almost 60 percent being younger than 40). Any origin country whose age structure deviates by the share of younger individuals being, say, 5 percentage points higher than the average, will typically display an increase in its migration rate to almost 0.06 percent.

The importance of the country-specific variance component is only slightly reduced in these estimates, indicating relatively persistent age-shares during the sample period. No substantial impact can be detected on the estimate of the persistence parameter as well. Overall, these results seem sufficiently stable to serve as the basis for our predictions. In particular, the variation captured by the variance components implies that the location of any prospective origin country in the distribution of country-specific effects will be decisive for the predicted accumulation over time of migration flows from that source. The temporal component will – due to its negative value at the end of the sample period – likely dampen

Table 6.4 GMM results – age-share as regressor (×100)

	Exactly identified model	*Overidentified model*
Common intercept	−0.254	−0.254
	(0.0045)	(0.0045)
Share of core-age pop.	0.483	0.483
	(0.005)	(0.0005)
Variance of		
Time-specific component	0.008	0.005
	(0.002)	(0.001)
Country-specific component	0.002	0.002
	(0.0006)	(0.0006)
Unsystematic component	0.003	0.006
	(0.003)	(0.0026)
Persistence parameter	0.630	0.635
	(0.235)	(0.192)
Overidentification test	–	4.21

Note: Standard errors are reported in parentheses.

prospective migration flows for several years to come. To ward off any downward bias in our predictions, we will disregard this dampening factor in our simulations.

Forecasting scenarios

Our approach identifies the overall population size in the CEEC-4 and its age-structure as the principal driving forces of future migration to Germany. To predict future migration flows, we therefore need the projected population size and age structure for these countries. Starting from the current age structure, we again construct these demographic projections using the German life-table of 1970/72, ignoring any loss of population due to emigration, and predicting the birth of future cohorts according to a common set of age-specific fertility rates. Specifically, it is assumed that reproduction rates in the CEEC-4 do not differ substantially from that observed for a typical cohort of post-World War II German women, the cohort born in 1936, which started its reproduction around 1950 and continued up to approximately 1984.

While initially the Polish population is relatively young, indicating a relatively high migration potential, that of Hungary is relatively old, with Estonia and the Czech Republic being somewhere in between. None of the countries displays a spectacularly high share of young individuals, and the overall development is towards an aging population, a phenomenon quite familiar from Western economies. Our particular choice of demographic parameters is likely to overpredict the young population. In our projections we combine this predicted age structure for each year in 1998–2017 with our estimated parameters reported in the previous section.

Since the CEEC-4 have no previous record of migration to Germany, choosing the likely location of the country-specific intercepts in the distribution whose variance has been estimated from the data for those countries which actually had such a migration record is of crucial importance for the validity of the results. To explore the impact of different invariance assumptions, we compare scenarios for the "typical country" with $\varepsilon_s=0$ with a "high-emigration" country whose value of ε_s is determined as plus one standard deviation apart from the typical country.

For both principal scenarios we predict migration to Germany over the period 1998–2017 using the standard migration rates applied to overall population (scenarios I and IV in Table 6.5) and to the overall population and age-structure (scenarios III and VI), and using the age-adjusted migration rates (scenarios II and V). Using the latter implicitly assumes that it is only the net migration of the young that is of importance in the future, and that the migration of old individuals that we observe in the historical data exclusively reflected the specific institutional setting before the turn of the century.

Irrespective of the particular specification chosen for the predictions, it is the choice of the country-specific component that is decisive for the magnitude of the forecasts. If the CEEC-4 behaved as a typical source country for the migration to Germany, annual net migration for all four countries taken together would fluctuate around 15,000–18,000 individuals during the forecasting period, leading to an accumulated figure of 300,000 –400,000 people by 2017. By contrast, if it were a high-emigration region, between 49,000 and 63,000 people would arrive in Germany – net of countervailing emigration flows – each year, leading to an accumulated influx of between 900,000 and 1.2 million people.

Although this figure is much higher than those of the scenarios I to III, it nevertheless seems moderate when compared to the high figures that fuel the public debate on this issue. While we explicitly refrain from any more concrete speculation on the impact that the large initial differences

Table 6.5 Summary of forecasting scenarios, 1998–2017

Scenario	*Average annual inflow*	*Accumulated inflow*
I: Standard rates	17,964	359,285
II: Age-adjusted rates	14,656	293,122
III: With age-share as regressor	15,079	301,583
IV: Standard rates plus one std.-deviation	62,656	1,253,129
V: Age-adjusted rates plus one std.-deviation	48,551	971,011
VI: With age share as regressor plus one std.-deviation	57,377	1,147,533

Note: All figures comprise the CEEC-4, i.e. Czech Republic, Estonia, Hungary, and Poland.

in economic prosperity between the CEEC-4 and the rest of the EU might have on the country-specific components to be realized, the high-immigration scenarios are likely to provide an upper bound on what to expect after EU accession of the CEEC-4.

Concluding remarks

In this chapter, we have reviewed aggregate-level migration studies with a particular emphasis on their potential and their limits as tools for forecasting future migration streams. As we have emphasized, the task of assessing migration potential and predicting future migration flows requires strong identification assumptions to hold, particularly when following the usual approach of fitting a relatively saturated specification to the observed migration data, typically including a substantial number of economic variables on the right-hand side of the regression. Over and above the necessary assumptions of temporal stability of the behavioral relationships, one has to have a relatively precise notion about the development of these conditioning variables in the future. Unfortunately and in contrast to key demographic variables, economic variables are notoriously difficult to predict.

Moreover, whenever a new origin region enters the scene, the extrapolation exercise has to extend from predictions out of the sample horizon to predictions out of the spatial realm of experience. This requirement is an almost prohibitive challenge to any saturated model of aggregate migration intensity. The specific application that our chapter addresses is the prediction of migration flows to be expected from the most likely accession countries in Eastern Europe. No previous migration record to Germany exists for these countries that can be used to gauge future emigration propensities from these countries, once they are to enjoy the freedom-of-movement privileges held by other EU member countries. Consequently, it hardly seems surprising that current predictions of the expected migration flows from these countries appear to vary widely.

In developing our own approach to the problem, we depart from the received migration literature – whose emphasis is typically on the explanation of migration activity, not its prediction into the future – and pursue a very parsimonious specification of migration rates that is fitted to historical data on the German post-World War II immigration experience. Its formulation explicitly allows for persistent economic and non-economic differences to be captured by a set of country-specific random effects which, together with a time-specific and a white noise component, drive the fluctuation of migration rates around its average across time and space. The relative magnitudes of these unobserved orthogonal variance components lends itself naturally to a discussion of the prediction problem raised by EU enlargement.

Specifically, if the new EU members were to display the emigration behavior to Germany that has characterized the typical origin country during the (high-immigration) post-World War II era, prospective net immigration would be of almost negligible magnitude. If, by contrast, they were to display a substantially more pronounced emigration propensity, future net immigration could be much larger, albeit still relatively moderate when considering the figures circulating in the public debate on this issue. Notably, while the proponents of large migration forecasts are likely to emphasize the large economic differences between the prospective EU members and the existing member states, it is very difficult to predict – if it materializes at all – the pace of any economic convergence towards the EU average within the next two or three decades. Moreover, the existing migration literature does not at all provide a convincing body of evidence for the actual relevance of economic variables to migration activity. At best, this evidence is mixed. It is also quite likely that the large economic discrepancies are balanced to some degree by considerable migration cost.

Most importantly, our approach to the problem emphasizes the crucial role of demographics for what is primarily a demographic process. It is the size of the population in the origin region, and particularly the size of the young population, which is of principal importance for the expected migration flows. Large fluctuations in economic differences would exert little impact on migration activity if the population in the source regions were to be old, a simple truth that seems to be neglected in many migration forecasts. Thus, in combining the estimates from our parsimoniously specified model for the aggregate migration rate with the projected population size and structure in the prospective EU member countries, we have exploited the fact that demographic circumstances can be predicted relatively precisely into the future. To assess the robustness of our forecasts to a variation of the model structure, we have pursued several specifications and several forecast scenarios, all yielding qualitatively similar results. If our emphasis were on explaining past migration behavior, rather than forecasting into the future and into different spatial circumstances, we would of course have pursued less parsimonious specifications, a task that we leave to future research.

Notes

We are grateful for helpful comments by David Card and participants of the European Science Foundation conference "Migration & Development" and to Katharina Türpitz for research assistance. All correspondence to Christoph M. Schmidt, Department of Economics (Econometrics), University of Heidelberg, Grabengasse 14, 69117 Heidelberg, Fax: +49 6221 543640, Email: schmidt@uni-hd.de.

1 There are two prominent alternatives to this approach: (i) using intentions data (e.g. Papapaganos and Sanfey, 2000; Bauer and Zimmermann, 1999) – since it is the manifestation of intentions, not some verbal account of desires, which are at issue, this approach risks being very unreliable; (ii) inference based on historical precedent – very rarely will it be possible to detect a closely comparable situation in historical data, however, making it very likely that this approach remains anecdotal.

2 These differences are caused by underlying forces such as – among others – participation in wars (see for instance the comparison of Germany, Poland and Sweden, and the effect of World War II on their respective population age structure in Schmidt, 1996, differences in the system of education and public health (in developing countries, education of the mother is a prime determinant of fertility and child mortality, and child mortality is still substantially different from that in the OECD), or differences in tax or social security systems.
3 The received literature frequently pays particular attention to the distinction of economic and non-economic migrants, with the latter comprising migrants pursuing family re-unification and political and war refugees. Our argument applies to voluntary migration.
4 Needless to say that this precludes a separate inclusion of country-specific effects.
5 Country-fixed effects are a problem for forecasting future streams from countries not being in the sample. However, this problem may be solved by modeling these effects directly (see below) or by a two-step procedure whose second step re-parameterizes the estimated intercepts by a set of time-invariant regressors (Fertig,1999).
6 A similar approach for southern European migration flows is adopted by (Faini and Venturini (1994).

References

Ashenfelter, Orley and David Card (1985) "Using the Longitudinal Structure of Earnings to Estimate the Effects of Training Programs," *Review of Economics and Statistics*, 67: 648–660.

Baevre, Kare, Christian Riis and Tore Thonstad (forthcoming) "Norwegian Cohort Emigration," *Journal of Population Economics*.

Bauer, Thomas and Klaus F. Zimmermann (1999) "Assessment of Possible Migration Pressure and its Labor Market Impact Following EU Enlargement to Central and Eastern Europe," a study for the Department for Education and Employment, London.

Dustmann, Christian and Christoph M. Schmidt (2000) "The Wage Performance of Immigrant Women: Full-Time Jobs, Part-Time Jobs, and the Role of Selection," Discussion Paper 233, Bonn: IZA.

Faini, Ricardo and Alessandra Venturini (1994) "Migration and Growth: The Experience of Southern Europe," Discussion Paper 964, London: CEPR.

Fertig, Michael (forthcoming) "The Economic Impact of EU-Enlargement: Assessing the Migration Potential," *Empirical Economics*.

Greenwood, Michael J. (1975) "Research on Internal Migration in the United States: A Survey," *Journal of Economic Literature*, 13: 397–433.

Harris, David and Laszlo Matyas (1998) "Introduction to the Generalized Method of Moments Estimation," in L. Matyas (ed.), *Generalized Method of Moments Estimation*, Cambridge: Cambridge University Press.

Harris, J.R. and Todaro, M.P. (1970) "Migration, Unemployment and Development: A Two-Sector Analysis," *American Economic Review*, 60: 126–142.

Karras, Georgios and Carmel U. Chiswick (1999) "Macroeconomic Determinants of Migration. The Case of Germany: 1964–1988," *International Migration*, 37: 657–677.

Katseli, Louka T. and Nicolas P. Glytsos (1986) "Theoretical and Empirical Determinants of International Labor Mobility: A Greek-German Perspective," in

I. Gordon, and A.P. Thirlwall (eds), *European Factor Mobility: Trends and Consequences*. London: Macmillan.

Papapaganos, Harry and P. Sanfey (forthcoming) "Intention to Emigrate in Transition Countries: The Case of Albania," *Journal of Population Economics*.

Plakans, Andrej S. and Charles Wetherell (1995) "Migration in the Later Years of Life in Traditional Europe," in David I. Kertzer, and Peter Laslett (eds), *Aging in the Past: Demography, Society, and Old Age*, Berkeley and Los Angeles: University of California Press.

Ravenstein, E. (1889) "The Laws of Migration," *Journal of the Statistical Society*, 52: 214–301.

Rogers, Andrei and Louis J. Castro (1986) "Migration," in Andrei Rogers and Frans J. Willekens (eds), *Migration and Settlement: A Multiregional Comparative Study*. Dordrecht: D. Reidel.

Schmidt, Christoph M. (1996) "Cohort Sizes and Unemployment: Lessons for Poland," in Hartmut Lehmann and Jonathan Wadsworth (eds), *Labor Markets by Design?*, Ifo Studies on Eastern Europe and the Economies of Transition, 21: 126–154.

Schmidt, Christoph M. (1997) "Immigrant Performance in Germany: Labor Earnings of Ethnic German Migrants and Foreign Guest-Workers," *Quarterly Review of Economics and Finance*, 37: 379–397.

Schmidt, Christoph M. (1999) "Knowing What Works – The Case For Rigorous Program Evaluation," Discussion Paper 77, Bonn: IZA.

Schmidt, Christoph M. (2000) "Reconstructing Germany: The Demographic Impact of Immigration During the Post-War Era." mimeo, University of Heidelberg.

Schmidt, Christoph M. and Klaus F. Zimmermann (1992) "Migration Pressure in Germany: Past and Future," in Klaus F. Zimmermann (ed), *Migration and Economic Development*, Berlin: Springer.

Sinn, Hans-Werner (1999) "EU Enlargement, Migration, and Lessons from German Unification," *German Economic Review*, 1: 299–314.

Sinn, Hans-Werner (forthcoming) "EU Enlargement, and the Future of the Welfare State," *Scottish Journal of Political Economy*.

Sjaastad, Larry A. (1962) "The Cost and Returns of Human Migration," *Journal of Political Economy*, 70: 80–93.

United Nations (1996) *Demographic Yearbook 1994*, Department for Economic and Social Information and Policy Analysis, 46.

Vogler, Michael and Ralph Rotte (2000) "The Effects of Development on Migration: Theoretical Issues and New Empirical Evidence," *Journal of Population Economics*, 13: 485–508.

Zimmermann, Klaus F. (1991) "Ageing and the Labor Market," *Journal of Population Economics*, 4: 177–200.

7 Illegal immigration trends, policies and economic effects

Slobodan Djajić

Introduction

Foreigners who enter, reside, or work in a country unlawfully are usually referred to as illegal, irregular or undocumented immigrants. The number of such persons residing in the industrial countries, as well as in some of the rapidly growing developing countries, has increased significantly over the last couple of decades. This phenomenon reflects a growing imbalance between the supply of migrants and the limited scope for legal immigration in the relatively prosperous economies. It also reflects the persistent demand for both documented and undocumented foreign labor in the advanced countries.

Illegal immigration presents a range of problems from the host-country perspective. It undermines the authority as well as the objectives of legal immigration programs. There are particular concerns about the impact of illegal immigration on fiscal programs, wages and employment opportunities of native workers, and the overall economic effect on local communities and industries employing undocumented foreign workers. In addition, in some countries, the authorities worry that illegal aliens may alter the composition of the population in a way that may one day challenge the cultural hegemony of the natives or pose a threat to internal security and national cohesiveness.

Confronted with an expanding stock of illegal immigrants, the receiving countries have implemented a variety of measures designed to bring the problem under control. These include internal measures to restrict employment opportunities of illegal aliens and their access to public services, large increases in expenditures on border control measures, new tighter rules under which a person can claim asylum, new laws to accelerate deportation procedures and increase the number of removals of illegal aliens, and tougher penalties and fines for participation in alien smuggling activity. Progress is also being achieved in deterring illegal inflows by means of various agreements with the governments of the source and transit countries to facilitate the removal of aliens and open new possibilities for legal, temporary migration. Finally, efforts are being made to discourage potential illegal immigrants from leaving their country of origin by means of advertising campaigns and agreements with the authorities of the source countries to prevent their citizens from exiting without authorization to enter their country of destination.

The purpose of this chapter is to review the recent experience of host countries with illegal immigration and examine their policies designed to control the inflows and activities of illegal aliens. The chapter ends with an overview of the economic impact of illegal immigration.

Recent trends

The hot spot on the global map of illegal immigration, in terms of volume, has been for some time the US–Mexico border. The problem of large-scale illegal flows in that region originated with the Bracero program in 1942, which imposed rigid rules under which Mexican workers may be employed in US agriculture (see Martin, this volume). Employers were required to arrange for the transport of Braceros from Mexico, provide them with housing, and pay wages no lower than those received by similar US workers. At the same time Mexican workers were expected to sign up on their side of the border and wait to be recruited officially. Both employers and Mexican workers found these ground rules excessively rigid. As a result, large numbers of Mexicans came on their own as illegal immigrants. When the Bracero program was terminated in 1964, undocumented Mexican workers continued to cross the border seeking primarily seasonal jobs in the agricultural sector. Under pressure from the agricultural lobby, the Immigration Reform and Control Act of 1986 (IRCA) provided for legalization of most of these workers. The 1987–88 legalization programs eventually granted immigrant status to 2.7 million foreigners, 2 million of them being of Mexican origin. The legalization was accompanied by several measures designed to curb further inflows of illegal aliens into the US economy. These included a major increase in border control efforts along the US–Mexico frontier and employer sanctions designed to discourage employment of undocumented aliens.

In terms of stemming illegal immigration into the US, these measures proved to be only partly effective. According to the last official estimate, the number of illegal aliens residing in the US has grown from 3.9 million in 1992 to 5 million in 1996. In the year 2000, there was broad agreement that the figure was around 6 million. The inflows continue in spite of additional tough measures implemented by the US authorities in the 1990s. Although most of the inflow is from the south, across the land border with Mexico, a large proportion of illegal aliens (41 percent in 1996) come to the US legally, through airports, with tourist, student, and other types of visas (INS, 1999). They become illegal aliens by overstaying their visas and/or engaging in activities incompatible with their status, such as when tourists accept paid employment.

The characteristics of visa overstayers differ significantly from those of illegal border crossers (see Rivera-Batiz, 2000, and this volume). They tend to be better educated, better connected or related to well-established legal residents of the host country, enjoy higher earnings and occupational status and a lower probability of being bothered by the immigration authorities. In a sense, it may be appropriate to refer to such visa overstayers as "first-class" illegal aliens. By contrast, illegal border crossers come in "economy class." For them, however, transport costs can be much higher and the service considerably less satisfying. Their predicament reflects not having the right profile or contacts in the destination country to be granted a visa.

In many cases, Indian, Pakistani, Chinese and other immigrants (including Mexicans) find it easier to come legally into Canada and then slip into the US along the thinly guarded frontier, rather than trying to enter the US directly. Others learn what they need to say in order to be processed as refugees in Canada and arrive in groups of a hundred or more on boats. The majority of people who arrive in Canada and claim refugee status are not detained while their claim is being processed. In waiting for a hearing, which may take up to a year, they are free to circulate in Canada. Should they choose to continue their journey to the south, there is not very much on the way to stop them. Canadian officials argue, however, that there are as many people entering Canada illegally from the south as there are going the other way.

In Western Europe, large-scale illegal immigration is a relatively recent phenomenon in the sense that foreign workers were largely welcome during the period of rapid economic growth from the late 1950s to the mid-1970s. Those who came uninvited in search of a better life were usually able to legalize their residence status, provided they found employment. With increasing slack in the European labor market since the mid-1970s, foreigners seeking a better life are finding entry and settlement procedures ever more demanding and complex. Many now come as tourists or with other types of short-term visas and then become illegal immigrants by violating the conditions of entry. Others come as asylum seekers and become illegal aliens if their applications are rejected or if they obtain and then lose refugee status because of a change in circumstances. Finally, there are those who enter without inspection across land borders from Central Europe, or arrive by boat to the Mediterranean shores of Italy, Spain, France or Greece. According to the OECD (1999), most of the illegal aliens in Western Europe are concentrated in the southern states. A wide range of estimates exists.[1] While none of these can be considered reliable, it seems that Italy has the largest number, with probably around 500,000 to 800,000 illegal foreign residents. A rough estimate for Greece is around 650,000, for Germany around 500,000, France 300,000, Britain 200,000, Switzerland 150,000, and between 50,000 and 100,000 each for Belgium and the Netherlands.

In the case of Central and Eastern European countries (CEEC), large numbers of migrants also arrive legally as tourists, students and businessmen from other countries in the region, as well as from Asia and Africa. Once there, many attempt to move on to Western Europe, Canada and the US. If it takes time to organize and finance the necessary arrangements, they may stay in the region illegally. Particularly affected by this mode of irregular migration are Poland and the Czech Republic, which have a common border with Germany. Bulgaria, Hungary and Slovakia are in a similar position because of their proximity to EU members Greece and Austria. Further north, the Baltic states serve as transit stations for illegal immigration to Sweden, Norway and Finland. While waiting for an opportunity to move West, illegal immigrants in transit countries can support themselves by participating in the flourishing informal or "underground" economy. Many migrants, however, become discouraged after a while and decide to return to their countries of origin.

In China, millions of potential immigrants, mostly males, are preparing for travel to the West in search of lucrative jobs which they believe are waiting to be filled. According to recent reports (e.g. Litke, 2000), alien smugglers or "snakeheads" charge their clients about $1,000 up front in order to arrange for transport to the US. If delivered to the destination successfully, the migrant must pay the trafficking network the full fee, often in the range of $10,000–50,000, out of future income. Work is arranged in restaurants, laundries, factories and sweatshops in the major cities such as New York and Los Angeles. In many cases the employer is connected to the trafficking network in one way or another, facilitating an orderly repayment of the "loan," which can carry interest charges of up to 30 percent per annum. Those who do not pay have been brutally beaten or held for ransom until their family pays.

The business of smuggling Chinese immigrants is a highly lucrative one, involving sophisticated international networks which are sufficiently powerful to bribe or intimidate government officials, transport companies, ship captains and crews, and willing to do whatever it takes to deliver illegal aliens successfully to their destination. Efforts by the authorities to curtail the most popular modes of transport and entry usually fail to reduce the inflows as traffickers quickly switch to other modes with lower probabilities of failure. For a number of years, snakeheads have been using retrofitted fishing vessels to transport loads of Chinese illegal immigrants across the Pacific. Once the US authorities began to intercept such ships, the smugglers switched to a tactic of sending migrants inside 40 foot metal containers aboard merchant vessels for a two- to three-week journey to the West Coast.

Australia is also experiencing an increase in illegal immigrant arrivals along its shores. In 2000, Chinese smugglers were said to be spreading rumours that it would be easy to work in Australia due to the increase in the demand for labor associated with the Summer Olympic Games in

Sydney. Illegal immigration in Australia is mostly from Asian countries, including Afghanistan, Iraq, Turkey, China, Iran, and Pakistan. In a typical case, migrants first arrive legally in Indonesia by air, where they prepare for the final clandestine boat trip to Australia. However, most of Australia's illegal aliens arrive legally through the country's airports and then overstay their visas.

Illegal immigration in Africa, Central and South America, and the Caribbean is also large in magnitude, although it receives less coverage in the media. The source countries tend to be those experiencing economic stagnation, severe income-distribution problems, political instability or armed conflicts, while the host countries are typically regional leaders in terms of economic growth and employment opportunities. Only the names of the source and host countries change over time with changes in the economic, social and political conditions in the local environment.

Regional conflicts such as those in Sri Lanka, Afghanistan and Kurdistan have created large numbers of refugees who seek stability and a better life, not only in the West, but primarily in other countries of the region. There are approximately two million refugees in Iran, mostly from Afghanistan, who became illegal immigrants by accepting unauthorized employment.

Malaysia has been for a number of years a major destination country for illegal immigrants from Indonesia. The number of undocumented aliens from Bangladesh and the Philippines is also significant. Men find work primarily on plantations and in the construction industry, while women find it in the household services sector. Thailand, which has borders that are very difficult to monitor, has a large number of illegal foreign workers from neighbouring Burma, Laos and Cambodia. According to the OECD (1999), in October 1997 Thailand had a population of illegal workers of approximately 935,000.

In the more developed of the Asian economies, the presence of a large number of illegal foreign workers reflects the recent shortage of unskilled labor, supported in part by official restrictions on entry of unskilled workers. This encourages those already in the country to remain illegally after their visas or "trainee" work permits expire. In the cases of Korea and Japan, most of the illegal immigrants have entered the country legally, but overstayed their visas and work permits.

In South Asian countries such as Bangladesh, India, Nepal and Pakistan, persistent poverty makes women and children particularly vulnerable to trafficking for sexual exploitation. Similarly, Southeast Asian women are trafficked to Europe and the relatively more prosperous Asian countries, East European women are trafficked to Western Europe and North America, Nigerian, Dominican and Latin American women are trafficed to Western Europe, and the list goes on. While some arrive with forged documents, many have an officially issued visa. A number of legal channels exist for obtaining visas that facilitate travel and entry. For example, traffickers who bring Filipinas to Belgium have used a wide range of instruments to obtain permits, including fake marriage, family reunion, adoption, student status, the au pair system, exchange programs, and tourism (IOM, 1999: 6)

Some years ago women were being lured by traffickers with promises of good jobs in restaurants, bars and factories, and then forced into prostitution upon arrival at the destination. Currently, that pattern of recruitment is becoming increasingly rare. Most trafficked women seem to be better informed about the conditions of employment in the host country and knowingly seek work in the sex industry. Many of those who return to their countries of origin do so with considerable amounts of savings and serve as an example for girls with aspirations to pull themselves out of poverty in a similar manner.

Trafficking in minors is also becoming increasingly common, particularly in Asia. Children from the least developed countries are brought by traffickers to neighbouring and more advanced economies where they work as beggars, street-corner drug dealers, but also in the sex industry.[2]

Efforts to control illegal immigration

Enforcement of immigration laws typically consists of a wide range of activities designed to achieve the overall objectives of maintaining adequate control over the national borders and reducing the number of illegal residents. In most countries, the goal is not "zero" illegal immigration. That would imply excessive levels of enforcement for which the societies are not prepared to pay, nor would they necessarily consider total enforcement to be desirable, even if it was costless.

US immigration policy is implemented by the Immigration and Naturalization Service (INS). Among its responsibilities, it conducts immigration inspections of travelers entering the US through one of the 250 official ports of entry, controls the 8,000 miles of US borders, and identifies and removes individuals lacking lawful immigration status (see INS, 1999: 163–5). Immigration inspectors at the official ports of entry are trained and equipped to identify and intercept terrorists, alien and narcotic smugglers, imposters, criminals, undocumented aliens and those making false claims to US citizenship. In addition, INS inspectors work in some foreign countries to preinspect passengers before boarding aircraft destined for the US, provide fraudulent document training to airline personnel and foreign officials, and assist them in identifying undocumented or unauthorized passengers.

The Border Patrol branch of the INS operates primarily in areas between the official ports-of-entry. Its mission is to detect and prevent smuggling and entry of illegal aliens into the country. The Investigations Division is the internal enforcement branch whose task is to identify and remove criminal aliens in the federal and state prison systems, as well as those currently on probation or parol, counter immigrant smuggling and document fraud, enforce restrictions on employment of illegal aliens, and respond to complaints regarding criminal illegal alien activity. Finally, the

Detention and Deportation branch is responsible for the detention, transport, processing, and supervision of illegal aliens awaiting removal. The overall objective of the INS is to reduce the number of illegal residents in the US, particularly targeting criminal aliens.

Other advanced countries have developed similar enforcement structures and use similar methods and technologies to deter, intercept and control the activities of illegal aliens. The constant evolution and increase in sophistication of smuggling and employment of undocumented workers requires continuous efforts on the part of the authorities to adapt and maintain their optimal level of enforcement. It also requires large increases in enforcement expenditures. Budget of the INS has increased from 1.5 to 3.8 billion dollars from 1993 to 1998 and its staff has grown over that same period from 19,000 to 31,000 officers. For the fiscal year 2000, the INS budget is at 4.3 billion dollars. With more resources and new legislation, host countries have been able to implement in the 1990s a wide range of initiatives designed to curtail illegal immigration. The following subsections discuss some of these measures in greater detail, although limitations on space allow for only a selective review that illustrates the general trend. The emphasis is on the developments in North America.

Border control

In the US, IRCA of 1986 provided for an increase in the effectiveness of border control, particularly along the US–Mexico frontier. The number of inspectors at the official ports of entry, Border Patrol agents between official ports, and expenditures on equipment have been increased significantly. The strategy was to concentrate personnel and resources initially in those sectors with the highest levels of illegal immigration activity and then spread out to other areas where the problem was less significant. In September 1993, the INS began Operation Hold-the-Line in El Paso, Texas, followed by Operation Gatekeeper in San Diego in October 1994. The two operations were designed to reduce the very large illegal inflows that were observed in those two sectors and divert the traffic to rural routes in the more remote areas along the border where INS agents expected to have a tactical advantage. In the San Diego district, between October 1994 and October 1996, 8 miles of steel fencing and 5 miles of permanent high-intensity lighting were installed along the border. In addition, equipment such as helicopters, night-vision devices, motion sensors, and other instruments to detect and prevent illegal entry were made available to the Border Patrol in the San Diego district. The Illegal Immigration Reform and Immigrant Responsibility Act (IIRIRA) of 1996 provided for two more layers of fencing with roads between fences, for the 14 miles of border extending eastward from the Pacific Ocean.

All these efforts in the El Paso and San Diego districts have made it more difficult for illegal aliens to enter the US without inspection along the more tightly controlled segments of the border. As a result, there was: (i) an increase in the number of persons attempting to enter with fraudulent documents through the official ports of entry, many making false claims to US citizenship; (ii) a large shift of illegal alien traffic to other sectors along the border; (iii) an increase in attempts by illegal aliens to enter the US by gathering near the official ports of entry and trying to overwhelm inspectors by running in large groups through the official ports; (iv) greater use by Mexicans of border-crossing cards for legal entry at the official ports, but then overstaying the terms of their visa and accepting unauthorized employment;[3] (v) an increase in alien smuggling activity as well as in the fees charged by the smugglers. In addition, it seems that the smugglers have become more organized and sophisticated, and that they transport migrants further into the interior of the US via interstate highways (GAO, 1997: 22).

Due to the shift of illegal alien traffic, apprehensions have decreased in areas of greater concentration of Border Patrol resources and increased in more remote areas. Moreover, it seems that Operation Hold-the-Line was successful in diminishing illegal immigration activity of local crossers, while long distance labor migrants were merely diverted to other locations along the southwest border (GAO, 1997: 23). Resources of the INS, however, were not sufficient to apprehend aliens traversing these more remote segments of the frontier.

While INS resources were being directed to the US–Mexico border, the US–Canada border became increasingly understaffed. Of the approximately 6,500 Border Patrol agents working for the INS nationwide as of July 21, 1997, about 6,000 were stationed along the Mexican border while the remaining 500 agents were given the task of monitoring and controlling entry along the east coast, the west coast and along the US–Canada frontier.[4] Some land stations were staffed with just one or two officers and only for a part of the day. As a result, smugglers have increased their focus on bringing illegal immigrants to the US from the north.

Other migrant-receiving countries are similarly enhancing their border control measures. This is particularly true along the external borders of the EU. In cooperation with the EU, border controls have also been enhanced by the prospective future members of the EU. Moreover, all destination countries have increased surveillance at the airports, with an emphasis on improving the effectiveness of identity checks of arriving passengers. Considerable improvements in coastal surveillance are also being implemented, as is tighter and more sophisticated monitoring of road and rail traffic. However, every time a particular surveillance technique proves to be effective, new modes of illegal alien smuggling seem to emerge. Tighter border controls and other policies that raise the cost of transporting illegal aliens across international borders serve to change the modalities but not the substance of alien trafficking.

From the theoretical perspective, it is important to distinguish between the effectiveness of border controls in dealing with temporary as opposed to permanent illegal immigration. When illegal immigration is seasonal or "guest-worker" in nature, tighter border controls may not necessarily reduce the stock of illegal aliens residing in the economy (see, e.g., Hill, 1987; Djajić and Milbourne, 1988; and Djajić, 1999). While tighter entry and border control measures discourage illegal immigrants from attempting to cross the border, those who are not deterred are likely to succeed at some point, although at a higher expected cost (see Donato, Durand and Massey, 1992; and Espenshade, 1994). The higher cost may reflect a larger required number of attempts to gain entry or the requirement to use the services of a professional alien smuggler. Either way, an illegal immigrant who makes it across the border has an incentive to remain in the host country for a longer period of time (Kossoudji, 1992). How much longer depends on the degree of concavity of his or her utility function. For a very low elasticity of marginal utility with respect to consumption, it can be shown that a migrant's desired stay is extended almost as much as required to cover the increase in transport cost with additional savings, while keeping the rates of consumption in the destination and source countries relatively stable (Djajić and Milbourne, 1988).

A large proportion of illegal aliens in the southwest of the US, in the economies of southern Europe or southeast Asia, enter and reside in the host country illegally for the purpose of taking advantage of seasonal employment opportunities. By raising transport costs, tighter border controls may at some point convert what would otherwise be temporary illegal immigrants into permanent ones. Thus, while reducing inflows, such measures may nonetheless serve to increase the stock of illegal aliens residing in the economy (Djajić, 1999). By contrast, when illegal immigration is of the permanent type, tighter border controls serve to diminish both the flow *and* the stock of illegal aliens.

Measures affecting asylum seekers

Most countries now consider that the majority of asylum seekers are "economic refugees" rather than individuals fleeing persecution. Faced with an ever increasing number of asylum seekers, and the tendency for asylum seekers to vanish and become illegal aliens if their applications are turned down, they are tightening the rules under which a person can claim asylum and speeding up processing of applications and appeals against negative decisions. They are also restricting employment opportunities for asylum seekers and, in many countries, keeping them in detention centers and local jails while awaiting a decision. All these measures are designed to shorten the stay of applicants on their territory and discourage individuals from migrating with the view of claiming refugee status.

In the majority of the OECD countries, application for asylum is now restricted to persons that (i) come from countries that have not signed the UN Convention on Refugees and the UN Convention on Human Rights and, in addition, (ii) have not passed through a country that has signed both conventions. Within the EU, recent agreements determine which of the member countries is responsible for any given application for asylum. An application can be submitted to one member state only, with the verdict determined by jointly established criteria. In theory, this prevents applicants from submitting a claim for asylum in several countries at a time. In support of that policy, the Eurodac Convention, which took effect in October 1998, provides for a joint fingerprint database of asylum seekers in the EU.

Members of the EU, as well as of the CEEC waiting to join the EU, are now applying these principles which make it possible for the authorities to determine that an asylum application is "manifestly unfounded" if they consider the applicant to be from a country where there is no serious risk of persecution, or if he or she has transited through a third country where protection may have been available (OECD, 1999: 72). This enables countries like Germany to turn back asylum seekers transiting through neighbouring countries like Poland and the Czech Republic.

Battling document fraud

As the benefits of being "documented" in an advanced country become more and more valuable, so do the official documents which serve to identify individuals as legal workers, residents or citizens. While the authorities continuously improve the technology of document production, this seems to provide only a temporary solution as counterfeiters quickly adopt new technologies and tactics. Those who need the documents can always find them one way or another. Depending on the nature of documents, however, it may be at a high price.

Travellers from advanced countries typically do not require a visa to travel to other advanced countries. A Western passport is therefore sufficient to have a good chance of arriving safely at almost any destination. Immigrant smugglers are said to charge up to $5,000 for an expertly modified Western-country passport (Ruppe, 2000). They sometimes even provide training to help clients impersonate the rightful bearer of the document. In an effort to curb such practices, the authorities are continuously adding new features to documents, making it easier for inspectors to detect alterations. However, such measures are in most cases quickly countered by innovative criminals.

When passports are difficult to modify, blank originals are sometimes stolen from Western country embassies and consular offices and then "issued" by the traffickers to their clients. If a Western passport is too expensive, there is also a market for altered passports from the immigrant's own country with an authentic visa for entry to an advanced country. With enough luck, skill, and calm nerves, it is often possible to complete the journey successfully.

Once in the host country, an illegal alien needs to obtain host country documents in order to be able to work, settle down, and be eligible for the range of public services offered only to legal residents or citizens. A breeder document, such as a birth certificate, which can be used to obtain other official documents, is issued in the US by 7,000 different offices and in more than 1,000 different formats. This makes birth certificates relatively easy to fake, but also difficult and time-consuming for the authorities to verify. And while major efforts are on the way to standardize birth certificates, improve document security, and legislate tougher penalties for document fraud in many countries, it will take years of work to obtain meaningful results.

Employer sanctions

Most advanced countries have implemented a wide range of new enforcement measures aimed to discourage employment of illegal aliens. The 1986 IRCA has made intentional employment of undocumented foreign workers an illegal act in the US, punishable by fines and prison sentences. Adequately enforced, such legislation can discourage employers from hiring illegal aliens and remove the attraction of good employment prospects which draws most illegal aliens to the US. Enforcement, however, has not been adequate under the Reagan, Bush and Clinton administrations. As a result, IRCA did not have a significant impact on the employment of illegal aliens in the US (Papademetriou, 1991a, 1991b). While employers were required to examine a worker's documents and keep records of such examinations, they were not expected to be experts in distinguishing between real and fraudulent documents. Availability of fraudulent documents quickly increased to meet the demand and employment of illegal aliens continued almost as usual.[5]

The IIRIRA of 1996 calls for three separate pilot programs to confirm an individual's employment eligibility to be set up in at least five states with the largest illegal alien populations. Participation in these programs, however, is on a voluntary basis for private employers, meaning that the project's aim is not enforcement, but rather learning how to set up an effective control system at some point in the future.

The American Federation of Labor and Congress of Industrial Organizations (AFL-CIO), which has fought for years to stop illegal immigration and the employment of undocumented workers in the US, is now calling for a legalization of unauthorized foreign workers and an end to employer sanctions. Considering that the sanctions have not been effectively enforced and are not likely to be enforced in the years to come, AFL-CIO sees greater potential benefits in absorbing legalized foreign workers into its movement, rather than trying to keep them out of the workplace and the country. Efforts to keep the illegal aliens out have indirectly supported discriminatory employment practices against them, which may have served to erode some of the benefits and standards enjoyed by unionized workers in occupations with high concentrations of undocumented aliens. In addition, employer sanctions have stimulated growth of underground economic activity in some industries, such as garment manufacturing, presenting both employers and workers in the official segment of that industry with a stiff competitive challenge.

In most EU countries, some CEECs, Canada, Switzerland, Australia, Singapore, Thailand, Malaysia, the Chinese province of Taiwan, South Korea, Japan, and other countries, it is also a criminal offence to employ illegal immigrants. Employers who intentionally hire undocumented workers are subject to fines and in some cases imprisonment. Enforcement, however, has not been fully effective due to lack of political will, technical capacity and enforcement resources. Employers who benefit directly from illegal immigration stand in the way of tighter enforcement, not only in the US, but in most other countries.

Legalizations

A number of countries have tried to reduce the stock of illegal immigrants by means of legalization programs. As noted above, IRCA enabled 2.7 million illegal aliens eventually to become permanent residents and citizens of the United States. Regularizations and illegal alien amnesties in some Asian economies led to issuing of temporary work permits in some specific sectors or activities. In other countries, such as South Korea, an amnesty merely permitted illegal aliens to leave the country without penalty.

A number of legalization programs of various types have also been implemented in Italy, Spain, France, Portugal, the Netherlands and Greece (see Sarris and Markova, this volume). In contrast with IRCA legalization, the aim of many of these programs was merely to bring the undocumented foreign workers out of the underground economy and into the official economy, where the activity contributes directly to fiscal programs and is subject to a greater degree of monitoring by the authorities. These legalizations typically granted only temporary work permits (rather than permanent residence), which expire in one or more years and thereby recreate, at least in part, the conditions prevailing before the legalization. A drawback of such "temporary" legalization schemes, from the perspective of addressing the illegal immigration problem, is their tendency to be repeated. Anticipation of similar future legalizations can serve to attract additional inflows of illegal aliens.

Advertising

Growth in the supply of illegal immigrants reflects to some extent the marketing efforts of traffickers who encourage potential migrants to go. In the Chinese provinces of Fujian and Guandong, "snakeheads" approach poor farmers and lower-middle-class workers with offers to take them to the land of opportunity, exaggerating what the opportunities are and downplaying the risks and hardships endured by Chinese illegal immigrants that land in the West. Those who experience hardships often attribute their misfortune to personal failure that may have been avoidable and do not find it in their interest to talk about such experiences. They prefer to portray themselves as being successful. Others who communicate to their families that they are suffering and not being adequately compensated for their clandestine work in the host country are sometimes accused of lying in an effort to justify transferring back to their families less funds than was anticipated.

For female workers in the sex industry, be they from Latin America, Asia, Africa or Eastern Europe, there is a strong incentive to conceal the nature of their occupation in the host country and the related abuses, both physical and economic, at the hands of their employers and traffickers. All these factors influence the flow of information between the migrants and their contacts in the source country, creating a biased, rosy picture of an illegal alien's experience in the host country.

To counter this tendency and perhaps go even further, authorities of the host countries, institutions such as the International Organization for Migration (IOM), and various non-governmental organizations have embarked on an advertising campaign designed to dissuade potential illegal immigrants from leaving their country of origin. The first IOM campaign was carried out in Romania in 1992–96, followed by ones in Albania (1992–95), the Philippines (1997–98), Vietnam (1998–99) and the Ukraine (1998). The more recent campaigns focus on trafficking in women, with the objective of providing information on the risks and dangers of being involved in that activity.

On a recent official visit to China, a regional director of the INS urged Chinese workers to remain in their home country: "The message we're trying to get across is that they should not believe what they're told by the snakeheads. The snakeheads tell them anything they can to trick them to go."[6] In addition, it seems that the Chinese government now issues warnings on television that immigrant smuggling is a deadly criminal activity (Litke, 2000).

The message that the authorities of the host countries are transmitting through various media usually consists of one or more of the following elements: the life of illegal aliens in the host country is more difficult than what it would have been had they stayed at home; the journey to the destination is extremely unpleasant, dangerous, and can result in the loss of life; there is a high probability that the ever more sophisticated detection methods of border patrols will result in apprehension and deportation; should the illegal immigrants manage to arrive successfully and evade the authorities within the host country, they are likely to be subjected to a wide range of abuses by the traffickers and networks that arrange for clandestine employment. For the time being, however, courses in "Restaurant English" continue to grow in popularity among the young Chinese. For as long as three-storey houses are mushrooming throughout villages of Fujian province, built with money earned in the US by illegal and legal immigrants, the desire to take a chance and become rich will continue to dominate any efforts to persuade people to stay in their villages.

International cooperation to curtail illegal immigration

International exchange of information on migrant smuggling is promoted by means of bilateral and multilateral technical cooperation agreements between Japan and Korea, Japan and China, Hong-Kong, China and the US, the EU and some of its neighbors, and other countries as well. In addition, the authorities are working very closely with international airlines and shipping companies in an effort to curtail smuggling. Chinese officials have also accepted US demands to pursue smugglers more aggressively and to impose more severe punishment on illegal immigrants. Chinese immigrants arriving by boat in Baja California, Mexico are now being apprehended by the Mexican authorities, detained in make-shift shelters, and returned back to China in application of an agreement financed by the US.

One of the problems experienced by the authorities in their attempts to deport illegal aliens is that they often destroy their own documents, making it difficult in some cases to identify their country of origin. And even if the country of origin is known, it is difficult to carry out the deportation without the cooperation of the relevant authorities. Multilateral and bilateral readmission agreements are therefore being concluded and used to facilitate the return of certain categories of immigrants back to their countries of origin or transit (OECD, 1999: 74). Such agreements are a potentially very useful instrument from the perspective of the advanced countries in relation to their efforts to deter and remove illegal immigrants and rejected asylum seekers from their territory. The agreements also serve to encourage transit countries to tighten their own border controls. In return, the transit countries have been able to secure for their citizens visa-free travel for short, 90-day stays in the more advanced partner countries (stays that often involve clandestine employment) as well as financial assistance for improving border controls and other forms of aid. Readmission agreements are now quite common in Europe, most importantly between the members of the EU and CEEC, former Soviet republics, and some states in North Africa and the Middle East.

Bilateral agreements are also being signed among OECD countries, as well as with non-member countries, regarding employment of foreign workers and social security arrangements with a view of regulating the employment of foreigners on their territory. By facilitating legal flows of workers across international borders, such agreements may serve to reduce the "pull" factors attracting illegal aliens from other countries.

Fines and penalties

In an effort to deter illegal immigration, the INS is seeking to increase prosecutions of alien smugglers, coyotes, and aliens with criminal records who re-enter the US after having been removed. Foreigners who are deported can also be prosecuted for re-entry under section 1326 of the US Code (GAO, 1997: 17). US Attorneys in the five INS districts along the southwest border have increased the number of prosecutions, focusing mainly on alien smugglers under section 1324 of the US Code, although the pattern varies from district to district.

The 1996 IIRIRA mandates new civil penalties for illegal entry into the US after April 1, 1997. An alien attempting to enter without inspection is subject to a civil penalty of at least $50 but not more than $250 for each entry or attempted entry. The penalty is doubled for repeat offenders. These penalties have not been enforced, however, due to high administrative costs and the fact that too few individuals have the money to pay the fine. There are, however, significant readmission penalties for those "unlawfully present" in the US. If the unlawful presence is for six months to a year, and the alien departs "voluntarily", inadmissibility to the US is for three years. Those unlawfully present for more than a year are not legally admissible to the US for a period of ten years. This can be a very severe punishment for illegal aliens with close family members, such as a spouse or children, who are legal residents in the US. Unlawful presence may result from overstaying a visa or entry without inspection (EWI). Those who EWI are inadmissible.

Removal procedures have also been simplified and give greater authority to the INS to proceed without being challenged in the courts. Moreover, under the new law, cancellation or suspension of removal is now granted only under very strict conditions and limited to 4,000 per year. The penalty for alien smuggling has been raised to 10 years' imprisonment, up to 15 years for more than two offenses, and possibly more if the trafficking activity results in injury or death. Similar measures have been or are in the process of being legislated in a large number of countries, including Belgium, the Netherlands, Denmark, Austria, and Switzerland. In an effort to combat trafficking, the Clinton administration is supporting a bill in Congress that would create up to one thousand T visas per year (which eventually lead to immigrant status) for trafficking victims who testify against traffickers.

In Britain, an increasing number of illegal immigrants have been found hidden in trucks, some of them suffocating along the way, as in the June 2000 incident involving 58 Chinese immigrants. In 1999, 20,000 asylum seekers arrived in Britain by truck. In response, a new law has come into force in April 2000, imposing an automatic fine of £2,000 on truck drivers for stowaways they bring into Britain, regardless of whether or not they are aware of their illegal cargo. Similar fines with respect to air, sea, and rail transport companies that bring aliens into the country without proper documents have been in force since 1987. Other countries, including the US, France, Spain, Germany and the Netherlands, also impose carrier sanctions.

In Italy, an Act of March 1998 includes an expulsion measure which allows the authorities to expel foreigners "if they enter the country illegally, if a residence permit is denied, if there is a lack of social integration, or if they threaten public order or national security" (OECD, 1999: 65). Individuals awaiting expulsion may be held in detention centers. Prior to the practice of detaining those ordered out of the country, the vast majority of them would not show up for the execution of the expulsion order. More detention centers for this same purpose are being built not only in Italy, but also in Australia, the US, Spain, Portugal, and Lithuania. The detention centers are also designed to accommodate asylum seekers while their cases are being assessed.

In Canada, the proposed Immigration and Refugee Protection Act would impose fines of up to C$1 million and life in prison for traffickers who bring ten or more migrants into the country. Similarly, the Irish government is planning to increase penalties for alien smuggling, imposing unlimited fines and confiscation of property as well as a 10-year prison sentence. Smuggling immigrants into Australia can lead to a 20-year prison sentence and a fine of A$220,000. In Malaysia the government is considering requiring landlords to check if their tenants are legally in the country. More than 300 people have been arrested in 1999 for harbouring illegal immigrants and 14 homeowners had their property confiscated (*Migration News*, 2000b). In France, the penalties for smuggling, transporting, or harboring illegal immigrants have been raised in 1991. Japan's Immigration Control and Refugee Recognition Act calls for fines of up to 300,000 yen, prison sentences of up to three years, deportation and a re-entry ban of five years for foreigners who overstay their visas. The maximum penalty for leaving China illegally has been raised under a new law from two weeks to one year in prison and more vigorous efforts are now made by the Chinese authorities to pursue vessels loaded with illegal immigrants (Kurtenbach, 2000). This is just a small sample of recently imposed fines and penalties designed to discourage alien smuggling and illegal immigration. The effectiveness of these measures is yet to be tested.

Economic impact of illegal immigration

Ethier (1986) provides the first formal theoretical analysis of the economic impact of illegal immigration. He considers the implications of alternative immigration policies and enforcement measures for the level of welfare and the distribution of income in the host country. Subsequent studies have extended and refined the analysis of how illegal immigration and the policies designed to control it affect the economy.[7]

The economic impact on the legal resident population of the host country can be both positive and negative. There are obvious welfare gains from trade with the illegal aliens in the market for labor services. This same trade, however, affects both commodity and factor prices, causing income to be redistributed from one group to another (see, for example, Ethier, 1986; Bond and Chen, 1987; Djajić, 1997; Hillman and Weiss, 1999; Grether, de Melo and Müller, this volume).

As illegal immigration alters the distribution of income, it gives rise to opposing views as to how strictly it should be controlled. Those who advocate tighter controls argue that illegal foreign workers displace low-skilled natives, depress wages, and neutralize market forces that would otherwise result in a rising trend of wages (see the survey by Greenwood and McDowell, 1986). In addition, it is said that the availability of unskilled legal and illegal immigrants lowers the pace of structural adjustment and technical progress, adversely affecting the economy's competitive position in the international market. If capital is mobile across sectors, illegal immigration may draw capital to the underground economy, depriving the rest of the economy of capital and causing it to stagnate. Illegal aliens are also said to draw benefits from the host country's social programs without always making the corresponding contribution to the programs' budgets.

Some of these views may be well founded, while others cannot be easily supported on the basis of either theoretical reasoning or empirical evidence. The notion that illegal immigration draws investment to the underground economy, depriving the rest of the economy of capital, falls into the latter category. Given the degree of openness of the industrial countries to international capital flows, such problems are not likely to materialize. And if some sectors are deprived of capital, this is likely to be due to a decline in their profitability that has nothing to do with illegal immigration.

Some attention is also given to the argument that illegal immigration, by maintaining downward pressure on wages, removes the incentives for restructuring and modernization of industry. This argument fails to recognize, however, that the host country's opportunity cost of using foreign labor is often one-tenth of the going domestic wage, due to barriers to international migration and to trade in goods and services that are highly intensive in the use of unskilled labor. Developing labor-saving technology of production under such conditions may well be privately profitable, but economically inefficient from a national point of view. However, to the extent that labor-saving technology can give rise to positive externalities or perhaps favorable terms-of-trade effects for the capital-abundant host country in the international market for goods and factor services, this argument should be appropriately modified.

Impact on the public sector

There is also the question of illegal alien participation in the use and financing of public services. In most countries, however, illegal aliens are virtually excluded from public sector benefits. Empirical evidence available for the US economy seems to indicate that a very small percentage of them do in fact receive free public services. Undocumented foreign workers are typically young males who are afraid of being apprehended if they request government assistance. Moreover, they are usually not accompanied by a wife or children who may be heavier users of public services. At the same time a large majority of them do pay social security and income taxes through the automatic withholding system.

A sample of illegal immigrants studied by North and Houstoun (1976) reveals that 77 percent paid social security taxes and 73 percent paid income taxes. There is overwhelming evidence pointing to the conclusion that illegal immigrants are in fact making a *positive net contribution* to the public coffers. As reported by Simon (1989: 295–96), "every study that provides dollar estimates shows that when the sum of the tax contributions to city, state and federal government are allowed for, these tax payments vastly exceed the cost of the services used by a factor of perhaps five, ten or more."

Even if illegal immigrants pay no taxes at all, while drawing benefits equal to those enjoyed by the natives, it can be shown that under plausible conditions they need not contribute to a public-sector deficit. In a simple neo-classical, general-equilibrium model where the government's budget is initially balanced and taxes are a constant proportion of "official" labor income, the budget can be shown to remain balanced in the long run following an inflow of illegal immigrants (Djajić, 1997). This budget-neutrality result reflects the adjustments that occur in the host country as an inflow of illegal aliens confined to only a particular segment of the economy (where undocumented workers are tolerated) gives rise to changes in the occupational and skill composition of the native labor force over time. Natives end up with a higher per capita income and pay correspondingly more in taxes. The long-run increase in the tax revenues of the government turns out to be proportional to the increase in the labor force resulting from illegal immigration. Thus, even if illegal immigrants pay no taxes out of their own income, their activities generate enough extra income for the natives, so that a fraction of that income (equal to the tax rate) is sufficient to cover the cost of public services enjoyed by the illegal aliens.

Immigrant children and their use of educational services have been at the center of the public debate on the public-sector impact of illegal immigration. According to Weintraub and Cardenas (1984), 85 to 93 percent of the cost of public services used by illegal immigrants goes for education. To the extent that many children of illegal immigrants eventually become naturalized citizens of the host country, it may be more appropriate to view such educational expenditures as an investment in the future productive capacity of the nation rather than a cost of illegal immigration.

Effect on wages

The impact of illegal immigration on wages of native workers is also an important and controversial issue. A number of empirical studies have attempted to quantify the effects of *legal* immigration on the wages of native workers. As noted in surveys by Greenwood and McDowell (1986), Borjas (1994), and Friedberg and Hunt (1995), most studies have identified only a small negative effect. Estimates of the elasticity of the native wage with respect to the number of immigrants are typically in the range of −0.01 to −0.02. That is, a 10 percent increase in the number of immigrants entails a fall in wages of native workers of 0.1 to 0.2 percent. The small magnitude of the wage effects may reflect a number of factors. Trade in goods and services, as well as capital and labor flows in and out of the area directly affected by immigration, probably absorb much of the effect of immigration on the wages of natives. One can use this same reasoning to argue that wages of natives would not have increased significantly in the absence of immigration. Any major tendency for wages to rise would have been neutralized to a large extent by capital outflows from the region and adjustments in the pattern of trade.

A study by Bean, Lowell and Taylor (1988) deals explicitly with the effects of *illegal* immigration from Mexico and its impact on the US labor market in the southwest. They summarize their findings as follows: "The concern that undocumented immigration from Mexico may be depressing the earnings of native-born workers is not borne out by these results ... It is also noteworthy that the effects of increases in the supply of this group are negligible on native-born Mexican Americans, the group that a priori may be expected to be most affected . . ." (1988: 46).[8]

Economic activities of illegal immigrants

Foreign workers lacking legal status normally take jobs which are at the bottom of the social ladder. These are jobs which typically involve low wages, tend to be temporary, and where working conditions are harsh, unpleasant, often unsafe and fail to comply with labor legislation. The jobs involve seasonal help in agriculture, work in hotel and restaurant trades, food processing, garment making, light manufacturing, the construction industry, the personal services sector, and as street vendors and throughout the underground economy.

One should not forget, however, the "first-class" illegal immigrants, a group that consists of more privileged visa overstayers, whose occupational and earnings experience is much more favorable. Such individuals typically have a higher level of education and skills, benefit from family networks in marketing their human capital, and tend to be more resourceful in becoming legal residents more quickly than the "economy class" aliens that cross the border surreptitiously. Regardless of class, however, illegal status typically translates into very little legal protection in many dimensions and potential abuses by the employers. Although in many countries the rights of workers are protected regardless of their legal status, the majority of illegal aliens do not complain about abuses to the authorities. They face the threat, explicit, implicit, or imagined, but usually very effective, that complaints could prompt the employer to call the authorities and have them deported.

The weak bargaining position of illegal aliens in the labor market is reflected not only in harsh, unsafe, and unpleasant working conditions, but also longer work days, no overtime, no holiday pay, and no benefits. In addition, their earnings tend to be considerably lower than those of comparable native workers (Rivera-Batiz, 1999).

Concentration of undocumented foreign workers in certain sectors of the economy reflects the supply and demand conditions and various constraints influencing the markets for illegal foreign labor. The technology of production may render certain activities more conducive for employment of illegal aliens. Internal enforcement of legislation on the employment of foreign workers may vary from one sector to another (Hill and Pearce, 1990). The skill profile of illegal aliens may not be similar to that of the natives, implying different occupational choices and preferences. Existing migration networks may serve to channel illegal immigrants to some geographic locations and occupations and not to others. Discriminatory practices of the natives may have similar effects. Whatever the case may be, illegal aliens are particularly concentrated in industries which are labor intensive, where economies of scale do not play a significant role, where compliance with health and safety regulations (and other labor legislation) is relatively costly per unit of labor, and where the labor demand conditions are volatile or seasonal in nature. In such an environment, use of undocumented foreign workers offers employers major possibilities for reducing labor costs, while at the same time increasing the efficiency of production.

The availability of cheap clandestine labor presents a significant advantage for entrepreneurs initiating new businesses and reduces the risk of embarking on new ventures. To the extent that it promotes start-ups of small businesses, the availability of illegal aliens in the economy may be an important factor in stimulating economic growth, investment, and a competitive business environment. In turn, a healthy and dynamic small business sector is at the heart of jobs creation for the native workers in most market economies.

In the agricultural sector, particularly in the case of perishable fruits and vegetables, the availability of undocumented foreign workers generates higher land rents and new employment opportunities for the natives whose labor services are complementary to those of the illegal aliens. The very existence of economic activity in some rural communities is now dependent on the availability of cheap foreign labor.

In the construction industry, the presence of illegal aliens employed as manual workers reduces the cost of construction. At the same time, however, it deprives native workers of similar employment opportunities. But is this undesirable from the national perspective? Not necessarily! Manual construction work is a seasonal occupation with a relatively high accident rate and without much prospect for occupational advancement. Displaced natives are compelled to seek other more rewarding employment and human capital accumulation activities. While that my imply some short-term adjustment costs at the time undocumented foreign workers become available in the construction sector, the long-run implications of natives being excluded from dead-end jobs can be rather positive. This is particularly true if market imperfections result in a suboptimal level of human capital accumulation on the part of natives prior to the inflow of illegal immigrants. The same is true with respect to the presence of undocumented foreign workers in the sex industry, hotel and restaurant services (particularly of the seasonal type) and all other jobs to which illegal aliens are usually given relatively easy access. The willingness of host-country authorities to tolerate certain types of illegal alien activity can be largely explained by the weight of these benefits from the perspective of the natives.

Generally speaking, if labor-market conditions and enforcement policies result in concentration of illegal aliens in dead-end occupations, where labor services are complementary to native factors of production, illegal alien inflows serve either to raise the earnings of complementary factors by increasing their productivity and rents or to raise the real income of natives by lowering the prices of goods and services produced with undocumented foreign labor (Djajić, 1997). Given the current experience of the advanced destination countries, and allowing for the adjustment costs imposed on the adversely affected natives, the economic impact of illegal immigration still seems to be rather positive.

Household services

A large number of illegal aliens are also employed in the household services sector. The nature of the production process in that sector makes transactions between natives and illegal immigrants potentially very rewarding for both parties. Even top American lawyers, including those with aspirations to head the US Justice Department, have not been able to resist hiring illegal aliens to perform services in their home and garden.

From the perspective of an illegal immigrant, a native household can offer not only a steady source of employment, income, food and in some cases shelter, but also a high degree of protection from immigration authorities and possible abuses in the outside world.[9] The native household may also serve illegal immigrants as a source of useful personalized information that helps them cope with their illegal status and improves their prospects of eventually becoming a legal immigrant. In addition, the flexibility of the household production function, and the substitutability of factors within it, can shield the illegal alien from activities that may give rise to frequent and more direct contacts with the authorities.

In return for this "compensation bundle," which derives its value to a large extent from the worker's lack of legal status, the illegal alien serves the household with a much greater degree of loyalty, effort, skill, and dedication than do documented workers in the same sector, but at a fraction of the price. For a professional couple in an advanced country it is now possible to hire an illegal alien with an MA degree to care for their school-age child or a medical doctor to look after an elderly parent around the clock. While such cases may not be frequent, there is no doubt that the presence of illegal aliens in the household services sector can give rise to significant improvements in household productivity at a low cost. At the same time it serves to release members of native households from repetitive, menial tasks and allows them to improve their marketable skills and pursue more rewarding professional or leisure activities. Significance of the resulting efficiency and welfare gains for the natives should not be underestimated.

Other negative effects

The possibility of enjoying low cost labor in an economy that tolerates some illegal immigration may, however, impose a cost on the next generation. The fact that illegal aliens have lower earnings in relation to the natives prevents them from offering their children the support for human capital accumulation that native children enjoy. The contribution of children of illegal aliens (who in most cases eventually become citizens) to the host country economy is correspondingly lower, while the cost of lifetime benefits drawn from social programs by these same individuals is likely to be higher. Thus, illegal immigration causes income to be redistributed from the future generation of taxpayers to the present generation. To put it in more concrete terms, while much of the benefits of illegal immigration are privatized by the employers of illegal aliens, the potential cost of assimilating their children into the mainstream of the society are shifted on to third parties. One should also take into consideration the possible congestion effects of large inflows of illegal immigrants and the resulting pressures on the available infrastructure. All that imposes costs that need to be contrasted with the potential benefits.

Concluding remarks

Technological, institutional and organizational advances and improvements in the industrial countries over the last few decades, as well as their policies on trade and foreign investment, have had enormous success in channelling global income flows in the direction of the advanced economies. The resulting increase in the per capita income gap between the rich and poor countries is becoming increasingly more apparent to the people of the developing countries. Along with demographic forces, this will continue to fuel migratory pressures and illegal immigration in the years to come. Trying to stop or control these pressures puts the authorities of the destination countries in conflict with one of the most powerful market forces. Chances of success are slim and any partial success is likely to come at a high cost.

Notes

1 On the problem of estimating the stock of illegal aliens, see, e.g., Warren and Passel (1987), Espenshade (1995), and Tapinos (1999).

2 For a more extensive discussion on the pattern of illegal immigration in various countries, see Ghosh (1998).

3 Data that would make possible estimates of overstays have not been collected by the INS for border crossers from Canada and Mexico. This is scheduled to begin in the year 2001.

4 GAO (1997). The shortage of Border Patrol agents and the plan to add only 1,500–2,500 additional agents between 1998 and the year 2000 reflected a lack of INS capacity to absorb staff at a faster pace, given the availability of infrastructure, equipment, training, and supervisory capacity. In fiscal year 1999, 1,100 new Border Patrol agents were hired. However, due to high turnover, this resulted in a net addition of only 369 new agents, far short of the 1,000 mandated by Congress.

5 To illustrate the effectiveness of INS enforcement methods, it is useful to quote from *Migration News* (2000a): "under operation Vanguard, the INS subpoenaed records from meatpacking employers in Nebraska, compared employee information on I-9 forms against Social Security Administration and INS records, and then told employers to ask employees who appeared to be unauthorized to clear up discrepancies in their records or face INS interviews. The INS then visited the plants . . . Most of those to be questioned disappeared before the INS arrived."

6 Kurtenbach (2000). It is interesting to note, however, that the same INS officer, on a stopover in Hong Kong, suggested that members of the Falun Gong meditation movement, claiming fear of persecution, might receive asylum in the United States. While this policy, if implemented, is likely to have a significant positive impact on the rate of growth of Falun Gong membership, it will also serve to stimulate interest in illegal immigration in the belief that it may be possible to use Falun Gong membership as a "green card" once the migrant reaches US territory.

7 See, e.g., Bond and Chen (1987), Chiswick (1988a, 1988b), Dell'Aringa and Neri (1987), Djajić (1987, 1997, 1999), Hill and Pierce (1990), Hillman and Weiss (1999), Jahn and Straubhaar (1995), Lianos, Sarris and Katseli (1996), and Sarris and Zorgrafakis (1999), to name a few.

8 See Grossman (1984) for an attempt to measure the impact of illegal immigration on the wages of native workers by means of a simulation.

9 One should not overlook, however, that the household itself may be an important source of illegal immigrant abuse. See Weinert (1991).

References

Bean, F.D., B.L. Lowell and L.J. Taylor (1988) "Undocumented Mexican Immigrants and the Earnings of Other Workers in the United States," *Demography*, 25: 35–51.

Bond, E.W. and T.-J. Chen (1987) "The Welfare Effects of Illegal Immigration," *Journal of International Economics*, 14: 315–328.

Borjas, G.J. (1994) "The Economics of Immigration," *Journal of Economic Literature*, 32: 1667–1717.

Borjas, G.J. (1995) "The Economic Benefits from Immigration," *Journal of Economic Perspectives*, 9: 3–23.

Chiswick, B.R. (1988a) "Illegal Immigration and Immigration Control," *Journal of Economic Perspectives*, 2: 101–115.

Chiswick, B.R. (1988b) *Illegal Aliens: Their Employment and Employers*, Kalamazoo, Mich.: W.E. Upjohn Institute for Employment Research.

Dell'Aringa, C. and F. Neri (1987) "Illegal Immigration and the Underground Economy in Italy," *Labor*, 1: 107–126.

Djajić, S. (1987) "Illegal Aliens, Unemployment and Immigration Policy," *Journal of Development Economics*, 25: 235–249.

Djajić, S. (1997) "Illegal Immigration and Resource Allocation," *International Economic Review*, 38: 97–117.

Djajić, S. (1999) "Dynamics of Immigration Control," *Journal of Population Economics*, 12: 45–61.

Djajić, S. and R. Milbourne (1988) "A General Equilibrium Model of Guest-Worker Migration," *Journal of International Economics*, 25: 335–351.

Donato, K.M., J. Durand and D.S. Massey (1992) "Stemming the Tide? Assessing the Deterrent Effects of the Immigration Reform and Control Act," *Demography*, 29: 139–157.

Espenshade, T.J. (1994) "Does the Threat of Border Apprehension Deter Undocumented US Immigration," *Population and Development Review*, 20: 871–892.

Espenshade, T.J. (1995) "Using INS Border Apprehensions Data to Measure the Flow of Undocumented Migrants Crossing the US–Mexico Frontier," *International Migration Review*, 29: 545–565.

Ethier, W.J. (1986) "Illegal Immigration: The Host-Country Problem," *American Economic Review*, 76: 56–71.

Friedberg, R.M. and J. Hunt (1995) "The Impact of Immigrants on Host-Country Wages," *Journal of Economic Perspectives*, 9: 23–44.

GAO (1997) *Illegal Immigration: Southern Border Strategy Results Inconclusive; More Evaluation Needed*. Washington, D.C.: US General Accounting Office.

Ghosh, B. (1998) *Huddled Masses and Uncertain Shores*, The Hague: Kluwer.

Greenwood, M.J. and J.M. McDowell (1986) "The Factor Market Consequences of US Immigration," *Journal of Economic Literature*, 24: 1738–1772.

Grossman, J.B. (1984) "Illegal Immigrants and Domestic Employment," *Industrial and Labor Relations Review*, 37: 240–251.

Hill, J.K. (1987) "Immigrant Decisions Concerning the Duration of Stay and Migratory Frequency," *Journal of Development Economics*, 25: 221–234.

Hill, J.K. and J.E. Pierce (1990) "The Incidence of Sanctions Against Employers of Illegal Aliens," *Journal of Political Economy*, 98: 28–44.

Hillman, A. and A. Weiss (1999) "A Theory of Permissible Illegal Immigration," *European Journal of Political Economy*,15: 595–604.

INS (1999) *Statistical Yearbook of the Immigration and Naturalization Service, 1997*, Washington, D.C.: US Government Printing Office.

IOM (1999) *Trafficking in Migrants: Quarterly Bulletin*, 19, July 1999.

Jahn, A. and T. Straubhaar (1995) "On the Political Economy of Illegal Immigration," paper presented at the CPER workshop on "The Political Economy of Illegal Immigration," September 14–16, 1995, Halkidiki, Greece.

Kossoudji, S. (1992) "Playing Cat and Mouse at the US–Mexico Border," *Demography*, 29: 159–180.

Kurtenbach, E. (2000) "Taking a Hard Line", ABCNews.go.com. Online. Available HTTP: http://abcnews.go.com/sections/world/DailyNews/china000217.html (5 April 2000).

Lianos, T.P., A. Sarris and L.T. Katseli (1996) "The Impact of Illegal Immigration on the Local Labor Markets: The Case of Northern Greece," *International Migration*, 34: 449–484.

Litke, M. (2000) "Striking a Deal with the Devil," ABCNews.go.com. Online. Available HTTP: http://abcnews.go.com/onair/WorldNewsTonight/wnt_000207_smugglers_feature.html (5 April 2000).

Migration News (2000a) "INS: Sanctions, Border," vol. 7, no. 4 (April). Online. Available HTTP: http://migration.ucdavis.edu/archive/april_2000–04.html (24 May 2000).

Migration News (2000b) "Malaysia: More Migrants," vol. 7, no. 4 (April). Online. Available HTTP: http://migration.ucdavis.edu/archive/april_2000–17.html (24 May 2000).

North, D.S. and M.F. Houstoun (1976) "The Characteristics and Role of Illegal Aliens in the US Labor Market: An Exploratory Study", Washington, D.C.: US Department of Labor.

OECD (1999) *Trends in International Migration*, Paris: OECD.

Papademetriou, D. (1991a) *Employer Sanctions and the US Labor Market: First Report*, Washington, D.C.: US Department of Labor.

Papademetriou, D. (1991b) *Employer Sanctions and the US Labor Market: Second Report*, Washington, D.C.: US Department of Labor.

Rivera-Batiz, F.L. (1999) "Undocumented Workers in the Labor Market: An Analysis of Earnings of Legal and Illegal Mexican Immigrants in the United States," *Journal of Population Economics*, 12: 91–116.

Rivera-Batiz, F.L. (2000) "Underground on American Soil: Undocumented Workers and US Immigration Policy," *Journal of International Affairs*, 53: 25–37.

Ruppe, D. (2000) "False Identities," ABCNews.go.com. Online. Available HTTP: http://more.abcnews.go.com/sections/world/dailynews/passportfraud000105.html (5 April 2000).

Sarris, A. and S. Zorgrafakis (1999) "A Computable General Equilibrium Model of the Impact of Illegal Immigration on the Greek Economy," *Journal of Population Economics*, 12: 155–182.

Simon, J. (1989) *The Economic Consequences of Immigration*, Basil Blackwell: Oxford.

Tapinos, G. (1999) "Clandestine Immigration: Economic and Political Issues," in OECD, *Trends in International Migration*, OECD: Paris.

Warren, R. and J.S. Passel (1987) "A Count of the Uncountable: Estimates of the Undocumented Aliens in the 1980 United States Census," *Demography*, 24: 375–93.

Weinert, P. (1991) "Foreign Female Domestic Workers: Help Wanted," Working Paper No. 50, International Labor Office: Geneva.

Weintraub, S. and G. Cardenas (1984) "The Use of Public Services by Undocumented Aliens in Texas," Public Research Project Report, Lyndon Johnson School of Public Affairs, University of Texas: Austin.

8 The decision to legalize by Bulgarian illegal immigrants in Greece

Alexander Sarris and Evgenia Markova[1]

Introduction and background

From the early 1900s until the late 1970s Greece had been a labor exporting country. After 1980 Greece became a labor importing country, and since 1990 immigration inflows have been very large. Illegal immigration into Greece has been a relatively recent phenomenon, which started in the 1980s and increased considerably in the 1990s, after the collapse of communist regimes in Central and Eastern Europe. Estimates vary, but they suggest that in the mid-1990s the number of illegal aliens residing in Greece was about 400,000, or near 4 percent of the Greek population (Lianos et al., 1996).

The response of the Greek government to this new phenomenon was as follows. In 1991 it passed an Immigration Law (L1975/1991) which included a series of provisions dealing with the legal stay of aliens, family reunification and work permits (Petrinioti, 1994). It also included rules on aliens' obligations, and permitted administrative deportations. It put severe limits on the extension of public services to illegal immigrants and also regulated the legal status of refugees. The policy to combat illegal immigration incorporated into this law was based on the penal treatment of illegal foreigners, but not their employers, and included increased policing of border areas and deportations.

In the face of widespread employment of illegal aliens throughout the economy and especially in the rural sector and in domestic services, policy shifted in recent years towards legalization of illegal foreigners and the signing of specific agreements with neighboring countries regarding temporary visas and permits.

Two Presidential Decrees (358/1997 and 359/1997) that granted "amnesty" to illegal immigrants were published in the government gazette in November 1997, following years of consultations, false starts and protests by local labor unions. The Decrees foresaw two phases of legalization. The first phase involved registration, and it started on January 2, 1998 and ended on May 31, 1998. Illegal immigrants who had registered during this five-month period and submitted the necessary certificates were issued the Alien's Temporary Residence Card, the so-called white card. The white card expired on April 30, 1999, by which time those migrants who managed to provide all the papers stipulated by the law were eligible to obtain the so-called green card that entitled them to a more permanent stay. The requirements included the acquisition by white cardholders, by April 30, 1999, of social security stamps corresponding to at least 40 workdays, at the equivalent of an unskilled laborer's wage.

Most green cards are valid for a one- to three-year period. The duration depends on the kind of work migrants are engaged in, the duration of stay and work in Greece, the state of the labor market and the general interests of the Greek economy. It may be renewed for another two-year period depending on the conditions named above. Illegal immigrants who met all the requirements for a green card, and could also prove that they have been living in Greece for at least five years and have the means to cover their living expenses, may get a five-year permit. These "old" migrants may apply to have their immediate families join them in Greece or to prevent their deportation.

About 370,000 formerly illegal immigrants registered in the first phase of the amnesty program. Of those, 64.9 percent were Albanian, 6.5 percent Bulgarian, and 4.5 percent Romanian, followed by Pakistanis, Ukranians, Poles, Georgians, and Indians, each constituting between 2 and 3 percent of those registering, and about 10 percent for all other nationalities. The majority of those registering (49.2 percent) have completed high school, while 37.1 percent have completed secondary school, and 8.9 percent hold university degrees.

The interesting observation is that despite the minimal requirements involved in the registration and amnesty program, there was a significant number of illegal aliens who did not register. While their exact number is not known, the survey reported later suggests that its magnitude is large. This raises the issue of why some illegal immigrants chose to stay illegal while others chose to legalize. The purpose of the present study is to explore this issue, by examining the factors that affected Bulgarian illegal immigrants' decision to take part or not in the amnesty program of the Greek government initiated on January 2, 1998.

The plan of the chapter is as follows. First a brief review of related literature is given. Subsequently we outline the essentials of a model of the decision to register in the legalization program. Then the survey utilized to obtain the data for the study is described, and a profile of those interviewed is presented. Subsequently the empirical model is outlined, and results from the empirical estimates are given. The final section summarizes the conclusions.

Relevant previous literature

There has been considerable previous research into the economics of international labor migration (for useful reviews see Borjas, 1994; Stark

1991; Straubhaar, 1988; and van den Broeck, 1996), but almost all of it concerned legal immigration. Research into illegal immigration is much more limited and recent (for a recent compendium devoted solely to illegal immigration, including references to earlier literature, see the articles in the special issue of the *Journal of Population Economics*, 12, 1, 1999). Even then most of the research into illegal immigration has been of a theoretical nature due to the understandable lack of appropriate data. There appears, however, to be no previous theoretical or empirical literature dealing with the decision of illegal immigrants to legalize. Hence the discussion below concerns literature that is related to this issue.

Neoclassical microeconomic migration theory, originating largely in Todaro's pioneering article (Todaro, 1969), focuses on individuals as rational actors who make their migration decisions based upon cost-benefit calculations that indicate a positive net return from the action. According to this approach, the individual would decide to legalize based on individual expected utility maximization. An illegal foreigner will approach the registration offices when his expected benefits exceed the perceived costs involved. One would expect that an illegal foreigner would register to minimize risks of being caught by the authorities, penalized and expelled from the country, thus securing a longer and safer stay. In addition, by registering, the illegal immigrant could assure social security coverage for him and his family (in case of a family migration). He is willing to legalize to attain access to public services (education etc.), to widen his prospects of climbing up a higher step on the professional ladder, and to improve his social status.

The above approach assumes that the individual illegal immigrant acts rationally. According to Ghosh (1996), however, it is only opportunity-seeking migrants that can act rationally. For them, the move is more a matter of choice than of compulsion. They tend to be more sensitive to the economic opportunities. We would expect them, when illegal in the host country, to be more flexible towards legalization opportunities. On the other hand, there are also the so-called survival migrants. For them, the search for basic economic security becomes a decisive factor in shaping their migration decisions. As they leave the home country under compulsion, it is certain that they would not normally possess valid residence and work permits. They would often hold irregular jobs in the underground economy of the receiving country. They normally operate at the periphery of the organized sector, making it difficult to reach the migrants effectively through the regular labor market mechanisms and measures. Survival migrants are the major target group of government amnesty programs.

The new economics of migration emphasizes family strategies to diversify sources of income, minimize risks to the household, and overcome barriers to credit and other market imperfections and constraints. The migrant is not necessarily the major decision-making entity responsible for his/her migration (Stark, 1991). Possible legalization of the stay and work of a family member can significantly reduce the costs and increase the returns to migration. For example, one important component of the direct returns to the non-migrating family from the migration of a family member is his/her remittances. Thus, amnesty might safeguard legal channels for remitting. Moreover, legalization maybe part of the overall family strategy to minimize risk. The decision to register can thus be a family decision and the attitude toward legalization part of family strategy.

The network theory is an efficient and necessary supplement to the new economics of migration. Assistance from prior emigrants in the host country is important to explain patterns of international migration. This implies that migrant networks may play a significant role in reducing the costs of the regularization process. In earlier research, the networks are assumed to operate on the base of primary kinship ties but the relationship can be widened to include all friendship patterns that exist in the communities of the sending country (MacDonald and MacDonald, 1964; King 1996). Government policies of the host country often facilitate the development of such networks, thus providing better management of the amnesty program.

Institutional theory could be very helpful in explaining the whole organization and management of the regularization program. The theory points to the fact that in the presence of international migration, there are a variety of legal and illegal entities that provide transport, housing and other services, which are often difficult for governments to register and regulate (Russel, 1997). Such institutions could facilitate migrants' participation in the amnesty program by offering legal and other services, as, for example, the filling of the application forms. It might be expected that once legalized, the foreigners would minimize their use of services provided by illegal institutions.

Dual labor market theory could also be reinterpreted to suggest the critical factors shaping migrants' decision whether to take part in the regularization process. Under the traditional dual market approach, employers seek for low-wage migrant workers, documented as well as undocumented, in an effort to control their labor costs. Straubhaar (1988) suggests that the existence of employers willing to employ illegal immigrants forms the demand side in the destination country and can be specified as a necessary and sufficient condition for migration to take place. Things radically change when it comes to the adaptation of dual labor market theory to explain illegal migrants' decision to register. Regularization *per se* intends to give migrants equal rights and obligations with the natives. According to the theory, the legalization of foreigners is supply-determined. The opportunity to legalize (to obtain the so-called green card) depends on the supply of employers willing to declare their employees and cover their social insurance obligations. The existence of such employers could be specified as a necessary and sufficient condition, the other documents having been submitted, for the successful completion of a migrant's regularization procedure.

A model of the illegal immigrant's decision to legalize

All the theories of migration reviewed above deal with different specific aspects of the migration decision, and offer interesting insights although not designed to deal with the problem at hand. Given that the issue of legalization concerns the decision by individual immigrants, who, nevertheless, operate among a particular socioeconomic environment and family background, it appears that ideas of the new economics of migration, which emphasize family decisions, risk, asymmetric information, etc., are an appropriate framework within which to think about the legalization decision.

The decision of immigrants to legalize can be thought of as part of an overall cycle of emigration, remittances, possible regularization and eventual repatriation. The Greek immigrant legalization program aims at regulating the short-term work-related residence of previously illegal foreigners, and does not aim at their eventual integration into Greek society and permanent residence. In this way it is different in concept from, for instance, the US legalization programs that basically aim at permanent residence and eventual integration of the immigrants. The decision to legalize by an illegal immigrant is markedly different in the American context, as in that case there basically is no cost to not legalizing. This would imply that on theoretical grounds there is no incentive or reason for an illegal immigrant into the US to stay illegal, given a chance to legalize. It is perhaps for this reason that the decision to legalize by illegal immigrants has not been much of a concern among policy and research circles in the US. It is taken for granted in that context that illegals would prefer to become permanent residents.

The fact that the law of legalization in Greece foresees a given fixed period of legality, implies that issues and timing of repatriation may be significant determinants of the decision to legalize. In other words, one would expect that the decision of an immigrant to legalize would depend on how close to the intended repatriation time the immigrant is.

Consider the decision of a potential immigrant to enter a country of destination (legally or illegally) for the purpose of illegally working there. This decision has been analyzed considerably in the context of the new economics of immigration. Factors that enter this decision would include push variables, such as family composition and dependency ratio, absolute and relative family income, the number of previously emigrated family members, the family asset position in the source country, the immigrant's working conditions in the source country, the costs of immigration, the initial level of his assets, etc. It would also include pull variables such as income differentials between the source and destination country, the existence of migrant networks in the destination country, the level of transactions cost for finding a job at destination, the distance to the country of destination, the degree of border controls and enforcement, etc.

The anticipation or probability of legalization would tend to affect the decision to emigrate. Hence if the legalization program were anticipated, this would tend to be interrelated with the other overall variables that shape an immigrant's decision to immigrate. On the other hand, if legalization was not anticipated, then the decision to legalize may not be related to variables that affect the decision to migrate.

The amnesty law and the form of the subsequent legalization program in Greece, albeit debated considerably within government and other interested circles, such as unions and employers, was not widely anticipated. Nevertheless, there was a considerable period during which immigrant legalization was publicly debated, and this suggests that some degree of anticipation could be justified. Hence it may be hypothesized that in some way the decision of immigrants to come to Greece, especially those that entered not long before the implementation of the amnesty program, may have been interrelated with the decision to legalize.

Consider an illegal immigrant who is already in the destination country and is working illegally, or is looking for employment. What is the major incentive that he has for registering in an amnesty program? It seems that the major incentive is to lower the risk of getting apprehended and sent back. In Greece, as in other countries, the rate of apprehension and repatriation of illegal aliens is not constant, and varies with economic conditions, the degree of protest by domestic unions and other interests, the changes in the political climate with neighboring countries, the budget for enforcement, etc. In summary, for an illegal alien there is a substantial non-zero probability of getting apprehended and sent back. This forced repatriation entails substantial cost, as the illegal has to pay for his/her ticket back to the source country.

If it is accepted that the major incentive to legalize is related to the risk of apprehension, and deportation, then what are the variables that depend on that risk? It seems that the main variable that depends on the risk of deportation is the amount of time that an immigrant can stay and work in the destination country. In fact it can be easily shown that if the risk of deportation in a given period t is constant and equal to p, then the expected time of stay in the destination country is equal to $1/p$.[2] Hence the lower the risk of deportation, the higher the expected length of stay.

The length of time an immigrant wishes to stay and work in a given destination country in turn depends on the overall optimization problem he or his family implicitly solve before coming to the destination country. Such a problem in turn depends on the family situation of the immigrant, and the particular incentives that lead him/her to migrate. For instance if the main objective of the immigrant is survival of his family, then it may be hypothesized that the desired length of time to spend in the destination country is large, and hence this type of immigrant would have a grater tendency to legalize. The variables that would determine in turn whether the immigrant is a survival type of immigrant are family characteristics and income/asset variables.

On the other hand, if the main objective of the immigrant is economic, such as to accumulate a given amount of money with which to start a small business in the source country, then his objective would be a rather fixed length of time to stay in the destination country, and he would plan to return back. In that case the closer to the intended departure time the legalization process would be, the lower the incentive to legalize.

The above hypotheses are reinforced by consideration of the cost of legalization for the prospective legalized immigrant. First, one must consider the direct cost of legalization, in terms of paying somebody (a lawyer or someone that speaks the language) to help with the various papers involved, and in terms of the travel costs to the appropriate office. Then one must consider the likelihood of lowering his/her wage when legalized. The reason that this involves a non-zero probability is that legalization implies according to the law that someone must pay for the social security contributions of the formerly illegal alien, when working. However, as was found by Lianos et al. (1996), the basic productivity adjusted difference in the wages (namely the total cost to the employer) between legal and illegal immigrants in Greece is the cost of social security contributions. Hence an employer, when faced with the requirement to pay social security contributions for the formerly illegal aliens, may opt either not to do so, and force the immigrant to pay them, or opt to fire the immigrant and hire an already legal or native worker instead. Thus, besides the direct cost that may lower the immigrant's wage, there is also a non-zero probability of losing one's job if working, or diminishing the likelihood of finding a job if not working. It is not clear what factors affect these probabilities, but they may be related to the type of job an illegal immigrant is doing.

Empirically the decision to legalize can be modeled as a binary choice variable y_i ($y_i=1$ if the i'th immigrant chooses to legalize and 0 otherwise). The value of this choice variable will in turn be determined by an underlying response variable y_i^*, where:

$$y_i^*=x_i\beta+u_i \tag{1}$$

And x_i is a row vector of variables for the i'th immigrant, β is a vector of contants and u_i is an error term.

The binary variable will be defined as follows

$$\begin{aligned} &y=1 \textit{ if } y_i^*>0 \text{ (the eligible foreigner will choose to legalize)}\\ &y=0 \text{ otherwise (the eligible foreigner will choose not to legalize)} \end{aligned} \tag{2}$$

Thus, from (1) and (2), the probability that a migrant i will choose to legalize is given by:

$$P(y_i=1)=P(u_i>-\beta' x_i)=1-F(-\beta' x_i) \tag{3}$$

where F( ) is the cumulative distribution function of u_i.

The data and a profile of the Bulgarian immigrants

The empirical analysis in this study is based on data obtained in a survey conducted among Bulgarian immigrants, mainly in the Athens area but a small part of it in the village of Moires, on the island of Crete. Some 153 Bulgarian immigrants were questioned in detail about their migration history, their current living and working conditions, and their participation in the legalization process.

A major statistical issue concerning a survey of this type involves the representative nature of the sample. It has been always difficult to give reliable estimates of the number of Bulgarian immigrants illegally residing and working in Greece. According to a survey conducted by the Greek Labor Observatory (quoted in the newspaper *Ependitis*, on April 17 and 18, 1999) 23,027 Bulgarian immigrants applied for the white/green card during the period January–May 1998. When they first went to register, migrants gave some information concerning residence address and other characteristics that could have theoretically allowed the design of a proper random sample. However, such a sample would not include those that did not register. Furthermore, in many cases the address information was wrong, due to migrant fears of getting caught. Thirdly, when it comes to talking to illegal migrants or migrants in an uncertain situation as the ones being half-legalized (with the certificate type I, namely the white card), the information obtained may not be reliable. For the reasons stated above, the method employed in this survey was to locate the major concentrations of Bulgarian migrants, and then to interview among those identified a number that, in our judgement, was thought to be representative.

The idea was to build some trust between the interviewer and the interviewed person, so as to increase the reliability of information. This was attempted by the fact the interviewer was a native Bulgarian (namely Markova, one of the two authors), and also by the fact that repeated visits were done in order to build some trust, and several immigrants were approached through their acquaintances. Clearly this procedure cannot guarantee to produce a scientifically random sample. However, the experience gained in the process suggests that the sample is reasonably representative of the Bulgarian immigrants in Greece and of those illegal Bulgarians that took part in the amnesty program. The characteristics of the interviewed Bulgarians were not much different in aggregate from those obtained in an earlier similar survey (Markova and Sarris, 1997), despite the fact that there was only 6 percent overlap between the new and the old samples. The final sample consists of 153 Bulgarians over age 19 who had worked in Greece for at least two weeks during their most recent stay. The interviews were conducted in the period March–May 1999.

Some 63 percent of all registered Bulgarian immigrants in the sample first learned about the amnesty program from other Bulgarians living in Greece, such as friends and relatives, a fact that proves the role of migrant networks in the migration process generally and in the regularization process in particular. Some 23 percent of the registered migrants pointed out the Greek mass media as their first source of information about the amnesty program while 11 percent learned about it through their Greek friends and employers.

Sixty-nine percent of the interviewed took part in the amnesty program of the government during January–May 1998 and 15 percent of them failed subsequently to submit all the paperwork necessary for receiving the green card. This means that those people benefited from the legal status for around 16 months and after 31 April 1999 became illegal again. Five of the interviewed did not register because of legal residence in the country at the time of the registration period. Forty-two of the interviewed (28 percent of the sample) declared that they did not have the chance to register. As primary reason some stated their late entrance in Greece, after the registration deadline on May 31, 1998. Others were living outside Athens at the time of registration, where it was difficult for them to obtain reliable information concerning legalization. A small fraction of the interviewed were obstructed by their employers from registering. Others preferred illegality because of fear of losing money or fear of been caught by the police when declaring address and passport information. They were usually people planning to return very soon to Bulgaria.

Of those among the sample that registered, 71 percent declared that their primary reason for doing so was to live and work in Greece without fear of expulsion. Another 15 percent stated as the main reason their desire to travel freely to Bulgaria. Other reasons accounted for the rest. About 48 percent of the registered migrants went to legalize during the first two months of the amnesty program, January and February 1998. Thirty-eight percent went in March or April 1999, and only a small fraction (15 percent) went in May 1999, the last month of the registration phase. Sixty-three percent of the interviewed Bulgarians that registered reported the positive attitude of their employers towards their decision to register. Twenty-two percent (23 people) of the registering migrants encountered serious objections from their employers, while 15 percent did not have an employer at the time of registering. Employment was not necessary for registration. More than half of the immigrants who encountered objections by their employers were forced to change job. Nine of those migrants changed job once, three changed job twice and one migrant had to change four employers in order to find one that would agree with his/her decision to register. Ten of the registering migrants who encountered employer objections did not change job, even though their employers were absolutely against their registration. Sixty percent of the registering immigrants went to register alone. Twenty-two percent went to register together with Bulgarian friends or relatives. Seven percent reported going to register accompanied by their immediate family and another 7 percent went with their employer.

Almost 20 percent of all interviewed registered Bulgarians confided having paid for obtaining one or more documents. Most of those paid for speeding up the issue of their certificate from the Ministry of Justice and almost all of them paid a lawyer an amount between 5,000 to 50,000 GrDr (the equivalent of 18 to 170 USD). Some reported having paid other intermediaries various amounts.

The payment of social insurance contributions is considered to be the main criterion for successful legalization. Of those obtaining the green card, 18 percent arranged with their employers to pay their social security contributions themselves. Another 3 percent shared the payment with their employers in the proportion stated by law, and the employers of 43 percent of the migrants paid the insurance. For the rest (28 percent) the solution was to pay themselves 15,000 GrDr (about 50 USD) at the Agricultural Bank of Greece for the insurance fund of those occupied in agriculture (OGA), although their occupation was not related to agriculture. These observations suggest, as discussed earlier, that the payment of social insurance is a major factor in the overall wage contract with an immigrant, and that many legalizing immigrants pay it themselves, in effect lowering their net wage.

About 60 percent of those interviewed (registered and non-registered) had completed high school, with the proportions similar among those registering and those not registering. Another 34 percent had partial or completed higher education. Among them there were economists, accountants, lab assistants, electricians, welders, etc., and almost all of them were previously occupied in the public sector in Bulgaria. The bulk of the interviewed (86 percent) was aged 19 to 49, and 42 percent were married, but their spouse accompanied few of them. The big cities (between 100,000 and 350,000 inhabitants) and medium-sized cities (with 50,000 to 99,000 inhabitants) of Northern Bulgaria had a dominant share in supplying migrants.

Fourteen migrants changed their job after legalization. Their new job usually differed in terms of higher pay and possession of social insurance. Ninety-one of the registered migrants did not change job because of their legalized status and more than half of them did not intend even to do so.

The majority of those who had already obtained the green card or the certificate for the card declared they just wanted to have a better quality of life for themselves and their families or to earn money to build houses for their children. Those with few years of stay in Greece put as their primary expectation to help their families to survive. Ninety percent of all Bulgarian immigrants interviewed would stay in Greece in the near future. Twenty-five percent of them believed they would stay illegally in the country.

Almost 80 percent of the interviewed immigrants would return to Bulgaria in the long term. The other 20 percent were not certain at the time of the interview; these were mainly members of young families with newborn babies that wanted to settle more permanently in Greece.

When asked what they would do upon their return to Bulgaria, most of the interviewed declared they would try to start their own business, usually joint with a Greek firm. Just a very small number answered that they would try to find a better-paid new job. There were some people who wanted to return to their old jobs. These were mainly high school teachers, although they had fears that in a few years there would not be enough children at school given the high rates of emigration of young people and the low birth rates. A considerable proportion of women would retire when back in Bulgaria. They plan simply to consume what was earned in Greece or go back to their villages and cultivate their land.

Empirical results

Given the information in the survey, we will attempt to explore whether the decision of the Bulgarian illegal immigrants in Greece to take part or not in the amnesty program of the government (January 1998–May 1998) can be explained by a set of migrants' attributes. The model described in equations (1)–(3) was estimated by binary logit and probit.[3]

The dependent variable is a binary variable that is equal to unity if the migrant went to register and zero if he decided not to do so. There are two major groups of explanatory variables introduced. The first concerns socio-demographic ones that comprise sex, education, the number and proportion of family members in Greece, and network variables. The second group includes labor market variables such as migrants' daily wages, type of job, time spent in Greece, and future intentions to leave Greece.

The first explanatory variable is gender, represented by the variable SEX, a dummy variable equal to one if the interviewed person is female and zero if male. Given the fact that the bulk of the interviewed were females, employed in households on a 24-hour live-in basis, one would expect very restricted contacts with the other migrants, hence not sufficient information about changes in the migration legislation. The expected sign of this variable is negative.

The variable for years of schooling completed, EDUCAT, reflects the transferability of education obtained at home and its effect on migrants' assimilation in the host society. Ghosh (1996) discusses the category of opportunity-seeking migrants that act rationally. More educated migrants could be considered as likely to not more rationally and to be more sensitive to economic opportunities, and therefore should be more sensitive to legalization as a unique opening for increased income and economic opportunities. Thus, we expect education to be positively related to an immigrant's decision to legalize.

A variable equal to the proportion of total family members (both in Bulgaria as well as in Greece) that reside in Greece, SHAREFGR, is constructed. If the legalization decision is part of a family decision involving also the family that remained in Bulgaria, then a variable related to this must be included. Its expected sign is positive.

Another variable designed to capture family relations is SHAREREMIT. It is equal to the share of immigrant income that is sent back to the family in Bulgaria. The larger this share, the tighter the relations with the family back home, and the more the risk from losing one's legal status and being expelled, hence the higher likelihood of legalization. The expected sign is positive.

The influence of a Bulgarian-friends network, FRIENDBG, is estimated to reflect whether immigrants have Bulgarian friends in Greece. It is a dummy variable that equals one if the interviewed keep regular relations with the other Bulgarians and zero otherwise. Migrant networks play a significant role in the information dissemination concerning migrants' legalization issues, and we expect this variable to be positively related to the decision to legalize, as networks would facilitate information sharing, and perhaps lessen the transaction cost of registering. Another related but different variable is NETWORJOB. This variable is defined to be equal to one if the immigrant found his/her last job in Greece through Bulgarian friends and zero otherwise. It is supposed to indicate the strength of Bulgarian networks and its sign is expected to be positive. A final variable designed to capture the flow of information about legalization is FRIENDGR. This dummy is equal to one if the immigrant has Greek friends and zero otherwise. As contacts with Greeks are supposed to facilitate information about legalization that is published mainly in Greek newsmedia, its expected sign is positive.

The second set of explanatory variables refers to migrants' participation in the host labor market and its effect on their decision to legalize. The variable for hourly earnings is introduced (DRH_HOUR). Since the mid-1960s, it has been increasingly common to analyze the migration decision as an investment decision. Migration is generated only when the present discounted value of the expected real benefits from migration exceed costs (Becker, 1962; Sjaastad, 1962; Cebula, 1979). Following the literature, we assume that the probability of legalization is positively associated with migrants' present income as well as the expected income increases from legalization. It is possible that this variable contains some measurement errors, given the fact that some migrants were paid on a basis different from an hourly rate, such as per day, week, or piece. For them, the hourly wage was computed using some additional information on hours worked per day, days worked per week, etc.

Higher migrant earnings are usually attributed to the comparative advantage of being illegal in certain sectors of a dual labor market. Such a hypothesis would suggest a possible negative sign of the coefficient. Another version also exists. It supports the idea that higher remunerated illegal migrants would be eager to legalize to secure future high income. Thus the expected sign of this variable is uncertain.

Another variable is constructed to capture the effect of the length of stay in Greece on irregular migrants' decisions to regularize their stay and work in Greece. The variable, TIMEGR, is measured as the period since the date of first entry in Greece minus the product of the number of times a migrant returned to Bulgaria and the average duration of stay there per return visit. The variable reflects also involuntary returns to Bulgaria, in case of illegality and expulsion. The length of time in Greece provides a measure of immigrants' assimilation in the host labor market and society. A larger value suggests better knowledge of the Greek language, access to networks and even closer relations with native workers. Its expected sign is positive, as more time in Greece is expected to lead to the higher probability of a desire to be assimilated through regularization. The variable TIMEGR2, the quadratic form of the duration of stay in Greece, is intended to capture the possible diminishing return of the length of stay in Greece, and is expected to have a negative sign.

A variable for years spent with the current employer, YCUREMPL, is introduced to reflect the effects of migrants' duration of stay at a job or with an employer on his/her decision to legalize. Employers play a decisive role in migrants' participation in the amnesty program. Their role could be informative–supportive. They could first inform their employed migrants about the legalization procedures and then assist them when applying. The expected sign is thus positive. A variable denoted EMPLATT is designed to reflect the attitude of the employer of the immigrant at the time of legalization. It is equal to one if the employer was positively inclined toward legalization, and zero otherwise or if the immigrant had no employment. The expected sign in the regression is positive.

The type of job a migrant was doing at the time of the interview – skilled or unskilled – is included as an explanatory variable. It is denoted by TYPEJOB, a dummy variable that equals one if the migrant was working at the time of legalization as an electrician, a banker, a chemist, a carpenter, a welder, a plumper, or a tailor and zero otherwise. Its expected sign is positive, for the same reasons as explained above for the education variable.

Migrants' intentions to stay in Greece in the short run are captured by the variable PLANSTAYG. It is expected that this variable is closely related to migrants' decisions regarding legalization. The variable is a dummy that equals one if the migrant was planning to stay in Greece in the near future, and zero if otherwise. As we have hypothesized that migrants' intentions to register are negatively related to their intentions to leave Greece in the short run, the expected sign of this variable is positive.

The variable EMPLORNOT is a dummy that is equal to one if the immigrant was employed at the time of legalization and zero otherwise. It is hypothesized that employment would give the immigrant a positive incentive to legalize and hence the expected sign is positive.

The existence of compensating wage differentials in the labor market, together with differences in working conditions and work-time schemes, implies that various occupations may offer illegal migrants different incentives for legalization other things being equal. Therefore, we introduce a set of occupational dummy variables. These are: CONSTR, equal to one if the migrant was employed in construction and zero otherwise; HOUSEWORK, equal to one if the interviewed person was employed in elderly care/baby-sitting and/or housework and zero otherwise; MANUF, equal to one if the migrant was employed in manufacturing and zero otherwise. The excluded occupations are services and agriculture. There is no *a priori* expectation concerning the signs of these dummies.

In the estimations data from 119 questionnaires were utilized from the 153 collected. The reason was that 5 of the interviewed immigrants were either students or married legally to a Greek, and hence were not subject to the legalization law. Another 25 immigrants had entered Greece after the end of the registration period, namely May 1998, and hence the analysis described earlier does not apply to them. Finally there were 4 immigrants who left Greece at the end of December 1997, namely before the start of the registration period, and returned to Greece after the end of May 1998, namely after the deadline for the initial registration. Whether they did so because of ignorance of the law or for other reasons is not known, but we cannot treat them on an equal basis to the ones that were in Greece during the period of registration. Of the remaining 119 immigrants, 84 chose to register, and 35 chose not to.

Tables 8.1 and 8.2 exhibit the results of binary logit and probit regressions respectively of the decision to legalize with the above variables. The results

Table 8.1 Bulgarian immigrants' choice for legality – maximum likelihood binary logit estimation results

Variable	*Expected sign*	*Estimated coefficient*	*z-statistic*	*Significance level*
CONSTANT	?	−11.156	−3.006	***
SEX	−	−0.808	−0.962	
EDUCAT	+	0.592	2.709	***
SHAREFGR	+	1.607	1.392	
SHAREREMIT	+	−0.00701	−0.616	
FRIENDBG	+	0.0408	0.0817	
NETWORJOB	+	−0.819	−1.007	
FRIENDGR	+	−0.823	−1.833	*
DRH_HOUR	?	0.00312	2.388	**
TIMEGR	+	−0.540	−0.704	
TIMEGR2	−	0.101	1.017	
YCUREMPL	+	0.223	0.828	
EMPLATT	+	0.966	1.340	
TYPEJOB	+	0.0701	0.0722	
PLANSTAYG	+	3.290	2.433	**
EMPLORNOT	+	2.030	2.351	**
CONSTR	?	0.105	0.105	
HOUSEWORK	?	1.503	1.484	
MANUF	?	1.443	0.983	
McFadden R^2		0.390		

Note: ***=statistically significant at 1% , **=statistically significant at 5%, *=statistically significant at 10% . The z-statistic is similar to the standard t-statistic and is the ratio of the coefficient estimate to its standard error.

Table 8.2 Bulgarian immigrants' choice for legality – maximum likelihood binary probit estimation results

Variable	*Expected sign*	*Estimated coefficient*	*z-statistic*	*Significance level*
CONSTANT	?	−6.911	−3.175	***
SEX	−	−0.497	−1.013	
EDUCAT	+	0.365	2.856	***
SHAREFGR	+	0.883	1.331	
SHAREREMIT	+	−0.00504	−0.767	
FRIENDBG	+	0.0105	0.0373	
NETWORJOB	+	−0.434	−0.957	
FRIENDGR	+	−0.471	−1.848	*
DRH_HOUR	?	0.00176	2.469	**
TIMEGR	+	−0.323	−0.708	
TIMEGR2	−	0.0606	1.044	
YCUREMPL	+	0.110	0.751	
EMPLATT	+	0.567	1.350	
TYPEJOB	+	−0.0328	−0.0620	
PLANSTAYG	+	1.946	2.519	**
EMPLORNOT	+	1.245	2.497	**
CONSTR	?	0.417	0.0749	
HOUSEWORK	?	0.869	1.473	
MANUF	?	0.956	1.124	
McFadden R^2		0.396		

Note: ***=statistically significant at 1% , **=statistically significant at 5%, *=statistically significant at 10% . The z-statistic is similar to the standard t-statistic and is the ratio of the coefficient estimate to its standard error.

are quite similar in the two regressions as far as significant coefficients and signs are concerned, and both of the regressions are significant, so it appears that the nature of the residuals in the regressions does not make much difference.

There are only five significant variables that seem to affect the decision to legalize. They include the years of education, the dummy variable that indicates friendship with Greeks, the level of wage the immigrant obtains in the Greek labor market, the variable indicating whether the immigrant plans to stay in Greece, and the variable indicating whether the immigrant was employed at the time of registration. All of these variables have the expected (positive) signs except the variable for friendship with Greeks, which is negative, and weakly significant. As recalled it was hypothesized that such a variable was a proxy for the degree of contacts of Bulgarian immigrants with Greeks and hence easier access to information. We cannot think of major reasons why contacts with Greek would bias negatively the decision of Bulgarians to legalize, and perhaps this variable is correlated with some other one that has been omitted.

The strong significance of education, the wage, the variable reflecting whether the immigrant plans to return to Bulgaria, and the variable reflecting whether the immigrant was employed at the time of registration suggest that the decision to legalize is more dictated by individual rational choice than by factors having to do with family decision making. This is also evidenced by the uniform lack of significance of variables related to family situation. Of interest also is the finding that all network-related variables seem to be not significant. Thus the results support a more individualistic and less household-based view of the attitudes of immigrants toward legalization.

Concluding remarks

Legalization of illegal immigrants is a policy that has been tried in several European countries and is contemplated by more. The results of this survey contribute towards our understanding of the factors that make illegal immigrants take part in a legalization program. The first interesting finding, of course, is that not all illegal immigrants are bound to legalize. The survey and empirical results revealed that apart from labor market variables and education, the key determinant of the decision to legalize is the expected period of stay in the host country. This finding is compatible with the notion that legalization is not without its costs for the illegal immigrants, and these costs must be balanced against the expected benefits.

From the survey it appears that a major issue also is the degree to which legalizing immigrants will be subject to social security payments. For some, the survey revealed that the expected benefits were so large that they agreed to pay the social security costs themselves. This, to some extent, also gives an indirect evidence about the costs of being illegal. If an illegal alien is willing to sacrifice about 20 percent of his wage (this is roughly the extent to which the reduced social security contributions for legalized immigrants amount to in Greece), this indicates a minimum lower bound for the value of legality.

The majority of the interviewed registered migrants pointed out as their primary reason for registering their human desire to work and live freely in the country, without fears of police and expulsion. As a second reason they ranked the opportunity to travel freely to Bulgaria every time they need to. These were migrants, usually young in age and educated, who considered legalization as a chance for climbing up the social ladder in the host country. This is compatible with the fact mentioned above that legalization entails a premium that immigrants are willing to pay for the change of status. It is also compatible with the survey finding that many legalizing immigrants were willing to pay a rather high transactions cost for legalization.

There were certain changes in migrants' lives after legalization. A great part of those interviewed did not report any changes in their status in the labor market. They remained doing the same job for the same employer and for the same reward. However, the social insurance coverage made the difference, especially the medical insurance. Legalization gave many migrants the chance to return home for the first time after many years of absence. Legalization gave migrants the chance to open bank accounts in Greek banks, thus reducing money transfers through informal channels or hiding money "under the pillow." This is another risk-reducing factor of legalization.

The majority of those who had already obtained the green card, or the certificate for it, declared that they wanted to save money for a better life in Bulgaria or for buying houses for their children. However, many migrants wanted only a better quality of life for them and their families in Greece. These are the ones that prefer to stay in Greece for extended periods.

About 80 percent of the interviewed would return to Bulgaria in the long term, but others were not certain at the time of the interview. They belonged mainly to young families, with children studying in Greece, who wanted to settle more permanently in the host country. In the former case legalization may by hypothesized to speed up repatriation, in the sense that it makes it easier and faster for formerly illegal immigrants to achieve their income objectives from immigration. On the other hand it may encourage others to emigrate, or those that stay for a long period to pressure openly for further extensions of their stay. Thus it not clear if legalization on the whole is helpful towards stemming the immigration flow or not. This, however, is a subject for further research.

Notes

1 Alexander Sarris is a professor and Eugenia Markova a Ph.D. candidate in the Department of Economics, University of Athens, Greece. This research was undertaken with support from the European Commission's Phare ACE program 1997.

2 To see this, note that the probability of an illegal immigrant surviving exactly t periods is equal to $(1-p)^{t-1}p$. Thus the expected length of stay s is equal to:

$$s = \sum_{t=0}^{\infty} t(1-p)^{t-1} p = \frac{1}{p}$$

3 The difference between logit and probit concerns whether the cumulative distribution of the error term in equation (1) is assumed to be logistic (logit) or normal (probit). As we do not know *a priori* which distribution is more appropriate, both were estimated.

References

Becker, G.S. (1962) "Investment in Human Capital: A Theoretical Analysis," *Journal of Political Economy*, Supplement 2, 70, (5): 9–49.

Borjas, G.J. (1994) "The Economics of Immigration," *Journal of Economic Literature*, 32(4): 1667–1717.

Cebula, R. (1979) *The Determinants of Human Migration*, Lexington: D.C. Heath.

Ghosh, B. (1996) "Economic Migration and the Sending Country." in Julien van den Broeck (ed.) *The Economics of Labour Migration*, Cheltenham and Brookfield: Edward Elgar.

Jahn, A. and T. Straubhaar (1995) "On the Political Economy of Illegal Immigration", paper presented at the CEPR workshop on "The Political Economy of Illegal Immigration", Halkidiki, Greece, September 14–16, 1995.

King, R. (1996) "Migration in a World Historical Perspective," in Julien van den Broeck (ed.), *The Economics of Labor Migration*, Cheltenham and Brookfield: Edward Elgar.

Lianos, T.P., A.H. Sarris and L. Katseli (1996) "Illegal Immigration and Local Labor Markets: The Case of Northern Greece," *International Migration*, 84 (3): 449–484.

MacDonald, J.S. and L.D. MacDonald (1964) "Chain Migration, Ethnic Neighborhood Formation and Social Networks," *Millbank Memorial Fund Quarterly*, 41(1): 82–97.

Markova, E. and A. Sarris (1997) "The Performance of Bulgarian Illegal Immigrants in the Greek Labor Market," *South European Society and Politics*, 2(2): 57–77.

Petrinioti, X. (1994) *Migration towards Greece*, Athens: Odysseas.

Russel, S.S. (1997) "International Migrations: Implications for the World Bank." HRO Working Paper 54, Washington, D.C.: World Bank.

Sjaastad, L.A. (1962) "The Costs and Returns of Human Migration," *Journal of Political Economy*, 70, Supplement 10: 80–93.

Stark, O. (1991) *The Migration of Labour*, Massachusetts: Blackwell Publishers.

Straubhaar, T. (1988) *On the Economics of Labor Migration*, Stuttgatt: Haupt.

Todaro, M. (1969) "A Model of Labor Migration and Urban Unemployment in Less Developed Countries," *American Economic Review*, 59(1): 138–148.

Wood, C.W. (1981) "Structural Changes and Household Strategies: A Conceptual Framework for the Study of Rural Migration," *Human Organization*, 40(4): 338–343.

Van den Broeck (ed.) (1996) *The Economics of Labour Migration*, Cheltenham and Brookfield: Edward Elgar.

9 Illegal immigrants in the US economy

A comparative analysis of Mexican and non-Mexican undocumented workers

Francisco L. Rivera-Batiz

Introduction

The prevailing image of undocumented workers in the United States is that of a population with low levels of educational attainment, employed in sectors supplying low-skilled jobs. This stereotypical view is reinforced by the frequent images portrayed in the press of the millions of unskilled Mexican immigrants who illegally cross the border into the US every year. It is a perception that is shared by most migration scholars. For example, in an analysis of a sample of illegal immigrants in Chicago, Illinois, Chiswick (1988: 143) concludes that "most illegal aliens have low levels of schooling." Similarly, a recent report from the National Research Council (1997: 7) observes that, compared to legal immigrants, "illegal immigrants ... are generally more poorly educated." And in a recent book, Borjas refers to the employers of illegal immigrants in the US as "large agricultural enterprises, sweatshops, and native households that hire illegal aliens as maids or nannies" (Borjas, 1999b: 206). This is a common perception, as reflected in the following statement by Ray Borane, the mayor of Douglas, Arizona, in a bitter *New York Times* editorial condemning the employers of undocumented workers: "Do you have any idea what havoc you cause in our area and in other border towns, all because some of you hire illegal immigrants to make your beds, mow your lawns and cook your meals?"[1]

Since most undocumented workers remain in the US economy largely undetected, existing profiles of illegal immigrants emerge mostly from the accounts of journalists or from particular case studies (with small samples) carried out by social scientists. The study by Chiswick, for example, consisted of a sample of 292 illegal immigrants, most of them from Mexico. And the studies upon which the National Research Council based its earlier statement about illegal immigrants were predominantly of Mexican migrants.[2] The comments by Mayor Borane, like most surfacing in the press, are based on immigrants close to the US–Mexico border. The fact is that the views currently displayed in public discussions of illegal immigration are subject to the limited data utilized to describe this population.

This chapter provides an analysis of the labor market performance of illegal immigrants in the United States through the use of a national sample of undocumented workers surveyed by the US Department of Labor in 1989. The survey, released for public use in 1996, is the Legalized Population Survey (LPS), which includes a random sample of 6,193 illegal immigrants who were residing in the US in 1987/88 when they sought legal permanent residence through the Immigration Reform and Control Act of 1986 (IRCA). This Act had as one of its major components an illegal immigrant amnesty program, through which illegals meeting certain requirements were able to obtain lawful permanent resident status.[3] The sample of undocumented workers in the LPS was interviewed in 1987 and 1988, before they became legal permanent residents. Detailed information was collected from them relating to their labor market and general socioeconomic experience in the US at the time that they applied for legalization. The LPS data provide the most extensive information available yet on the experiences of illegal immigrants in the United States.[4]

Despite the widespread perception of illegal immigrants as predominantly unskilled persons with low levels of schooling, our analysis of the LPS data provides a sharply different picture. Because close to half of all the undocumented in the US come from Mexico, one must make a differentiation in the analysis between Mexican and non-Mexican illegals. This has a major impact, as the characteristics of the Mexican immigrants, who have been frequently studied in the previous literature, are quite different from those of the rest of the illegal immigrant population. The chapter shows that the central image of the illegal immigrant in the US, presented on television and newspapers as well as in academic journals, as an unskilled, low-income worker surreptitiously crossing the Rio Grande is misleading and ignores the great diversity present in this population.

First of all, the chapter provides an overview of illegal immigration in the United States, including a comparison of the characteristics of visa overstayers and illegal border crossers, as determined from the LPS, and a comparison of undocumented workers with the overall immigrant population, as determined from Census data. It then proceeds to compare the socioeconomic status and labor market situation of Mexican and non-Mexican illegal immigrants. Next it focuses on the factors determining differences in earnings between Mexican and non-Mexican undocumented workers, presenting the empirical human capital model utilized to analyze the role of education, age, location, and an array of other factors in explaining wages. The results of the empirical earnings functions are then presented, and there is a discussion of the differences in the estimated labor market rates of return to various individual characteristics among Mexican and non-Mexican illegal immigrants. The final section summarizes the conclusions of the chapter.

Illegal immigration in the United States

The illegal immigrant population residing in the United States has been gradually rising over the last 15 years. Since by definition this population cannot be officially counted, one must rely on indirect methods to estimate its size. The most reliable estimates of undocumented workers in the US have been obtained using the so-called residual methodology. This technique calculates the number of illegal immigrants as the difference between the total number of immigrants who are counted in the US at any given time and the number of legal immigrants in the country. For instance, Warren and Passel (1987) found that there were 8.0 million immigrants counted in the 1980 US Census of Population while there were 5.9 million legal immigrants residing in the US at the time, as determined by Immigration and Naturalization Service (INS) data, leaving a residual of 2.1 million undocumented immigrants counted in the 1980 Census.

As Table 9.1 presents, studies using the residual methodology conclude that the number of undocumented immigrants in the US rose to a peak of 4.8 million in 1987, going down to 2.2 million in 1988 after the legalization component of the 1986 Immigration Reform and Control Act went into effect. Since that time, the number of illegal immigrants has gradually climbed again. The most recent estimates of the US Bureau of the Census place the number of undocumented immigrants at 3.7 million in 1994. Since the average net increase of the illegal population each year between 1988 and 1994 was 275,000, one can impute that the number of illegal immigrants in the year 1998 was about 4.7 million, about the same as it was in 1987.[5]

Among the population of illegal immigrants, the largest share comes from Mexico. Approximately one out of every two undocumented workers residing in the United States originates in Mexico. Table 9.2 presents the composition of illegal immigrants residing in the US by country of origin. In terms of

Table 9.1 Estimates of the illegal immigrant population in the US, 1980–1998

	Number of undocumented immigrants
1980	2,100,000
1986	3,200,000
1987	4,800,000
1988	2,200,000
1990	2,600,000
1992	3,400,000
1994	3,750,000
1998	4,700,000

Sources: Warren and Passel (1987), Woodrow and Passel (1990) and Fernandez and Robinson (1994). The 1998 estimate is an extrapolation of the growth for 1994–98 based on the 1988–94 average annual increase.

Table 9.2 Undocumented immigrants in the US, by country of origin, 1998

Country of origin	*Total number of undocumented immigrants*	*Percentage of total undocumented population*
Total, US	4,700,000	100.0
Mexico	2,538,000	54.0
El Salvador	315,000	6.7
Guatemala	155,000	3.3
Canada	113,000	2.4
Haiti	99,000	2.1
Philippines	89,000	1.9
Honduras	85,000	1.8
The Bahamas	66,000	1.4
Nicaragua	66,000	1.4
Poland	66,000	1.4
Colombia	61,000	1.3
Other	1,047,000	22.3

Source: The distribution of illegals is based on INS estimates for October 1996. The total number of illegals by country for 1998 is based on the 1996 distribution multiplied by the total number of illegals estimated for 1998.

population size, Mexican illegals are followed by migrants from El Salvador, Guatemala, Canada, Haiti, the Philippines, and Honduras.

What are the characteristics of undocumented workers in the US? Are the stereotypes mentioned in the introduction correct? The existing literature is not much help on this issue since it uses small samples consisting mostly of illegal immigrants who entered the country through the US–Mexico border. But according to Immigration and Naturalization Service (INS) statistics, the majority of undocumented workers have not entered the US unlawfully but instead have come in by legal means, with tourist, student or work visas that are later allowed to expire. The INS has estimated that slightly over half of the illegals residing in the US in 1994 had first entered the country legally. With legitimate visas on their hands, prospective illegals can simply walk through the inspection booths at US ports of entry. Once they overstay their visas, they blend quietly into American society, avoiding detection and any contacts with the INS.

The characteristics of visa overstayers appear to be quite different from those of illegal border crossers. For instance, the country of origin of illegal immigrants varies significantly according to the method used by the migrants to enter the US. As estimated by the INS, most migrants from Mexico have entered the country by crossing the border illegally. So do many from Central America (El Salvador and Guatemala). However, most illegals from Canada, Poland, the Philippines, Haiti, the Bahamas and Italy initially entered the country lawfully. In the case of Polish citizens, the INS estimates that, in 1994, only 1 percent had initially crossed the US border unlawfully.

The geographical distribution of illegal immigrants in the US also diverges by the method of entry into the country. Undocumented workers crossing the US–Mexico border stay mostly in the US southwest. By contrast, the majority of those who initially enter the country legally end up in the northeastern United States, mostly in New York or New Jersey. Table 9.3 displays INS estimates showing that the illegal immigrant population in New York and New Jersey is dominated by countries such as Ecuador, Ireland, Israel, Italy, Egypt, Pakistan, the Phillippines, Poland, Portugal and Yugoslavia. Most of these migrants first entered the country legally, with lawful visas, through the international airports at Newark in New Jersey and Kennedy in New York.

The limited existing profiles of visa overstayers tell us that the characteristics of these immigrants differ greatly from the traditional picture of the illegal immigrant. They appear to have superior educational attainment and to have achieved greater socioeconomic progress when compared to illegal border crossers. For instance, consider the case of Nuccio R., a 24-

Table 9.3 Illegal immigrants in New York and New Jersey, 1994

Country of origin	*Number of illegal immigrants*
A. New York	
Italy	31,000
Poland	27,000
Ecuador	27,000
Dominican Republic	24,000
Trinidad & Tobago	24,000
Colombia	22,000
Jamaica	21,000
El Salvador	20,000
Ireland	20,000
Israel	15,000
Pakistan	15,000
New York total	**529,000**
B. New Jersey	
Portugal	17,000
Poland	11,000
Italy	9,000
Colombia	9,000
Ecuador	7,000
Philippines	7,000
Haiti	6,000
El Salvador	6,000
Yugoslavia	4,000
Egypt	4,000
Mexico	4,000
New Jersey total	**137,000**

Source: The data is for 1994, from the Immigration and Naturalization Service.

year-old Italian immigrant who came to the US on a tourist visa but stayed after the visa expired. Interviewed by the *New York Times* after four years of illegal residence in the US, Nuccio, a high school graduate, had "a full-time job in a relative's delicatessen, a car, a driver's license, credit cards and his own apartment."[6]

This vision of visa overstayers as a population with sharply different characteristics from those who cross the border illegally is confirmed by the Legalized Population Survey (LPS). Because the LPS represents a national cross-section of illegal immigrants in the US, it includes overstayers as well as illegal border crossers. Based on the public use LPS sample, Table 9.4 presents data on the characteristics of illegal border crossers and visa overstayers in 1987–88 and compares them with those of the overall immigrant population as determined by the 1990 US Census of Population and Housing.

One can notice, first of all, that illegal border crossers are on average younger than visa overstayers and have a greater concentration of men. On both of these accounts, visa overstayers have a profile that is closer to the

Table 9.4 Characteristics of illegal border crossers, visa overstayers and all immigrants

	Illegal border crossers	*Visa overstayers*	*All immigrants in 1990 Census*
Sex (% male)	60.3%	51.9%	50.6%
Age (average, in years)	31.9	36.6	37.5
Recent migrant (% who moved to the US in the last ten years)	84.5%	80.0%	43.2%
Educational attainment (average years of schooling completed by persons aged 25 or older)	7.1	11.6	10.7
College attendance (% of persons 25 years of age or older who completed at least one year of college)	6.7%	41.0%	37.5%
Professional and technical occupations (% of all persons 16 years of age or older in these occupational categories)	8.3%	28.2%	34.6%
Family income (annual, 1989)	$18,808	$21,372	$42,241
Family income per person (family income divided by number of persons in the family)	$6,218	$9,054	$11,775
Residence in California (%)	54.5%	31.4%	12.9

Source: Legalized Population Survey and 1990 US Census of Population and Housing; authors' computations.

average immigrant residing in the US than to illegal border crossers. The same holds true for schooling. The average educational attainment of visa overstayers is much higher than that of illegal border crossers. According to the data in the LPS, the average years of schooling of adult visa overstayers in 1987–88 was 11.6, compared to 7.1 among illegal border crossers. In fact, the schooling of visa overstayers was closer to – and even exceeded – that of the overall immigrant population, which had an average of 10.7 years of schooling in 1990. Furthermore, 41 percent of all visa overstayers had received at least one year of college education, compared to only 6.7 percent among illegal border crossers. Again, this compares favorably with the overall immigrant population, 37.5 percent of whom had completed at least one year of college.

These differences in educational attainment are reflected in the diverse occupational distributions of the visa overstayers and illegal border crossers. For instance, although only 8.3 percent of illegal border crossers aged 16 years or older were holding professional and technical occupations in 1987–88, as many as 28.2 percent of the visa overstayers were in this category. The latter is very close to the corresponding proportion among the overall immigrant population, which was 34.6 percent in 1990.

Despite the similar demographic characteristics of visa overstayers and the overall immigrant population in the US, there are also major differences. Both visa overstayers and illegal border crossers have been residing in the US for a shorter period of time than immigrants in general. As Table 9.4 shows, close to 80 percent of both groups of illegal immigrants arrived in the US in the ten years previous to the LPS survey interview, compared to 43.2 percent among the overall immigrant population. There are also significant income gaps. In 1989, the annual family income per person (measured by annual family income divided by the number of persons in the family) of the overall immigrant population in the US was $11,775. The annual family income per person of visa overstayers (in 1989 dollars) was substantially lower, equal to $9,054. The latter, however, sharply exceeds the family income per worker prevailing among illegal border crossers, equal to $6,218 (in 1989 dollars).

This discussion suggests that the stereotypical perception of illegal immigrants in the US as unskilled Mexican workers dashing across the Rio Grande is a severely distorted one since it represents only a fraction of the overall illegal immigrant population in the country. The almost exclusive attention paid by both the press and the academic literature on Mexican illegal immigrants means that we know very little on non-Mexican illegal immigrants, who are estimated to constitute close to half of all undocumented workers residing in the US. Using data available from the LPS, the following section focuses on examining the comparative economic and labor market situation of Mexican and non-Mexican illegal immigrants in the US, showing the substantial differences that exist between these two groups of workers.

Mexican and non-Mexican illegal immigrants: a comparative profile

This section presents a comparative profile of the socioeconomic status of Mexican and non-Mexican illegal immigrants in the US. We start with a discussion of differences in basic demographic and socioeconomic variables, moving later to discuss labor market variables, including a breakdown of labor force participation rates, unemployment rates and wages. As noted before, the data are from the LPS study and represent the situation of illegal immigrants when they applied for legalization in 1987 or 1988. The distribution of the countries of origin of non-Mexican immigrants is the following: Central America, 48.6 percent; Asia and Pacific, 15.2 percent; South America, 13.5 percent; the Caribbean, 9.8 percent; Europe, 7.5 percent; and Africa and the Middle East, 5.4 percent.

Table 9.5 shows that both Mexican and non-Mexican illegal immigrants tend to have an over-representation of men in their midst. Among the Mexican contingent, 58.7 percent are men while among non-Mexicans the corresponding percentage is 56.6 percent. The Mexican illegals are younger than non-Mexicans, with the average age among Mexicans equal to 31.6 years and among non-Mexicans equal to 35 years. Both groups consist mostly of migrants who moved to the United States in the ten years prior to interview, with over 80 percent in this category for both groups. However, the method of entry into the country diverges considerably among Mexican and non-Mexican migrants. For Mexican illegals, 84.8 percent entered the country by crossing the border illegally, while for non-Mexicans only 53.2 percent entered through these means, the remainder crossing the border legally and later overstaying their visas.

The educational attainment of Mexican illegals is substantially lower than that of non-Mexican migrants. As Table 9.5 shows, the average years of schooling of Mexican illegal immigrants of 25 years of age or older was 6.3 years, compared to 10.4 years among the non-Mexican group. This

Table 9.5 Characteristics of Mexican and non-Mexican illegal immigrants

	Mexican immigrants	*Non-Mexican immigrants*
Sex (% male)	58.7%	56.6%
Age (average, in years)	31.6	35.0
Educational attainment (average years of schooling completed by persons aged 25 or older)	6.3	10.4
Family income per person (family income divided by number of persons in the family)	$5,662	$8,429

Source: Legalized Population Survey; authors' computations.

significant difference in schooling is also reflected in the proportion of persons 25 years of age or older who had completed more than 12 years of schooling (which, in the US, would correspond to having received some college education). For Mexican undocumented migrants, only 4.5 percent had completed more than 12 years of schooling, while for non-Mexican illegals, the corresponding proportion was 29.2 percent.

The divergence in educational attainment of the two groups of migrants is mirrored by the gap in family income. This is measured by annual family income in 1987 (expressed in 1989 dollars). To take into account the differences in the number of persons in a family existing in Mexican and non-Mexican groups, we compute per capita family income, obtained by dividing family income by the number of persons in the family. Table 9.5 shows that family income per person among non-Mexican illegals exceeds the one among Mexican illegals by close to 50 percent. The average per capita family income among Mexicans was $5,662, while for non-Mexicans it was $8,429.

Table 9.6 presents data on the major labor market indicators for Mexican and non-Mexican illegal immigrants. By definition, labor force participation rates represent the proportion of the economically active population that is either employed or actively seeking employment. The age group considered in our analysis ranges from 18 to 64 years of age, and the data are for 1987 and 1988, as obtained by the Legalized Population Survey. As can be seen in Table 9.6, the average labor force participation rate among men diverges very little between Mexican and non-Mexican immigrants. There are, however, significant differences among women. For Mexican women, illegal immigrants had a labor force participation rate of 62.4 percent, compared to 77.7 percent for the non-Mexican immigrant population.

The unemployment rates for both Mexican and non-Mexican illegal immigrants range between 3.2 and 4.1 percent depending on gender.

Table 9.6 Comparative labor market indicators: Mexican and non-Mexican illegal immigrants

	Mexican immigrants		*Non-Mexican immigrants*	
	Male	*Female*	*Male*	*Female*
Labor force participation rate	96.2%	62.4%	95.8%	77.8%
Unemployment rate	3.6%	4.1%	3.2%	3.3%
Weekly wage (1989 dollars)	$287.8	$191.9	$369.6	$234.8

Source: Legalized Population Survey.

Note: Data are for 1987 and 1988 (wages adjusted to 1989 dollars).

These figures lie substantially below the unemployment rates of the overall American labor force. The national unemployment rate in the US in 1987 was 6.2 percent, and in 1988 it was 5.5 percent. Although differences in demographic and human capital characteristics may help explain the lower unemployment rates of undocumented workers, the very nature of the illegal immigration decision means that these workers are willing to take jobs at wages and working conditions below those accepted by other workers. With lower reservation wages when compared to other workers in the US labor market, it is not surprising that their unemployment rate is lower.

Table 9.6 also presents the weekly wages earned by employed illegal immigrants. Gender patterns observed in the general working population are reproduced among immigrants. For example, male Mexican illegal immigrants earn close to 50 percent more than their female counterparts. And among the non-Mexican undocumented population, male workers earn 57.4 percent more than female workers. There are also substantial earnings differences between Mexican and non-Mexican illegal immigrants, with the latter receiving 37.8 percent higher wages among men and 22.4 percent higher wages among women.

What explains the differences in earnings between Mexican and non-Mexican illegal immigrants? Are the gaps in educational attainment specified earlier the major force or are other, yet unidentified factors more important? The next two sections explore in detail the variables behind the wage disparities.

The earnings of Mexican and non-Mexican illegal immigrants: the empirical model

The framework adopted here to examine wage determinants follows the standard empirical human capital literature in postulating that the natural logarithm of the wage rate of a worker i of sex j is given by:

$$\log W_{ij} = \beta' X_{ij} + U_{ij} \qquad (1)$$

where W_{ij} is the weekly wage rate received by the worker, β is a vector of coefficients to be estimated, X_{ij} is a vector of individual human capital, occupational and demographic characteristics affecting wages, and U_{ij} is a stochastic disturbance term.

The human capital variables in the vector X_{ij} include, first of all, years of schooling, represented by the variable EDUCAT. In addition, to reflect the skills acquired by the person through seniority and aging in the labor market, we include years of on-the-job experience, proxied by the variable EXPER (measured as age minus years of schooling completed minus six). The variable EXPERSQ, equal to the square of the years of on-the-job experience, is also introduced in the equation to reflect variable returns to experience. On the assumption of positive, but diminishing, returns to on-the-job experience, the variable EXPER would have a positive coefficient and EXPERSQ a negative coefficient in the earnings equation.

English language proficiency has been found to be a key human capital variable influencing the earnings of immigrants. Employment opportunities may be severely limited if the immigrant's knowledge of the English language is not sufficient. On the other hand, ethnic enclaves can allow broad leeway for immigrants to find jobs even if their English proficiency is absent. The measure of English proficiency utilized in this chapter is symbolized by the variable NOENGLISH, which is equal to one if the person does not know how to speak English at all, and zero otherwise. The existing research examining the role played by English language proficiency on labor market outcomes generally finds a positive impact of English proficiency on earnings (see, for example, Chiswick and Miller, 1996; Gonzalez, 2000; and Rivera-Batiz, 1990, 1996).

The presence of disequilibria in the labor market, as well as the existence of compensating wage differentials, implies that various occupations may be endowed with different wages, holding worker characteristics constant. As a result, our wage equations introduce a set of occupational dummy variables. These are: PROFTECH, equal to one if the person was employed in managerial, professional, technical, sales and administrative occupations, and zero otherwise; FARMING, equal to one if the immigrant was employed in agricultural occupations, and zero otherwise; OPERAT, if the worker was an operator, fabricator or laborer, and zero otherwise; and PRODUCT, if the person was in precision production, craft and repair occupations, and zero otherwise. The excluded, baseline, occupations are service occupations. Since the baseline service jobs generally offer comparatively lower wages in the American economy, we expect the occupational dummy variables to be positively associated with earnings, perhaps with the exception of FARMING.

Workers supply various amounts of hours per week on their jobs. Labor supply can influence earnings, not only because more hours worked per week (at a given hourly wage rate) will increase weekly earnings, but also because the hourly rate for overtime work may be higher than for the regular workday. To incorporate variable labor supply into our earnings analysis, we include a variable denoted by HOURS, equal to the number of hours per week that the person supplies in the labor market. It can be expected that, holding other things constant, increased hours of work per week will be associated with higher weekly wages.

Migratory and work decisions are influenced by family considerations. The necessities of a married couple may lead heads of households to a more intensive job search process, and higher earnings, when compared to single workers, especially if the family has children. In addition, if spouses and children are residing in source countries, married immigrants will have a stronger incentive to increase their employment search efforts, in order to increase the amount of remittances that they can send to their spouses waiting abroad. A dummy variable, SINGLE, is included in the analysis to reflect possible differences in earnings between single and married persons. The variable is equal to one if the person is single and zero otherwise.

The longer immigrants reside in a country, the higher their earnings. There are two explanations for this connection. Firstly, as postulated by Chiswick (1978) and Duleep and Regets (1999), immigrants make a wide range of investments over time after they arrive in a country. These investments may be in the form of increased schooling or on-the-job training, both of which would be proxied by variables already included in our analysis. However, immigrants also make other types of productive investments, such as developing employment networks that can assist them in finding employment opportunities, and acquiring greater information on local, host-country labor market institutions, which can improve job search efficiency and lead to higher-paying job offers. Alternatively, Borjas (1995, 1999a) has suggested that more recent immigrant cohorts in the US have lower "quality" than previous ones, thus also receiving inferior wages, holding everything else constant. The longer an immigrant has been in the US, the older the immigrant cohort with which he or she is associated, and the higher the earnings. To incorporate the impact of recency of immigration into the analysis, we define a dummy variable RECENT to be equal to one if the immigrant moved to the US within the ten years previous to interview, and zero otherwise. Note that, whether because of labor market assimilation or because of cohort effects, one expects the variable RECENT to have a negative impact on immigrant earnings.

Another explanatory variable utilized in the wage equations is geography, which is represented by the variable CALIF, a dummy variable equal to one if the migrant resided in California and zero otherwise. Since the largest share of both Mexican and non-Mexican immigrants locates in California, the agglomeration of these migrants can be expected to generate ethnic enclaves and networks that could exert a positive impact on earnings. In addition, the extent of the labor market for undocumented workers may be greater in California, as illegal immigrant employers seek to locate near their employees. On this basis, it can be expected that, holding other things constant, illegal immigrants will be more likely to find higher-paying employment opportunities in California than elsewhere. This may be particularly the case for Mexican illegal immigrants since California represents the prime location of both legal and illegal Mexican immigrants. Portes and Bach (1985) have explained the superior economic performance of the Mariel Cuban immigrants relative to that of Haitian immigrants in the 1980s as deriving from the employment opportunities available to the Cuban immigrants in the Cuban-American ethnic enclave of the Miami area. A similar case can be made regarding the employment of Mexican illegal immigrants in Mexican ethnic enclaves in California.

The discussion so far suggests that the wage equation to be estimated should be given by:

$$\log W_{ij}=\beta_0+\beta_1 EDUCAT_{ij}+\beta_2 EXPER_{ij}+\beta_3 EXPERSQ_{ij}+\beta_4 NOENGLISH_{ij} +\beta_5 PROFTC_{ij}+\beta_6 FARMING_{ij}+\beta_7 OPERAT_{ij}+\beta_8 PRODUCT_{ij} +\beta_9 HOURS_{ij}+\beta_{10} SINGLE_{ij}+\beta_{11} RECENT_{ij}+\beta_{12} CALIF_{ij}+U_{ij} \quad (2)$$

where all the variables are as defined above.

The earnings of Mexican and non-Mexican illegal immigrants: results

The empirical model discussed in the last section is applied here to examine the weekly wages of Mexican and non-Mexican illegal immigrants in the United States using the LPS data.[7] Individuals with no responses on the relevant questions used to determine individual characteristics (such as earnings, educational attainment, etc.) were eliminated from the analysis. In addition, following the custom in the literature, the sample was circumscribed to persons 18 to 64 years of age, the age group most likely to be fully-involved in the labor market. Only employed workers were considered. With these restrictions, the samples utilized in the wage equations estimated in this chapter include 2,171 Mexican and 2,569 non-Mexican immigrants.

The LPS sample provides information on the weekly wages of illegal immigrants in the week before they applied for legalization. Since the window for applications was from May 5, 1987 to May 4, 1988, the data available on wages for illegal immigrants corresponds to either 1987 or 1988. In order to convert them to a common denominator, both the 1987 and 1988 data were adjusted for inflation and expressed in 1989 dollars. It is these adjusted, real wages (expressed in 1989 dollars) that are discussed throughout the following analysis.

Table 9.7 presents the sample means for the variables introduced in the wage equations, by Mexican/non-Mexican origin (place of birth) and gender. The first row shows the average values for the dependent variable, the logarithm of the weekly wage. The average weekly wages for men are substantially higher than for women and this is reflected in the data presented in Table 9.7, for both Mexican and non-Mexican immigrants. At the same time, the wages of Mexican immigrants are significantly lower than those of non-Mexican immigrants. This gap holds for both men and women.

The lower earnings of Mexican illegals compared to non-Mexican workers may be the reflection of mean differences in the characteristics of the two groups. Table 9.7 documents some of these key differences. Mexican illegal immigrants have substantially lower levels of education than non-Mexican undocumented workers. The sample means for the variable EDUCAT show that the average years of schooling of male Mexican illegal immigrant workers in the LPS sample was 6.8 years, compared to 10.7 years among their non-Mexican counterparts. There is a similar educational gap among women. For female Mexican illegal immigrant workers, the mean years of schooling was 6.8 years, compared to 10.0 years among non-Mexicans.

Table 9.7 Sample means, Mexican and non-Mexican illegal immigrants

Variable	*Mexican*		*Non-Mexican*	
	Male	*Female*	*Male*	*Female*
Log weekly wage	5.569	5.138	5.730	5.323
EDUCAT (average years of schooling completed)	6.8	6.8	10.7	10.0
EXPER (years of experience)	18.7	19.1	17.7	19.5
EXPERSQ (experience squared)	466.0	486.3	411.9	490.6
ENGLISH (proportion who does not speak English)	0.463	0.561	0.233	0.345
PROFTC (proportion employed in professional, technical, sales and managerial occupations	0.069	0.126	0.242	0.263
FARMING (proportion employed in agricultural occupations)	0.125	0.037	0.022	0.004
OPERAT (proportion employed as operators, fabricators and laborers)	0.391	0.377	0.294	0.201
PRODUCT (percentage employed as precision production, craft and repair workers)	0.195	0.051	0.186	0.024
SERVICE (percentage employed in services)	0.220	0.409	0.254	0.508
HOURS (number of hours worked per week)	42.6	39.0	42.9	39.0
SINGLE (proportion never married)	0.313	0.318	0.355	0.320
RECENT (proportion who migrated to the US ten years or less before survey)	0.840	0.764	0.865	0.862
CALIF (proportion residing in state of)	0.612	0.656	0.380	0.457
Number of observations	1,494	677	1,569	1,000

Another major difference between Mexican and non-Mexican workers is their English language proficiency. Table 9.7 shows that the proportion of Mexicans who expressed that they could not speak English at all was 46.3 percent among men and 56.1 percent among women. By comparison, the equivalent percentages for non-Mexican workers was 23.3 percent for men and 34.5 percent for women.

The distribution of employment by sector also varies between Mexican and non-Mexican workers. The latter have a substantially greater proportion of employment in professional, technical, managerial and administrative occupations. Among men, 24.2 percent of non-Mexican illegals were employed in these occupations, compared to only 6.9 percent among Mexicans. For women, 26.3 percent of non-Mexican workers were employed in this sector, compared to 12.6 percent among Mexicans. On the other hand, Mexican undocumented workers are over-represented in agricultural occupations.

There are also some differences in the length of time that immigrants have been in the United States. Mexican illegal immigrants have resided in the US for a somewhat longer period of time than non-Mexicans. Among Mexican illegal immigrants, 84 percent of all men and 76.4 percent of all women arrived in the US during the decade before their interview in 1987 or 1988. But for the non-Mexican group, 86.5 percent of all men and 86.2 percent of all women declared that they had arrived in the US in the decade before their interview in 1987 and 1988. Note, however, that eligibility requirements under IRCA, including the need to present acceptable documentation of residence in the US, could influence survey respondents on this question.

The majority of Mexican immigrants in the data, over 60 percent, resided in California. Given the geographical proximity to Mexico, and the fact that the comparatively large Mexican ethnic enclave in Los Angeles and in other parts of California provides a comparative advantage for the employment of legal and illegal immigrants, it is not surprising that most Mexican immigrants locate in that state.

Table 9.7 shows that there are no major differences between Mexican and non-Mexican workers in terms of marital status or years of on-the-job experience. The average value of these variables is similar in the two groups of illegal immigrants.

Tables 9.8 and 9.9 present the key results of our empirical analysis. Table 9.8 shows the coefficients of the estimated wage equations for men while Table 9.9 depicts the results for women. Note that the signs of the regression coefficients on the explanatory variables are all identical in the four equations. Furthermore, the signs are all in line with our expectations, as stated earlier. On the other hand, there are some significant differences in the magnitude of the coefficients across equations.

Tables 9.8 and 9.9 show that rates of return to education are significantly higher among non-Mexican illegal workers. For instance, holding other things constant, an additional year of schooling provides a 1.5 percent increase in the weekly earnings of male Mexican workers, but for non-Mexican illegals the corresponding increase is more than twice, 3.2 percent. Among Mexican women, an additional year of schooling increases earnings by approximately 2 percent, but for non-Mexicans, the rate of return is much higher, equal to 3.5 percent. The superior rate of return to education among non-Mexican immigrants may be due to several factors. One possibility is that the non-Mexican immigrants moving to the US may be self-selected on the basis of having a greater transferability of their

Table 9.8 Regression estimates, Mexican and non-Mexican illegal immigrants, male wage equation

Independent variable	*Mexican illegal immigrants*		*Non-Mexican illegal immigrants*	
	Parameter estimate (s.e.)	*T-statistic*	*Parameter estimate (s.e.)*	*T-statistic*
INTERCEPT	4.4495* (0.0886)	50.23	4.2961* (0.0933)	46.03
EDUCAT	0.0145* (0.0036)	4.01	0.0317* (0.0036)	8.77
EXPER	0.0205* (0.0036)	5.71	0.0220* (0.0043)	5.12
EXPERSQ	−0.0004* (0.0001)	−6.10	−0.0004* (0.0001)	−4.02
NOENGLISH	−0.0997* (0.0209)	−4.76	−0.1084* (0.0320)	−3.39
PROFTECH	0.1164* (0.0425)	2.74	0.2168* (0.0357)	6.08
FARMING	0.0097 (0.0347)	0.28	−0.0344 (0.0823)	−0.42
OPERAT	0.0994* (0.0256)	3.88	0.0551 (0.0319)	1.73
PRODUCT	0.2713* (0.0298)	9.10	0.2679* (0.0358)	7.47
HOURS	0.0161* (0.0011)	14.21	0.0167* (0.0011)	14.82
SINGLE	−0.1114* (0.0237)	−4.72	−0.0731* (0.0270)	−2.71
RECENT	−0.0517 (0.0271)	−1.91	−0.0503 (0.0353)	−1.43
CALIF	0.1009* (0.0200)	5.05	0.0243 (0.0245)	0.99
Adjusted R-SQ	0.26	–	0.28	–

Notes: *=Statistically significant at a 99 percent confidence level.
**=Statistically significant at a 95 percent confidence level.

schooling to the American labor market. For example, if non-Mexican immigrants perceive their move to the US as permanent, then prospective migrants with human capital skills easily-transferable to the US will have a stronger incentive to migrate. Once in the US, they will benefit from this by obtaining higher-paying jobs. If Mexican immigrants, on the other hand, perceive their move as temporary, then the transferability of their skills to the American labor market is not as significant in their migratory decision and the immigrant contingent will not be positively self-selected on the basis of human capital characteristics (see Chiswick 1999 and Taylor 1985). The lower mean level of schooling among Mexican illegal immigrants may also explain the lower rates of return to education. With US rates of return

Table 9.9 Regression estimates, Mexican and non-Mexican illegal immigrants, female wage equation

Independent variable	*Mexican illegal immigrants*		*Non-Mexican illegal immigrants*	
	Parameter estimate (s.e.)	*T-statistic*	*Parameter estimate (s.e.)*	*T-statistic*
INTERCEPT	3.9641* (0.1316)	30.11	3.9526* (0.0957)	41.31
EDUCAT	0.0197* (0.0067)	2.94	0.0354* (0.0418)	8.50
EXPER	0.0113 (0.0059)	1.91	0.0158* (0.0047)	3.37
EXPERSQ	−0.0002 (0.0001)	−1.87	−0.0002** (0.0001)	−2.34
NOENGLISH	−0.1868* (0.0392)	−4.77	−0.1850* (0.0319)	−5.79
PROFTECH	0.2833* (0.0574)	4.93	0.3418* (0.0347)	9.85
FARMING	0.2554* (0.0947)	2.70	0.3721 (0.2060)	1.81
OPERAT	0.2990* (0.0407)	7.35	0.1580* (0.0349)	4.53
PRODUCT	0.3679* (0.0789)	4.66	0.0726 (0.0854)	0.85
HOURS	0.0170* (0.0018)	9.49	0.0158* (0.0012)	13.36
SINGLE	−0.0855** (0.0389)	−2.20	−0.0893* (0.0291)	−3.07
RECENT	−0.0936** (0.0407)	−2.30	−0.0503 (0.0385)	−1.31
CALIF	0.1528* (0.0368)	4.16	0.0568** (0.0266)	2.14
Adjusted R-SQ	0.32	–	0.40	–

Notes: *=Statistically significant at a 99 percent confidence level.
**=Statistically significant at a 95 percent confidence level.

to education and employment opportunities expanding rapidly at the top of the distribution (for college graduates), non-Mexican illegals may find many more profitable job opportunities than those in the collapsing low-wage labor markets facing Mexican undocumented workers.

The economic returns to labor market experience also vary across the various groups considered, although the major differences are on the basis of gender. As with the rate of return to education, the rate of return to experience among both men and women is somewhat higher for non-Mexican immigrants. To understand this result, note that the variable RECENT, associated with years of residence in the US, is being held constant while we consider changes in EXPER. Given the number of years that an immigrant has been residing in the US, changes in the EXPER variable are directly related to changes in the number of years of experience the worker has had abroad. One way to interpret the higher EXPER coefficient in the non-Mexican wage equation is that it shows that the returns in the US labor market of an increase in years of experience abroad are proportionally higher for the non-Mexican worker than for the Mexican immigrant.

This pattern, in turn, may be determined by the relative success of non-Mexican illegal immigrants in matching their occupational experience abroad with that in the United States. The LPS data set does include information on the occupations held by undocumented workers in their countries of origin just before moving to the US. When one compares the occupations held by illegals in the US with those they held abroad, 22.5 percent of the non-Mexican workers had jobs in the same occupational category, while only 14.2 percent of Mexicans had matching jobs. For many non-Mexican undocumented workers, then, their labor market experience abroad is more valuable in the US because they are more likely to find jobs in the US labor market similar to those they held in their own countries before emigrating. This may be the case for workers emigrating from industrialized countries. But it may also be associated with the fact that there are more visa overstayers among the non-Mexican migrants. The greater, initial stability provided by legal entry into the country may allow non-Mexican immigrants to seek and obtain jobs that more closely match their job experience abroad.

The lack of ability to speak English, as reflected by the variable NOENGLISH, has a consistently negative influence on earnings, for both Mexican and non-Mexican migrants. The impact, however, appears to be much more significant for women. Among Mexican and non-Mexican men, the inability to speak English lowers earnings by approximately 10 percent, holding other things constant. But among women, the corresponding drop is approximately 19 percent, almost twice as high. This result reproduces previous research on the impact of English proficiency on earnings (see Rivera-Batiz, 1990, 1996). Women may be penalized more heavily for lower English proficiency due to the types of jobs that they tend to hold (such as clerical or service sector jobs), which require more frequent usage of English.

The occupational dummies are generally positive in Tables 9.8 and 9.9, suggesting that the various categories, including professional and technical, managerial, sales and administrative support workers, operators, fabricators and laborers, all tend to have higher earnings than service sector occupations. This positive association of certain occupational categories with higher earnings is quantitatively important. For instance, non-Mexican male and female undocumented workers employed in professional, technical, managerial or administrative support occupations can earn on average 22 and 34 percent higher earnings, respectively, than service sector employees.

The occupational wage premium received by white-collar workers is also positive, though smaller, for Mexican illegals.

Hours worked are significantly related to weekly earnings for all groups considered. In addition, single workers earn substantially less than married workers, and residence in California is generally linked to greater earnings, everything else held constant, especially among Mexican immigrants.

Conclusions

The results of this survey contradict many of the prevailing views held by both the public and academics alike on undocumented workers in the United States. Using the 1989 Legalized Population Survey, the research presented here provides data that are based on a national sample of illegal immigrants, instead of relying on the small samples of predominantly Mexican undocumented workers utilized in the existing literature.

The analysis first shows that the perception of illegal immigrants as unskilled workers with low levels of schooling is incorrect since it only characterizes Mexican immigrants. Among non-Mexican illegals, the chapter shows that the mean years of schooling for persons aged 25 years of age or older was 10.4 years, which is about the same as the average years of schooling of the overall immigrant population counted in the 1990 US Census of Population. By contrast, Mexican illegal immigrants were found to have an average of 6.3 years of schooling.

The schooling differences between Mexican and non-Mexican undocumented workers are even stronger when one looks at the proportion of the population 25 years of age or older who had completed at least one year of college (more than 12 years of schooling). Among Mexican illegals, the proportion was 4.5 percent but among non-Mexican undocumented workers the proportion was equal to 29.2 percent. For comparison purposes, 37.5 percent of all adult immigrants in the 1990 Census had completed at least one year of college education.

These figures coincide with data on the proportion of the workforce employed in professional, technical, managerial and administrative occupations, which was equal to approximately 9 percent among Mexican illegals and 25 percent among non-Mexican illegals, compared to 35 percent for the overall immigrant population residing in the US in 1990.

This chapter shows not only that educational attainment among non-Mexican illegal immigrants was sharply higher than among Mexican undocumented workers, but also that the rates of return to education were significantly greater for the former. Estimating empirical human capital earnings equations, the chapter shows that the average rate of return to education among Mexican undocumented male workers was 1.5 percent per additional year of schooling, while for non-Mexican male workers the corresponding figure was 3.2 percent, more than twice. Among women, the Mexican rate of return to education was 2 percent, compared to 3.5 percent among non-Mexican workers. Returns to experience were also greater for non-Mexican immigrants.

The higher rates of return to human capital among non-Mexican illegal immigrants are consistent with the view that non-Mexicans moving to the US may be self-selected on the basis of a greater transferability of their schooling to the American labor market. If, for instance, non-Mexican immigrants perceive their move to the US as permanent, then prospective migrants with human capital skills that are more productive in the US will have a stronger incentive to migrate. Once in the US, they will benefit from their "special" skills by obtaining higher-paying jobs. If Mexican immigrants, on the other hand, perceive their migratory move as temporary, then the transferability of their skills to the American labor market is not as significant for their future economic progress and the Mexican immigrant cohort will not be positively self-selected on the basis of human capital characteristics.

The lower rates of return to education among Mexican illegal immigrants may also reflect the lower mean level of schooling compared to non-Mexican migrants. With US rates of return to education and employment opportunities expanding rapidly at the top of the distribution (especially for college graduates), non-Mexican illegals may find more profitable job opportunities than Mexican undocumented workers, who are facing a collapsing low-wage labor market. Finally, the fact that a large share of non-Mexican illegal immigrants are visa overstayers means that their initial entry into the country is legal and, for a certain period of time, allows the workers the stability to seek higher-paying employment opportunities. Among Mexican illegal immigrants, the great majority of whom enter the US by crossing the border illegally, the situation may not be as propitious.

Despite the substantially higher earnings that non-Mexican illegal immigrants display compared to Mexican illegals, one must not forget that both groups of workers earn substantially less than the overall immigrant population. Non-Mexican male illegal workers earned 73 percent less than their counterparts in the general immigrant population; among women, the shortfall was 71 percent. For Mexican workers, male illegals earned 35 percent less than the overall immigrant population, with the gap equal to 39 percent among women.[8] Although a fraction of these wage gaps are due to differences in educational attainment and other demographic characteristics, a substantial share is due to the presence of discrimination and exploitation of undocumented workers in US labor markets.[9]

This chapter has shown the great heterogeneity present among undocumented workers in the United States. Recognizing this diversity has appreciable policy relevance. For instance, it has often been argued that illegal immigrants represent a continuous, massive influx of unskilled migrants entering the US labor market with sharply negative effects on other unskilled workers in the country. But this study finds that a significant fraction of illegal immigrants are highly-skilled and may be complementary to – rather than substitute of – unskilled workers.[10] Unfortunately, public policy discussions regarding illegal immigrants in the US too often rely on stereotypical images that do not adequately represent the totality of this population. It is hoped that, by presenting a more comprehensive profile of illegal immigrants, this chapter will help in generating more informed debate on undocumented workers in the future.

Notes

1 Borane (1999: A10).

2 Other major studies upon which most profiles of illegals are based include a 1975 sample of 793 illegal Mexican immigrants apprehended by the INS at the border (see North and Houstoun, 1976), and another sample of 232 Mexican illegal immigrants interviewed in their region of origin in Mexico (see Massey, 1987). See also Borjas (1990), Chiswick (1984), and Reichert and Massey (1979).

3 For more details on IRCA's amnesty and its implementation, see Gonzalez Baker (1990, 1997) and Rivera-Batiz (1991).

4 IRCA allowed undocumented immigrants who had been continuously residing in the US since January 1, 1982 to be eligible for temporary resident status. Once a person applied for temporary resident status, he or she was also eligible for permanent resident status, so long as the application was filed on or before November 6, 1990. The LPS sample is representative of all illegal immigrants in the US who came forward with the necessary documentation to seek legalization. Although most observers agree that a large portion of the undocumented population residing in the US in 1987 and 1988 was identified by IRCA's amnesty program, it is also likely that short-term, temporary workers were not as widely reached by the program. IRCA did make a special provision for the amnesty of illegals working in agriculture (the Special Agricultural Worker or SAW program), but the LPS survey did not include this population in its sample. Because of these caveats, one may consider the LPS data (and the analysis in this chapter) as representing those illegal immigrants who intend to remain permanently in the United States, and not temporary migrants. For more details on the LPS data, see Smith, Kramer and Singer (1996). See also Tienda et al. (1991).

5 Insofar as the residual methodology estimates represent a count of illegal immigrants responding to Census surveys, they may suffer from an undercount problem. Recently, the INS has estimated the illegal immigrant population in 1996 to be 5 million (see INS 1999; and Massey and Singer, 1995).

6 Dunn (1995: B5).

7 Previous analysis of the LPS data set has examined the earnings of the overall illegal immigrant population, the Mexican subgroup, and Latin American workers, but it has not focused on studying the differences between Mexican and non-Mexican workers; see Borjas and Tienda (1993), Chiswick and Miller (1996), Cobb-Clark and Kossoudji (1996, 2000), and Rivera-Batiz (1999).

8 These figures are based on weekly wages earned by each group, expressed in 1989 dollars.

9 See Rivera-Batiz (1999, 2000) for an analysis of the shortfall in the earnings of illegal Mexican workers. See also Kossoudji and Cobb-Clark (1999).

10 An increase in the supply of factors of production complementary to unskilled labor will, by definition, raise the wages of unskilled workers. Studies examining the substitution and complementarity of skilled and unskilled labor find that skilled immigrants are generally complementary to unskilled workers (see, for example, Gang and Rivera-Batiz, 1994).

References

Borane, Ray (1999) "Do You Hire Illegal Immigrants?," *New York Times*, August 30: A10.

Borjas, George J. (1990) *Friends or Strangers: The Impact of Immigrants on the US Economy*, New York: Basic Books.

Borjas, George J. (1995) "Assimilation and Changes in Cohort Quality Revisited: What Happened to Immigrant Earnings in the 1980s?," *Journal of Labor Economics*, 13: 201–245.

Borjas, George J. (1999a) "The Economic Analysis of Immigration," in O. Ashenfelter and R. Freeman (eds), *Handbook of Labor Economics*, Amsterdam: North Holland.

Borjas, George J. (1999b), *Heaven's Door: Immigration Policy and the American Economy*, Princeton: Princeton University Press.

Borjas, George J. and Marta Tienda (1993) 'The Employment and Wages of Legalized Immigrants,' *International Migration Review*, 27: 712–747.

Chiswick, Barry R. (1978) "The Effects of Americanization on the Earnings of the Foreign-Born," *Journal of Political Economy*, 86: 897–922.

Chiswick, Barry R. (1984) "Illegal Aliens in the United States Labor Market: An Analysis of Occupational Attainment and Earnings," *International Migration Review*, 18: 714–32.

Chiswick, Barry R. (1988) *Illegal Aliens: Their Employment and Employers*, Kalamazoo, Mich.: W.E. Upjohn Institute for Employment Research.

Chiswick, Barry R. (1999) "Are Immigrants Favorably Selected?," *American Economic Review*, 89: 181–185.

Chiswick, Barry and Paul Miller (1996) "Language Skills and Earnings among Legalized Aliens," paper presented at the 1997 American Economic Association Meetings, New Orleans, mimeo.

Cobb-Clark, Deborah A. and Sherrie A. Kossoudji (1996) "Finding Good Opportunities within Undocumented Markets: US Occupational Mobility for Latino Workers," *International Migration Review*, 30: 901–924.

Cobb-Clark, Deborah A. and Sherrie A. Kossoudji (2000) "IRCA's Impact on the Occupational Concentration and Mobility of Newly-Legalized Mexican Men," *Journal of Population Economics*, 13: 311–324.

Duleep, Harriet and Mark Regets (1999) "Immigrants and Human-Capital Investment," *American Economic Review*, 89: 186–191.

Dunn, Ashley (1995) "Greeted at Nation's Front Door, Many Visitors Stay On Illegally," *New York Times*, January 3: A1, B5.

Fernandez, E. and J. Gregory Robinson (1994) "Illustrative Ranges of the Distribution of Undocumented Immigrants by State," Technical Working Paper 8, US Bureau of the Census.

Gang, Ira N. and Francisco L. Rivera-Batiz (1994) "Labor Market Effects of Immigration in the United States and Europe: Substitution vs. Complementarity," *Journal of Population Economics*, 7: 157–175.

Gonzalez, Arturo (2000) "The Acquisition and Labor Market Value of Four English Skills: New Evidence from NALS," *Contemporary Economic Policy*, 18: 259–269.

Gonzalez Baker, Susan (1997) "The Amnesty Aftermath: Current Policy Issues Stemming from the Legalization Programs of the 1986 Immigration Reform and Control Act," *International Migration Review*, 31: 5–27.

Gonzalez-Baker, Susan (1990) *The Cautious Welcome: The Legalization Programs of the Immigration Reform and Control Act*, Lanham, MD: University Press of America.

Immigration and Naturalization Service (1999) "Illegal Alien Resident Population," mimeo, United States Department of Justice, August 11; <http://www.ins.usdoj.gov/illegalalien/index.html>.

Kossoudji, Sherrie A. and Deborah A. Cobb-Clark (1999) "Coming Out of the Shadows: Learning about Legal Status and Wages from the Legalized Population," mimeo, Center for Economic Policy, Australian National University, Canberra.

Massey, Douglas S. (1987) "Do Undocumented Immigrants Earn Lower Wages than Legal Immigrants: New Evidence from Mexico," *International Migration Review*, 21: 236–274.

Massey, Douglas S. and Audrey Singer (1995) "New Estimates of Undocumented Mexican Migration and the Probability of Apprehension," *Demography* 32: 203–213.

National Research Council (1997) *The New Americans: Economic, Demographic, and Fiscal Effects of Immigration*, Washington, D.C.: National Academy Press.

North, Douglas S. and Marion Houston (1976) "The Characteristics and Role of Illegal Aliens in the United States Labor Market: An Exploratory Study," mimeo, Linton and Co., Washington, D.C.

Portes, Alejandro and R. Bach (1985) *Latin Journey: Cuban and Mexican Immigrants in the United States*, Berkeley: University of California Press.

Reichert, Josh and Douglas Massey (1979) "Patterns of US Migration from a Mexican Sending Community: A Comparison of Legal and Illegal Immigrants," *International Migration Review*, 13: 599–623.

Rivera-Batiz, Francisco L. (1990) "English Language Proficiency and the Economic Progress of Immigrants," *Economics Letters*, 34: 295–300.

Rivera-Batiz, Francisco L. (1991) "Introduction to US Immigration Policy Reform in the 1980s," in Francisco L. Rivera-Batiz, Selig Sechzer and Ira Gang (eds), *US Immigration Policy Reform in the 1980s: A Preliminary Assessment*, New York: Praeger Publishers.

Rivera-Batiz, Francisco L. (1996) "English Language Proficiency, Quantitative Skills and the Economic Progress of Immigrants," in H. Orcutt Duleep and P. Wunnava, (eds), *Immigrants and Immigration Policy: Individual Skills, Family Ties and Group Identities*, Greenwich, Conn.: JAI Press.

Rivera-Batiz, Francisco L. (1999) "Undocumented Workers in the Labor Market: An Analysis of the Earnings of Legal and Illegal Mexican Immigrants in the United States," *Journal of Population Economics*, 12: 91–116.

Rivera-Batiz, Francisco L. (2000) "Underground on American Soil: Undocumented Workers and US Immigration Policy," *Journal of International Affairs*, 53: 485–502.

Smith, Shirley, Roger Kramer and Audrey Singer (1996) *Characteristics and Labor Market Behavior of the Legalized Population Five Years Following Legalization*, Immigration Policy and Research Division, Bureau of International Labor Affairs, US Department of Labor, Washington, D.C.

Taylor, J. Edward (1985) "Selectivity of Undocumented Mexico–US Migrants and Implications for US Immigration Reform," Working Paper PDS-85–4, The Urban Institute, Washington, D.C.

Tienda, Marta, G.J. Borjas, H. Cordero-Guzman, K. Neuman and M. Romero (1991) "The Demography of Legalization: Insights form Administrative Records of Legalized Aliens," NORC, University of Chicago, Chicago.

United States Department of Commerce (1993) *1990 US Census of Population and Housing 5%* Public Use Microdata Sample, Bureau of the Census, Washington, D.C.

United States Department of Labor (1996) *Legalized Population Survey Public Use File*, Bureau of International Labor Affairs, Washington, D.C.

Warren, Robert and Jeffrey Passel (1987) "A Count of the Uncountable: Estimates of Undocumented Aliens Counted in the 1980 United States Census," *Demography*, 24: 120–135.

Woodrow, Karen and Jeffrey Passel (1990) "Post-IRCA Undocumented Immigration in the United States: An Assessment Based on the June 1988 CPS," in F. Bean, B. Edmonston and J. Passel (eds), *Undocumented Migration to the United States: IRCA and the Experience of the 1980s*, Washington, D.C.: The Urban Institute.

10 Immigrant adjustment in Israel

The determinants of literacy and fluency in Hebrew and the effects on earnings

Barry R. Chiswick and Gaston Repetto

Introduction

This chapter is concerned with an econometric analysis of the determinants of Hebrew language proficiency among adult male immigrants in Israel and the effect of this proficiency on the labor market earnings of these immigrants. The analysis is based on the 1972 Census of Israel and parallels an analysis performed for the 1983 Census (Chiswick, 1998). It is not possible to perform a similar analysis for the 1995 Census of Israel as this census did not include any questions on Hebrew language proficiency.

This study differs from analyzes of language and earnings of immigrants in Israel performed using the various immigrant absorption surveys (see, for example, Beenstock 1993, 1996a, 1996b; Beenstock and Ben-Menahen, 1997; Eckstein and Shachar, 1995; Eckstein and Weiss, 1998; Neuman, 1998, and the references therein). The census contains a much larger sample size, and includes immigrants over a wide range of durations of residence and from all countries of origin, in contrast to the absorption surveys which have smaller samples, with limited duration in Israel (usually three or fewer years), and sometimes limited to specific origins (e.g. Jews from the former Soviet Union).

The motivation for this study is twofold. One is to develop even further and to sharpen the tests for the robustness of models for the acquisition by immigrants of the destination language and the effects of destination language skills on their earnings. Most such studies have been performed for the US, Canada and Australia, three highly developed, English-speaking countries of overseas settlement. English is an international language which may have value in the labor market even in the non-English speaking countries of origin. Are the models of language acquisition and impact also useful for a less well developed economy (Israel in 1972) in which the destination language is not English? Moreover, unlike the US, Canadian and Australian censuses, which ask only about speaking ability, the 1972 Census of Israel includes information on literacy in Hebrew, through a question on the ability to write in Hebrew, as well as on speaking Hebrew.[1]

Another motivation is to learn more about the immigrant absorption process in Israel. Israel expends considerable resources on Hebrew language training for new immigrants. What are the basic determinants of Hebrew language proficiency and what are the consequences for labor market earnings in the Israeli economy? The answers to these questions will provide insights that can guide immigration policy in countries that ration immigration visas on kinship, skill or refugee criteria, and can guide absorption (adjustment) policy in Israel and elsewhere.

The chapter begins with a thumbnail sketch of the language and earnings models. The details of these models are presented elsewhere. There follows a description of the variables in the 1972 Census of Israel that form the basis for this study. The empirical results are then presented. The chapter closes with a summary and conclusion.

The models – immigrant language acquisition and earnings

The theoretical models of immigrant acquisition of the destination language and immigrant earnings adjustment are presented here in thumbnail fashion as they have been developed elsewhere in detail. For the basic model development for earnings see Chiswick (1978), and for language see Chiswick and Miller (1992, 1995), with an application of these approaches to Israel presented in Chiswick (1998).

Hebrew language proficiency

The model of destination language proficiency among immigrants is based on a human capital framework. Language skills among immigrants are expected to be productive in the labor market and in consumption activities, are acquired at a sacrifice of time and out-of-pocket (direct) expenditures by the immigrant and those financing the immigrant's language acquisition, and these skills are embodied in the person. Therefore, language skills satisfy the three components of the definition of human capital.

The model of acquisition of dominant language proficiency is based on three conceptual explanatory variables: exposure, efficiency and economic factors. These three conceptual variables are discussed in turn with the development of variables to measure their influences.

Proficiency in Hebrew among immigrants in Israel is expected to be greater the more they are exposed to Hebrew. Exposure can be thought of as having three components: exposure prior to immigration, exposure measured in units of time in Israel, and exposure per unit of time in Israel.

The Census does not include any information on exposure to Hebrew prior to immigration.[2] Although country of birth is known, there is no country other than Israel in which Hebrew is a dominant language and most immigrants to Israel do not arrive with a working knowledge of the language. Some absorption surveys, however, do include information on pre-immigration knowledge of or study of Hebrew, and find that it enhances proficiency after immigration (see, for example, Beenstock 1996a).

Exposure in units of time is usually measured by duration of residence in the destination. It is typically measured as the number of years since the person first came to the destination as a permanent migrant. For most immigrants to Israel this is a one time event, although among North American immigrants there is a greater propensity for return migration that sometimes results in re-immigration. It is to be expected that the effect of duration on language skills is initially large and that the incremental effect on proficiency diminishes with duration of residence, suggesting a quadratic specification.

The intensity of exposure per unit of time in the destination is measured by several proxy variables. One is the ability to avoid using Hebrew, which is proxied by the extent to which others in the region within Israel in which the respondent lives speak the same non-Hebrew language as the respondent. The ability to avoid using Hebrew is greater if one speaks a language other than Hebrew that is common in the area (e.g. English) compared to a language that is rare (e.g. Greek).

The ability to avoid using Hebrew is also greater if one immigrates with a spouse who speaks the same origin language. This suggests that linguistic interactions within the household are important, and that proficiency would be lower among those whose current marriage was prior to immigration (married overseas). There is no particular hypothesis for the effect of being married after immigration in contrast to remaining single.

Children, especially children born in Israel, may have partially offsetting impacts on parental proficiency. Parents may learn Hebrew from their Israeli-born or Israeli-educated children. On the other hand, children would detract from parental acquisition of language skills if they serve as translators for their parents. Children as translators is likely to be more relevant for consumption activities than for labor market activities.[3] Children also detract from parental destination language proficiency if the parents speak the origin language to preserve it among their children, or among women if children have an adverse effect on female labor supply. Previous research suggests that children born in the destination have a positive effect on the destination language proficiency of their fathers, but that the effect of children is less positive or more negative on their mother's language skills.

Efficiency in language acquisition refers to the process by which exposure is converted into destination language proficiency (human capital). Developmentally children are more efficient in language acquisition than are adults (Long, 1990). It is expected that proficiency would fall with a rise in age at immigration. It is also expected that those with a higher level of schooling would be more proficient.[4] Persons with more schooling may be more efficient (more able) learners; they would also have greater proficiency in their origin language and may have a greater understanding of the structure of languages.

Another factor relevant for the acquisition of destination language skills is the "linguistic distance" between that language and the origin languages. The closer are origin and destination languages, the greater the expected proficiency in the new destination language. Although a measure of linguistic distance between English and other languages has been developed and used successfully for the study of immigrants in the US and Canada (Chiswick and Miller, 1998a), no comparable index has been developed for Hebrew. Yet some languages, such as Arabic, are linguistically closer to Hebrew than are other languages, such as English. Indeed, of all the major immigrant languages, Arabic is linguistically closest to Hebrew.

Labor market factors also effect the incentives to acquire destination language proficiency. Those who expect to receive higher wages if they were to become proficient have a greater incentive to become proficient. This is difficult to model empirically, and while sample selectivity tests have been performed on this proposition for English-speaking immigrant-receiving countries, this will not be done here, in part because of the lack of identifying instruments (Chiswick and Miller, 1992, 1995). It has also been shown elsewhere that immigrants with a higher level of schooling receive a larger increase in earnings from proficiency in the host language (Chiswick and Miller, 1995). That is, it appears that schooling and language skills are complementary inputs in the generation of earnings. As a result, the education variable in the language equation will, in part, reflect the effect of greater economic benefits to the more educated to becoming proficient.

Immigrants to Israel from some countries have higher rates of emigrating, either to return to their origin or to go to a third country, than from others. The higher the probability of an immigrant leaving Israel, the shorter is the expected duration of residence, and given the country-specific nature of Hebrew, the weaker the incentive to invest in the language. Indeed, to the extent that immigrants to Israel from the US and Canada have high propensities for return migration and immigrants from the Arab countries of North Africa and the Middle East have virtually no return migration, one would expect lesser fluency in Hebrew among the former than among the latter, other things being the same (Beenstock, 1996b, Blejer and Goldberg, 1980).

As a result of this discussion the analysis of Hebrew language proficiency for adult males is based on the following equation:

$$\begin{aligned} \text{LANG} = f(&\underset{+}{\text{YSM}}, \underset{-}{\text{YSMSQ}}, \underset{-}{\text{AGE}}, \underset{+}{\text{EDUC}}, \underset{?}{\text{MARR}}, \underset{-}{\text{MARROVER}}, \underset{-}{\text{CONPR}}, \\ &\underset{?}{\text{Children}}, \underset{+}{\text{Children born in Israel}}, \underset{?}{\text{Region of Residence}}, \underset{?}{\text{Country of Birth}}), \end{aligned}$$

where LANG is a measure of proficiency in Hebrew, YSM, YSMSQ, AGE and EDUC denote years since migration and its square, age and educational attainment, respectively, while MARR and MARROVER are dichotomous variables that are unity for those currently married and those whose marriage occurred prior to immigration, respectively. CONPR is a language concentration measure. The actual measures of these variables available from the 1972 Census are discussed below. The hypothesized signs of the partial effects are indicated below the variables.

Earnings

The modeling of the effect of Hebrew language skills on earnings is much more straightforward. The approach uses the "human capital earnings function" which relates the natural logarithm of earnings to human capital (e.g. schooling and years of labor market experience) and demographic variables (e.g. gender, marital status, region of residence, etc.). It has been expanded to incorporate immigrant-related variables, including duration of residence, citizenship, country of origin, and of special interest here, destination language skills (Chiswick, 1978; Chiswick and Miller, 1995).

The earnings equation may be written as:

$$LNY=f(\underset{+}{EDUC}, \underset{+}{EXP}, \underset{-}{EXPSQ}, \underset{+}{YSM}, \underset{-}{YSMSQ}, \underset{+}{MARR}, \underset{+}{LANG}, \underset{+}{CITIZ},$$
$$\underset{?}{\text{Region of residence}}, \underset{?}{\text{Country of Birth}}),$$

where LNY is the natural logarithm of earnings, EXP and EXPSQ are years of potential labor market experience and its square, and CITIZ is a dichotomous variable for citizenship.[5] The hypothesized signs are indicated below the explanatory variables.

The data – 1972 Census of Israel

The data under study are the microdata sample created by the Central Bureau of Statistics from the 1972 Census of Israel. This is a 20 percent (one-in-five) simple random sample of the Israeli population. The data drawn from this sample for this study are limited to foreign-born Jewish men age 25 to 64 years in 1972 who were not enrolled in a Yeshiva in 1972. The age limits include the prime labor force years and are beyond the usual age of compulsory military service. Those enrolled in a Yeshiva are not labor market participants. The analysis is limited to males at this exploratory stage.

The language questions in the 1972 Census are questions (11) and (12). Translated into English they are:

11) Do you know how to write (at least a simple letter)?
   a) Do you know how to write in Hebrew? Yes, No
   b) Do you know how to write in Arabic? Yes, No

c) Do you know how to write in another language or languages? Yes, No

Respondents were not asked to specify the other languages in which they could write.

12) What is the language (or languages) that you speak every day?
_________ Record the sole language or the primary language.
_________ Record the second language.
_________ Record the third language.
(Do not record languages that you know but do not speak every day).

There is no information on the degree of literacy or the degree of fluency in spoken Hebrew. Literacy is expressed in this study as a dichotomous variable taking the value of unity for those who can write at least a simple letter in Hebrew, and zero otherwise (HEBWRIT). For speaking fluency four categories are considered: only speaks Hebrew (HEBONLY), speaks Hebrew as a primary but not only language (HEBPRIM), speaks it as a secondary or tertiary language (HEBSECTH), and does not speak Hebrew on a daily basis (HEBNONE). In some analyzes the Hebrew fluency variable is dichotomous, where HEBSOP equals unity for those for whom it is the only or primary language spoken daily, and it is zero otherwise.

The earnings variable is the gross annual salary for male wage and salary workers in Israeli Liras, the currency used in Israel at that time. The earnings analysis is performed only for those with positive earnings.

Most of the explanatory variables used in the analysis are fairly straightforward. Age (AGE) is measured in years since birth. Education (EDUC) is measured as years of schooling attended, with a top coding of 22 years. The maximum potential labor market experience is measured as age minus schooling minus five (EXP=AGE–EDUC–5), and is defined to equal zero for any negative values. Duration in Israel (YSM) is measured as the current year (1972) minus the year of "aliya" (immigration) to Israel.

Marital status (MARR) is unity for those who are currently married and zero otherwise. Married overseas (MARROVER) is unity for those in their first marriage if this took place prior to immigration (year of first marriage equal to or earlier than year of immigration), otherwise it is zero. The two children variables are a dichotomous variable equal to unity if there are children under age 20 living in the household (CHILDREN) and a dichotomous variable that equals unity if any of the married, widowed or divorced women living in the household has a child born in Israel (HCHILBIS).

The region of residence dichotomous variables are defined for Tel Aviv and Jerusalem, with the rest of the country as the benchmark. The various countries of birth are combined into seven regions: Asia (nearly all coming from the Asian countries of the Middle East), North Africa (from Morocco to Somalia), English-speaking countries (US, Canada, UK, Ireland, Australia, New Zealand, South Africa), Western Europe (other than the UK and

Ireland), USSR and Latin America, with Eastern Europe (i.e. the post-war Communist bloc countries of Europe other than the USSR) as the benchmark.

The language concentration measure (CONPR) is constructed in the following manner. The foreign-born adult male Jewish population is divided into the "natural regions" of the country.[6] Within each region (i), the percentage of the group speaking each of the 12 most frequently reported only or primary languages other than Hebrew (j) is computed.[7] This percentage is the CONPR for each respondent in the region (i) reporting language (j) as their only or primary language. Thus, for a French speaker in Jerusalem the CONPR is the percent of foreign-born adult Jewish men in Jerusalem who speak French as their only or primary language. For those who speak only Hebrew, CONPR is defined to be zero since CONPR refers to the concentrations speaking languages other than Hebrew. It is also defined to equal zero for those reporting a primary language not in the top 12 languages other than Hebrew because the population density of these language speakers is so low.

Empirical analysis

This section reports the statistical analysis of spoken Hebrew language usage and ability to write in Hebrew, followed by the statistical analysis of annual earnings among wage and salaried workers.

Hebrew language proficiency

The distribution of language skills among adult foreign-born Jewish men in Israel is reported in Table 10.1. Hebrew is the only language spoken on a daily basis among 24 percent of the men, and for another 52 percent it is the primary but not the only language, making a total of 75 percent for whom it is the only or primary language. All told, including second and third languages reported, 89 percent report Hebrew as spoken daily.

The second most frequently spoken language is Arabic, which is spoken primarily by North African and Middle Eastern immigrants. It is spoken by 5 percent of the Jewish immigrants as an only or primary language, but by 23 percent if second and tertiary languages are included. Yiddish, the traditional language of East European Jews, is in third place. English, an important international language, is spoken as the only or primary language of only 1 percent of the sample, but if second and third languages spoken are included, the proportion increases to 9 percent. The top 12 languages after Hebrew are spoken as the only or primary language by 22 percent of the adult foreign-born men, or by 88 percent of those reporting an only or primary language other than Hebrew.

There is a strong relation between duration in Israel and proficiency in Hebrew (Table 10.2). The proportion of foreign-born men reporting Hebrew

Table 10.1 Frequency distribution of languages spoken in Israel, 1972 (foreign-born Jewish men, age 25 to 64)

Language	*Only and primary*[(a)]	*Only, primary and second*	*Only, primary, second and third*
Hebrew	75.4	86.5	88.9
Arabic	4.8	20.0	22.9
Yiddish	4.0	14.3	17.7
Romanian	3.4	8.4	9.9
French	1.9	7.7	10.7
Spanish-Ladino	1.6	4.9	6.0
English	1.3	5.4	8.6
Hungarian	1.1	3.3	4.1
Kurdish	0.9	1.8	2.1
Russian	0.8	2.0	3.0
German	0.8	3.9	5.9
Persian	0.7	2.2	2.3
Polish	0.7	3.2	5.2
Other	2.9	2.3	2.2
Total	100.0	(b)	(b)

Source: 1972 Census of Population and Housing, Israel, Public Use Sample, Demographic File, 20 percent sample of the population.

Notes: Sample size: 92,797.
(a) Hebrew is the only language spoken by 23.7 percent.
(b) Column adds to more than 100 percent due to dual and triple language fluency.

Table 10.2 Hebrew speaking skills by duration in Israel, 1972 (foreign-born Jewish men, age 25 to 64)

Duration (years)	*Sample size*	*Only lang. (%)*	*Primary lang (%)*	*Second+ third lang. (%)*	*Does not speak (%)*	*Unknown (%)*	*Total (%)*
0–5	5,799	3.22	21.54	31.63	39.14	4.47	100.00
6–10	9,377	8.37	43.50	25.10	20.65	2.38	100.00
11–15	8,858	12.10	49.73	21.64	14.41	2.12	100.00
16–20	8,043	21.19	55.94	13.96	6.39	2.52	100.00
21–25(a)	42,582	27.46	55.38	10.56	4.64	1.97	100.00
26–30	4,574	33.95	59.93	5.18	2.32	1.62	100.00
31–35	3,831	31.66	59.07	5.69	2.01	1.57	100.00
Over 35	9,733	38.42	54.43	3.82	1.80	1.53	100.00
Total	92,797	23.65	51.70	13.52	8.97	2.15	100.00

Source: 1972 Census of Population and Housing, Israel, Public Use Sample, Demographic File, 20 percent sample of the population.

Note: (a) These immigrants arrived in 1947–51, encompassing the year of independence and the subsequent large immigration from Europe, North Africa and the Middle East.

as the only or primary language increases with duration in Israel. The pattern of improvement is similar to the one observed 11 years later in the 1983 Census (Chiswick, 1998).[8] This suggests that the pattern is not due to inherently poorer Hebrew language ability among the more recent cohorts of immigrants that would put them at a linguistic disadvantage throughout their life in Israel, but rather reflects a longitudinal effect–Hebrew language skills improving with duration of residence.

The means and standard deviations of the variables used in the analyzes are reported in Table 10.3 by the degree of Hebrew usage. Those who are more proficient in Hebrew, that is, they speak it as their only or primary language, compared to those with lesser proficiency, tend to be younger, better educated, resided longer in Israel, were married in Israel and have children, with at least some children born in Israel. These are, however, simple relationships.

The multiple regression analysis of spoken Hebrew language usage is reported in Table 10.4 using Ordinary Least Squares (OLS) and Logit analysis. Both procedures tell essentially the same story: using Hebrew as the only or primary language is greater the higher the level of education, the longer the duration of residence, and the younger the age at immigration (age when duration in Israel is held constant).[9] Those who married their current spouse prior to immigration are less likely to use Hebrew. The comparison of those who married after immigration with those not married shows an ambiguous pattern: lesser fluency for the former in the OLS analysis but no significant difference in the logit analysis. Children, especially if born in Israel, are associated with a greater use of Hebrew among their fathers.

Compared to the rest of Israel, those living in the more religiously observant and traditional Jerusalem are more likely to use Hebrew as their only or primary language. Compared to the rest of Israel other than Jerusalem, Hebrew is less likely to play this role in Tel Aviv. Even after controlling for place of residence in Israel through the Tel Aviv/Jerusalem city variables, the linguistic concentration variable (CONPR) is statistically significant. That is, immigrants living in a region in which a larger proportion of the foreign-born speak the same non-Hebrew language as the respondent are less likely to report they speak Hebrew as their only or primary language. This suggests that the greater the ease among immigrants to rely on their origin language, the less likely are they to use Hebrew.

Country of birth matters. Compared to Jewish immigrants born in Eastern Europe, those from North Africa and the Middle East (Asia) are more likely to use Hebrew as their only or primary language. These immigrants share with those of Eastern Europe a negligible propensity for return migration, but the language of their countries of origin (primarily Arabic) is linguistically closer to Hebrew than are the European languages. At the other extreme, those from Western Europe, and especially those from the English-speaking developed countries, have a much lower use of Hebrew.

It is the immigrants from the English-speaking developed countries in particular that have a high degree of return migration (see Beenstock, 1996b; Blejer and Goldberg, 1980). Indeed, Hebrew usage by country of

Table 10.3 Means and standard deviation of variables used in language analysis, Israel, 1972 (foreign-born Jewish men, age 25 to 64)

Variable	*All*	*Hebrew only*	*Hebrew primary*	*Hebrew second or third*	*No Hebrew*
AGE	44.63	41.08	44.09	49.00	51.25
	(11.63)	(11.51)	(11.29)	(10.64)	(10.39)
EDUC	9.09	9.65	9.49	8.04	7.02
	(4.45)	(4.04)	(4.21)	(5.01)	(4.92)
YSM	21.14	25.19	22.29	15.87	12.35
	(9.81)	(8.82)	(8.96)	(9.02)	(9.31)
YSMSQ	543.00	712.53	576.89	333.34	239.10
	(466.97)	(513.69)	(453.38)	(331.32)	(317.08)
MARR	0.90	0.90	0.91	0.92	0.89
	(0.30)	(0.30)	(0.29)	(0.27)	(0.32)
MARROVER	0.37	0.16	0.33	0.71	0.79
	(0.48)	(0.36)	(0.47)	(0.45)	(0.41)
CHILDREN	0.68	0.74	0.72	0.61	0.48
	(0.47)	(0.44)	(0.45)	(0.49)	(0.50)
HCHILBIS	0.69	0.81	0.76	0.52	0.32
	(0.46)	(0.39)	(0.43)	(0.50)	(0.47)
TEL-AVIV	0.35	0.39	0.36	0.31	0.30
	(0.48)	(0.49)	(0.48)	(0.46)	(0.46)
JERUSALEM	0.07	0.07	0.08	0.07	0.04
	(0.26)	(0.26)	(0.26)	(0.25)	(0.21)
ASIA	0.21	0.30	0.21	0.15	0.11
	(0.41)	(0.46)	(0.41)	(0.35)	(0.31)
NORTHAFR	0.23	0.19	0.24	0.26	0.22
	(0.42)	(0.40)	(0.43)	(0.44)	(0.42)
USSR	0.06	0.06	0.05	0.05	0.12
	(0.23)	(0.25)	(0.21)	(0.22)	(0.32)
EASTEURO	0.41	0.37	0.41	0.44	0.48
	(0.49)	(0.48)	(0.50)	(0.50)	(0.50)
WESTEURO	0.06	0.06	0.06	0.05	0.03
	(0.23)	(0.24)	(0.24)	(0.21)	(0.18)
ENGLSPEA	0.01	0.005	0.01	0.04	0.02
	(0.12)	(0.07)	(0.10)	(0.20)	(0.15)
LATIAMER	0.01	0.005	0.02	0.02	0.02
	(0.12)	(0.08)	(0.12)	(0.13)	(0.14)
CONPR	10.19	0	13.62	14.07	13.84
	(10.18)	(0)	(9.42)	(9.76)	(9.83)
Sample size	92,797	21,947	47,977	12,550	8,328

Source: 1972 Census of Population and Housing, Israel, Public Use Sample, Demographic File, 20 percent sample of the population.

Note: The variables are defined in the text.

Table 10.4 Analysis of determinants of speaking Hebrew used as only or primary language, Israel, 1972 (foreign-born Jewish men, age 25 to 64)

Variables	*OLS*	*Logit*
CONSTANT	0.4544	0.0769
	(47.67)	[0.96]
AGE	−0.0073	−0.0595
	(−47.41)	[−42.59]
EDUC	0.0142	0.1137
	(45.53)	[42.25]
YSM	0.0339	0.2022
	(77.70)	[51.25]
YSMSQ	−0.0004	−0.0019
	(−44.94)	[−21.52]
MARR	−0.0190	0.0139
	(−4.10)	[0.35]
MARROVER	−0.0716	−0.4560
	(−20.20)	[−15.81]
CHILDREN	0.0262	0.3125
	(7.80)	[11.16]
HCHILBIS	0.0755	0.2811
	(21.04)	[9.88]
TEL-AVIV	−0.0080	−0.0776
	(−3.00)	[−3.23]
JERUSALEM	0.0143	0.1522
	(2.99)	[3.41]
ASIA	0.0556	0.4876
	(15.87)	[14.88]
NORTHAFR	0.0809	0.6203
	(23.01)	[20.17]
USSR	0.0012	0.0392
	(0.21)	[0.76]
WESTEURO	−0.0671	−0.6127
	(−12.23)	[−11.56]
ENGLSPEA	−0.1703	−1.2923
	(−16.25)	[−16.93]
LATIAMER	0.0552	0.0734
	(5.27)	[0.90]
CONPR	−0.0035	−0.0307
	(−28.02)	[−28.32]
R^2 adj.	0.3339	
Chi Square		28,299.44
Sample Size	81,594	81,594

Source: 1972 Census of Population and Housing, Israel, Public Use Sample, Demographic File, 20 percent sample of the population.

Notes: Dependent variable: HEBSOP=1 if speak Hebrew as only or primary language, otherwise it is zero.
t ratios are in parentheses.
Asymptotic t ratios are in brackets.

origin seems to be greater the lower degree of return migration and the closer the language of origin is to Hebrew.

There is a strong relationship between Hebrew speaking frequency and ability to write in Hebrew, but the correlation is far from perfect.[11] Table 10.5 reports the OLS and logit analysis of the determinants of being able to write (a simple letter) in Hebrew. The patterns are generally the same as for speaking. Those with more schooling, who have been in Israel a longer period of time, who immigrated at a younger age, who did not marry prior to immigration, and who have children, especially children born in Israel, are more likely to be able to write a letter in Hebrew. Those who live in Jerusalem are more likely to be able to write in Hebrew in the logit analysis, but there is no difference between Tel Aviv and the rest of the country. Those who live in areas where more immigrants speak their origin language (CONPR) are less able to write in Hebrew.

Country of origin also matters for writing, with the patterns being similar to that for speaking. Those from North Africa and the Middle East have a greater propensity to be able to write in Hebrew, compared to Eastern European immigrants, even though the Arabic alphabet is very different from the Hebrew alphabet. Those from Western Europe and the English-speaking countries are less able to write in Hebrew than Eastern European immigrants.

Although the dependent variables are not strictly comparable, and the general patterns are very similar, there are some interesting differences in the partial effects of some of the explanatory variables on speaking and writing Hebrew. Education has a much larger impact on writing skills than on speaking, whereas duration in Israel has a larger impact on improving speaking than on improving writing. The negative impact on Hebrew proficiency of the linguistic concentration measure is stronger for speaking than for writing. These patterns for the differential effect on speaking and writing of these explanatory variables are remarkably similar to what was found in a study of English speaking and reading proficiency among illegal aliens who obtained legal status (primarily of Hispanic origin) in the United States (Chiswick and Miller, 1999). This provides additional support for the robustness of the findings within and across countries. The comparison with the US study also suggests very similar determinants of the two dimensions of literacy, reading and writing skills.

As a further refinement of the analysis, Table 10.6 reports the multinomial logit analysis of the four category Hebrew variable: only Hebrew, Hebrew primary, Hebrew secondary (or tertiary) and no Hebrew spoken daily.[11] Although the signs and levels of statistical significance are indicated in Table 10.6, the magnitudes can be difficult to interpret. To facilitate interpretation, Table 10.7 reports the probabilities that an individual with a particular set of characteristics will be in each of the four language groups, based on the multinomial logit analysis in Table 10.6. The probabilities in a row sum to unity.

Table 10.5 Analysis of determinants of Hebrew writing, Israel, 1972 (foreign-born Jewish men, age 25 to 64)

Variables	*OLS*	*Logit*
CONSTANT	0.4164	−1.2570
	(48.41)	[−13.39]
AGE	−0.0051	−0.0468
	(−36.22)	[−29.34]
EDUC	0.0339	0.3186
	(120.36)	[92.79]
YSM	0.0195	0.1488
	(49.46)	[32.82]
YSMSQ	−0.0002	−0.0012
	(−27.19)	[−10.86]
MARR	0.0104	0.2023
	(2.49)	[4.37]
MARROVER	−0.0408	−0.3965
	(−12.71)	[−11.69]
CHILDREN	0.0010	0.2172
	(3.28)	[6.65]
HCHILBIS	0.0453	0.2309
	(13.95)	[6.91]
TEL-AVIV	0.0033	0.0008
	(1.36)	[0.03]
JERUSALEM	−0.0041	0.1277
	(−0.95)	[2.45]
ASIA	0.0237	0.3574
	(7.48)	[9.65]
NORTHAFR	0.0347	0.4277
	(10.91)	[12.17]
USSR	−0.0165	0.0568
	(−3.30)	[0.96]
WESTEURO	−0.0533	−0.3764
	(−10.78)	[−5.31]
ENGLSPEA	−0.0170	−0.5139
	(−1.799)	[−4.65]
LATIAMER	0.0303	0.1167
	(3.22)	[1.06]
CONPR	−0.0005	−0.0038
	(−4.47)	[−3.11]
R^2 adj.	0.3077	
Chi Square		26,293.33
Sample Size	81,025	81,025

Source: 1972 Census of Population and Housing, Israel, Public Use Sample, Demographic File, 20 percent sample of the population.

Notes: Dependent variable: HEBWRIT=1 if know how to write at least a simple letter in Hebrew, otherwise it is zero.
t ratios are in parentheses.
Asymptotic t ratios are in brackets.

Table 10.6 Multinomial logit analysis of Hebrew language usage, Israel, 1972 (foreign-born Jewish men, age 25 to 64)

Variable	*Primary lang. relative to only Hebrew*	*Second and third lang. relative to only Hebrew*	*No Hebrew relative to only Hebrew*
INTERCEPT	0.9195	0.6451	1.5274
	(11.44)	(5.84)	(11.95)
AGE	0.0442	0.0890	0.1126
	(36.24)	(48.41)	(50.88)
EDUC	−0.0031	−0.1025	0.1859
	(−1.30)	(−29.28)	(−43.18)
YSM	−0.0979	−0.2406	−0.3628
	(−22.23)	(−40.55)	(−56.59)
YSMSQ	0.0006	0.0018	0.0038
	(8.36)	(13.87)	(28.31)
MARR	−0.0814	0.0012	−0.1883
	(−2.35)	(0.02)	(−3.05)
MARROVER	0.1704	0.6542	0.5125
	(6.03)	(16.69)	(10.24)
CHILDREN	0.1033	−0.2151	−0.4807
	(0.39)	(−5.68)	(−10.92)
HCHILBIS	0.0081	−0.1810	−0.4631
	(0.28)	(−4.56)	(−9.96)
TEL-AVIV	−0.0065	0.0169	0.0076
	(−0.34)	(0.56)	(0.20)
JERUSALEM	0.0628	−0.0551	−0.3454
	(1.79)	(−0.99)	(−4.59)
ASIA	−0.3054	−0.6780	−1.0507
	(−12.36)	(−16.54)	(−19.40)
NORTHAFR	0.0403	−0.3462	−0.7519
	(1.49)	(−8.72)	(−15.24)
USSR	−0.2621	−0.4518	−0.1865
	(−6.35)	(−6.58)	(−2.56)
WESTEURO	0.2613	0.7274	0.5233
	(6.72)	(11.29)	(5.95)
ENGLSPEA	0.3041	1.6422	1.0617
	(2.60)	(12.85)	(7.04)
LATIAMER	0.5341	0.3305	0.2425
	(5.04)	(2.53)	(1.64)
Chi Square	34,923.53	34,923.53	34,923.53
Sample Size	81,602	81,602	81,602

Source: 1972 Census of Population and Housing, Israel, Public Use Sample, Demographic File, 20 percent sample of the population.

Notes: Dependent variable: HEBPRIML=3 if speaking Hebrew only, HEBPRIML=2 if Hebrew is primary language, HEBPRIML=1 if Hebrew is used as second or third language, and HEBPRIML=0 if individual does not speak Hebrew. Base category HEBPRIML=3.
z statistics are in parentheses.

Table 10.7 Predicted probability of being in each language category, Israel, 1972 (foreign-born Jewish men, age 25 to 64)

Variable	*Value*	*Only Hebrew*	*Hebrew primary*	*Hebrew second or third*	*No Hebrew*
MEANS		0.2068	0.6477	0.1096	0.0359
BASE		0.1594	0.6538	0.1455	0.0412
AGE	34	0.2502	0.6416	0.0887	0.0196
	45	0.1567	0.6532	0.1478	0.0423
	56	0.0891	0.6042	0.2238	0.0829
EDUC	5	0.1409	0.5854	0.1957	0.0780
	10	0.1629	0.6661	0.1354	0.0356
	15	0.1782	0.7177	0.0888	0.0154
YSM	16 (256)	0.1093	0.6243	0.2050	0.0613
(& YSMSQ)	27 (728)	0.2528	0.6528	0.0786	0.0158
	38 (1444)	0.4083	0.5519	0.0327	0.0071
MARR	1	Base	Base	Base	Base
	0	0.1498	0.6667	0.1366	0.0468
MARROVER	1	0.1242	0.6041	0.2181	0.0536
	0	Base	Base	Base	Base
CHILDREN	1	Base	Base	Base	Base
	0	0.1600	0.5919	0.1811	0.0669
HCHILBIS	1	Base	Base	Base	Base
	0	0.1521	0.6189	0.1664	0.0625
TEL-AVIV	1	0.1596	0.6505	0.1482	0.0416
JERUSALEM	1	0.1559	0.6809	0.1347	0.0285
Rest of Israel	0	Base	Base	Base	Base
EASTEURO	0	0.2104	0.6645	0.0928	0.0323
ASIA	1	0.2774	0.6456	0.0621	0.0149
NORTHAFR	1	0.2140	0.7038	0.0668	0.0155
USSR	1	0.2605	0.6332	0.0732	0.0331
WESTEURO	1	Base	Base	Base	Base
ENGLSPEA	1	0.1249	0.5349	0.2848	0.0554
LATIAMER	1	0.1389	0.7486	0.0853	0.0271

Source: 1972 Census of Population and Housing, Israel, Public Use Sample, Demographic File, 20 percent sample of the population.

Notes: Sample Size=81,602.
The base or reference person is a 44.6 year old Jewish male born in Western Europe with 9.1 years of schooling, who has lived in Israel 21.1 years, and is married but married after coming to Israel, has children born in Israel and does not live in Tel Aviv or Jerusalem.
Row totals may not add to 1.0000 due to rounding.
Multinomial logit coefficients obtained from Table 10.6.

The top row of Table 10.7 reports the probabilities for the person with "mean" characteristics, while the second row reports the probabilities for the base or reference person. The base or reference person in Table 10.7 has a mean age (age 44.6), level of education (9.1 years), and duration in Israel (21.1 years), is married, but married after immigration, and has children that were born in Israel. The reference person was born in Western Europe and does not live in Jerusalem or Tel Aviv.

The analysis indicates that the probability of speaking only Hebrew or speaking Hebrew as a primary language increases with education. The probability of speaking Hebrew as the only or primary language increases from 83 percent for those with base characteristics and 10 years of schooling to 90 percent for those with 15 years of schooling. Although the probability of speaking Hebrew as a primary but not only language decreases from 61 percent to 55 percent from 16 to 38 years duration in Israel, the probability that it is the only language spoken daily increases from 11 percent to 41 percent. The effect of an older age at migration on speaking Hebrew (the age variable for the base duration in Israel) is dramatic; Hebrew usage is lower the older the age at migration.

Those who married overseas are less likely to speak only Hebrew or to speak it as a primary language. Not having children or having children who were not born in Israel is associated with lesser use of Hebrew.

The analysis also shows important differences by country of origin. Immigrants from English-speaking countries are much more likely to report Hebrew as their second (or third) language spoken or that they speak no Hebrew. English is presumably being predicted as the primary or only language spoken on a daily basis by 34 percent of those from English-speaking countries (28.5 percent speak Hebrew as the second or third language and 5.5 percent do not speak Hebrew on a daily basis).

Earnings

The mean annual earnings of wage and salary workers in 1972 in Israeli Liras are reported in Table 10.8 for adult Jewish immigrants by Hebrew speaking and writing proficiencies.[12] These simple relationships show that for each level of speaking Hebrew, earnings are higher for those who can write in Hebrew. For each writing level, earnings are higher for those who speak Hebrew as their only or primary language, compared to those for whom it is a second or third language or who do not speak Hebrew. The highest earnings are received by those for whom Hebrew is the primary language, but they also speak another language on a daily basis, and they can write a letter in Hebrew (IL 12,518). The lowest earnings are received by those who neither speak Hebrew on a daily basis, nor can they write in Hebrew (IL 8,045).

The statistical analysis of earnings is reported in Tables 10.9 and 10.10 to ascertain the effects of Hebrew speaking usage and Hebrew literacy, when other variables are held constant. Table 10.9 column (1) reports the basic earnings equation without the language variables, while speaking skills are added in the next three columns. In Table 10.10 the effects on earnings are examined for writing skills and for speaking and writing combined.

Table 10.8 Mean earnings by Hebrew language skills, Israel, 1972 (foreign-born Jewish men, age 25 to 64, with positive gross annual earnings, wage and salaried workers)

	Speaking Hebrew				
Writing Hebrew	*Only*	*Primary*	*Second or third*	*No Hebrew*	*Total*
Yes	12,310.88 (14,708) [7,315.59]	12,518.10 (32,160) [7,736.96)	11,034.99 (5,352) [8,276.64]	9,996.84 (1,840) [7,217.98]	12,229.08 (54,060) [7,686.70]
No	7,594.10 (705) [4,983.46]	8,024.56 (2,865) [4,956.33]	7,782.43 (3,029) [4,894.87]	6,952.52 (3,286) [5,975.12]	7,563.29 (9,885) [5,319.15]
Total	12,095.13 (15,413) [7,292.14]	12,150.54 (35,025) [7,647.83]	9,859.47 (8,381) [7,405.50]	8,045.29 (5,126) [6,611.50]	11,507.81 (63,945) [7,561.08]

Source: 1972 Census of Population and Housing, Israel, Public Use Sample, Demographic File, 20 percent sample of the population.

Notes: Number of cases (N) are in parentheses.
Standard deviations (STD) are in brackets.
Earnings in 1972 Israeli Lira.

The effects of the basic variables on earnings are largely invariant with respect to the inclusion of speaking and writing variables. Earnings increase with additional human capital (Table 10.9, column 1). Earnings increase by about 4 percent per year of schooling (EDUC), which is lower than the 6 percent found in the analysis of immigrants in the 1983 Census, as well as lower than in the United States and Canada (Chiswick, 1998; Chiswick and Miller, 1992).

Earnings increase with pre-immigration labor market experience (EXP), at about 1.8 percent per year when evaluated at 10 years of experience. Experience in Israel (YSM) has a larger effect. Evaluated at 10 years, the effect of an extra year in Israel on earnings rather than an extra year in the country of birth is 2.1 percent when language skills are not held constant and about 1.7 percent when they are. Some of the effect of duration in Israel on earnings operates through language skills, that is, Hebrew language proficiency increases with duration and greater proficiency enhances earnings. Married men earn considerably more than observationally similar men who are not married. These patterns are similar to effects found in the 1983 Census and for other immigrant receiving countries.

Place of residence in Israel matters. Earnings are about 5 percent lower in Jerusalem and 1.6 percent lower in Tel Aviv than in the rest of the country (Table 10.9, column 1). This is slightly different from the pattern in the 1983 Census, an 8 percent lower earnings in Jerusalem and no significant difference in earnings in Tel Aviv. More striking is the difference between Israel, on the one hand, and the US and Canada on the other, where earnings tend to increase with population density or city size (Chiswick and Miller, 1992).

Country of birth also matters. Compared to immigrants from Eastern Europe, earnings are lower by about 20 percent among those from Asia (Middle East), 14 percent among those from North Africa, and 11 percent among those from the USSR (Table 10.9, column 1). There is no significant difference in earnings between Western European and Eastern European origin immigrants. Some immigrants, on the other hand, have earnings significantly higher than Eastern Europeans – about 20 percent higher for those from English-speaking developed countries and 7 percent higher among Latin American immigrants.

When the language variables are added to the earnings equation it is clear that Hebrew language skills matter. Speaking only Hebrew or speaking it as a primary language raises earnings by about 13 percent (Table 10.9, column 2). Compared to those who speak only Hebrew, there is no difference in earnings on the part of those who speak it as a primary language, but earnings are lower by about 9 percent for those who report it as a second or tertiary language, and by over 20 percent for those who do not speak it on a daily basis (Table 10.9, column 3).

Other variables being the same, speaking English on a daily basis is associated with about 15 percent higher earnings (Table 10.9, column 4).[13] On the other hand, speaking Arabic is associated with about 2 percent lower earnings. These patterns are very similar to the earnings differences for English and Arabic speakers in the 1983 Census (Chiswick, 1998). Greater earnings for English language skills, even when country of origin is held constant, may arise because English is an international language.[14] Those engaged in foreign trade or in tourism in Israel may have expanded opportunities if they have some degree of proficiency in English. Moreover, immigrants from the high income English-speaking developed countries have a high opportunity cost of remaining in Israel and a high propensity for return migration. Perhaps mainly those who "do well" in Israel remain.

Harder to explain are the lower earnings of those who speak Arabic on a daily basis, even after controlling for country of origin. Jewish immigrants from the Middle East and North Africa who speak Arabic on a daily basis may be less well skilled in Hebrew and less integrated into the mainstream Israeli economy than those who do not speak Arabic, other things being the same.

The analysis of literacy indicates that those who can write a letter in Hebrew earn about 12 percent more than those who cannot (Table 10.10, column 1). When Hebrew speaking and writing are both included in the analysis, each is statistically significant (Table 10.10, columns 2 and 3). Of particular note is Table 10.10, column (4). The benchmark is those for whom Hebrew is the only or primary language and who can write a simple letter in Hebrew. Those who can speak Hebrew but not write it have 8 percent lower earnings (YSPNWR). Those who do not speak Hebrew as an

Table 10.9 Analysis of earnings with language variables, Israel, 1972 (foreign-born Jewish men, age 25 to 64, with positive gross annual earnings, wage and salaried workers)

Variables	*(1)*	*(2)*	*(3)*	*(4)*
CONSTANT	7.8380	7.7994	7.9506	7.9545
	(416.80)	(412.21)	(401.86)	(400.71)
EDUC	0.0441	0.0433	0.0429	0.0413
	(63.97)	(62.70)	(62.07)	(59.01)
EXP	0.0304	0.0305	0.0300	0.0305
	(36.14)	(36.25)	(35.51)	(36.04)
EXPSQ	−0.0006	−0.0005	−0.0005	−0.0005
	(−40.43)	(−38.81)	(−38.00)	(−38.25)
MARR	0.3044	0.3038	0.3029	0.3032
	(35.25)	(35.14)	(35.06)	(35.15)
YSM	0.0273	0.0224	0.0212	0.0216
	(33.76)	(26.27)	(24.66)	(25.17)
YSMSQ	−0.0003	−0.0002	−0.0002	−0.0002
	(−17.60)	(−14.18)	(−13.06)	(−14.01)
TEL-AVIV	−0.0163	−0.0159	−0.0159	−0.0168
	(−3.19)	(−3.10)	(−3.10)	(−3.28)
JERUSALEM	−0.0457	−0.0484	−0.0498	−0.0524
	(−4.99)	(−5.28)	(−5.45)	(−5.73)
ASIA	−0.2037	−0.2117	−0.2136	−0.2069
	(−30.45)	(−31.60)	(−31.86)	(−27.47)
NORTHAFR	−0.1376	−0.1482	−0.1523	−0.1419
	(−20.87)	(−22.42)	(−23.04)	(−19.24)
USSR	−0.1142	−0.1166	−0.1121	−0.1117
	(−10.45)	(−10.69)	(−10.28)	(−10.25)
WESTEURO	0.0073	0.0150	0.0141	0.0016
	(0.68)	(1.39)	(1.30)	(0.15)
ENGLSPEA	0.1989	0.2229	0.2078	0.0867
	(9.02)	(10.11)	(9.42)	(3.65)
LATIAMER	0.0799	0.0722	0.0680	0.0708
	(3.57)	(3.23)	(3.04)	(3.18)
HEBSOP	–	0.1282	–	–
	–	(18.79)		
HEBPRIM	–	–	0.0047	−0.0015
			(0.81)	(-0.24)
HEBSECTH	–	–	−0.0854	−0.0941
			(−9.53)	(−10.05)
HEBNONE	–	-	−0.2082	−0.2217
			(−18.80)	(−19.36)
ENGLOPS	–	–	–	0.1597
				(14.02)
ARABOPS	–	–	–	−0.0240
				(−3.21)
R^2 adj.	0.2427	0.2466	0.2483	0.2510
Sample Size	61,622	61,416	61,416	61,416

Source: 1972 Census of Population and Housing, Israel, Public Use Sample, Demographic File, 20 percent sample of the population.

Notes: Dependent variable: natural logarithm of gross annual earnings for wage and salaried workers.

t ratios are in parentheses. Earnings in 1972 Israeli Lira.

Table 10.10 Analysis of earnings with language and writing variables, Israel, 1972 (foreign-born Jewish men, age 25 to 64, with positive gross annual earnings, wage and salaried workers)

Variables	*(1)*	*(2)*	*(3)*	*(4)*
CONSTANT	7.8042	7.7814	7.7780	7.9769
	(411.01)	(407.96)	(402.11)	(400.43)
EDUC	0.0405	0.0408	0.0408	0.0408
	(56.12)	(56.39)	(56.37)	(56.37)
T	0.0299	0.0301	0.0301	0.0301
	(35.37)	(35.60)	(35.53)	(35.53)
TSQ	−0.0005	−0.0005	−0.0005	−0.0005
	(−38.35)	(−37.46)	(−37.42)	(−37.42)
MARR	0.3033	0.3030	0.3030	0.3030
	(35.02)	(34.90)	(34.90)	(34.90)
YSM	0.0247	0.0213	0.0213	0.0213
	(29.73)	(24.67)	(24.67)	(24.67)
YSMSQ	−0.0003	−0.0002	−0.0002	−0.0002
	(−15.82)	(−13.45)	(−13.43)	(−13.43)
TEL-AVIV	−0.0176	−0.0171	−0.0171	−0.0171
	(−3.43)	(−3.32)	(−3.33)	(−3.33)
JERUSALEM	−0.0477	−0.0499	−0.0500	−0.0500
	(−5.20)	(−5.42)	(−5.43)	(−5.43)
ASIA	−0.2041	−0.2096	−0.2097	−0.2097
	(−30.37)	(−31.13)	(−31.14)	(−31.14)
NORTHAFR	−0.1408	−0.1484	−0.1485	−0.1485
	(−21.23)	(−22.31)	(−22.32)	(−22.32)
USSR	−0.1120	−0.1143	−0.1141	−0.1141
	(−10.25)	(−10.47)	(−10.45)	(−10.45)
WESTEURO	0.0140	0.0188	0.0187	0.01867
	(1.29)	(1.734)	(1.72)	(1.72)
ENGLSPEA	0.2014	0.2214	0.2200	0.2200
	(9.15)	(10.05)	(9.96)	(9.96)
LATIAMER	0.0808	0.0752	0.0748	0.0748
	(3.62)	(3.36)	(3.35)	(3.0.35)
HEBWRIT	0.1216	0.0888	0.0959	–
	(15.60)	(10.97)	(9.08)	
HEBSOP	–	0.1072	0.1183	–
		(15.00)	(9.23)	
HEBSPWR	–	–	−0.0153	–
			(−1.05)	
YSPNWR	–	–	–	−0.0806
				(−7.16)
NSPYWR	–	–	–	−0.1030
				(−12.60)
NSPNWR	–	–	–	−0.1989
				(−20.52)
R^2 adj.	0.2430	0.2453	0.2453	0.2453
Sample Size	60,893	60,689	60,689	60,689

Source: 1972 Census of Population and Housing, Israel, Public Use Sample, Demographic File, 20 percent sample of the population.

Notes: Dependent variable: natural logarithm of gross annual earnings for wage and salaried workers.
t ratios are in parentheses. Earnings in 1972 Israeli Lira.

only or primary language but who can write Hebrew (NSPYWR) have 10 percent lower earnings. While those who neither speak nor write Hebrew (NSPNWR) have 20 percent lower earnings.

The analysis of earnings indicates that the skills of immigrants matter. Earnings increase with schooling and pre-immigration labor market experience. Post-immigration labor market experience and both speaking and writing Hebrew language skills are also important determinants of earnings. Earnings also vary by origin, with North African and Middle Eastern Jewish immigrants having the lowest earnings, perhaps because of the lower quality of schooling in their origins and their pre-immigration human capital was formed in economies at a much lower level of economic development than was Israel in 1972. Immigrants from the English-speaking developed countries have the highest earnings, in part because they speak the most important international language, come from highly developed economies with advanced school systems, and the high wages, political freedom and absence of persecution in their origin countries means that they have a high opportunity cost of staying in Israel. The high propensity for return migration and the high opportunity cost of staying is Israel may account for the high earnings of the immigrants from English-speaking countries that remain in Israel.

It is possible to estimate the rate of return on the investment in Hebrew language proficiency. It was found here that, at least in 1972, proficiency in Hebrew increased earnings by 20 percent, all other variables being the same. Suppose that this level of Hebrew proficiency can be obtained through a six-month full-time intensive Hebrew language ("ulpan") training program. The cost of this program is the forgone earnings plus the costs of the teachers, classroom, supplies, etc. For simplicity of exposition let us assume that these latter costs are also equal to six months' forgone earnings. If the total cost is the equivalent of a full year's potential earnings and if a long work life is assumed (and 30 years would be sufficiently long), the real social rate of return on this investment would be approximately 20 percent.[15] This would be a high rate of return on an investment in human capital. The rate of return would, of course, be lower if the immigrant is older (shorter remaining working life) or if the immigrant requires a longer or more expensive training period, and would be higher if the training costs were lower than what was used in this example.

Summary and conclusions

This study has used the 1972 Census of Israel to analyze the determinants of Hebrew speaking and writing proficiency among adult male Jewish immigrants. It also analyzes the effects of these skills on labor market earnings.

Hebrew speaking proficiency is measured by whether it is spoken on a daily basis as the only language or in conjunction with other languages, or not at all. Writing proficiency is measured by the ability to write a letter in Hebrew. The analysis demonstrates that the acquisition of these skills is consistent with the model of immigrant language acquisition developed for English-speaking destinations. In particular, Hebrew language proficiency among adult male immigrants is greater among those who: immigrated at a younger age, have been in Israel longer, and have more schooling. Hebrew skills are lower among those who married their current wife prior to immigration, and are greater among those with children, especially if they were born in Israel. Thus, skills and family structure matter.

Hebrew language skills are associated with where one lives in Israel. Those living in Tel Aviv are less likely to speak Hebrew, while those living in Jerusalem are more likely to speak and write Hebrew than immigrants living in the rest of the country. Those living in areas where many others use their origin language are less likely to speak Hebrew or to be able to write in Hebrew. That is, linguistic concentrations or enclaves retard Hebrew language acquisition.

Immigrants from North Africa and the Middle East show the greatest use of Hebrew, perhaps because it is linguistically close to Arabic and they have a low propensity for return migration. Those from Western Europe, and especially those from the developed English-speaking countries, have the least proficiency in Hebrew. The high propensity for return migration and the importance of English as an international language may discourage English language speakers from investing in the Hebrew language.

Hebrew language skills influence earnings. Those who speak Hebrew as an only or primary language earn about 13 percent more per year than those who use it less frequently or not at all, while those who can write in Hebrew have a similar earnings advantage. Although they are related, Hebrew speaking and writing proficiency have separate effects and both matter. Those who possess both skills earn about 20 percent more than those who lack both skills.

Hebrew is not the only language that effects earnings. Immigrants who speak English have an earnings advantage of about 16 percent, while those who speak Arabic have a 2 percent earnings disadvantage, other variables being the same.

The similarity of the findings with other immigrant receiving countries suggests that the underlying processes determining Hebrew language usage in Israel and its effect on earnings are the same as elsewhere. The large effects on earnings of Hebrew language skills indicates its importance in the labor market and for the successful absorption of immigrants.

Notes

This chapter is an outgrowth of Barry Chiswick's collaborative research with Paul W. Miller on the Economics of Language. This chapter was presented at the Conference on the Economics of Judaism and Jewish Human Capital, co-sponsored by the Departments of Economics at the University of Illinois at Chicago and Bar-Ilan University (Ramat Gan, Israel), held in Chicago, June 2000. Comments from Carmel U. Chiswick, Evelyn Lehrer, and Paul W. Miller on an earlier draft were very helpful. An earlier version was published in Sergio DellaPergola and

Judith Evans (eds), *Papers in Jewish Demography, 1997*, Jerusalem: Hebrew University, Jewish Population Studies 29 (2000). We appreciate the assistance of Michael Beenstock, Department of Economics, Hebrew University, and of Michal Peleg, Director, and Natasha Volchkima, both of the Social Science Data Archive, Hebrew University, in making available the 1972 Census of Israel.

1 Few survey data sets on immigrants include information on literacy, that is, reading and/or writing skills. Studies that have examined immigrant literacy in the destination language include Beenstock (1993) for Israel, Rivera-Batiz (1996), Chiswick (1991), Chiswick and Miller (1998b and 1999) for the United States, Kee (1993) for the Netherlands and Dustmann (1994) for Germany. Compared to the census, these studies tend to analyze relatively small samples of selected foreign-born populations.

2 The Israeli Census is similar to censuses in other major immigrant receiving countries in not asking about specific pre-immigration experiences, other than country of birth.

3 For an interesting newspaper article on children serving as translators for their immigrant parents in the United States, see Hedges (2000).

4 Unlike the case of English among immigrants in the English-speaking developed countries, immigrants to Israel with a higher level of schooling are not more likely than their less educated counterparts to have been exposed to Hebrew in their pre-immigration secular schooling.

5 The automatic granting of Israeli citizenship to Jewish immigrants at entry means that this is not a relevant variable for Israel.

6 These regions are Jerusalem, Northern, Haifa, Central, Tel Aviv, Southern, and two very small groups, Jewish localities in the occupied territories (West Bank and Gaza) and area not specified.

7 These languages in order of frequency are Arabic, Yiddish, German, Romanian, French, Spanish-Ladino, Polish, English, Hungarian, Persian, Russian, and Kurdish. The substantive findings are unchanged if CONPR is expanded to include second or tertiary languages spoken.

8 For example, although in the 1972 Census among immigrants in Israel 6 to 10 years 8 percent spoke only Hebrew and 52 percent spoke Hebrew as an only or primary language, eleven years later in the 1983 Census, the cohort in Israel 16 to 20 years reported 19 percent and 79 percent, respectively. This is very similar to the 21 percent and 77 percent speaking only Hebrew or Hebrew as the only or primary language, respectively, among immigrants in the country 16 to 20 years as reported in the 1972 Census. See Table 10.2 and Chiswick (1998).

9 As the mean of the dependent variable is 0.75, multiplying the logit coefficients by 0.188 gives a partial effect that can be compared to the OLS coefficients. The majority of the effects in the logit model are slightly stronger than in the OLS model.

10 The cross-tabulation of writing and speaking among adult foreign-born men, expressed in percentage, is:

	Speaking Hebrew				
Writing	*Only*	*Primary*	*Second or third*	*No Hebrew*	*Total*
Yes	23.2	47.9	8.5	3.1	82.7
No	1.3	4.8	5.2	6.1	17.3
Total	24.5	52.7	13.7	9.2	100.0

11 Because the construction of the language concentration variable (CONPR) involves assigning values of zero to all individuals in the "Only Hebrew" category, the language concentration variable cannot be included in the multinomial logit model.

12 Other studies of the labor market adjustment of immigrants in Israel using various census and survey data include Beenstock (1993, 1996b), Beenstock and Ben-Menachem (1997), Chiswick (1998), Eckstein and Shachar (1995), Eckstein and Weiss (1998), Friedberg (2000), Neuman (1998), and Raijman and Semyonov (1998).

13 The dichotomous variables ENGLOPS and ARABOPS are unity for those who speak English and Arabic, respectively, on a daily basis as their only, primary or secondary language.

14 The effect of country of origin on earnings among immigrants in Israel from the high wage, high return migration English-speaking developed countries is presumably reflected in the coefficient of the English-speaking country of origin variable.

15 If going from lacking proficiency to having proficiency increases annual earnings by 100b percent, and if k is the cost of the investment expressed in full-year potential earnings, the rate of return on the investment is approximately $r=b/k$. In this example, $b=0.20$, $k=1.0$ and the rate of return on the investment is approximately 20 percent. If the cost were nine months' potential earnings, the rate of return would be approximately $r=0.20\ /.75=26.6$, or approximately 27 percent.

References

Beenstock, Michael (1993) "Learning Hebrew and Finding a Job: Econometric Analysis of Immigrant Absorption in Israel," Discussion Paper 93.05, Falk Institute, Hebrew University, Jerusalem.

Beenstock, Michael (1996a) "The Acquisition of Language Skills by Immigrants: The Case of Hebrew in Israel," *International Migration*, 34 (1): 3–30.

Beenstock, Michael (1996b) "Failure to Absorb: Remigration by Immigrants to Israel," *International Migration Review*, 30 (4): 950–978.

Beenstock, Michael and Yitzhak Ben-Menahem (1997) "The Labor Market Experience of CIS Immigrants to Israel: 1989–1994," *International Migration*, 35 (2): 187–224.

Blejer, Mario I. and Itzhak Goldberg (1980) "Return Migration-Expectations versus Reality: A Case Study of Western Immigrants in Israel," *Research in Population Economics*, 2: 443–449.

Chiswick, Barry R. (1978) "The Effect of Americanization on the Earnings of Foreign-Born Men," *Journal of Political Economy*, 86 (5): 897–922.

Chiswick, Barry R. (1991) "Speaking, Reading and Earnings Among Low-Skilled Immigrants," *Journal of Labor Economics*, 9 (2): 149–170.

Chiswick, Barry R. (1998) "Hebrew Language Usage: Determinants and Effects on Earnings Among Immigrants in Israel," *Journal of Population Economics*, 11 (2): 253–271.

Chiswick, Barry R. and Paul W. Miller (1992) "Language in the Immigrant Labor Market," in Barry R. Chiswick (ed), *Immigration, Language and Ethnicity: Canada and the United States*, Washington: American Enterprise Institute.

Chiswick, Barry R. and Paul W. Miller (1995) "The Endogeneity Between Language and Earnings: International Analyzes," *Journal of Labor Economics*, 13 (2): 245–287.

Chiswick, Barry R. and Paul W. Miller (1998a) "English Language Fluency Among Immigrants in the United States," *Research in Labor Economics*, 17: 151–200.

Chiswick, Barry R. and Paul W. Miller (1998b) "Language Skill Definition: A Study of Legalized Aliens," *International Migration Review*, 32 (4): 877–900.

Chiswick, Barry R. and Paul W. Miller (1999) "Language Skills and Earnings Among Legalized Aliens," *Journal of Population Economics*, 12 (1): 63–91.

Dustmann, Christian (1994) "Speaking Fluency, Writing Fluency and Earnings of Migrants," *Journal of Population Economics*, 7 (2): 133–156.

Eckstein, Zvi and Ron Shachar (1995) "On the Transition to Work of New Immigrants: Israel 1990–92," mimeo, Department of Economics, Tel Aviv University.

Eckstein, Zvi and Yoram Weiss (1998) "The Absorption of Highly Skilled Immigrants: Israel, 1990–1995," mimeo, Department of Economics, Tel Aviv University.

Friedberg, Rachel (2000) "You Can't Take it With You? Immigrant Assimilation and the Portability of Human Capital," *Journal of Labor Economics*, 18 (2): 221–251.

Hedges, Chris (2000) "Translating America for Parents and Family," *New York Times*, Monday, June 19, New York Report, p. A19 (Midwest Edition).

Kee, Peter (1993) *The Economic Status of Male Immigrants in the Netherlands*, Amsterdam: University of Amsterdam.

Long, Michael H. (1990) "Maturational Constraints on Language Development," *Studies in Second Language Acquisition*, 12 (3): 251–285.

Neuman, Shoshana (1998) "Immigration: The Israeli Case," mimeo, Department of Economics, Bar Ilan University, Ramat Gan, Israel.

Raijman, Rebeca and Moshe Semyonov (1998) "Best of Times, Worst of Times, and Occupational Mobility: the Case of Russian Immigrants in Israel," Working Paper 98–04, Research on Immigration and Integration in the Metropolis, Vancouver.

Rivera-Batiz, Francisco L. (1996) "English Language Proficiency, Quantitative Skills, and the Economic Progress of Immigrants," in Harriet Orcutt Duleep and Phanindra V. Wunnava, (eds), *Immigrants and Immigration Policy: Individual Skills, Family Ties, and Group Identities*, Greenwich, Conn. JAI Press: 55–77.

11 Why go back?

Return motives of migrant workers

Christian Dustmann

Introduction

Most of the theoretical and empirical literature on migration has paid little attention to the fact that many migrants return to their home countries after having spent a number of years in the host country. This is surprising, since many migrations today are in fact temporary. For instance, labour migrations from Southern to central Europe in the 1950s–1970s were predominantly temporary. Böhning (1984: 147) estimates that "more than two thirds of the foreign workers admitted to the Federal Republic [of Germany], and more than four fifth in the case of Switzerland, have returned." Glytsos (1988) reports that of the 1 million Greeks migrating to West Germany between 1960 and 1984, 85 percent gradually returned home. Dustmann (1996) provides evidence for a substantial outmigration over that period for other European countries. Return migration is also considerable for the United States. Jasso and Rosenzweig (1982) report that between 1908 and 1957 about 15.7 million persons immigrated to the United States and about 4.8 million aliens emigrated. They found that between 20 and 50 percent of legal immigrants (depending on the nationality) re-emigrated from the United States in the 1970s. Warren and Peck (1980) estimate that about one-third of legal immigrants to the United States re-emigrated in the 1960s.

The decision of migrants to return to their home countries is not only an important issue in its own right. It also has crucial implications for immigrants' behavior. Migrants who have the intention to remain for shorter periods in the host countries could be expected to accumulate less human capital which is specific to the host country economy than migrants with more permanent intentions. This has implications for assimilation patterns of immigrant workers. A number of empirical studies[1] have found considerable differences in the economic assimilation of migrant workers of different origin. If origin is correlated with expected durations in the host country (return could be less costly for some origin countries, and more costly for others), then this may contribute to explaining divergent assimilation profiles.

There is some earlier work on the effect of return plans on migrants' behaviour. Djajić (1989) shows that in a guest-worker system, levels of wages and prices in the home country affect the migrant's consumption and labour supply in the host country. Galor and Stark (1990, 1991) show that the probability of return also affects migrants' saving behavior and performance in the host country. Evidence in Merkle and Zimmermann (1992), stating that return probabilities of migrants affect their saving behavior, is compatible with these considerations.

In these studies, the return time of the migrant is assumed exogenous. Most temporary migrations in Europe and in the US, however, are migrations where it is the migrant who decides about whether and when to return. These return migrations often take place despite persistently more favourable economic conditions in the origin countries. Simple static models, where migration takes place in response to positive wage differentials between host and home country, cannot explain return migrations. In these models, migrants should only be expected to return if the economic situation changes so that real earnings at home increase relative to those in the host country.

There are some models explaining return migrations, which take place without a reversal of the economic situation in host-country and home country. Stark (1992) uses the theory of relative deprivation to explain why migrants may return to a less rich economy or region. Mesnard (2000) identifies capital market imperfections in the home country as a reason which may lead to return migrations. Djajić and Milbourne (1988) explain return migration by assuming that migrants have a stronger preference for consumption at home than abroad. Raffelhüschen (1992) uses an individual-specific location parameter in the utility function to introduce return migration in an overlapping generations model. Hill (1987) shows that migration may be temporary and repetitive if the migrant has a preference for certain locations.

This chapter develops a general life-cycle model, where a return is motivated by locational preferences, as in Djajić and Milbourne (1988), Hill (1987), and Raffelhüschen (1992). In addition, it offers in a unified setting two further motives for a return: first, higher purchasing power in the home country of assets accumulated in the host country. This motive has first been identified in a paper by Djajić (1989). A second motive is higher returns in the home economy on human capital, acquired in the host country. The last motive has first been identified in an earlier paper of mine (Dustmann, 1995), but this chapter provides a more in-depth analysis. A combination of these three motives appears to provide a more general framework which helps to explain migration behaviour, which may seem irrational in simpler models. For instance, human capital considerations may explain migrations which take place despite negative wage differentials, and a locational preference for the host country.

If migrations are temporary, then behavioral choices, like consumption and labour supply, are taken in conjunction with the choice of the migration duration. This has important implications for the way we need to specify empirical models. I briefly discuss some of these implications at the end of the chapter.

The structure of the chapter is as follows. The next section develops the basic model, and the remaining section investigates the different motives for return. The interaction between immigrants' behavior and their optimal return plans is then discussed, along with implications for empirical work. The final section summarizes the key findings and gives some conclusions.

The model

In the following analysis, only the productive life of an individual is considered. A *return migrant* is defined as a migrant who works for a chosen period in a host country, and returns *before* retirement age. Accordingly, a *permanent* migrant is a migrant who does not intend to return before retirement. Denote the migrant's active lifetime, or remaining time in the labour force, by T, and the optimal time to remain in the host country by $\hat{t}$. Consider the maximization problem of a migrant at the start of his migration history. He maximizes a utility function over the horizon T, with respect to consumption c and the optimal return point $\hat{t}$:

$$J = \int_0^{\hat{t}} u\left(c^I(\tau), \xi^I\right) e^{-\rho\tau} d\tau + \int_{\hat{t}}^{T} u\left(c^E(\tau), \xi^E\right) e^{-\rho\tau} d\tau \qquad (1)$$

where ρ is the rate of time preference, and c^I and c^E are the optimal flows of consumption abroad and at home respectively. The variables ξ^I and ξ^E summarize factors which are locationally fixed, and complementary to consumption. Examples are social relations, and subjectively perceived life quality parameters (climate, social regulations). Although both ξ^I and ξ^E may change over time, it is assumed here that they are considered as constant by the migrant when solving his optimization problem. This assumption is not as restrictive as it seems to be; a decision of how long to remain in a certain location is very likely to be affected by the subjective perception of the location at that moment, relative to the alternative location, rather than the path of possible perceptions over the optimization period. I discuss possible extensions below.

Since the migrant can influence ξ^i, $i=I, E$, only by a change in the location, ξ^I and ξ^E are treated as parameters rather than as variables. The utility functions exhibit the following properties: $u_1>0$, $u_2>0$, $u_{11}<0$, $u_{22}<0$, $u_{12}>0$, where the subscripts 1,2 denote derivatives with respect to the first and second argument. To simplify matters, the following notation will be used: $u(k,\xi^E)=v^E(k)$, $u(k,\xi^I)=v^I(k)$. Furthermore, the utility functions have the properties that $v_I^i(k)_{k\to\infty}\to 0$, $v_I^i(k)_{k\to 0}\to\infty$, $v^i(0)=0$, $i=I,E$. Throughout the analysis, it is assumed that $\xi^I\leq\xi^E$. A strictly larger home location parameter ($\xi^I<\xi^E$) is assumed to correspond to a higher utility from a constant consumption flow k in the home country both in marginal as well as in absolute terms: $v_1^E(k)>v_1^I(k)$, $v^E(k)>v^I(k)$.

The migrant maximizes (1), subject to the following intertemporal budget constraint:

$$\int_0^{\hat{t}} y^I e^{-r\tau}d\tau + \int_{\hat{t}}^T y^E(\hat{t})\,e^{-r\tau}d\tau + K_0 - \overline{K}e^{-rT} - \int_0^{\hat{t}} c^I(\tau)\,e^{-r\tau}d\tau - \int_{\hat{t}}^T pc^E(\tau)\,e^{-r\tau}d\tau = 0 \tag{2}$$

where r is the (time-constant) interest rate. To simplify matters, fixed cost of re-migration is set to zero.

The relative price level between emigration- and immigration country is given by p, where $p<1$ denotes a lower price level in the home country than in the host country. In this case, purchasing power of savings accumulated in the host country is higher in the home country. The stock of savings at $t=0$ is denoted by K_0, and $\bar{K}$ is the desired stock of savings at the end of the planning horizon, T.

Earnings per unit of time in the immigration and the emigration country are given by y^I and y^E respectively. Earnings y^I are assumed to be constant over time. However, earnings y^E may depend positively on the duration $\hat{t}$, with $y_{\hat{t}}^E\geq 0$, $y_{\hat{t}\hat{t}}^E\leq 0$. Accordingly, the time spent in the host country may enhance a migrant's human capital endowment which will only become earnings effective after re-migration.

This is a rather simple way to model the accumulation of human capital. Killingsworth (1982) and Rosen (1972) refer to this formulation of human capital acquisition as the *experience model*. It captures some basic features of many real migration situations. For the economies of origin countries which are in the process of industrialization, knowledge about working patterns, institutional features, incentive structures, and the language of highly industrialized countries is likely to be very valuable. Immigrants acquire such knowledge, and they may therefore considerably enhance their productivity in the home economy.[2] This human capital, though not sufficient to raise the earnings position in the host country considerably, raises potential wages in the home country. It is this increase in the migrant's potential wage which may trigger a return, as will be shown below. Notice that for obtaining this result, it suffices to assume that experience or training abroad increases potential home country wages by more than host country wages. To simplify the analysis, host country wages are assumed constant.

Consider first consumption flows in the two countries, which are implied by maximization of (1) s.t. (2). Denoting the marginal utility of wealth at t by $\pi(t)$, with $\pi(t)=\pi^0\,e^{(\rho-r)t}$, where $\pi^0=\pi(0)$, it follows that:

$$c(t) = \begin{cases} v_1^{I-1}(\pi) & : \quad 0 \le t < \hat{t} \\ v_1^{E-1}(\pi p) & : \quad \hat{t} \le t \le T \end{cases} \tag{3}$$

where the superscript $^{-1}$ denotes inverse functions. Strict concavity of the utility functions implies that the path of consumption increases if $\rho<r$. Only this case, which is consistent with increasing consumption profiles, is considered in the following analysis.

It follows from (3) that the migrant's consumption profile will "jump" upwards at the point of return if $\xi^I<\xi^E$, or if $p<1$. This model generates savings patterns which are understood as characterizing return migrations: an accumulation of savings in the host country, a peak of the savings profile upon return, and a decumulation of savings after a return (see Piore, 1979).

Writing consumption as a function of the marginal utility of income, $\pi(t)$, the budget constraint (2) implicitly determines π^0 as a function of $\hat{t}$:

$$\int_0^{\hat{t}} y^I e^{-r\tau} d\tau + \int_{\hat{t}}^{T} y^E(\hat{t})\, e^{-r\tau} d\tau + K - \int_0^{\hat{t}} c^I(\pi(\tau)) e^{-r\tau} d\tau - \int_{\hat{t}}^{T} pc^E(\pi(\tau)\,p)\, e^{-r\tau} d\tau = \Gamma(\pi^0, t), \tag{4}$$

with $K=K_0-\bar{K}e^{-rT}$. From the first order condition with respect to $\hat{t}$ follows:

$$\underbrace{\pi^0 e^{(\rho-r)\hat{t}}\left[\left[(y^I - c^I) - (y^E - pc^E)\right] + \frac{1}{r} y_{\hat{t}}^E \left[1 - e^{r(\hat{t}-T)}\right]\right]}_{\text{Benefit of staying abroad}} - \underbrace{\left[v^E - v^I\right]}_{\text{Cost of staying abroad}} = \Delta(\pi^0, \hat{t}) \tag{5}$$

Relations (4) and (5) determine the optimal π^0 and the optimal point of return $\hat{t}$. At the optimum, $\Delta(\pi^0,\hat{t})=\Gamma(\pi^0,\hat{t})=0$.

The return decision

I now investigate in detail the various reasons for a return migration which can be explored within the framework set out above. It is useful and illustrative to distinguish between cost and benefit of an additional unit of time spent in the host country. Using (4) to determine π^0 as a function of $\hat{t}$, (5) becomes a function of $\hat{t}$ alone. The first term in (5) corresponds to the benefit ($B(\hat{t})$) of lengthening the time spent abroad (every unit of time abroad increases resources for lifetime consumption, and enhances human capital); the second term reflects the cost $C(\hat{t})$ (staying longer abroad deprives the migrant of the possibility to consume during that unit of time in the home country):

$$B(\hat{t})-C(\hat{t})=D(\hat{t}) \tag{6}$$

where $D(\hat{t})$ is the difference in benefit and cost of remaining a further unit of time abroad. At the optimal return point $\hat{t}$, the cost of staying longer abroad is equal to the benefit of doing so, or $D(\hat{t})=0$.

For a migration to occur it is necessary that the cost of migration for $\hat{t}\rightarrow 0$ is smaller than the benefit, or $D(\hat{t})_{\hat{t}\rightarrow 0}>0$. An interior return point occurs if cost and benefit profiles cut at some $\hat{t}<T$. An intersection of cost and benefit schedules may be caused independently by three scenarios:

$(a)\ \xi^E>\xi^I,\ y^E_t=0,\ p=1,$

$(b)\ \xi^E=\xi^I,\ y^E_t=0,\ p<1,$

$(c)\ \xi^E=\xi^I,\ y^E_t>0,\ p=1.$

In scenario (a), differences in locational complementarities trigger a return. This explanation for return migrations has been explored by Djajić and Milbourne (1988). In scenario (b), lower prices in the home country encourage the migrant to return home. In scenario (c), an increase in the migrant's potential wage back home may cause a return. All three return motives are now investigated in detail.

To ensure that $D(\hat{t})_{\hat{t}\rightarrow 0}>0$, the wage differential between host and home country, y^I-y^E, is assumed to be positive for some initial $t, 0\leq t\leq T$. The cost $C(\hat{t})$ is positive whenever $\xi^E>\xi^I$ or/and $p<1$ (since in this case $[v^E-v^I]>0$). For scenario (c), the cost of remaining abroad equals zero.

Necessary for an interior return point is that $D(\hat{t})$ decreases in $\hat{t}$. That this is the case for each of the three return motives can be easily shown. It is instructive to derive the marginal cost and benefit schedules. For this purpose, differentiate the cost schedule with respect to $\hat{t}$. This yields an expression for the *marginal cost* $MC(\hat{t})$ of remaining a further unit of time abroad:

$$MC(\hat{t})=\pi\left[\dot{\pi}+e^{(\rho-r)\hat{t}}\frac{\partial\pi^0}{\partial\hat{t}}\right]\left[c^{E'}p-c^{I'}\right], \tag{7a}$$

where $c^{i'}$, $i=E,I$ are the derivatives of consumption with respect to $\pi(t)$, with $c^{i'},<0$. Furthermore, $\dot{\pi}$ is the change in π with respect to t, and π is evaluated at $\hat{t}$.

It can be shown that $\frac{\partial\pi_0}{\partial\hat{t}}\leq 0$ (see (11), Appendix A). For $\xi^E>\xi^I$ and/or $p<1$, it follows from (3) that $[c^{E'}p-c^{I'}]\leq 0$. Since $p<0$, the expression in

(7-a) is positive (or zero), indicating that the cost of staying in the host country increases over time (or remains constant).

The marginal benefit of remaining a further unit of time abroad, $MB(\hat{t})$, is given by:

$$MB(\hat{t}) = \pi\left[\dot{\pi} + e^{(\rho-r)\hat{t}}\frac{\partial\pi^0}{\partial\hat{t}}\right]\left[c^{E'}p - c^{I'}\right] + \left[\dot{\pi} + e^{(\rho-r)\hat{t}}\frac{\partial\pi^0}{\partial\hat{t}}\right]\left[\left(y^I - c^I\right) - \left(y^E - c^E p\right) + \frac{1}{r}y_{\hat{t}}^E\left(1 - e^{r(\hat{t}-T)}\right)\right] + \pi\left[y_{\hat{t}\hat{t}}^E\left(1 - e^{r(\hat{t}-T)}\right)\frac{1}{r} - y_{\hat{t}}^E e^{r(\hat{t}-T)}\right] \tag{7b}$$

Notice that the first term in (7-b) is identical to the marginal cost $M\,C(\hat{t})$, (expression 7-a). To show that $D(t)$ decreases in t, it remains to show that the second and third terms are negative for each of the three scenarios (a)–(c). If a return is motivated by (a) or (b), the third term equals zero, and the second term is negative (which follows from (5)). In case (c), the third term is clearly negative. It follows from (5) that the second terms is negative, and approaches zero as $t \to \hat{t}$. Consequently, $D(\hat{t})$ decreases in $\hat{t}$, and the benefit schedule is flatter than the cost schedule for all three scenarios $M\,B(\hat{t}) - M\,C(\hat{t}) < 0$.

To illustrate the implications of the model, each of the three return motives is now investigated in more detail, and simulations are performed for specific functional forms of the utility function and the accumulation of potential earnings in the home country (for details, see Appendix B). As a benchmark, the case where $\xi^E = \xi^I$, $y_t^E = 0$, and $p = 1$ is considered. This situation is referred to as the *classical case* – migration is only characterized by a positive wage differential between sending and receiving country.

The classical case

First consider the case where migration occurs as a consequence of positive wage differentials. Price levels are equal in both countries ($p = 1$), and $y_t^E(t) = 0$. The migrant is indifferent between consumption at home and abroad ($\xi^E = \xi^I$), and wages are higher abroad ($y^E < y^I$). Consequently, the cost of spending an extra unit of time abroad, $C(\hat{t})$, is equal to zero, and the benefit is simply $\pi(y^I - y^E)$, which is positive. Although $M\,B(\hat{t}) - M\,C(\hat{t}) = \dot{\pi}(y^I - y^E) < 0$, the benefit of staying abroad never approaches zero for a finite T. Accordingly, the migrant will never want to return to his home country. Migration, in this case, becomes permanent.

Figure 11.1 illustrates the cost and benefit schedules. Since the migrant is indifferent between consumption at home and abroad, the cost schedule is a horizontal line through 0. The benefit schedule decreases since $r > \rho$.

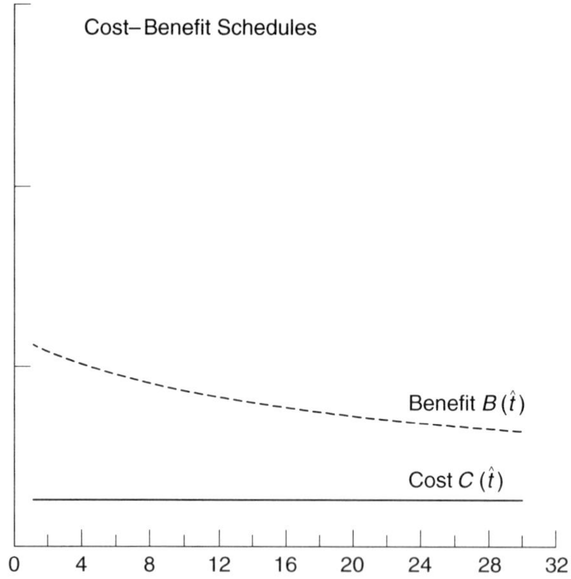

Figure 11.1 Cost and benefit schedules, classical case.

Figure 11.2 illustrates the consumption and earnings profiles. Consumption follows a typical life-cycle pattern which evolves when $r>\rho$. If, on the contrary, $y^E>y^I$, migration from the home country does not occur. Consequently, if wage differentials are the only driving force of migration, as is often assumed in the literature, only these two migration patterns are possible.

Return motive 1: locational preferences

Now consider a situation where the wage differential is again positive, with $y_t^E=0$, but assume that the migrant has a preference for consumption in his home country: $\xi^E>\xi^I$. This corresponds to situation (a). Cost and benefit of staying abroad are now both positive. If the initial benefit is sufficiently high, relative to the cost of migration ($D(\hat{t})>0$ for $\hat{t}\rightarrow 0$), migration occurs. However, the differential $D(\hat{t})$ decreases in $\hat{t}$, and there exists an interior return point, where $D(\hat{t})=0$. Whether an interior solution or a corner solution (permanent migration) occurs depends, for a given utility structure, on the size of the locational parameters and on the wage advantage abroad. For an interior solution, Figures 11.3 and 11.4 illustrate the path of earnings and consumption and the benefit and cost schedules respectively. Note that life-cycle consumption has a discontinuity at $t=\hat{t}$. The consumption profile follows a typical pattern for return migrants. While being abroad, migrants accumulate savings. After returning to the home country, they increase consumption, drawing on the previously accumulated stock of savings.

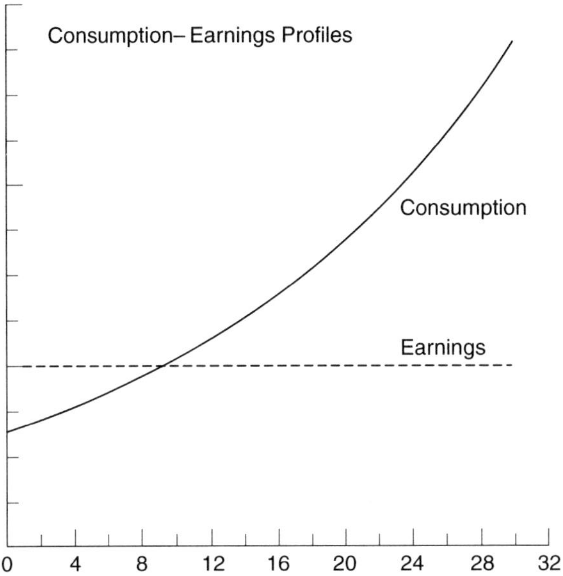

Figure 11.2 Earnings and consumption profiles, classical case.

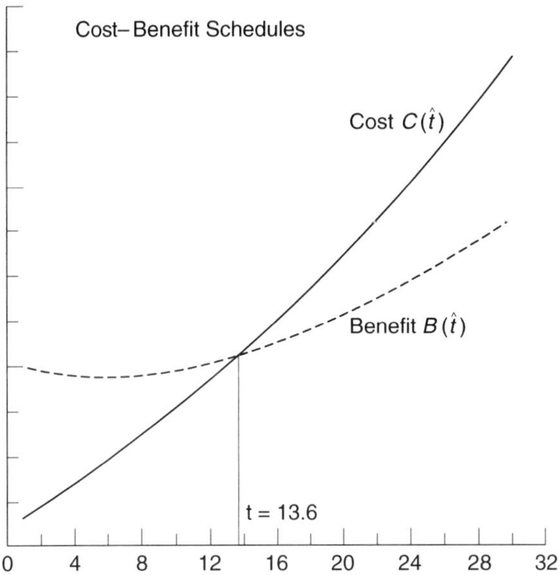

Figure 11.3 Cost and benefit schedules, preference for home country.

Return motive 2: purchasing power of savings abroad

Assume now that the migrant is indifferent between consumption at home and abroad ($\xi^I = \xi^E$), $y^I > y^E$ and $y^E_t = 0$, but the purchasing power of the host

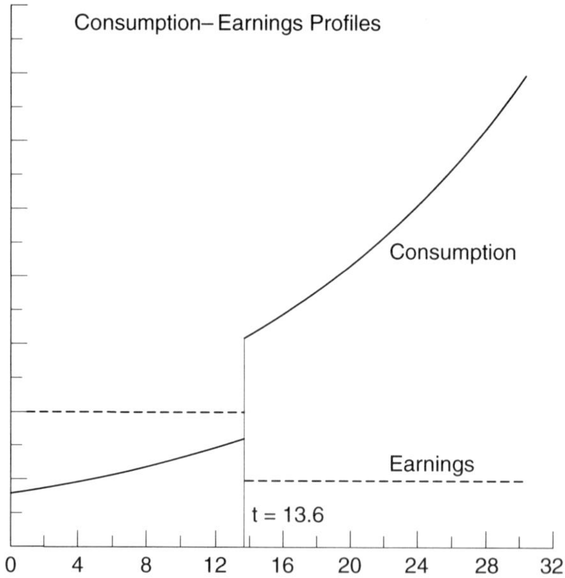

Figure 11.4 Earnings and consumption profiles, preference for home country.

country currency is higher in the home country ($p<1$). Since wages are higher in immigration countries, non-traded goods and services tend to be more expensive in host countries than in home countries. Furthermore, migrants often exhibit different consumption habits than natives, which may be due to cultural or religious differences. They may demand goods which need to be imported, and are accordingly more expensive.

A higher purchasing power of the host country currency in the migrant's home country leads to lower consumption abroad, and higher consumption at home (see (3)). Accordingly, costs $C(\hat{t})$ and benefits $B(\hat{t})$ are both positive. Migration occurs if $D(\hat{t})>0$ for $\hat{t}\rightarrow 0$. But $M\ B(\hat{t})-M\ C(\hat{t})<0$, and an interior solution occurs if the benefit schedule cuts the cost schedule before $\hat{t}=T$. The individual, although indifferent between locations, first migrates, but then returns to take advantage of both high wages abroad and low prices at home. This situation is illustrated in Figures 11.5 and 11.6.

Note also that this return motive creates a target saving behavior. Interestingly, savings do not necessarily peak at the return point; in the case depicted in Figure 11.6, the migrant reduces his savings stock while still residing in the host country.[4] A target saving behavior of return migrants, which has often been emphasized in the literature (see, for instance, Piore, 1979), seems to be compatible with scenarios (a) and (b).

Return motive 3: human capital

Lastly, consider the case where wages are initially higher abroad, the purchasing power of the foreign currency is equal in both countries ($p=1$),

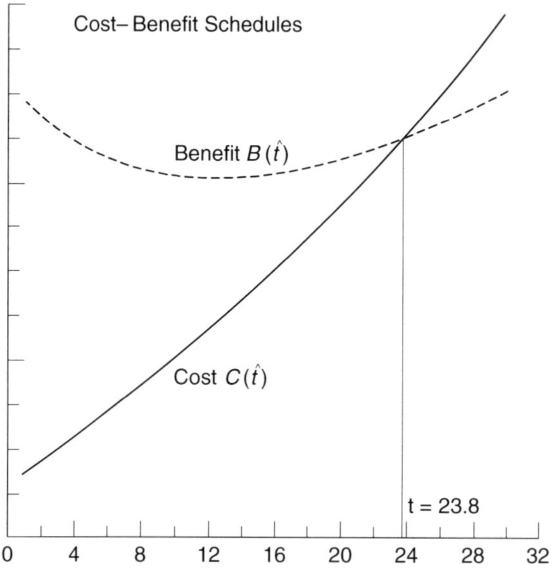

Figure 11.5 Cost and benefit schedules, higher price level abroad.

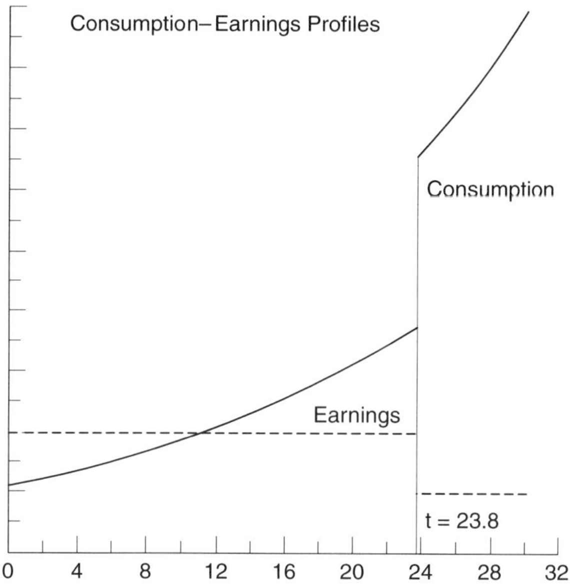

Figure 11.6 Earnings and consumption profiles, higher price level abroad.

and the migrant is indifferent between consumption at home and abroad ($\xi^I = \xi^E$). The time the migrant spends abroad, however, increases his earnings potential at home ($y_t^E > 0$), while it has no impact on the earnings potential abroad. Since the migrant is indifferent between consuming at home and abroad, the cost of migration $C(\hat{t})$ is equal to zero, and the benefit reduces to:

$$B(\hat{t}) = y^I = y^E + \frac{1}{r} y_i^E \left[1 - e^{r(\hat{t}-T)}\right], \tag{8}$$

which is positive for $\hat{t} \to 0$. However, since potential earnings at home are increasing over time, $B(\hat{t})$ will decrease, and eventually become zero. This is exactly the point when the migrant returns. Notice that at this point, the potential wage in the home country must be strictly higher than the wage received in the host country.

This situation is illustrated in Figures 11.7 and 11.8. The cost schedule is now equal to the zero line, but benefits decrease as the migrant improves his potential earnings position in the home country.

The model leads to a number of further interesting insights and results. One immediate implication is that migration and re-migration may occur, despite an initially *negative* wage differential. To see this, consider (8). The last term measures the benefits from human capital acquired in the host country over the remaining period in the home country. If this term is sufficiently large, benefits may well be positive, although the initial wage differential $y^I - y^E$ is negative. Migration in this case is purely an investment decision, and solely triggered by the future return to human capital.

Combinations of the different scenarios may now serve to describe specific types of migration. For instance, student migrations are frequently

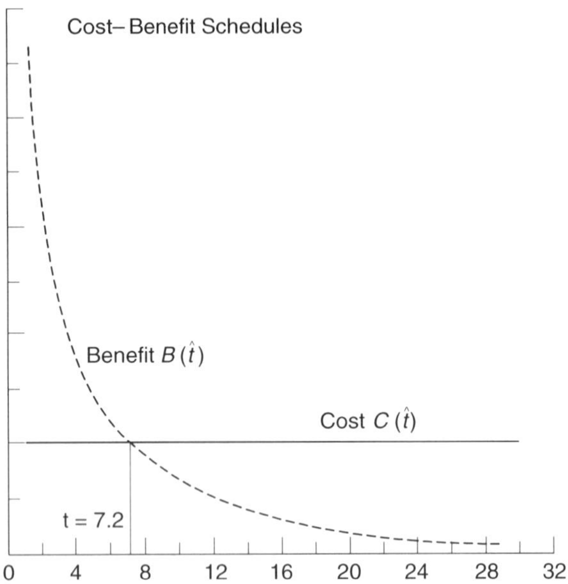

Figure 11.7 Cost and benefit schedules, human capital.

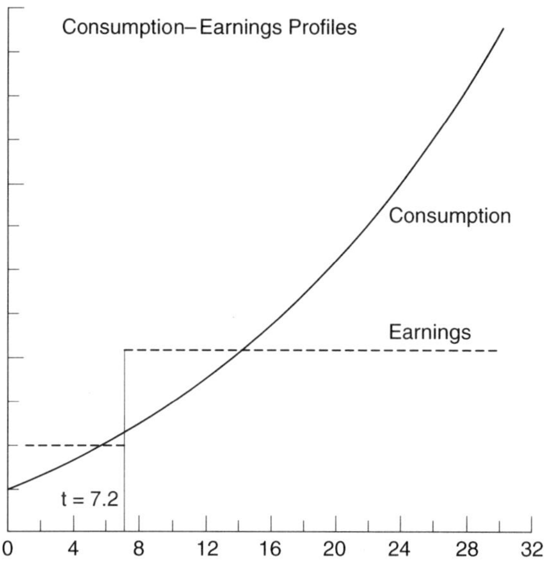

Figure 11.8 Earnings and consumption profiles, human capital.

characterized by a negative wage differential (consisting of forgone earnings in the home country, and possibly negative earnings abroad, such as fees etc.). However, migration occurs if the return to human capital acquired abroad is sufficiently large over the remaining time in the home country (last term in (8)).

The above considerations show that dynamic modelling is crucial to understand migrations which may seem non-rational in simple static models. Furthermore, a single return motive may not suffice to explain some of the observed migratory behavior. The above framework allows us to study a large range of empirical migration situations.

Comparative statics

To investigate how parameter changes affect the migrant's optimal duration abroad, comparative statics can be performed on the system described by equations (4) and (5). The partial effects of an increase in the parameters y^E, y^I, p, K and T on the optimal return time $\hat{t}$ are derived in the Appendix,[5] and they are reported in Table 11.1.

If return migration is caused by locational preferences or purchasing power considerations ($\xi^E > \xi^I$ or/and $p<1$), a change in any of these parameters has a direct as well as an indirect effect on the optimal duration $\hat{t}$, corresponding to an income and a substitution effect. The indirect effect results from changes in the marginal utility of wealth π^0, which in turn affects $\hat{t}$. However, if return migration is caused by scenario (c) only, the indirect effect vanishes, and only the direct effect is at work. The reason is that in this case the optimal paths of consumption and income are separable. These two situations are distinguished in the discussion which follows. In Table 11.1, the first row refers to the situation where a return is induced by motives (a) or/and (b); the second row refers to the situation where a return is induced by situation (c) only.

The effects of an increase in the home country wage y^E is unambiguously negative. Both the direct and the indirect effect point in the same direction. However, the effect of an increase in the host country wage on the optimal duration is not clear-cut for (a), (b). The reason is that now the direct effect and the indirect effect point in different directions. Intuitively, the migrant would like to prolong the stay abroad as a direct response to higher wages; but the gain from a further stay abroad decreases, and this has a counteracting effect on the optimal duration. Dustmann (1999b) provides some empirical evidence, which is compatible with the observation that the migration duration may decrease if the wage differential increases.

Notice that, if the return is solely induced by the human capital argument (situation (c)), an increase in host country wages has an unambiguously positive effect on the length of migration. The reason is that in this situation, the optimal paths of consumption and income are separable. Accordingly, changes in the marginal utility of wealth π^0 do not affect the optimal return time, and the indirect effect is equal to zero.

Consider next the effect of a decrease in purchasing power (increase in p) on the optimal return time. Again, the total effect is ambiguous. The direct effect is clearly positive: a decrease in purchasing power increases the optimal duration in the host country. However, the indirect effect is not clear-cut, since the effect of an increase in p on the marginal utility of wealth itself (π^0_p) is ambiguous. These are the conventional counteracting effects on the marginal utility of wealth: an increase in p decreases the flow of consumption c^E, but, at the same time, increases expenditures. Depending on the magnitude of these two effects, π^0 increases or decreases. Consequently, the total effect of an increase in p on the total duration is ambiguous, implying that an increase in purchasing power may decrease or increase the optimal migration duration.

Again, if human capital considerations are the only reason for a return migration (scenario (c)), then the indirect effect vanishes, and the effect of an increase in purchasing power on the optimal return time is unambiguously positive.

Table 11.1 Comparative statics

Increase in	y^E	y^I	p	K_0	$\bar{K}$	T
Motives (a), (b)	<0	$\gtrless 0$	$\gtrless 0$	<0	>0	$\gtrless 0$
Motive (c)	<0	>0	>0	<0	>0	>0

A further interesting variable is the length of the migrant's remaining active lifetime, T. Empirically, heterogeneity among immigrants with respect to T is reflected by heterogeneity in the age at entry to the host country. The direct effect of an increase in T (term $\hat{t}_T$) appears to be positive. The indirect effect is positive if expenditures at the end of an active working life are higher than earnings ($p\, c^E - y^E > 0$, see Appendix). This clearly occurs if only locational preferences trigger a return migration. Accordingly, in this case migrants who are younger at entry to the host country remain abroad longer. Likewise, under return scenario (c), the indirect effect vanishes ($t_{\pi^0} = 0$), and migrants who are younger at entry stay abroad longer. If purchasing power considerations are the return motive, however, the effect is ambiguous in general.

Other parameters which influence the optimal time abroad are the initial wealth and the desired wealth at the end of the planning horizon. Effects of both parameters are clear-cut. While a higher stock of accumulated capital at the beginning of the planning period (K_0) decreases the optimal duration abroad, a higher desired stock of capital at the end of the planning period ($\bar{K}$) has the opposite effect.

Extensions and implications for empirical work

The above model does not allow for the choice of leisure. Also, the mechanism of human capital accumulation is simple. Extensions, which allow for labour supply choices, and choices about human capital investments, are straightforward. Economists are typically interested in understanding and modelling these behavioral decisions of individuals. The model set out above provides a powerful framework to study behavior of migrant workers within a life-cycle model. Other than native workers, migrants who plan to return take these return plans into account when making choices in the host country. This has important implications for empirical work. Neglecting the simultaneity between, for instance, consumption and labour supply choices on the one side, and return plans on the other, may lead to misspecified empirical models.

To illustrate this point, consider savings and consumption behavior of migrants. Within the framework set out above, conditions (3), (4) and (5) determine simultaneously consumption $c(t)$, the marginal utility of wealth, $\pi(t)$, and the optimal return point, $\hat{t}$. To obtain an estimable specification, linearize these three equations, and solve out for $\pi(t)$. This leaves us with a system of two simultaneous equations, determining consumption and the optimal return time. Dropping, for simplicity, time indices, and adding error terms, results in the following statistical model:

$$
\begin{aligned}
c &= \alpha_1 + \alpha_2 \hat{t} + \alpha_3 x + u, \\
\hat{t} &= \beta_1 + \beta_2 c + \beta_3 z + v,
\end{aligned} \tag{9}
$$

where α_i and β_i, $i=1,2,3$ are parameter (vectors), and u and v are error terms. The (vectors) x and z contain variables which determine consumption and the return time, respectively. Suppose that one element of x is the wage in the host country, and that the respective parameter in α_3 is the parameter of interest.

It is obvious that estimation of the consumption equation, omitting the optimal return time, does not identify this parameter, because of a conventional simultaneous equations bias. The parameter identified in this case is a compound parameter, measuring the direct effect of changes in wages, conditional on the optimal return time, and the indirect effect, by way of changing the return time. For this particular example, it can be shown that, while the direct effect is positive, the indirect effect is ambiguous in general (see Dustmann, 1995, for details). Accordingly, when estimating consumption functions for return migrants without taking this simultaneity into account, the parameter estimate on wages in the host country is not the structural parameter which the analyst may want to identify.

Similar considerations apply in related models, where labour supply or human capital investments of immigrants are analysed. Dustmann (1997a) develops a simplified version of the above model, where individuals choose labour supply in addition. The model is estimated for females, where partner characteristics identify the model. Dustmann (1999a) develops a model where investments in human capital production are a further choice variable. The empirical application investigates investments in language capital of migrant workers.

Summary and conclusions

This chapter analyzes migration and re-migration decisions of migrant workers. A life-cycle model is developed where individuals decide simultaneously about their optimal consumption, and the optimal return time to their home countries. In previous studies, locational preferences (Djajić and Milbourne, 1988) and purchasing power differentials between countries (see Djajić, 1989) have been emphasized to explain temporary migrations. A further motive for a return migration, human capital enhancement while abroad, has first been identified by Dustmann (1995). This chapter combines all three motives within a unified framework, and provides further analysis of all three motives.

The model provides a general framework for studying the behavior of immigrants who choose their return time optimally. The analysis has also important implications for empirical work, as demonstrated above. Neglecting the fact that the migrant's return decision is taken simultaneously with other behavioral decisions in the host country may lead to misspecified empirical models.

The model is not without shortcomings, however. Although it explains a number of stylized facts, and provides some structure on the specification of empirical models, it is simplistic in many respects. It replicates a world where all decisions are taken at the time of immigration. Only in a completely deterministic world with fully informed agents, however, do intention and realization coincide. In a non-deterministic setting, and where agents are not fully informed at the time of immigration, migrants may re-optimize when obtaining additional information on host and home country. Furthermore, preference parameters, which have been assumed as constant in this model, may well change over time. As a consequence, migrations initially planned as permanent may become temporary, and vice versa. To model this process requires a dynamic model, where information about host and home country is updated in each period, and where return plans are adjusted accordingly. This is an interesting avenue for further research, and attempted in a paper by Adda and Dustmann (2000).

Notes

1 See, for instance, Borjas (1984), Chiswick and Miller (1993).
2 Gains in human capital were in fact emphasized during labor migration movements in Europe. Mehrländer (1980: 88), for instance, reports for the case of Germany that the countries of origin expected outmigration *to improve the training of the workers concerned, ultimately creating a larger reservoir of skilled labour in the countries of origin.*
3 This is always true for utility functions where the elasticity of the marginal utility of consumption is not decreasing in consumption.
4 See Dustmann (1995) for a detailed analysis of migrants' savings behavior under these three scenarios.
5 Changes in the wage $y^E(\hat{t})$ have to be understood as changes in the base wage at $\hat{t}=0$.

References

Adda, J. and C. Dustmann (2000) "A Dynamic Model of Return Migration," mimeo, University College London.

Böhning, W. (1984) *Studies in International Migration*, New York: St Martin's Press.

Borjas, G.J. (1984) "The Economic Status of Male Hispanic Migrants in the United States," in R.H. Ehrenberg (ed.), *Research in Labor Economics*, Greenwich, Comm., JAI Press.

Chiswick, B.R. and P. Miller (1993) "Language in the Immigrant Labor Market," in B. R. Chiswick (ed.), *Immigration, Language and Ethnicity: Canada and the United States*, Washington: AEI Press.

Djajić, S. (1989) "Migrants in a Guest-Worker System," *Journal of Development Economics*, 31: 327–39.

Djajić, S. and R. Milbourne (1988) "A General Equilibrium Model of Guest-Worker Migration: A Source-Country Perspective," *Journal of International Economics*, 25: 335–51.

Dustmann (1995) 'Savings Behaviour of Return Migrants', *Zeitschrift fuer Wirtschafts- und Socialwissenschaften*, 115: 511–535.

Dustmann, C. (1996) "Return Migration – The European Experience," *Economic Policy*, 22: 214–50.

Dustmann, C. (1997a) "Differences in the Labour Market Behaviour between Permanent and Temporary Migrant Women," *Labour Economics*, 4: 29–46.
Dustmann, C. (1997b) "Return Migration, Savings and Uncertainty," *Journal of Development Economics*, 52: 295–316.
Dustmann, C. (1999a) "Temporary Migration, Human Capital, and Language Fluency of Migrants," *Scandinavian Journal of Economics*, 101: 297–314.
Dustmann, C. (1999b) "Return Migration, Wage Differentials, and the Optimal Migration Duration," mimeo, University College London.
Galor, O. and O. Stark (1990) "Migrants' Savings, the Probability of Return Migration and Migrants' Performance," *International Economic Review*, 31: 463–7.
Galor, O. and O. Stark (1991) "The Probability of Return Migration, Migrants' Work Effort, and Migrants' Performance," *Journal of Development Economics*, 35: 399–405.
Glytsos, N.P.} (1988) "Remittances and Temporary Migration: A Theoretical Model and its Testing with the Greek-German Experience," *Weltwirtschaftliches Archiv*, 124: 524–549.
Hill, J.K. (1987) "Immigrant Decisions Concerning Duration of Stay and Migration Frequency," *Journal of Development Economics*, 25: 221–34.
Jasso, G. and M. R. Rosenzweig (1982) "Estimating the Emigration Rates of Legal Immigrants using Administrative and Survey data: The 1971 Cohort of Immigrants to the United States," *Demography*, 19: 279–290.
Killingsworth, M.R. (1982) "Learning by Doing and Investment in Training: A Synthesis of Two Rival Models of the Life Cycle," *Review of Economic Studies*, 44, 263–71.
Mehrläender, U. (1980) "The 'Human Resource' Problem in Europe: Migrant Labor in the FRG," in U. Raaman (ed.) *Ethnic Resurgence in Modern Democratic States*, New York: Pergamon.
Merkle, L. and K. Zimmermann (1992) "Savings, Remittances and Return Migration," *Economics Letters*, 46: 77–81.
Mesnard, A. (2000) "Temporary Migration and Capital Market Imperfections," mimeo, ARQADE, University of Toulouse.
Piore, M.J. (1979) *Birds of Passage*, Cambridge: Cambridge University Press.
Raffelhüschen, B. (1992) "Labor Migration in Europe: Experiences from Germany after Unification," *European Economic Review*, 36: 1453–1473.
Rosen, S. (1972) "Learning by Experience as a Joint Production," *Quarterly Journal of Economics*, 86: 366-382.
Stark, O. (1992) *The Migration of Labor*, Oxford: Blackwell.
Warren, R. and J.M. Peck (1980) "Foreign-Born Emigration from the United States," *Demography*, 17: 71–84.

Appendix A: comparative statics

Comparative statics on equations (4) and (5) may be performed by using the implicit function theorem. To apply the implicit function theorem, one has to ensure that a unique local differentiable solution exists at $(\hat{t},\pi^0)$ Necessary for $(\hat{t},\pi^0)$ being an optimal solution to (4) and (5) is that $\Gamma(\pi^0,\hat{t})$ and $\Delta(\pi^0, \hat{t})=0$. Sufficient is that the Jakobian H of the system described by (4) and (5) fulfills $\partial\Gamma/\partial\pi^0>0$, $\partial\Delta/\partial\hat{t}<0$ and Det $(H)=0$, with H:

$$H = \begin{bmatrix} \frac{\partial \Gamma}{\partial \pi^0} & \frac{\partial \Gamma}{\partial \hat{t}} \\ \frac{\partial \Delta}{\partial \pi^0} & \frac{\partial \Delta}{\partial \hat{t}} \end{bmatrix} \tag{10}$$

Deriving the elements of H (see below), it can be shown that this condition is fulfilled. Totally differentiating equation (4), and re-arranging terms yields:

$$\begin{aligned} d\pi^0 &= \frac{b_1}{b} d\hat{t} + \frac{b_2}{b} dy^E + \frac{b_3}{b} dy^I + \frac{b_4}{b} dp + \frac{b_5}{b} dK + \frac{b_6}{b} dT \\ &= \pi_{\hat{t}}^0 d\hat{t} + \pi_{yE}^0 dy^E + \pi_{yI}^0 dy^I + \pi_p^0 dp + \pi_K^0 dK + \pi_T^0 dT \end{aligned} \tag{11}$$

where

$$b = -\left[\int_0^{\hat{t}} c^{I'} e^{(\rho - 2r)\tau} dt + \int_{\hat{t}}^{T} pc^{E'} e^{(\rho-2r)\tau} dt\right] > 0,$$

where $c^{i'}$, i=E,I, are the derivatives with respect to π.

$$\begin{aligned}
b_1 &= \left[\left(y^E - c^E p\right) - \left(y^I - c^I\right) - \frac{1}{r} y_{\hat{t}}^E \left(1 - e^{r(\hat{t}-T)}\right)\right] e^{-r\hat{t}} \leq 0, \\
b_2 &= -\left[1 - e^{-r(T-\hat{t})}\right] \frac{1}{r} e^{-r\hat{t}} < 0, \\
b_3 &= -\left[1 - e^{-r\hat{t}}\right] \frac{1}{r} < 0, \\
b_4 &= \int_{\hat{t}}^{T} \left[c^E + \pi p \frac{\partial c^E}{\partial (p\pi)}\right] e^{-r\tau} d\tau \lesseqgtr 0 \quad \text{as} \quad c^E \lesseqgtr \pi p \frac{\partial c^E}{\partial (p\pi)}, \\
b_5 &= -1 < 0, \\
b_6 &= \left[pc^E - y^E\right] e^{-rT} > 0 \quad \text{for} \quad pc^E > y^E \quad \text{at} \quad t = T.
\end{aligned}$$

The effect of an increase in the price level on the budget constraint is ambiguous in sign. It depends on whether the direct effect of a price change on the cost of consumption is smaller than the indirect effect of a change in the consumption flow as a consequence of a change in the price. An increase in T has a positive effect on lifetime expenditure (tightening the migrant's budget constraint, and increasing the marginal utility of wealth) if expenditures are higher than earnings at t=T.

Totally differentiating (5) with respect to $\hat{t}$, π^0, p, y^E, y^I, K and T results in the following expression:

$$d\hat{\imath} = \frac{a_1}{a} d\pi^0 + \frac{a_2}{a} dy^E + \frac{a_3}{a} dy^I + \frac{a_4}{a} dp + \frac{a_5}{a} dK + \frac{a_6}{a} dT$$
$$= \hat{\imath}_{\pi 0} d\pi^0 + \hat{\imath}_{yE} dy^E + \hat{\imath}_{yI} dy^I + \hat{\imath}_p dp + \hat{\imath}_K dK + \hat{\imath}_T dT \qquad (12)$$

where

$$a = \dot{\pi}\left[\left(y^I - c^I\right) - \left(y^E - c^E p\right) + \frac{1}{r} y_{\hat{\imath}}^E \left(1 - e^{r(\hat{\imath}-T)}\right)\right]$$
$$+ \left[\pi \frac{1}{r} y_{\hat{\imath}\hat{\imath}}^E \left(1 - e^{r(\hat{\imath}-T)}\right) - y_{\hat{\imath}}^E \left(1 - e^{r(\hat{\imath}-T)}\right)\right] < 0,$$
$$a_1 = e^{(\rho - r)\hat{\imath}}\left[\left(y^E - c^E p\right) - \left(y^I - c^I\right) - \frac{1}{r} y_{\hat{\imath}}^E \left(1 - e^{r(\hat{\imath}-T)}\right)\right] \leq 0$$
$$a_2 = \pi > 0,$$
$$a_3 = -\pi < 0,$$
$$a_4 = -\pi c^E < 0,$$
$$a_5 = 0,$$
$$a_6 = -\pi\left[y_{\hat{\imath}}^E e^{r(\hat{\imath}-T)}\right] < 0.$$

Notice that a_I and b_I are both equal to zero for scenario (c). As a consequence, $\hat{\imath}\,\pi^0 = 0$ in this case. Rewrite (11) and (12):

$$\begin{bmatrix} 1 & -\hat{\imath}_{\pi 0} \\ -\pi_{\hat{\imath}}^0 & 1 \end{bmatrix} \begin{bmatrix} d\hat{\imath} \\ d\pi^0 \end{bmatrix} = \begin{bmatrix} \hat{\imath}_{yE} dy^E & \hat{\imath}_{yI} dy^I & \hat{\imath}_p dp & \hat{\imath}_K dK & \hat{\imath}_{\xi I} d\xi^I & \hat{\imath}_{\xi E} d\xi^E & \hat{\imath}_T dT \\ \pi_{yE}^0 dy^E & \pi_{yI}^0 dy^I & \pi_p^0 dp & \pi_K^0 dK & \pi_{\xi I}^0 d\xi^I & \pi_{\xi E}^0 d\xi^E & \pi_T^0 dT \end{bmatrix}$$

Using Cramer's rule produces the partial effects in Table 11.1, where $D = 1 - \hat{\imath}_{\pi^0} \pi_{\hat{\imath}}^0 = 1 - \frac{a_I b_I}{a\, b} > 0$.

Appendix B: simulations

For the simulations, the utility functions are specified as follows:

$$\upsilon^I(c) = \frac{1}{(1-\alpha)} \xi^I c^{(1-\alpha)},$$
$$\upsilon^E(c) = \frac{1}{(1-\alpha)} \xi^E c^{(1-\alpha)}. \qquad (13)$$

Furthermore, earnings in the host country are $y^E(\hat{t})=\bar{y}^E+\gamma ln(1+\hat{t})$. If $\gamma>0$, staying longer abroad increases the migrant's earnings potential in the home country. It then follows from (4) and (5) that the optimal time of return, $\hat{t}$ and the marginal utility of wealth in $t=0$, π^0, together with the realized stock of savings in $t=T$ is determined by the following system of equations:

$$\pi^{\frac{1}{\alpha}}\left[y^I - y^E(\hat{t}) + \gamma\frac{1}{r(1+\hat{t})}\left[1-e^{r(\hat{t}-T)}\right]\right] + \frac{\alpha}{(1-\alpha)}\left[\xi^{I\frac{1}{\alpha}} - p\left(\frac{\xi^E}{p}\right)^{\frac{1}{\alpha}}\right] = 0, \tag{14a}$$

$$\begin{aligned}\bar{K}e^{-rT} - K_0 = {} & \frac{1}{r}\left[y^I\left[1-e^{-r\hat{t}}\right] + y^E\left[e^{-r\hat{t}} - e^{-rT}\right]\right] \\ & -\frac{1}{b}\left[\left[\frac{\xi^I}{\pi^0}\right]^{\frac{1}{\alpha}}\left[1-e^{-b\hat{t}}\right] + \left[p\frac{\xi^E}{\pi^0 p}\right]^{\frac{1}{\alpha}}\left[e^{-b\hat{t}} - e^{-bT}\right]\right],\end{aligned} \tag{14b}$$

where $b=\frac{1}{\alpha}(\rho-r)+r$.

The basic parameter configuration for the simulations is: $\alpha=0.4$, $\rho=0.08$, $r=0.1$, $T=30$, $\xi^E=1.3$, $\xi^I=1$, $\gamma^I=4$, $\bar{y}^E=2$, $K_0=0$, $\gamma=0$, $p=1$, $\bar{K}=0$.

For these parameters, consumption–earnings profiles and the profile of savings are given in Figures 11.3 and 11.4. The optimal point of return, $\hat{t}$, equals 13.67, and $\pi^0=0.82$. In Figures 11.1 and 11.2, $\xi^I=\xi^E=1$. In Figures 11.5 and 11.6, the price level p is chosen to be equal to 0.8. The optimal return point and the marginal utility of wealth in $t=0$ are $\hat{t}=23.8$ and $\pi^0=0.71$. Finally, Figures 11.7 and 11.8 show profiles where $\xi^I=\xi^E=1$, but $\gamma=2$. Optimal return point and marginal utility of wealth are now given by $\hat{t}=7.2$ and $\pi^0=0.63$, respectively.

12 Determinants and effects of migrant remittances

A survey

Nicholas P. Glytsos

Introduction

This chapter reflects an effort to provide a critical synthesis of the literature on remittances, their generating factors and their effects in the economy of the migrant sending country. The discussion will focus on the theoretical and methodological issues as well as empirical analysis, where greater emphasis will be given to the analytical approaches and the nature of the findings and less on the specific quantitative results in various countries. An attempt will be made to pinpoint and explain some of the similarities and contrasts of theories and realities and interpret the empirical findings with respect to the theoretical hypotheses to which they are related.

Determinants of remittances

Theoretical approaches

The first noticeable and systematic effort to build a theory of remittance determination came from the literature of rural–urban migration by Lucas and Stark (1985) and Stark and Lucas (1988). As declared by these two pioneers, by 1985 no comprehensive theory of remittances existed and there was little statistical evidence on the motives of remitting. In their own 1985 contribution they argued that the intuitively implied altruistic motive for remittances–even after they turned it into a theoretical hypothesis of migrant derived utility–is a simplification inadequate to explain remittance flows. According to them, pure altruism and pure self-interest are extremes within which "tempered altruism" and "enlightened self-interest" are more realistic explanations.

They proposed a theory of remittance determination, in a family framework of decision making, which is conceptualized as a "self-enforcing co-operative contractual arrangement" between the migrant and the family. The migrant anticipates inheriting from his parents and invests on his return home with the aim of enhancing his prestige with "family and friends" or enlarging his political influence. Remittances take the form of an insurance premium for the finance of migration risk by the family, and it covers, on the other hand, the family risks with respect to agricultural production and technological investment. One safeguard that the contract is not breached by either side is provided by the element of altruism that is present in the family relation.

Remittances are part and parcel of a series of elements related to the option of migration as a strategic effort for raising family welfare. In this respect, Katseli and Glytsos (1986) and Glytsos (1988) consider remittances as an indispensable part of the migration decision and a manifestation of the migrant choice of strategy for attaining the saving goal. This being the case, remittances are expected to be determined by the attitudes of the migrant and of each member from the rest of the family in their contribution to the collective decision on migration. According to Katseli and Glytsos (1986) and Glytsos (1988), this is not a once and for all decision, but a continuous process of revisions and adjustments to the changing conditions at home and abroad. Everything and at any moment is under revision. The migrant and the family have to deal with a series of intertemporal decisions that have implications for the savings target, the duration of stay abroad, the timing of return, the family members to migrate, and the size and regularity of remittances. The collective criterion on the basis of which adjustments are determined is the change in the intertemporal indirect utility functions in the home and host countries.

Poirine (1997), building on the idea of a "loan element" in the contract between the migrant and the family, implied in several of the Stark studies, gives an alternative dimension to the self-interest motivation to remit. He considers his hypothesis not universal but as a partial explanation of remittances, *pari passu* with other explanations, such as the altruistic motive and the self-insurance provision. The core of his thesis is that the family functions as an informal financial market, with the main purpose "to finance investments in human capital" with "informal loans" that are repaid by remittances.

He claims that the particular remitting motive prescribes also the manner in which remittances are used. Thus, given the nature of the "loan", remittances are not used, according to Poirine, for investment by the family, and cannot consequently be reduced over time, as the altruistic theory predicts, whereas the size of their flows should be analogous to the loan. This is in contrast to remittances in the form of an insurance payment which, as he states, should be invested and can be expected to have a negative association with the family income, giving rise to possible fluctuations. The regularity of remittance flows found for Tonga and Western Samoa leads Poirine (1997: 590) to suggest that the loan hypothesis is more relevant than the co-insurance or altruistic theory.

Hoddinott (1994), referring also to rural households, questions the micro-approach to migration and remittances (i.e. household utility maximization), on the grounds that it does not give adequate weight to the prospective migrant. He proposes a model that takes the migrant outside the family nest and diversifies the migrant behavior from that of the rest of the family, in a joint utility maximization.

What makes the difference in relation to the unique family utility maximization is the possession of some wealth by the migrant, in addition to his expectation of future parental inheritance. This makes migrants less depended on family support. He considers the Todaro (1969) individualistic model and the household collective model as special cases of his more global approach. Interestingly enough, he introduces an element of possible disagreement between the potential migrant and his parents and discusses the consequences of that disagreement. In particular, he claims that "there exists some benchmark, or minimum remittance level, that all migrants are expected to provide" (1994: 461), which has some resemblance to Glytsos's (1988) well-defined required remittances as we will shortly see. Hoddinott also recognizes that migrant earnings could be a function of remittances, because of the obligatory threshold that may force the migrant, just as in Glytsos's model, to work harder and longer to fulfil this obligation.

One issue that is raised in the literature concerns the determinants of return migration that, for our interest here, has an impact on remittances. Katseli and Glytsos (1986) view return migration as an internal part of a strategy embracing the whole migration process that involves the emigration-stay-repatriation cycle. They consider repatriation as an intertemporal discrete choice problem, where the decision to repatriate is closely tied to the *ex ante* decision to emigrate and the desired length of stay abroad.

More specifically, they demonstrate that the timing of migration and the length of stay abroad will be determined endogenously as a result of the intertemporal utility maximization in the home and host countries, which takes the form:

$$V_{ij} = f(Y_{ij}^e, E_{ij}, S_{ij}^e, \varepsilon_{ij})$$

where V=utility, Y^e=expected income, E=probability of employment, S^e=expected savings accumulation, i=individual migrant, j=a, h stand respectively for abroad and home, and ε=a random variable including unobservable socioeconomic characteristics of the migrant. With this tool they indicate the conditions of no migration, permanent migration, and temporary migration and return. Their hypothesis predicts that an increase in a migrant's expected income–which is an element in the utility function–will initially prolong the length of stay for the purpose of accumulating savings. But when enough savings are accumulated, as a result of which the utility of the migrant at home becomes relatively higher, additional increases of income will shorten the stay. This makes the savings target as well as remittances "an integral part of the emigration-repatriation decision making process" (Glytsos, 1988: 524–25). Other authors have further developed and refined the analysis of optimal return time and savings behavior of temporary migrants in the host country, generating a large body of literature on this topic. Dustmann's contribution to this volume provides a review.

Modelling remittance determination

A number of models, some explanatory and others empirical, follow from the theories of the previous section. One of them by Glytsos (1988) is cast in a demand and supply scheme, according to which the ability of the migrant to remit is the supply side and the claim of the family on the migrant's income is the demand side. He considers the two sides as a tug-of-war situation, behind which lies the relative bargaining power of the two parties. The migrant tries to minimize the leakages and the family to maximize the benefits from the migrant's income. This kind of approach seems to be an analytical expression of the view that recognizes the migrant as a separate entity in the family framework of decision making, that allows him some individual discretion and initiative in pursuing his self-interest within the family framework. Hoddinott's (1994) joint utility maximization of the migrant and the family, instead of a unique utility maximization for the family as a whole, also provides for the possibility of a "disagreement" between the migrant and his family.

Glytsos (1988, 1997) points to two major "leakages" that drain migrant's income and set at risk his savings target, i.e. migrant living expenses in the host country, and the remittances he is obliged to send to the family at home. In the framework of the general strategic choice of migration as a means of improving the future family welfare at home, the migrant makes various tactical moves for protecting his goals and minimizing these leakages, in accordance with the conditions he faces in the host country. He is continuously revising his expectations of future income and adjusting a nexus of interrelated factors, including the length of stay, the intensity of work, and the flow of remittances above the required level, all of which have a bearing on his savings target.

The relative bargaining power of the two parties is represented as two corresponding parameters in Glytsos's (1988) respective expressions of "affordable" and "warranted" remittances. The former are determined by the migrant surplus savings over the savings target, as this target is set each time, and the latter are determined by the excess of the average family income at home over the income in the "neighbourhood" of the family. This is the exact definition of Glytsos's "required" remittances, which constitute an *ex ante* remittance threshold, similar to Hoddinott's (1994), beyond which migration becomes profitable and takes place. In line with the Lucas and Stark (1985) implicit contract theory discussed above, Glytsos's required remittances are more a social rather than an economic prerequisite for the family. They are required to "save face" in the local community and justify, in the eyes of the neighbors, the wisdom of the decision to send some family members abroad. This seems to fit well the "relative deprivation" model by Stark (1984) and Stark and Taylor (1991), attaching a dual character to the impact of remittances on family welfare, i.e. increasing the level of its income and improving its income position with respect to the income of other villagers.

More specifically, Glytsos's p_1 parameter, which determines a withholding from the migrant's surplus savings, as defined above, seems to give meaningful support to the Stark and Lucas (1988) argument that the higher the risk of migration (expressed by parameter p_1) the higher the "value of the family-provided insurance" (expressed by the surplus savings withheld). This is verified by a theoretically expected (and empirically supported by Greek data), positive association between remittances and the current and one-year lagged value of the family income. In counterpart, Glytsos's p_2 parameter, reflecting the strength of the family bargaining power, is expected to have, and is empirically found to have, as shown by his equation (16), a positive impact on remittances. This provides additional support for the Stark and Lucas hypothesis.

Apart from these endogenous remittances that are interrelated with migration flows and the incomes earned abroad, some remittances do not fall into this category, because of their exogenous character to the system of migration. They may be in the form of savings transfer for the purpose of reaping higher yields. The flows of these remittances, that in the terminology of Katseli and Glytsos (1986) are called "desired" remittances, to contrast them with the "required" remittances, depend on the relative profitability of savings in the home and host countries, and can be explained in a framework of a portfolio management choice. Required remittances generate an obligation of financial support for those left behind, while desired remittances depend on relative macroeconomic factors in the host and home country (see Katseli and Glytsos, 1986, 1989; Glytsos, 1988; and Djajić, 1989).

Any amount of remittances over the threshold is a matter of the relative bargaining power between the migrant and the family. One can argue here that their implicit contract includes some non-negotiable terms of principle – the guarantee of required remittances – and some flexible, negotiable terms concerning remittances above this level. Such terms may refer to a whole package of interrelated elements, including a moving savings target, the length of stay abroad and the return, as well as the number of family members that may decide to migrate.

Empirical analysis

Two major methodologies of empirical analysis emerge from the theoretical approaches and the explanatory models of the previous sections. The first identifies variables that reflect the microeconomic behavior of the migrant and the family, and the second uses macroeconomic variables of remittance determination. More often than not, econometric analysis applies jointly these two kinds of variables.

The impact of the microeconomic behavioral variables is *ex ante* determined by the theoretical approaches described above, but the impact of macroeconomic variables need some elaboration. Corresponding to the family utility maximization and the portfolio management choice hypotheses, there are two distinct and rather opposite ways that variables such as the foreign exchange rate, the interest rates in the home and host countries, and the inflation rate in the home country may affect remittances. The first is by changing the value of the portion of remittances sent out of altruism or for the purpose of fulfilling the conditions of an implicit contract with the family. In this sense, the exchange rate is expected to have a negative impact on remittances–the same level of consumption or household finance can be sustained with fewer foreign currency units ("negative income effect").

The portion of remittances in the form of savings transfers is, on the other hand, affected positively by the rate of return on capital in the home country, raising the yield of savings or the return to investment ("positive return effect") (Glytsos, 1988: 532). The impact of the host country interest rate could be either positive or negative. It can be positive as a factor raising migrant wealth and negative as a factor raising the relative profitability of deposits in the host country (Katseli and Glytsos, 1989: 110–11). Finally, the inflation rate in the home country, by reducing *per se* the purchasing power of income, may have a positive effect on the portion of remittances that go to family support. And yet, its overall impact is ambiguous, because it can signal economic uncertainty and political instability that deter remittances. Given this dual character of macroeconomic effects, and the fact that remittance figures cannot be divided according to their purpose, only empirical case studies can indicate the relative strength of these opposing influences of macroeconomic variables.

The few existing econometric studies on remittance determination concentrate mostly on the effects of macroeconomic variables and pay lip-service to the estimate of the impact of microeconomic behavior of the migrant and the family. In this respect, the empirical work by Lucas and Stark (1985) for Botswana produced a statistical verification of their implicit contract hypothesis, but they also recognize in combination the importance of the altruistic motive for remitting as it comes from their statistical analysis on the basis of household data.

Glytsos (1988) rigorously derives the testable equation below from his dynamic hypothesis of microeconomic motivation which includes assumptions for income and remittance expectations and adjustments,

$$R_t = f(y_{ht}, y_{ht-1}, y_{at}, y_{at-1}, R_{t-1}, R_{t-2})$$

where R=remittances per migrant, y_h=per capita income in Greece, y_a= per capita income in Germany, and t, t-1, t-2 designate correspondingly current, one-year lag and two-year lag values of the predetermined variables. The macroeconomic variables, i.e. the exchange rate (e), the interest rate in Greece (r) and the inflation rate in Greece (p), are also introduced in the equation. This is done in an effort to combine individual and family behavior with macroeconomic factors, in a joint explanation of overall remittances (including their required and desired components). In a log-linear form of this equation, the macroeconomic variables are introduced in linear form, as a kind of shift factors of the core behavioral equation. The equation is estimated with data from the Greek–German migration of the period 1960–82.

The estimated positive signs for domestic current and lagged per capita income in Greece support the bargaining model and they jointly point to some kind of permanent income notion as a basis of remitting. Let me note here that Katseli and Glytsos (1989), using the same period data, found a negative, instead of a positive, association between remittances and Greek per capita income, verifying the altruistic motive for remitting. This may be due to the different specification of the estimated equation, particularly its static nature, which ignores the various adjustment mechanisms accounted for in Glytsos's dynamic equation.

It is interesting to note here that using a similar equation but with data for the period 1960–93, the only different estimate is the reversal of the sign of Greek per capita income, turned from positive to negative, suggesting an altruistic motive of remitting. This could be explained by the fact that after the early 1980s the Greek temporary migrants in Germany turned more or less into permanent residents. As a result, the self-interest motive for remitting subsided and the altruistic motive took the upper hand, the migrants in Germany behaving in the same way as their permanent counterparts in the US and Australia, whose remittances are negatively related to the Greek per capita income (Glytsos, 1988: 545, Glytsos, 1997: 427).

The findings, on the other hand, of positive signs for current per capita income in Germany, and a negative sign for its lagged value, suggest a partial adjustment mechanism of remittances with respect to the migrant's income flows over time. In addition, an indication of overall adjustment of remittances is suggested by the positive sign of one-year lagged remittances and the negative sign of the two-year lagged remittances (Glytsos, 1988: 535).

Turning to the macroeconomic variables, econometric analysis for Greece (Katseli and Glytsos, 1986, 1989) shows a positive association of remittances with the interest rate in Germany, reflecting a wealth effect, and a neutrality with respect to the Greek interest rate and the foreign exchange rate. Roughly the same neutrality of these three variables is also found by Glytsos (1988: 536–37 and 1997: 427). Inflation in Greece has a negative sign, perhaps reflecting uncertainties from the perspective of remitters, but it can also be explained by the rise in the relative yield of savings in

Germany, as a result of the fall of the real Greek interest rate caused by inflation. Swamy (1981) and Straubhaar (1986) find that remittances of Southern European migrants in Germany were not associated with macroeconomic variables. Faini (1994: 242), using data of various Southern European migrants in Germany, finds that interest rates are not significant determinants, whereas the exchange rates have a positive impact. A positive effect of "financial incentives" is also found for the South Pacific (Brown, 1994: 364). For a detailed general survey of the literature on earlier empirical findings for the determinants, but also the uses, of remittances see Russell (1986), and for the Maghreb countries Garson (1994).

Feeding back the econometric estimates to his structural model, Glytsos (1988) measures the insurance provided by the family for sustaining the savings target, when it faces the risk of being run down by the vagaries of the economic conditions in the receiving country. As the empirical findings suggest, such unfavorable conditions generate unstable income expectations forcing the migrant to withhold, as predicted by the theoretical model, a portion – which under certain conditions was estimated to be up to 50 percent – of the surplus savings as a shock absorber of income fluctuations. This reduces the flow of remittances to the family at home. As it appears, the higher the level of uncertainty, the higher the risk premium of adjustment. On the part of the family, the payment of this insurance can be afforded under the already discussed permanent income notion. The reimbursement by the migrant is expected in good times.

Poirine (1997: 606) contemplates that empirical evidence for Tongan and Samoan immigrants in Australia is suggestive of the validity of the implicit loan theory, which "in many cases explains better remittance behaviors, remittance flows, and remittance uses, than the 'altruistic' 'self-interest', or 'co-insurance' theories". In counterpart, neither the self-interest nor the altruistic theoretical hypotheses are supported by these findings, according to Poirine (1997: 600). Brown's (1997) findings, on the other hand, reject, for the same areas, the altruistic but not the self-interest hypothesis. Considering that returns to human capital, financed by the informal loans, are potentially higher in international than in internal migration, Poirine points out that the implicit loan theory could be more relevant to the former and the co-insurance theory more relevant to the latter.

In cases of wide gaps between official and unofficial exchange rates, substantial amounts of remittances are channelled through the black market, where they can occasionally command a premium of more than 30 percent (Russell, 1986; Feiler, 1987). Official remittances therefore constitute only a part of the actual flow of remittances. The unofficial flows give particular content to the portfolio management model by elevating the role of the black market for foreign exchange to that of a major determinant of the distribution of savings between home and host countries (Wahba, 1989). Middle East and African countries, but others as well, are important cases in point. Empirical evidence shows that Egyptians respond promptly to the black-market premium, as do migrants from Bangladesh (Miranda, 1988) and the Maghreb (Rocha, 1989: 9–10). The case on the European side of the Mediterranean is ambiguous. Analysis for Yugoslavia, Greece, and Turkey shows that premium-free market exchange rates have no effect on remittances (Swamy, 1981: 684). Combined data for the period 1977–89 for Morocco, Portugal, Tunisia, Turkey, and Yugoslavia reveals, however, that a 10 percent increase in the black-market premium on the exchange rate reduces official remittances by 3 percent (Elbadawi and Rocha, 1992: 27–28).

Contrary to the claim by Elbadawi and Rocha (1992: 11), Katseli and Glytsos (1986, 1989) and Glytsos (1988) take into account the length of stay as a determinant of remittances. In fact, they use the same variable, i.e. a time trend, as Elbadawi and Rocha (in one of their alternatives). In particular, Glytsos (1988) uses this approach to test his concept of "return illusion," pointing to a positive sign, versus his "permanent settlement syndrome," pointing to a negative sign of time trend. He finds, in a log remittances equation, a positive, statistically significant coefficient of 0.54 for remittances from Germany to Greece, and a negative, statistically significant coefficient of −0.22 for remittances from the US to Greece. These findings verify, respectively, the return illusion for migrants in Germany and the permanent settlement syndrome for migrants in the US. For the period 1960–76 of mass emigration and repatriation, the positive coefficient of time trend can also be explained by the rapid turnover of the migrant stock, as indicated by an elasticity of 2.5 for return migration with respect to migrant stock of Greeks in Germany, estimated with data of the period 1968–76 (Glytsos, 1991). Accordingly, the average length of stay of migrants was relatively short.

Others have found, however, a negative impact of the time trend. This is the case of Elbadawi and Rocha (1992: 27–8), using data for various countries, and of Merkle and Zimmermann (1992), who, using panel data for Turkish, Italian, Greek, Spanish and Yugoslav households heads in Germany, estimated a negative coefficient of "planned future duration of stay." This is consistent with the standard explanation of temporary migrants, turning into permanent migrants over time, acquiring the latter's remitting attitudes (Glytsos, 1997: 428).

In a quite different spirit, Hoddinott (1994) estimates an equation derived from the migrant's joint utility maximization in which he includes as explanatory variable a "reward" for remittances above the benchmark obligatory level. In practice this reward takes the form of the amount of land obtained by the migrant from his father, and is expected to have a negative impact on remittances. The size of parental land holdings is also included in the equation, with an expected positive sign. Other explanatory variables are the migrant's wage and a set of household characteristics (age, marital status, number of adult sons in the family and the number of dependants in the family). As predicted by his model, the possession of land by the migrant in Western Kenya is found to reduce remittances and the parental land holdings are found to raise them.

Effects of remittances

Analytical approaches

There are two major channels through which remittances have an impact on the migrant sending country. First, as foreign exchange flows through the balance of payments (see Glytsos, 1998a), which is beyond the scope of this chapter, and second, as income spent and saved, which is the topic of this section. In this sense, remittance effects are discussed either as part of overall effects of migration, usually as a compensation making up for the losses produced by emigration, or on their own merit as injections of income into the home economy, detached from the other effects of migration. The dichotomy of direct versus indirect effects of remittances is an important issue of debate. One section of the literature concentrates on the discussion of the direct impact of remittances on income distribution, family welfare and poverty but is less concerned with their subsequent implications for the economy at large.

In this respect, more emphasis is placed on the immediate social aspect of the income flows and less on the direct and indirect economic contribution of remittances to production and growth. Another section of the literature leads a lively debate on the significance that remittance spending on consumption, housing and the purchase of land has on investment and growth. Only in recent years has it been recognized that even this manner of disposition of remittances contributes to growth and employment, producing in various ways indirect effects on the economy (see Glytsos, 1998b: 179–80), including the release of other resources to investment (e.g. Stark, 1980: 211) or generating multiplier effects after their diffusion in the economy at large (e.g. Russell, 1992: 270; Glytsos, 1993).

From a different perspective, a considerable portion of the literature is concerned with remittance flows to the rural sector, and particularly to farm households, partly because of the interest in rural–urban migration. However, in international migration many remittance recipients are not farmers but non-farm workers, from both the rural and urban sectors. This being the case, the distribution of remittances between these two groups of recipients influences their impact on the economy. The reason is that rural households are, in this respect, small productive units that finance their capital and material needs with remittances; in contrast, households that work for wages are only consuming units, financing with remittances the purchase of goods and services. Consequently, a dual theory of return migration and remittances is called for, one for farm households as production units and another for non-farm households as consumption units.

Modelling remittance effects

In the framework that is set by these introductory remarks, there are models that deal with the impact of remittances on income distribution, economic welfare and poverty, and others that deal with the impact on investment and growth. Let me say at the outset that the effects of remittances on income inequality and social welfare need not be unidirectional. An increase in income inequality does not always entail a social welfare loss, in fact it may turn out to be a positive development under Pareto criteria (Stark and Yitzhaki, 1982). Several authors (e.g. Djajić, 1986; Quibria, 1996) consider the role of remittances as a possible correcting factor for the decline in welfare caused by the loss of trading opportunities suffered by the remaining residents as a result of emigration. They build on earlier work of Rivera-Batiz (1982) that ignores the role of remittances in his analysis of the welfare implications of emigration.

Lundahl (1985), working on a similar remittance-migration model with traded and non-traded goods, and assuming that all remittances are spent on consumption, finds that the impact of remittances on workers' and capitalists' real incomes depends on the relative factor intensity of traded goods and the prices of non-traded goods. Using a model with two factors (capital and labor), two commodities (traded and non-traded) and two economic classes (capital-rich and capital-poor), Quibria (1996) concludes that if emigration is not accompanied by capital, including human capital ("pure migration"), and remittances per migrant are higher than the home wage rate–a condition that seems to be satisfied in most countries–welfare of the source country is unambigously raised. But if emigration is "bundled," i.e. accompanied by capital, the impact of remittances on welfare depends on the resulting changes in the capital/labor ratio.

The size of remittances is also a crucial parameter for shaping welfare in the Kirwan and Holden (1986: 52) investigation, which is conducted under the same analytical conditions of the overall impact of emigration, and the assumption that all remittances go to consumption. If remittances just make up for the lost pre-migration income, welfare will decline. This is due to the disruption in the internal exchange of internationally non-traded goods caused by the departure of workers from the service sector. Only remittances in excess of the income loss will increase welfare. A similar conclusion is also obtained by Rivera-Batiz (1986), referring to the restoration of the overall welfare loss due to the exodus of workers. He presents a model that is richer than others (e.g. Rivera-Batiz, 1982) in three respects. First, as the above authors, he considers migration effects in the presence of remittances; second, he relaxes the assumption made by others (e.g. Kirwan and Holden, 1986 and Djajić, 1986), that all remittances are spent on consumption; and third, he distinguishes between temporary and permanent migrants. This combines, in a way, Djajić's (1986) model on the welfare generated by permanent migrants and Kirwan and Holden's (1986) model with temporary migrants who produce abroad and consume at home, with remittances as a connecting link.

Going beyond the first direct effects of remittances, Taylor (1992, 1996) discusses the short-term indirect effects on income distribution, through the impact of remittances on the income from other sources, and the long-term effects, through the finance of asset accumulation. The direction of the indirect impact on income distribution is in the long run indeterminate because the influence on household-farm income is not known, due to the fact that remittances may change investment risks, leading to changes in production plans with further implications.

Taylor and Wyatt (1996), referring to rural households, argue that one element that plays a role in the strength of remittance effects, i.e. household-farms' initial asset holdings, is neglected in the literature. They state that "the impact of remittances on income inequality ... depends on the distribution of the initial constraints on household farm production that are relieved by remittances" (1996: 901), and they back their thesis with empirical evidence from Mexico. Thus, households in need of complementary investment will benefit most. Remittances may enhance farm production in households with limited liquidity and limited assets, and may have negligible effects on rich households with high liquidity. As a result, in the aggregate, the distribution of household assets will be a critical factor in the manner that remittances affect income distribution.

From a different perspective, Stark et al. (1986) draw attention to the role of the diffusion of information at successive stages of migration. They maintain and empirically support that the impact of remittances on income distribution is related to the migration history. At the initial stages, when information is still limited and the employment potential in destination very uncertain, migrants come mostly from village households with some substantial resources. At that stage, only a few of these households receive remittances, widening the income inequality in the village. As migration is gradually augmented and more widely spread over a greater range of income classes, remittances are analogously spread and income distribution turns less unequal.

In a recent contribution, Djajić (1998) enriches and refines further the model of the joint emigration-remittances effects on welfare. He introduces, apart from migrants and remaining residents, one more agent, i.e. foreign capital, into the model. Djajić reaches the conclusion that, in the presence of foreign capital, remittances spent on investment improve welfare, but the impact of remittances spent on consumption would depend on the relative factor intensities of traded and non-traded goods.

In one of the rare efforts to measure the overall (direct and indirect) effects of remittances on the home country economy, Glytsos (1993, 1998b) applies two different methods. The first Glytsos (1993) is to translate, through an appropriate matrix, the spending of remittances on consumption and non-consumption goods into demand by industrial product, and through an input-output table to estimate the overall, as well as the disaggregated effects on production, employment, capital formation and imports. The second method Glytsos (1998b) is to build a macroeconometric model, for the assessment of the growth-generating capacity of remittances. He uses a simple Keynesian-type model, with some dynamic elements, derived from a permanent income hypothesis. The econometric model consists of three behavioral equations, namely, a consumption function, an investment function and an imports function. It includes, in addition, a national income identity that introduces remittances as an exogenous factor.

Empirical findings

A word of warning is in order at the outset. Empirical analysis based on the official data of remittance flows leaves out remittances channeled through unofficial routes, which in some cases, as for the Arab countries, reach huge proportions. Particularly concerned with the consequences of these remittances for the economy, and especially for the money markets of home countries, Choucri (1986) refers to the predominance of a "hidden economy," exclusively generated by the unofficial transfer of remittances, that in various ways impedes the government policy and hinders its efficiency.

In their empirical evaluations, most of the studies on income inequality use the Gini coefficient. This way, Knowles and Anker (1981: 213) found that remittances reduce income inequality in Kenya. The same was found by Stark et al. (1986) for the overall income inequality, applying a Gini decomposition coefficient for Mexico to US migrants. But at the village level the impact varies. Using an extended Gini index (see Yitzhaki, 1983; Lerman and Yitzhaki, 1985) and data of two Mexican villages, Stark et al. established a rising inequality in one village and a falling inequality in the other. What makes the difference is the position of recipients in the income distribution of the village, and the distribution of remittances across recipients. Lipton (1980) found no reduction of income inequality, either because the size of remittances was not large enough or because they do not flow to low-income recipients.

To evaluate the robustness of their result, Stark et al. (1988) refine further their analysis by conducting a sensitivity test with the extended Gini index. The test shows that the bottom and top ends of income distribution do not give migrants. To take account of remittances that are spent on goods and services produced by poor households, some second phase indirect effects on income inequality are estimated. Their calculations confirm the robustness of their earlier results as to the village difference of remittance effects on income inequality. Evidence for Philippines shows that remittances increase disanalogously income inequality, particularly in the countryside (Rodriguez, 1998: 336). Despite their low share (4.3 percent) in rural household income, they contribute 7.5 percent to the rural income inequality.

As in the case of the income distribution–welfare dichotomy, opposing effects of remittances are possible in the income distribution–poverty dichotomy. Empirical evidence from three rural Egyptian villages shows this possibility (Adams jr., 1991). Remittances tend to reduce poverty (slightly), because a proportionate number of poor households do receive remittances. But at the same time, remittances widen income inequality as measured by the Gini coefficient, because of the large share of top-income brackets involved in migration. The inequality is reinforced by the strong correlation between remittances and total income. Income distribution turns also more unequal in Pakistan (Gilani et al., 1981), where remittances are received by upper-income villagers. By contrast, remittances decrease income inequality in Tonga, a small country in the South Pacific with agriculture and the public sector employing a very high proportion of the labor force, and where remittances represent 40 percent of GDP (Ahlburg, 1996: 392–6).

A great concern has been expressed that remittances contribute to a rise in inflation resulting from an increased demand for goods and services in the face of an unresponsive supply. But the empirical evidence seems to be inconclusive. For instance, in Turkey, supply responded promptly to the increased demand from remittances with no pressure on inflation (Martin, 1991). In Asian countries, although remittances may have raised land prices and construction costs, there is no evidence that the overall inflation has been affected (Stahl and Arnold, 1986: 916). For Greece, the evidence is contradictory. Papademetriou and Martin (1991) claim that the increased demand for building material induced by remittances generated inflation. This assertion is in contrast to the fact that, at least during the peak migration years in the 1960s, inflation in Greece was insignificant. Furthermore, as Glytsos (1993) found, the demand for housing out of remittances generated a multiplier of 2 on domestic production. In Egypt, on the other hand, remittances have, according to several authors, contributed to inflation through the land and housing price hikes (Sirageldin et al., 1983; Lesch, 1990; Adams jr., 1991), while according to others they have not (Choucri and Lahiri, 1983). In some Egyptian villages, as much as 73 percent of remittances went to housing (Wahba, 1996: 13). In Jordan, remittances are also found to have contributed to inflation (Keely and Saket, 1984).

The empirical results of Glytsos's (1993) model for Greece are articulated into three different levels, namely, *individual* (impact on consumer expenditure of recipients), *local* (impact in a region with high emigration) and *macroeconomic* (impact on output, employment and capital formation by industry). The findings show that remittance recipients almost doubled their consumption (in 1971), with priority spending on education and recreation, where expenditure increased by a factor of 3.3 and on transportation, where expenditure increased by a factor of 2.1. In the high emigration region of Florina, remittances raised consumption expenditure of recipients to a level exceeding the average expenditure of the rural areas of Greece as a whole by 60 percent. The pre-remittance level of recipient's consumption was in this region 28 percent lower than the average of the country's rural areas. For some particular items that serve as status symbols, such as beverages, apparel, footwear and durables, remittances raised recipient's expenditures even above the average level of the urban areas of the country. For the region as a whole, consumption increased to the average of all rural areas, from the pre-remittance level that stood 19 percent lower than the average.

At the macro-level, Glytsos's (1993) findings show a contribution of remittances of 4.1 percent to total gross output (in 1971), which was equivalent to half the growth rate of GDP of 8 percent in 1971, with a multiplier of 1.7 (one extra drachma of remittances generated 1.7 extra drachmas of gross output). In about one-third of industries, including construction, the multiplier was over 2.0. Imports made up 12.8 percent of induced gross production, whereas 22 percent of remittance original spending went to imports of both consumption and investment goods. However, at the aggregate level, induced imports represented only 4.9 percent of Greece's total imports, suggesting a negligible pressure on the balance of payments. Finally, remittances supported about 4.7 percent of employment and 8 percent of capital capacity in manufacturing. Obviously, these two effects were at the time rather significant for Greece as they were not for other countries (e.g. OECD, 1978: 28; MacMillen, 1982: 263). An empirical model by Kandil and Metwally (1990: 164–6), with similar macroeconomic variables as Glytsos's (1998b) model below, found for Egypt a multiplier of remittances with respect to GNP of 2.2 and a multiplier of 0.77 with respect to imports.

Glytsos's (1998b) econometric model estimated the impact of remittances on consumption, investment, imports and growth with a system of four corresponding simultaneous equations, using data individually for a number of countries from the two sides of the Mediterranean basin. The findings support, as expected, the permanent income hypothesis in the behavior of remittance spending and demonstrate a time distribution of the effects on output, consumption, investment and imports. The dynamic nature of the model allows for the possibility of estimating short-term and long-term effects. The estimated model demonstrates a uniform empirical performance of the countries examined. But the findings show a common phenomenon of instability in the impact of remittances on all variables with wide intra-country and inter-temporal fluctuations. One important specific finding is that changes in remittances have a considerable and occasionally strong impact on investment (including housing).

Concluding remarks

There is no unique theory of remittance determination, but combined or alternative theoretical hypotheses for different parts of remittances, distinguished according to their purpose. One part, which is endogenous to the whole emigration-repatriation cycle, is explained mostly by the microeconomic behavior of the migrant and the family, and another part, which is exogenous to the migration process, is explained mostly by macroeconomic factors. A number of different explanatory or econometric models have been constructed to assess or estimate the determinants of remittances. Some of these models reflect the tenets of particular theories, while others constitute straightforward applications with data from individual countries or groups of countries. The various empirical analyses from the application of these models verify, on occasion, one or the other of the theories of remittance determination. The different, often conflicting results depend on the nature of migration as temporary or permanent, the specification of the equations applied, the reference period or the country examined. This lends support to the view that there is a plurality of joint or alternative explanations of remittance determination.

There is hardly a comprehensive theory of remittance effects. Instead, various models assess the direct and/or the indirect effects of remittances on income distribution, social welfare, poverty, and also on production and growth. The impact of remittances is examined either in the framework of the emigration-repatriation cycle, as a compensating factor for the losses caused by emigration or as an independent income flow that is spent in the home country. The empirical analysis shows a variety of often contradictory results, especially on income inequality and the contribution to investment and growth.

Acknowledgement

The technical support of Yulie Papakonstantinou is gratefully acknowledged.

References

Adams jr, R.H. (1991) *The Effects of International Remittances on Poverty, Inequality and Development in Rural Egypt*, Research Report 96, International Food Policy Research Institute.

Ahlburg, D.A. (1996) "Remittances and the Income Distribution in Tonga," *Population Research and Policy Review*, 15 (4): 391–400.

Brown, R.P.C. (1994) "Migrant's Remittances, Savings and Investment in the South Pacific," *International Labour Review*, 133 (3), 347–367.

Brown, R.P.C. (1997) "Estimating Remittance Functions for Pacific Island Migrants," *World Development*, 24 (4): 613–626.

Choucri, N. (1986) "The Hidden Economy: A New View of Remittances in the Arab World," *World Development* 14 (6): 697–712.

Choucri, N. and S. Lahiri (1983) *Macroeconomic Impacts of Remittances in Egypt : An Exploratory Analysis*, Cambridge, Mass: Technology Adaptation Program, MIT.

Djajić, S. (1986) "International Migration, Remittances and Welfare in a Dependent Economy," *Journal of Development Economics*, 21: 229–234.

Djajić, S. (1989) "Migrants in a Guest-Worker System," *Journal of Development Economics*, 31: 327–339.

Djajić, S. (1998) "Emigration and Welfare in an Economy with Foreign Capital," *Journal of Development Economics*, 56: 433–445.

Elbadawi, Ibrahim A. and Robert de Rezende Rocha (1992) "Determinants of Expatriate Workers' Remittances in North Africa and Europe," Policy Research Working Paper, WPS 1038, World Bank.

Faini, R. (1994) "Workers Remittances and the Real Exchange Rate," *Journal of Population Economics*, 7: 235–245.

Feiler, G. (1987) "Scope and Some Effects of Remittances of Egyptian Migrant Workers in the Arab Oil-Producing Countries: 1973–1984," *Asian and African Studies*, 21: 305–325.

Garson, Jean-Pierre (1994) "The Implications for the Maghreb Countries of Financial Transfers from Emigrants," in OECD, *Migration and Development*, Paris: OECD: 275–287.

Gilani, I., M. Khan and I. Munawar (1981) *Labor Migration from Pakistan to the Middle East and its Impact on the Domestic Economy*, Research Report 126, Islamabad: Pakistan Institute of Development Economics.

Glytsos, Nicholas P. (1988) "Remittances in Temporary Migration: A Theoretical Model and Its Testing with the Greek-German Experience," *Weltwirtschaftliches Archiv*, 124 (3): 524–549.

Glytsos, Nicholas P. (1991) *Theoretical and Empirical Analysis of Migratory Movements and of Remittance Flows, between Greece and Germany*, Studies Series (New) 7, Athens: KEPE (in Greek).

Glytsos, Nicholas P. (1993) "Measuring the Income Effects of Migrant Remittances: A methodological Approach Applied to Greece," *Economic Development and Cultural Change*, 42 (1): 131–168.

Glytsos, Nicholas, P. (1997), "Remitting Behaviour of Temporary and Permanent Migrants: The Case of Greeks in Germany and Australia," *Labour*, 11 (3): 409–435.

Glytsos, Nicholas P. (1998a), "La migration comme moteur de l'intégration régionale: L'example des Transfers de Fonds," in OECD, *Migrations, Libre Échange et Intégration Régionale dans le Basin Mediterranéen*, Paris: OECD: 173–186.

Glytsos, Nicholas P. (1998b) "A Macroeconometric Model of the Effects of Migrant Remittances in Mediterranean Countries," paper presented at the ERF Conference on Population Challenges in the Middle East and North Africa: Towards the 21st Century, Cairo, November 2–4, 1998.

Hoddinott, John (1994) "A Model of Migration and Remittances Applied to Western Kenya," *Oxford Economic Papers*, 46: 459–476.

Kandil, M. and M.F. Metwally (1990) "The Impact of Migrants' Remittances on the Egyptian Economy," *International Migration*, 28 (2): 159–180.

Katseli, Louka, T. and Nicholas P. Glytsos (1986) "Theoretical and Empirical Determinants of International Labor Mobility: A Greek-German Perspective," Discussion Paper 148, Centre for Economic Policy Research (CEPR).

Katseli, Louka, T. and Nicholas P. Glytsos (1989), "Theoretical and Empirical Determinants of International Labor Mobility: A Greek-German Perspective," in Ian Gordon and A.P. Thirlwall (eds), *European Factor Mobility: Trends and Consequences*, London: Macmillan: 95–115.

Keely, C.B. and B. Saket (1984) "Jordanian Migrant Workers in the Arab Region: A Case Study of Consequences for Labour Supplying Countries," *Middle East Journal*, 38 (4): 685–698.

Kirwan, F. and D. Holden (1986) "Emigrants' Remittances, Non-Traded Goods and Economic Welfare in the Source Country," *Journal of Economic Studies*, 13 (2): 52–58.

Knowles, J.C. and R. Anker (1981) "An Analysis of Income Transfers in a Developing Country: The Case of Kenya," *Journal of Development Economics*, 8 (2): 205–226.

Lerman, R. and S. Yitzhaki (1985) "Income Inequality Effects by Income Source: A New Approach and Applications to the United States," *Review of Economics and Statistics*, 67 (1): 151–156.

Lesch, A.M. (1990) "Egyptian Labour Migration," in I.M. Oweiss (ed.), *The Political Economy of Contemporary Egypt*, Washington D.C.: Georgetown University.

Lipton, M. (1980) "Migration from Rural Areas of Poor Countries: The Impact on Rural Productivity and Income Distribution," *World Development*, 8 (1): 1–24.

Lucas, Robert E.B. and Odet Stark (1985) "Motivations to Remit: Evidence from Botswana," *Journal of Political Economy*, 93 (5): 901–918.

Lundahl, Mats (1985) "International Migration, Remittances and Real Incomes: Effects on the Source Country," *Scandinavian Journal of Economics* 87 (4): 647–657.

MacMillen, M.J. (1982) "The Economic Effects of International Migration," *Journal of Common Market Studies*, 20: 245–267.

Martin, P.L. (1991) *The Unfinished Story: Turkish Labour Migration to Western Europe*, Geneva: International Labor Organization.

Merkle L. and K. F. Zimmermann (1992) "Savings, Remittances, and Return Migration," *Economics Letters*, 38: 77–81.

Miranda, K. (1988) "Workers' Remittances, Commodity Aid Utilisation and Exchange Rate Unification", Washington, D.C.: International Monetary Fund, January, mimeo.

OECD (1978) *The Migratory Chain*, Paris: OECD.

Papademetriou, D.G. and P.L. Martin (eds) (1991) *The Unsettled Relationship: Labor Migration and Economic Development*, New York: Greenwood Press.

Poirine, Bernard (1997) "A Theory of Remittances as an Implicit Family Loan Arrangement," *World Development*, 25 (4): 589–611.

Quibria, M.G. (1996) "International Migration, Remittances and Income Distribution in Source Country: A Synthesis," *Bulletin of Economic Research*, 49 (1): 29–46.

Rivera-Batiz, F. (1982) "International Migration, Non-traded Goods and Economic Welfare in the Source Country," *Journal of Development Economics*, 11: 81–90.

Rivera-Batiz, F. (1986) "International Migration, Remittances and Economic Welfare in the Source Country," *Journal of Economic Studies*, 13 (3): 3–19.

Rocha, R. (1989) "Workers' Remittances in the Maghreb Countries: A preliminary Analysis," EMTTF, The World Bank, mimeo.

Rodriguez, E.R. (1998) "International Migration and Income Distribution in the Philippines," *Economic Development and Cultural Change*, 46 (2): 329–350.

Russell, Sharon Stanton (1986) "Remittances from International Migration: A Review in Perspective," *World Development*, 14 (6): 677–696.

Russell, Sharon Stanton (1992) "Migrant Remittances and Development," *International Migration*, 30 (3/4) (Special Issue): 267–287.

Sirageldin, et al. (1983) *Manpower and International Labor Migration in the Middle East and North Africa*, Oxford: Oxford University Press.

Stahl, C.W. and F. Arnold (1986) "Overseas Workers' Remittances in Asian Development," *International Migration Review*, 20 (4): 899–925.

Stark, Oded (1980) "On the Role of Urban-to-Rural Remittances in Rural Development," *Journal of Development Studies*, 16 (3): 369–374 (reprinted as chapter 14 in Stark, 1991).

Stark, Oded (1984) "Rural-to-Urban Migration in Less Developed Countries: A Relative Deprivation Approach," *Economic Development and Cultural Change*, 32: 475–486 (reprinted as chapter 7 in Stark, 1991).

Stark, Oded (1991) *The Mitigation of Labor*, Oxford and Cambridge, Mass: Blackwell.

Stark, O. and R.E.B. Lucas (1988) "Migration, Remittances and the Family," *Economic Development and Cultural Change*, 36: 465–481 (reprinted as chapter 15 in Stark, 1991).

Stark, Oded and J.E. Taylor (1991) "Migration Incentives, Migration Types: The Role of Relative Deprivation," in O. Stark, *The Migration of Labor*, Oxford and Cambridge, Mass: Blackwell: 140–166.

Stark, O., J. E. Taylor and S. Yitzhaki (1986) "Remittances and Inequality". *Economic Journal*, 96: 722–740 (reprinted as chapter 17 in Stark, 1991).

Stark, O., J.E. Taylor and S. Yitzhaki (1988) "Migration, Remittances and Inequality: A Sensitivity Analysis using the Extended Gini Index," *Journal of Development Economics*, 28: 309–322 (reprinted as chapter 18 in Stark, 1991).

Stark, O. and S. Yitzhaki (1982) "Migration, Growth, Distribution and Welfare," *Economic Letters*, 10: 243–249 (reprinted as chapter 21 in Stark, 1991).

Straubhaar, T. (1986) "The Determinants of Workers' Remittances: The Case of Turkey," *Weltwirtschaftliches Archiv*, 122: 728–739.

Swamy, G. (1981) "International Migrant Workers' Remittances: Issues and Prospects," Working Paper 481, World Bank, Washington, D. C.

Taylor, J.E. (1992) "Remittances and Inequality Reconsidered : Direct, Indirect and Intertemporal Effects," *Journal of Policy Modelling*, 14 (2): 187–208.

Taylor, J.E. (1996) "International Migration and Economic Development : A Micro Economy-Wide Analysis," in J.E. Taylor (ed.), *Development Strategy, Employment and Migration*, Paris: OECD: 87–104.

Taylor, J.E. and T.J. Wyatt (1996) "The Shadow Value of Migrant Remittances, Income and Inequality in a Household-farm Economy," *Journal of Development Studies*, 32 (6): 899–912.

Todaro, M. (1969) "A Model of Labor Migration and Urban Unemployment in LDC's," *American Economic Review*, 59: 138–148.

Wahba, J. (1996) "Remittances in the Middle East: A Review," paper presented at the Conference on Labor Markets and Human Resource Development, Kuwait, September 16–18, 1996. Sponsored by the Economic Research Forum for the Arab Countries, Iran and Turkey, mimeo.

Wahba, Sadek (1989) "Workers' Remittances as a Source of Foreign Earnings: A Study of Determinants of Recorded Remittances in Egypt," Washington, D.C.: International Monetary Fund, mimeo.

Yitzhaki, S. (1983), "On the Extension of the Gini Inequality Index," *International Economic Review*, 24 (3): 617–628.

Index

Note: Page references in *italics* refer to Figures; those in **bold** refer to Tables